Creating Kashubia

McGill-Queen's Studies in Ethnic History
Series One: Donald Harman Akenson, Editor

1 *Irish Migrants in the Canadas*
   A New Approach
   Bruce S. Elliott
   (Second edition, 2004)

2 *Critical Years in Immigration*
   Canada and Australia Compared
   Freda Hawkins
   (Second edition, 1991)

3 *Italians in Toronto*
   Development of a National Identity,
   1875–1935
   John E. Zucchi

4 *Linguistics and Poetics of*
   Latvian Folk Songs
   Essays in Honour of the Sesquicentennial
   of the Birth of Kr. Barons
   Vaira Vikis-Freibergs

5 *Johan Schroder's Travels in Canada, 1863*
   Orm Overland

6 *Class, Ethnicity, and Social Inequality*
   Christopher McAll

7 *The Victorian Interpretation*
   of Racial Conflict
   The Maori, the British, and
   the New Zealand Wars
   James Belich

8 *White Canada Forever*
   Popular Attitudes and Public Policy
   Toward Orientals in British Columbia
   W. Peter Ward
   (Third edition, 2002)

9 *The People of Glengarry*
   Highlanders in Transition, 1745–1820
   Marianne McLean

10 *Vancouver's Chinatown*
   Racial Discourse in Canada, 1875–1980
   Kay J. Anderson

11 *Best Left as Indians*
   Native-White Relations in the
   Yukon Territory, 1840–1973
   Ken Coates

12 *Such Hardworking People*
   Italian Immigrants in Postwar Toronto
   Franca Iacovetta

13 *The Little Slaves of the Harp*
   Italian Child Street Musicians in
   Nineteenth-Century Paris, London,
   and New York
   John E. Zucchi

14 *The Light of Nature and the Law of God*
   Antislavery in Ontario, 1833–1877
   Allen P. Stouffer

15 *Drum Songs*
   Glimpses of Dene History
   Kerry Abel

16 *Canada's Jews*
   (Reprint of 1939 original)
   Louis Rosenberg
   Edited by Morton Weinfeld

17 *A New Lease on Life*
   Landlords, Tenants, and Immigrants
   in Ireland and Canada
   Catharine Anne Wilson

18 *In Search of Paradise*
   The Odyssey of an Italian Family
   Susan Gabori

19 *Ethnicity in the Mainstream*
   Three Studies of English Canadian
   Culture in Ontario
   Pauline Greenhill

20 *Patriots and Proletarians*
   The Politicization of Hungarian
   Immigrants in Canada, 1923–1939
   Carmela Patrias

21 *The Four Quarters of the Night*
   The Life-Journey of an Emigrant Sikh
   Tara Singh Bains and Hugh Johnston

22 *Cultural Power, Resistance, and Pluralism*
   Colonial Guyana, 1838–1900
   Brian L. Moore

23 *Search Out the Land*
   The Jews and the Growth of Equality in British Colonial America, 1740–1867
   Sheldon J. Godfrey and Judith C. Godfrey

24 *The Development of Elites in Acadian New Brunswick, 1861–1881*
   Sheila M. Andrew

25 *Journey to Vaja*
   Reconstructing the World of a Hungarian-Jewish Family
   Elaine Kalman Naves

McGill-Queen's Studies in Ethnic History
Series Two: John Zucchi, Editor

1 *Inside Ethnic Families*
   Three Generations of Portuguese-Canadians
   Edite Noivo

2 *A House of Words*
   Jewish Writing, Identity, and Memory
   Norman Ravvin

3 *Oatmeal and the Catechism*
   Scottish Gaelic Settlers in Quebec
   Margaret Bennett

4 *With Scarcely a Ripple*
   Anglo-Canadian Migration into the United States and Western Canada, 1880–1920
   Randy William Widdis

5 *Creating Societies*
   Immigrant Lives in Canada
   Dirk Hoerder

6 *Social Discredit*
   Anti-Semitism, Social Credit, and the Jewish Response
   Janine Stingel

7 *Coalescence of Styles*
   The Ethnic Heritage of St John River Valley Regional Furniture, 1763–1851
   Jane L. Cook

8 *Brigh an Orain / A Story in Every Song*
   The Songs and Tales of Lauchie MacLellan
   Translated and edited by John Shaw

9 *Demography, State and Society*
   Irish Migration to Britain, 1921–1971
   Enda Delaney

10 *The West Indians of Costa Rica*
   Race, Class, and the Integration of an Ethnic Minority
   Ronald N. Harpelle

11 *Canada and the Ukrainian Question, 1939–1945*
   Bohdan S. Kordan

12 *Tortillas and Tomatoes*
   Transmigrant Mexican Harvesters in Canada
   Tanya Basok

13 *Old and New World Highland Bagpiping*
   John G. Gibson

14 *Nationalism from the Margins*
   The Negotiation of Nationalism and Ethnic Identities among Italian Immigrants in Alberta and British Columbia
   Patricia Wood

15 *Colonization and Community*
   The Vancouver Island Coalfield and the Making of the British Columbia Working Class
   John Douglas Belshaw

16 *Enemy Aliens, Prisoners of War*
   Internment in Canada during the Great War
   Bohdan S. Kordan

17 *Like Our Mountains*
   A History of Armenians in Canada
   Isabel Kaprielian-Churchill

18 *Exiles and Islanders*
   The Irish Settlers of Prince Edward Island
   Brendan O'Grady

19 *Ethnic Relations in Canada*
   Institutional Dynamics
   Raymond Breton
   Edited by Jeffrey G. Reitz

20 *A Kingdom of the Mind*
   The Scots' Impact on the Development of Canada
   Edited by Peter Rider and Heather McNabb

21 *Vikings to U-Boats*
   The German Experience in Newfoundland and Labrador
   Gerhard P. Bassler

22 *Being Arab*
   Ethnic and Religious Identity Building among Second Generation Youth in Montreal
   Paul Eid

23 *From Peasants to Labourers*
   Ukrainian and Belarusan Immigration from the Russian Empire to Canada
   Vadim Kukushkin

24 *Emigrant Worlds and Transatlantic Communities*
   Migration to Upper Canada in the First Half of the Nineteenth Century
   Elizabeth Jane Errington

25 *Jerusalem on the Amur*
   Birobidzhan and the Canadian Jewish Communist Movement, 1924–1951
   Henry Felix Srebrnik

26 *Irish Nationalism in Canada*
   Edited by David A. Wilson

27 *Managing the Canadian Mosaic in Wartime*
   Shaping Citizenship Policy, 1939–1945
   Ivana Caccia

28 *Jewish Roots, Canadian Soil*
   Yiddish Culture in Montreal, 1905–1945
   Rebecca Margolis

29 *Imposing Their Will*
   An Organizational History of Jewish Toronto, 1933–1948
   Jack Lipinsky

30 *Ireland, Sweden, and the Great European Migration, 1815–1914*
   Donald H. Akenson

31 *The Punjabis in British Columbia*
   Location, Labour, First Nations, and Multiculturalism
   Kamala Elizabeth Nayar

32 *Growing Up Canadian*
   Muslims, Hindus, Buddhists
   Edited by Peter Beyer and Rubina Ramji

33 *Between Raid and Rebellion*
   The Irish in Buffalo and Toronto, 1867–1916
   William Jenkins

34 *Unpacking the Kists*
   The Scots in New Zealand
   Brad Patterson, Tom Brooking, and Jim McAloon

35 *Building Nations from Diversity*
   Canadian and American Experience Compared
   Garth Stevenson

36 *Hurrah Revolutionaries*
   The Polish Canadian Communist Movement, 1918–1948
   Patryk Polec

37 *Alice in Shandehland*
   Scandal and Scorn in the Edelson/Horwitz Murder Case
   Monda Halpern

38 *Creating Kashubia*
   History, Memory, and Identity in Canada's First Polish Community
   Joshua C. Blank

Creating Kashubia

HISTORY, MEMORY, AND IDENTITY IN CANADA'S FIRST POLISH COMMUNITY

Joshua C. Blank

McGill-Queen's University Press
Montreal & Kingston • London • Chicago

© McGill-Queen's University Press 2016

ISBN 978-0-7735-4719-3 (cloth)
ISBN 978-0-7735-4720-9 (paper)
ISBN 978-0-7735-9851-5 (ePDF)
ISBN 978-0-7735-9865-2 (ePUB)

Legal deposit second quarter 2016
Bibliothèque nationale du Québec

Printed in Canada on acid-free paper that is 100% ancient forest free (100% post-consumer recycled), processed chlorine free

This book has been published with the help of financial assistance received from the Carleton Centre for the History of Migration and the Shannon Fund at Carleton University.

McGill-Queen's University Press acknowledges the support of the Canada Council for the Arts for our publishing program. We also acknowledge the financial support of the Government of Canada through the Canada Book Fund for our publishing activities.

LIBRARY AND ARCHIVES CANADA CATALOGUING IN PUBLICATION

Blank, Joshua C., 1984–, author
Creating Kashubia : history, memory, and identity in Canada's first Polish community / Joshua C. Blank.

(McGill-Queen's studies in ethnic history. Series two ; 38)
Includes bibliographical references and index.
Issued in print and electronic formats.
ISBN 978-0-7735-4719-3 (bound). – ISBN 978-0-7735-4720-9 (paperback). – ISBN 978-0-7735-9851-5 (PDF). – ISBN 978-0-7735-9865-2 (ePUB)

1. Polish Canadians – Ontario – Renfrew (County) – History.   2. Kashubes – Ontario – Renfrew (County) – History.   I. Title.   II. Series: McGill-Queen's studies in ethnic history. Series two ; 38

FC3095.R4Z7 2016   971.3'810049185   C2015-907876-8
                                             C2015-907877-6

Set in 10.5/13.5 Warnock Pro with Humanist 777 BT
Book design & typesetting by Garet Markvoort, zijn digital

CONTENTS

Preface and Acknowledgments • ix

Figures and Tables • xiii

Introduction • 3

Part I Revisiting Historical Memory

1 The Production of Knowledge and Canada's First Polish Community • 19

2 Poverty, Piety, and Political Persecution • 55

3 Migration Memories • 99

4 Intending Settlers: T.P. French and His Guidebook • 132

5 Poor Land and Victorian Science • 144

Part II Cultural Redefinition

6 The Origins and Development of the Kashubian Label • 177

7 Legacies of Promotion: Cultural Redefinition and the Wilno Heritage Society • 210

Epilogue • 238

Appendix: Emigrants from Prussian-Occupied Poland Who Settled on the Opeongo and Surrounding Townships • 253

Notes • 257

Bibliography • 313

Index • 343

PREFACE AND ACKNOWLEDGMENTS

Although I consider myself Canadian (as ambiguous as that seems), my ancestors were land-hungry peasants who emigrated from partitioned Poland as early as 1858. Shaped by the place and space of the Madawaska Valley, I am one of many descendants of European peasants. Familial and ethnic identities were always passed on to me and have largely influenced my career and research path. After high school, my study into the past became quite lengthy, its syllabus widespread and often unpredictable.

In the classroom, I have always conveyed that history evolves. Without questioning the past, the historical record does not evolve. As more sources are unearthed and examined and more questions are pondered, these findings, after discussion and analysis, can amend the current record. In much the same way, the significance and importance of some ethnic or cultural identifiers may change over time. We must teach and bring to light these developments, since "history is progress through the transmission of acquired skills from one generation to another," in the words of E.H. Carr. The purpose of this investigation is twofold: to query the past and present and to integrate primary and secondary material.

Its approach is multi-disciplinary. My intent is to query the past and present by resituating the migration in the nineteenth-century social, political, economic, and religious contexts of the land of departure. The study thus reimagines the history of migration to, and the ethnic and cultural redefinitions within, Canada's first Polish community. Rarely were descendants' voices used for this purpose. The study thus integrates both primary archival material and secondary material to marry micro-level movements with the macro-level narrative.

In recent years, several local authors and community boosters have appropriated notions of voice away from historians using archives, and attempted to expand the narrative of settlement in Canada's first Polish community. In the process, they have become knowledge makers and reinvented the community's history and identity with a Kashubian trope. However, although both groups have codified and bolstered their narratives from the migration and settlement periods, they have not made full use of the other's stores of knowledge. By querying and theorizing these gaps, this study examines how these two groups produced their knowledge of Kashubian migration, settlement, and identity by expanding, contextualizing, and problematizing certain narratives and memories. This is also a case study that shows how the politics of ethnic memory are important both locally and transnationally. In many instances, I deconstruct hegemonic or commonly held definitions and/or delineations of certain labels, events, and practices; I make no apologies for doing so. As Franca Iacovetta states, "No community or group is monolithic, of course, and the scholar is not obliged to agree with [his or her] subjects' point of view." Nonetheless, "choosing to disagree with one's community can be difficult."

The study also casts new light on the avenues of emigrant recruitment in Prussian-occupied Poland and examines, at length, the origins and diffusion of symbols and invented traditions that have been adopted by recent ethnic movements.

At times, readers might think my findings are iconoclastic, but my hope is that by reaching back to move forward we can all navigate our pasts and our futures more deeply. I hope this study will not only widen and deepen the narratives surrounding my ancestors but will also serve as a springboard for further investigations into the social, political, and institutional aspects of the settlement. Any errors, improper citations, or omissions in this analysis are either inadvertent or the product of an exhausted researcher.

Acknowledgments

I am indebted to many people. Their mere mention, I fear, does not adequately convey my gratitude.

Many thanks to my grandparents: Zita (Shalla) Glofcheskie and Bronas Glofcheskie, for their love of literature and the generous grant to purchase books while attending university. They, along with Frances (Shulist) Blank, always made sure that I was aware of my roots. I am also thankful for the hard work and resolve displayed by my Polish ancestors. They worked the land, were shaped by it, and survived.

Not only have my parents, Mary (Glofcheskie) and Clifford Blank, taught me countless lessons in life, given what they could afford, but they have always been a pillar of support in all my athletic and academic endeavours. Thanks are also due to Peter and Bev Glofcheskie, whose support and encouragement are always present. To my brothers, Aaron and Isaac, thank you for asking the question "Why does history matter?" and for throwing baseballs at my head. Nicole (Etterlin) Van Herk deserves thanks for her German-language and translation skills. Kinga Bielec deserves thanks for her Polish-language and translation skills.

Many individuals at Carleton University deserve thanks for their guiding suggestions, especially Dr Duncan McDowall, Dr Dominique Marshall, and Dr Jennifer Evans. I am truly fortunate to have been able to learn from Dr John C. Walsh, whose interest and "ways of knowing" are contagious. His collection of literature greatly aided in the writing of this book. He is a remarkable professor – one whose pedagogical and theoretical questions were invaluable. Thanks are also due to Dr Jan K. Fedorowicz. His keen eye sharpened several sections of Polish history. Dr Bruce S. Elliott has also been a fount of knowledge. He continually posed questions and guided me to think beyond the page in the many stages of my research. I thought I was dedicated (when writing emails to him at 12 a.m.) only to find that, quite often, he would reply a few minutes later. His desire to read and absorb all the scholarship surrounding the issue is one of his many commendable traits as a meticulous scholar. I can only hope to possess the cognitive archive for local and public history that Bruce wields. Many thanks for all your help!

Thanks are also due to several people in Poland: Katarzyna Kulikowska and Ewa Gilewska, curators at the Gdańsk branch of the *Muzeum Nardowe (Oddzial Etnografii)* for their guidance in my study of the material aspects of the Kaszubian region; Wojciech and Ola Etmanski, who welcomed me into their home with kindness and hospitality; and to Artur Jablonski for giving me books and graciously inviting me to a ZKP meeting in 2009.

I wish to thank Angela (Villeneuve) Lorbetskie and Karen Filipkowski, former and current librarians of the Barry's Bay and Area Public Library for granting me special access to archived newspapers and the oral history project products over the past few years. Over the years, Angela in particular has done a remarkable job in preserving copies of Barry's Bay's newspapers for generations of interested readers and researchers.

Generous support packages and bursaries from the Department of History, the Faculty of Graduate Studies and Postdoctoral Affairs, and the Estate of Frank Underhill at Carleton University enabled me to complete research into this subject. I also want to thank Dr Elliott and Dr Marilyn Barber of the Carleton Centre for the History of Migration and the Shannon Fund for a generous grant. I would also like to thank Teresa Berezowski and Fr Wojciech Blach with the Canadian Polish Congress's Canadian Polish Millennium Fund, Ewa Zadarnowski of the Polish-Canadian Women's Federation, Jose Semrau of the Polish Heritage Foundation of Canada, and Dr Alexander Jablonski of the Reubenbauer Foundation, for their generosity and financial assistance. Without their help, this book would not have appeared in print.

I am grateful to have received excellent support and patience from Kyla Madden at McGill-Queen's University Press. She has been most helpful in transforming a lengthy manuscript into the book you are reading today. This study has also benefitted from the three anonymous readers and their valuable comments. Also crucial to the development of this book are Ryan Van Huijstee, Helen Hajnoczky, John Zucchi, copy editor Gillian Scobie, and typesetter Garet Markvoort. Thank you for your suggestions and assistance throughout the publishing process.

Last but not least, I could not have done this without the one who supported me in every possible way – Kim Van Herk. She was there through it all. Whether in conversations about the research, retreats into the wilderness, or on stroller walks with our daughter Sophia, she's been the positive and bright shining star in my life. I hope that we're always, in the words of Jim Cuddy, "lost together."

FIGURES AND TABLES

Figures

0.1 Colonization Roads in Canada West from Spragge, "Colonization Roads in Canada West 1850–1867," 12. Used with permission • 4

0.2 Migrant origins map. Map credit: J. Blank • 5

1.1 The St Hedwig's White Eagles, 1936, from the *Barry's Bay Review*, 25 May 1961 • 39

1.2 Polish dance group at St Hedwig's Church in Barry's Bay (c. 1966), from the collection of Zita Glofcheskie • 41

1.3 The 1972 provincial plaque ceremony in Wilno, from the collection of Zita Glofcheskie • 43

2.1 Partitioned Poland at the turn of the nineteenth century. Source: H.G. Wells, *The Outline of History*, 800 • 61

2.2 The Opeongo Road migrants map. Map credit: Bill Nelson, after Mordawski, *Statystyka Ludnosci Kaszubskiej*, 2005 • 71

2.3a and 2.3b Photos of late nineteenth-century peasant hovels near the community of Liniewo, Poland. Source: Alexander Treichel, c. 1900 • 75

2.4 Bismarck is Coming! Source: Cartoon from *Der Flot*, May 1891 • 87

3.1 A cross-section of an immigrant ship showing ample room in steerage. Source: *Die Gartenlaube: Illustrirtes Familienblatt*. Liepzig: Ernst Keil, 1854: 450 • 113

3.2 The realities of steerage. A depiction of steerage on the *Samuel Hop* in *Leipziger Illustrirte Zeitung*, 1849, reprinted in Moltmann and Bickelmann, *Germans to America*, 66 • 113

3.3 The farm of Joseph Hildebrandt and Matilda Gutowski, from the collection of Beverly (Flynn) Glofcheskie • 120

3.4 A Prussian Pass Card belonging to Jan Pawel von Klopotek-Głowczewski, courtesy of Marie Landon • 127

4.1 The guidebook that reportedly brought Polish settlers to Canada. Source: French, *Information for Intending Settlers on the Ottawa and Opeongo Road and Its Vicinity* • 133

4.2 Caricature of an emigration agent. A woodcut, by Eduard Kretzchmar (1848). The image is reprinted in Moltmann and Bickelmann, *Germans to America*, 66 • 142

5.1 Devine's 1861 Map of the Ottawa-Huron Tract: *Government Map of Part of the Huron and Ottawa Territory Upper Canada Compiled under the direction of Thomas Devine F.R.G.S.C. & c. Head of Surveyors Branch U.C.* (1861). Map courtesy of the Ontario Archives • 154

5.2 The 1,000-acre sectional survey of Radcliffe Township. Archives of Ontario RG 19-20-2 (item 37.11). Map courtesy of the Ontario Archives • 155

5.3 A settlers' hut along the Opeongo in 1901. Archives of Ontario, Charles McNamara Collection, C-120-1-0-1.1 • 157

5.4 Settlers toiled with their hands and with animals to clear land for farming. Archives of Ontario, F-150-23-0-27 • 158

5.5 Road and rail cutting crew near Algonquin Park as photographed by John Walter Le Breton Ross in 1894. Courtesy of Algonquin Park Museum Archives #156 • 169

6.1 Slavic peoples in Central Europe during the tenth century. Map credit: Bill Nelson, after Zamoyski, *The Polish Way*, 9 • 180

6.2 Jan Jannsonius, *Accurata Prussiae description*, Amsterdam, c. 1645–60 • 184

6.3   Ramułt's ethnographic map of the Kaszubian speech. Source: back insert in *Statystyka Ludności Kaszubskiej* • 189

6.4   The Kaszubian coat of arms • 199

6.5   The Pomeranian coat of arms, c. 1530 • 200

6.6   Embroidery patterns adopted by Teodora Gulgowska, as printed in Stelmachowska, *Strój Kaszubski*, 50 • 203

6.7   A reconstructed Kaszubian ethnic costume printed on the inside cover of Stelmachowska, *Atlas Polskich Strojów Ludowych* • 206

6.8   The Kaszubian ethnic costume at Muzeum Kaszubskie. Photo credit: J. Blank, 2009 • 207

7.1   Kashub Day 2008, showing the stage and dance floor in Wilno. Photo credit: J. Blank, 2008 • 215

7.2   A Wilno blanket box. Photo credit: Beverly Glofcheskie, 2015 • 231

Tables

2.1   Population statistics, Powiat Kościerzyna, 1821–1890 • 71

2.2   Population statistics, Powiat Chojnicki, 1821–1871 • 72

2.3   Locality densities, c. 1870s • 72

2.4   Language and religion statistics in West Prussian counties • 81

3.1   Ships that brought Polish-Kashub emigrants to Canada • 107

3.2   Hamburg departures by ship type, 1859–1869 • 108

3.3   Nineteenth-century Hamburg ship types, captains, and owners • 108

3.4   Voyages on the Barque *Elbe* • 110

3.5   Voyages on the Barque *Franklin* • 110

3.6   Voyages on the Barque *Main* • 111

3.7   Voyages on the Barque *Donau* • 111

3.8 Voyages on the Barque *Oder* • 112

3.9 Forest to farmland clearance rates, c. 1862–1863 • 118

3.10 More forest to farmland clearance rates, c. 1874–1890 • 119

8.1 Summer visitors to Wilno Heritage Society's Heritage Park • 245

Creating Kashubia

INTRODUCTION

Nestled in the westernmost section of Renfrew County, Ontario, are a handful of small communities founded primarily by Polish-Kashub settlers. Between 1858 and 1910, several small waves of peasants from the northern part of partitioned Poland settled near the present-day communities of Wilno and Barry's Bay. The latter community is a village in the now-amalgamated Township of Madawaska Valley, about 200 kilometres west of Ottawa. Many of the 4,000 township residents trace their roots to nineteenth-century Irish and Polish settlers.[1] The hamlet of Wilno, a few kilometres east of Barry's Bay, was recognized by the Province of Ontario in 1972 as the first Polish settlement in Canada.

The landscape here, part of the Canadian Shield, is hilly and heavily forested. Known as the Madawaska Highlands, it is an area of fractured block mountains and stratified kame deposits.[2] The hills are rough and ragged compared with the flatter, lower-lying farmland closer to Renfrew. Before the 1850s, small bands of Algonquin hunters inhabited the area. They have never officially surrendered the territory.[3] In the early nineteenth century, timber barons, such as John Egan, and lumberjacks, moved into the area seeking the plentiful white pine coveted for ship masts and export. Even in the 1870s, after forty years of logging, pine still blanketed the area. In the words of one lumberjack, the "whole country was covered with an ocean of pine; as far as the eye could reach from any prominent height."[4]

In the 1850s, the government of Canada West launched a colonization scheme to open these lands for settlement. Thirteen colonization roads were hacked out of the wilderness; the most prominent was the Opeongo Colonization Road (see figure 0.1).[5] From its origins at the Ottawa River, east of the present-day city of Renfrew, the road was to wind through the hills, eventually to end at Lake Opeongo in present-day Algonquin Park. The road did not progress as far as planned, however, and was abandoned west of Barry's Bay. Nonetheless, groups of Irish, German, and Polish settlers sought land along the road – 100 acres, free, to any man over the age of eighteen.[6]

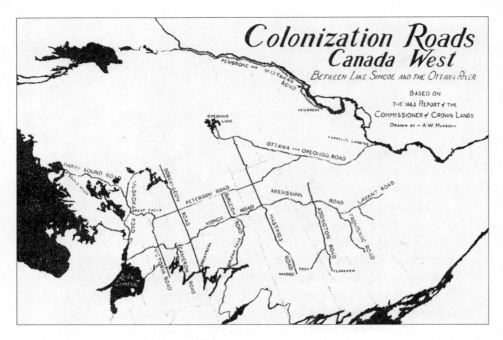

0.1   Colonization Roads in Canada West.

By the end of the 1870s, the attraction of land along the colonization roads had faded and was "replaced by the frontier settler fantasies attached to the Prairies and the American West."[7] Although some immigrants joined family or cohorts in the townships along the Opeongo Road, the tide of European immigration promoted by the Canadian government now turned toward the Prairies.

The arrival of peasants from Prussian-occupied Poland along the Opeongo Colonization Road was the first of several transatlantic migrations of Polish people to Canada. This first wave of settlers, consisting of roughly sixty families, were peasants from Prussian-occupied Poland who arrived between 1858 and 1871. At the end of this period, 617 Polish people were living in Canada – most of them along the Opeongo. The second wave of emigrants also originated in Prussian-occupied Poland. They came during Otto von Bismarck's Kulturkampf[8] and settled around Wilno and Barry's Bay between 1871 and 1907 (see Appendix).

In the 1880s and 1890s, a small group of Poles and their families from Galicia, the Austrian sector of partitioned Poland, also arrived in the

0.2 Migrant origins. Ironically, the two areas that sent many emigrants to the Ottawa Valley are poles apart on the map. Polish-Kashubs who left the north came from the counties of Kościerzyna and Chojnice. The Galician Poles departed from the voivodeships of Tarnów, Rzeszów, and Krosno.

vicinity, along with a group of Poles from Massachusetts and a few families from the Poznań region of Poland (see figure 0.2).

A priest assigned to St Stanislaus Kostka in Wilno, Fr Jankowski, was also said to have journeyed to Poland in the 1890s to recruit families. Among the Galician group were: John Maika of Tarnow and his wife Catherine Gumieny of Zawadka, Joseph Maika of Zasów, Jacob Yashinki of Błażkowa, Andreas Dudeck of Czudec, John and Apolonia Hudder of Straszęcin, Joseph Mysliwiec and Catherine Koznacka of Jaslo, the Jedrzejczyks (Andrechecks) from Jaslo, and John Brotton and Antonina Kaminska of Róża, along with Michael Zielny and Margaret

Beanish, John Beanish, Thomas Beanish, Stanislaus Stefaniak, Lawrence Yaskulski, Martin Koznaski and Agathe Smozowska, Carl Lechowitch and Franzeska Szczerba, Peter Jaroszkiewicz and Josephine Wojciekiewicz, and the Bielawski, Babij (Babinskie), and Wikiera families. They were only a few of the estimated 1.1 million people who emigrated from Austrian-occupied Poland between 1854–1914.[9] And in the 1890s, as Fr Joseph Legree writes, several families from Webster, Massachusetts arrived "after spending some fifteen years in the States amidst language difficulties, religious bigotry, and unemployment ... to settle in the Paugh Lake area."[10] The families who left Webster – in 1890 a textile mill city of 7,031 people – included August Cyra and Martha Gutoskie, John Pick and Anna Lubecki, John Buch and Marianna Trader, and Vincent Matuszewski and Helen Blaskavitch.[11] At the same time, several families moved to Renfrew County from the Poznań region, such as Joseph Mintha and Marianna Zmiślony, Paul Nadobny and Elizabeth Pierunek and the Tomczyks of Krotoszyn, the Baderskis of Mikstat, Vincent Kowalski of Poznań, John Strąk and Johanna Szreta, and the Krawczyks.

By 1900, there were 6,285 Polish people in Canada, with 2,918 in Ontario. At this time, many parishes, places of residence, stores, and rural schools were built in hamlets formed near the Opeongo, including Brudenell, Killaloe Station, Wilno, and Barry's Bay – all spurred by the 1897 construction of the Ottawa, Arnprior and Parry Sound Railway. After 1900, the westward shift of Polish migration began. Apart from the oft-mentioned Sifton-era migrations of the Eastern European "stalwart peasant" in the "sheepskin coat" to farms in the Prairies, the largest migration of Polish people to Canada came in the wake of the Second World War. This postwar group, comprising educated professionals, displaced persons, political exiles, and veterans, mainly settled in several cities in Ontario. Between 1941 and 1960, 76,975 Polish people immigrated to Canada, virtually doubling the Canadian Polish population, from 167,485 to 323,517. Toronto replaced Winnipeg as the centre of Polish organization, nearly quadrupling its Polish population, from 13,094 in 1941 to 51,180 in 1971. The occupational demographics within the Polish group in Canada also changed. Between 1941 and 1961, the percentage of those involved in agriculture or semi-skilled work decreased from 62 per cent to 25 per cent, whereas those involved in the manufacturing sector jumped from 19 per cent to 35 per cent.

The number of Poles in the professional and managerial sectors also rose, from 0.2 per cent to 15.8 per cent during the same period.[12]

Beginning in the 1950s, and with the benefit of higher salaries and more leisure time, the newer class of urban Polish professionals migrated to the Barry's Bay and Wilno area for the summer months. After this group established cottages and religious and scouting communities around Wadsworth Lake, the "first settlement" region become more culturally and linguistically significant for the Canadian-Polish diaspora. Nowadays, the townships surrounding the original settlement are known to many in the wider Polish-Canadian community as Kaszuby and serve as a focal point for ethnic travellers. Kaszuby also houses several Polish religious retreats, including the Cathedral in the Pines dedicated to Our Lady of Angels which was founded by Fr Ignatius (Rafał Grzondziel) in 1953.

Since the early twentieth century, the body of literature on these migrations and the emergence of the Polish and non-Polish communities of the Upper Ottawa Valley has become voluminous. As evidenced in local books, pamphlets, genealogical publications, films, and radio broadcasts, the Polish-Kashubs are well-represented in many media. In the process, several narratives and myths about ethnicity and identity have become attached to the migration. These narratives and myths, deeply rooted in local historical memory, have continued to surface in local historiography and oral history. However, the authors of these works, whether based within the community or outside, have largely neglected to examine these myths. They have either ignored them or accepted them uncritically.

My aim in part I is to delve into the processes by which such knowledge is produced and to apply what I find to illustrate how writings and oral histories have shaped commonly understood narratives of settlement in the Polish-Kashubian ethnocultural community. In part II, my aim is to illustrate how a newfound sense of authority – shared authority (in which locals/residents are a meaningful part of the product/process rather than just sources of old sayings and customs) – in the production of knowledge has contributed to the evolution of ethnic consciousness and the reinvention of ethnicity in this community. In sum, I wish to revisit the "complete sequence" of the migration process and provide context to many of the avenues opened by historical memory.[13]

To analyze how knowledge is produced, a sociological approach is needed to determine the influences on historical consciousness in the area of the first migration. Chapter 1, "The Production of Knowledge and Canada's First Polish Community" analyzes the influences of school and the Church, as well as trends in the writing of professional and local history that compete with memory and oral history in forming the historical record. In doing so, it becomes apparent that though each publication that addressed the Polish-Kashubs contributed to the narratives and myths of settlement, none of them took advantage of the many stores of knowledge available. Whereas professional historians wrote histories on the basis of archival evidence and included some local knowledge, local historians, or pastkeepers, wrote histories from the bottom up, often in filiopietistic tones. Each work by these authors, whether outside or inside the community, served a specific purpose, but also, unfortunately, excluded certain bodies of knowledge. Yet when both micro- and macro-level[14] research interact with one another on the meso level, as Dirk Hoerder calls it, we are able to see not only the self-determination of migrant men and women but the structural limitations (poverty, emigration restrictions, passport controls, the availability of transportation networks) and the political and national contexts that shaped their actions.[15] The chapters in part I integrate both the primary and secondary knowledge amassed along with additional archival materials and analytical frameworks to contextualize certain migration myths and narratives.

In the literature on the first Polish group in Canada, several authors have come to a consensus about what conditions explain why the migrants left Prussian-occupied Poland. Their consensus, heavily inflected by local memory, rests on a somewhat simplified narrative of poverty and political and religious persecution. This literature has influenced more recent written works, as well as local historical memory. These claims only prompt further inquiry because, for some authors, "the separation from homeland is a matter of family history and not personal experience, [thus] such knowledge is constructed from diverse sources of variable reliability: a matter of interpretation and, therefore, contestation."[16] In other words, because the scope of some publications is often too narrow, it prevents their authors from adding elements from the national and international levels.

Although early Polish migration to Canada occurred in two distinct phases, which were influenced by different factors, many authors do not address the causes of emigration before Bismarck's attempt to limit the power of the Vatican in Prussian-occupied Poland in 1871. In other cases, such as in the writings of Fr William O'Dwyer and Fr Aloysius Rekowski, the dominant motifs and rhetoric of exile dominate the migration narrative. To quote John Gaddis, because representations of the past can be swallowed up in "an anecdote so often repeated ... that it takes on a life of its own; [or] a photograph depicting a single moment that, by surviving, becomes all we can recall of a person, or a place, or a time,"[17] the following chapter digs deeper into both the causes of emigration and the reasons why certain narratives have dominated the discourse.

Chapter 2, "Poverty, Piety, and Political Persecution," examines the memory of the migration by revisiting the forces at work in the land of departure. This chapter gives greater context to the instigating factor of poverty in Prussian-occupied Poland, suggested by local memory; divides the migration of Polish-Kashubs into two phases: pre-Bismarckian (1858–71) and Bismarckian (1871–1907); and presents the greater colonization scheme at work in Prussian-occupied Poland. In the case of former migrants, poverty was their main reason for leaving, fuelled by recent emancipation, land reforms, insufficient precipitation levels, and population increases. The latter wave of migration was undoubtedly affected by these same conditions, although it was further prompted by conflict between Prussia and the Vatican. While the two powers fought over spiritual and administrative control, the peasant population felt the effects at a micro level as they tried to practise their faith.

Over the last few decades, the settlers have been portrayed in two conflicting ways. Relying on the trope of migration as a disrupter of settled ways of life, some works have continued the theme of exile in their portrayal of the inter-European and transatlantic migrations. In this light, the migrants were objects of empathy: hapless and naive victims tricked by emigration agents and diabolically swept up in the upheavals and alienation in their homeland. Although the migrants may have felt this way, their portrayal by some authors as hardy and brave stands in contrast to their supposed naiveté. What becomes apparent is that since numerous local authors are descendants of these migrants, they genuflect to them and, using various literary devices, invest the migrants with admirable, strong-willed qualities.

Such a contrast prevents a historical appraisal of who the migrants really were and masks the agency they exercised in the emigration process. In the wake of these conflicting interpretations, chapter 3, "Migration Memories," resituates the settlers and the movement as an impelled migration rather than an exile. It establishes the settlers as hardworking, faithful, illiterate, and poor but with a desire to emigrate. While downplaying their measured success in Poland, by twenty-first-century western standards, this chapter brings forth the migrants' self-determination and individual agency in their decision to migrate. It also queries why the meta-narrative was not challenged by Galician Poles, who joined the Polish-Kashubs in the Ottawa Valley.

Several authors writing about the Polish-Kashub group declare that the migrants' destination was Canada because they were promised free land – something desirable in Poland. Yet the way in which authors approach the historical question – "How did the Polish peasants know there was free land in Canada?" – varies. Some authors, such as O'Dwyer or William Makowski, do not mention this aspect of the process at all, continuing their narrative once the migrants set foot in Canada. Others, such as Henry Radecki, Benedykt Heydenkorn, and Shirley Mask-Connolly, speculate that they were informed by agents – an understanding engrained in local historical memory. Yet another group (Kazmierz Ickiewicz, Isabella Jost, Anna Zurakowski, and Rekowski) concludes that it was an 1857 English-language pamphlet written by the Crown Lands agent for the Opeongo Road, Thomas Patrick French, that brought the peasants to settle in Canada a year later.[18] However, these authors do not examine in detail or contextualize the colonization policies and initiatives of the government in the Canadas. As a result, no consensus has been reached on this matter.

I suggest that the settlers were informed through another avenue. During 1856, the Bureau of Agriculture and Statistics sent out advertisements across the country describing free lands for settlement along the Opeongo, Addington, and Hastings Roads. This notice was passed along by William Sinn, the Crown's German translator at the Port of Quebec, to his "underground" business partner, Charles Eisenstein of Berlin, Germany. It was Eisenstein's agents, operating across German lands, who spread the word about free land in Canada. This is not to deny that French's pamphlet renewed the idea that Canada was offering free land, but it is less likely to have been the instigator than the notice circulating through German agents in 1856. Chapter 4, "Intending Settlers: T.P. French and His Guidebook," proposes that potential emigrants were informed earlier than 1857 about free land in Canada and resituates French's publication as an informative emigrant guidebook.

Local historical memory in the Wilno and Barry's Bay region recalls the early settlement era as one of great disappointment. The notion that the settlers were given poor land by agents and officials was passed down through several generations as a subversive local memory in opposition to the state's official version, which stated that the land was good for settlement.[19] One local author, Rekowski, gave a political edge to this idea by arguing that the Polish settlers were given bad land on purpose – because they were Polish. In the most recent contributions to this debate, three authors, Rekowski, Mask-Connolly, and Theresa Prince, conclude that the agents knew the land was poor and not fit for settlement.[20] Unfortunately, to justify their claims that the soil was poor, Rekowski and Prince use soil surveys completed in the 1970s, making their argument anachronistic. Although this chapter does not deny that the soil was poor, the use of the modern soil survey only inflames the narrative. This approach also does not heed one of the historian's key responsibilities: to contextualize and historicize the time and space in which the immigrants lived.[21] Chapter 5, "Poor Land and Victorian Science" argues that many government officials at the time, heavily influenced by Victorian science and surveying techniques, actually believed the land was fertile.

Although most publications that address Canada's first Polish community end their narratives around the 1970s or 1980s, a surge of ethnic consciousness and cultural recreation has occurred since then, which is noteworthy for both the ethnic and the scholarly communities. After looking at the production of knowledge, memories, and myth-making in part I, part II analyzes how recent attempts at producing knowledge through shared authority has created a resurgence in historical consciousness and a reinvention of ethnicity in Canada's first Polish community. Further, it borrows scholarly approaches that address the fluidity of ethnicity to assuage the "community lost" fears of local authors and pastkeepers.

Long before recent attempts at re-ethnicization, and before the postwar influx of Polish immigrants into the Barry's Bay and Wilno area in the 1950s and 1960s, descendants of the early settlers thought of themselves as "Polish." Even though ships' lists and Crown documents initially referred to them as "Prussian" – because they departed from a land controlled by Prussia – from their perspective, their language and identity were Polish. They thus experienced a cultural awakening when they met postwar Poles. These recent migrants insisted that the ancestors of the Opeongo settlers were a specific group of people – Kaszubians – who spoke a different, Slavic tongue. Encountering this challenge to their self-understanding, the third-, fourth-, and fifth-generation descendants of the original settlers pondered their identity. Some local residents looked into their past for answers, a collective effort that resulted in the 1998 foundation of the Wilno Heritage Society (WHS), whose aim is to preserve the Polish-Kashubian heritage of the area. The society initially comprised a few descendants of the original settlers who looked back to their homeland in a search for their roots. They learned that a period of redefinition was simultaneously underway in the same area their ancestors had left behind, as many people in northern Poland were attempting to gain recognition for a new language, "Kaszubian," and a new cultural identity apart from Polish.

With the knowledge of this cultural redefinition taking place across the ocean, and to combat this loss of Polishness, the WHS partnered with its older cousin from Poland, the Zrzeszenie Kaszubsko-Pomorskie (the Kashubian Pomeranian Association or KPA), to mediate the situation. As a result of this partnership, some members of the WHS refashioned (or recreated) the identity for the group that settled in Canada, basing it on a Kaszubian identity in Poland. Since then, the WHS, as a community pastkeeper, has stepped into the realm of public memory, constructing new historical narratives while refashioning old ones, and overlaying them with a Kashubian trope. Comprising a few local inhabitants and several hundred donor members, the WHS is the dominant carrier, creator, and reinventor of ethnic identification in the area.[22] One of its larger endeavours was the creation of a museum and park in Wilno, which holds an annual May third weekend celebration attended by hundreds of people.

By reaching back into the past, the WHS joined with the KPA to concretize the identity of those in Canada's first Polish community.

The first chapter in part II, chapter 6, "The Origins and Development of the Kashubian Label," delves into the development and solidification of the ethnic group and the fluidity of identity in the homeland. Using local and international literature, it queries how and why the Kaszubian label has evolved from the word for a fold in a peasant garment, or a ducal title, to a language and an ethnic group.

Chapter 7, "Legacies of Promotion: Cultural Redefinition and the Wilno Heritage Society" further traces the reinvention of ethnicity and how the production, transfer, and sharing of knowledge has heightened ethnic consciousness. It also engages the Polish-Kashubian diaspora in the question, and looks at the cross-fertilization of ideas between the homeland and Canada's first Polish community. It takes the "culture as verb" activities promoted by the WHS – including the rebranded May third Polish Day festivities – and asks questions about ethnicity. While local populations and heritage tourists are caught up in the performance of ethnicity, I step back and analyze the cultural delineations of the WHS. Do all individuals agree on the newly created label? Do other multiple identities persist? Indeed, globalization and the metaphysical loss of "home" has prompted many to exercise symbolic forms of ethnicity by returning "home" or partaking in activities to recharge or revive ethnic identity. Participation in the WHS's sponsored events and activities serves various nostalgic functions. As several people from the Kaszubian area of northern Poland have attended the festivities in Wilno, this chapter examines the creation of the imagined community that links these people who are poles apart. The collapse of time and space between these two groups has meant that ethnicity, in many realms, has flourished.

Although multiple identities and markers of ethnicity exist among local participants, a central concern for all ethnic organizations is whether ethnicity can survive in the future. One of the reasons the WHS emerged was due to the perceived lack of ethnic consciousness and one group's desire to increase and promote it. Instead of approaching the issue with ideas subject to a teleological or organic life cycle such as "community lost" or "community saved," the epilogue explores the construction and persistence of ethnic identity via non-static and reinvented notions. Ultimately, and contrary to the binary statements of Wojciech Etmanski and Mask-Connolly,[23] I argue that ethnicity can survive in the face of the decline of an ethnic identifier, such as nguage, and suggest how ethnicity can be reimagined for future generations. Newly emerging concepts that use intersectional approaches, such as the influence of public history and ethnic identity, hold promise for scholars wanting to delve into contemporary ethnic reimaginings.

Investigations into these topics do not come without some barriers and complications. As a former resident of Barry's Bay, I understand the internal dynamics of the community, as well as its historical memory and the stories embedded in its oral history. As a trained historian and teacher, I am familiar with the scholarly methods involved in the practice of history as an academic discipline. Drawing on this dual identity, and the promising concept of shared authority, my intent is to combine both local and professional knowledge to provide a more complete account of the history of Canada's first Polish community, in which I evaluate and address the competing narratives and realities propounded in the historical record and local memory.

Integrating these methodologies with grassroots research presents complications with language, because source material and oral history can be found in English, German, Polish, and admixtures of Polish/Kashubian/German. As a result, many third-, fourth-, and fifth-generation descendants – including me – who have been educated in English experience language barriers. However, the fact that English-speaking Polish-Kashub descendants are querying and writing about their roots contributes to contemporary reimaginings of the ethnic group. The historical record evolves, even if it is not recorded in the traditional mother tongue.

Returning to the difficulties that an insider faces, it became apparent, when trying to share authority with residents, that they were apprehensive. In querying ethnicity and identity among fourteen local residents, I often faced degrees of willingness and unwillingness to participate in this study. Although researchers are required to obtain ethics approval from academic institutions to carry out oral interviews and research, local residents were often unwilling to sign the required consent form. Moreover, several people with whom I spoke on two Kashub Days were unwilling to be formally interviewed. Several of these descendants claimed that since I am a "historian," I am an "authority" and can write a better history than they could tell, a response similar to the difficulties faced by Franca Iacovetta when conducting research in her Italian-Canadian community. This does not, I hope, signal elitism on my part since Iacovetta also believes that the researcher "by virtue of years spent studying a variety of sources, might well 'know' more, or rather 'know differently,' about [his or her] topic than an individual informant without falling into the elitist trap." Despite bringing situated knowledge to an interview, I am not an outsider to both worlds. But because the researcher has greater knowledge and different ways of thinking, as well as professional authority, it is not always possible to have a pristine, shared relationship with interviewees that allows a researcher to explore contemporary topics. Sometimes subjects simply abstain from participating due to real and/or perceived apprehensions.[24] While spaces such as Wilno and Barry's Bay are crucial in the production and generation of knowledge and historical memory, they also condition the types of disagreements or questioning that can be posed. Certain sites, such as Wilno's Heritage Park, where locals gather, also illustrate the intimate connections between "location and locution ... [as] social spaces facilitate and condition discursive space." Space, just like groupthink, can both enable and constrain discourse.[25] And, despite the desire to include everyone, not everyone wishes to play an active role in the remaking or reimagining of a shared group history. For some, historical memory is static and uncontested. By linking historical memory and cultural redefinition in one publication, my hope is that this multifaceted study contributes to the field of migration history as well as the study of ethnicity.

A Note on Terminology

Since the borders of Poland have changed through conflict and partition, the definition of "Polish" has also changed over time. References to Polish in this study will encompass one or more of the following traits: those who speak the Polish language; those who define themselves – solely or hyphenated – as Polish; and those who lived within the borders of pre-partition Poland, or who emigrated from the territory delineated by the pre-partition boundaries. "Polish" will also be used to describe the political entities of pre-partition and post–First World War Poland. The terms "Kaszub," "Kashub," and "Kashubian" are used to refer to specific persons or areas where it has been argued that people of the "Kashubian culture" or the "Kashubian language" lived or currently live. It is also used when specific persons define themselves – solely or hyphenated – as Kashub. Other terms will be explained as needed when they arise.

PART I
REVISITING HISTORICAL MEMORY

1

The Production of Knowledge and Canada's First Polish Community

> The place of the past in any landscape is as much the product of present interest as of past history.
> David Lowenthal, *Past Time, Present Place*

The first Polish community in Canada has long escaped the lens of historians. These settlers emigrated to Canada West during an episode of political instability before Confederation, and early Canadian historians paid more attention to the political deadlock in the Unionist period than to broader social questions. Despite making several appearances in the *Sessional Papers of the Province of Canada* during the late 1850s and early 1860s, and in some correspondence within the Crown Lands Department, nineteenth-century documentation on the group is scarce. To complicate matters, the Poles who settled along the Opeongo left little written evidence.

Although authors' writings outside the Polish-Kashub group were based on research into archives or observation of the people in the area, the group's representation in various media in the past decade has greatly increased. Since this group tended not to analyze the micro-level movements and patterns of the Polish group in the Barry's Bay/Wilno area, local historians and genealogists attempted to fill the narrative void using oral history and more unconventional sources, such as newspaper obituaries and family lore, to write the history of a group that left few written records. As a result, an investigation into not only the written history but also the oral history and historical memory of the enclave is needed.

Though local historians and pastkeepers have enriched the narrative by incorporating oral history, to the academic eye many of their publications leave the reader desiring a more contextualized history rather than a compartmentalized or mythologized one. This is where the skills of the professional historian could shape the narrative. On the other hand, some local residents may read the work of the external expert and feel that the deep analysis and the density of the language crowds out the narrative of the settlers and their individual histories and life events. These tensions – between the archival and the oral, the professional and the amateur, and the external and the internal – have all contributed to the production of historical knowledge of Canada's first Polish community. Yet such tensions, and the space between the methodologies, have also created a gap in the historical record for the Polish group. What is known by each group at a given time has dictated their writings and narrative-making capabilities. As a result, a bridge of shared authority needs to be created to establish a more comprehensive historical and social account of the ethnic group and its history.

Many writings on the Polish group in Canada have traversed genres from the national narrative through the social polemic and filiopietist phases. It is thus necessary to trace their contents and claims. Each phase not only reflected the concerns of its era but helped to illustrate the knowledge gap from which community publications have emerged. Yet this historical memory and the identity of those in Canada's first Polish community were also defined by other forms of knowledge, such as oral history, lived experience, and the descendants' exposure to agents of socialization such as priests and postwar Polish immigrants. Also vital is the concept of shared authority. The increase in shared authority has resulted in a surge in local historical memory and a heightened sense of ethnic consciousness. Important throughout, however, is the question: How did each author arrive at their conclusions? What emerges is that since cultural knowledge is distributed and controlled, "who knows what" determined how portions of the population perceived and constructed themselves and which interpretations gained status. From this, several myths and narratives of migration and settlement can be further examined.

The Production of Knowledge and Recognition by Authority

Knowledge is the act or result of knowing or understanding something and is derived from many sources. It is "perception by means of the senses," which can also be accumulated overtime to form a collective storehouse of understanding. Because it is subject to the senses, knowledge can be obtained passively or actively through reading, writing, speaking, listening, and doing. Another conceptualization of knowledge – local knowledge– is "tacit knowledge embodied in life experiences and reproduced in everyday behavior and speech." Julie Cruikshank argues that "local knowledge is never crudely encapsulated in closed traditions, but is produced during human encounters."[1] Being educated does not necessarily result in knowledge. But, for better and/or worse, what is known often needs to pass through a vetting process to ensure that it gains legitimacy and is accurate. In the academic realm, this process is overseen by an authority – someone who holds power or who has been conferred the right to judge, like a political figure, professor or researcher. Authority is also a complicated concept, used by both enlightened leaders and unjust oppressors. At the same time, authority is a "social relationship in which some people are granted the legitimacy to lead and others agree to follow" and the right "of a person to give commands depends on others' belief in his or her legitimacy." When invoking the term "legitimacy," we must also weigh the components that determine legitimacy: experience, knowledge, memory, positionality, expression, and perception. Authority can be confusing "because people are both attracted to, and repulsed" by it, depending on how authentic and legitimate it appears.[2]

Max Weber's typology of authority states that there are five types of authority. Traditional authority is based on pre-existing beliefs that grant legitimacy for those in ruling positions. A charismatic authority figure has been endowed with supernatural or superhuman powers or qualities and their legitimacy depends on their ability to fulfill people's needs and interests. This resembles the authority of the parish priest. Legal-rational authority, sometimes known as bureaucratic authority, gives high-ranking officials the right to enforce and issue commands. Professional authority is based on expertise in a given field. Finally, authority is dependent upon the ability to communicate[3]– the medium delivers and shapes the message but also relies on memory for its existence and recall.

As many sociologists, anthropologists, historians, and ethnographers have shown, memory is also a complicated concept. John Gillis writes that memory helps us to make sense of the world in which we live and is often treated as a fixed object – as something that can be retrieved. Memory is individual and also collective – in the sense of being public, popular, shared, social, historical, local, regional, and national. Memory is not static, fixed, or even constant. The historical use of the concept of memory is not about cognition. Regardless of the aggregate data or frequency of recall, Maria Cattell and Jacob Climo tell us that memory is "reconstructed by the dialectics of remembering and forgetting, shaped by the semantic and interpretive frames, and subject to a panoply of distortions." Building on the last influence – distortion – we have in many cases made the past controllable through constructed memories.[4]

In the study of history, memory is widely used and analyzed, consciously and unconsciously, individually and collectively. We construct and select our individual memories through our experiences. Our memories are also influenced by external factors. It is often burdensome to study individual memory since we compose memories to help us feel relatively comfortable with our lives. For these reasons, historians were once reluctant to incorporate individual memory into scholarly discourse. This epistemological convergence has changed, however. Scholars have examined personal memories more closely to see how individual recollections fit, even unconsciously, into cultural scripts. Similar individual memories grouped together form the basis of a collective memory. This collective memory can be unique to a group, class, or gender. Once connected, these collective memories form the base of a shared cultural knowledge and are often furthered by vehicles of memory such as books, films, and museums.[5]

Closely connected to collective memory, public memory has been described as the "body of beliefs and ideas about the past that help a public or society understand both its past, present, and by implication, its future." Public memory, as Pierre Nora articulated, is prompted and crystallized through *lieux de memoire*; these sites can range from "archives to museums, parades to moments of silence ... [and] ruins to commemorative feast days."[6] In the case of the Polish-Kashub group, individual and collective memory has been brought into the public realm through churches, historical plaques, books, films, and a museum. Yet individual discussion, agreement, and disagreement has led some to ponder the implications of public or collective memory. Newer paradigms have explored individual memory and its epistemological intersections and challenges with public memory.[7]

Sometimes popular memory subverts official memory. In a Nova Scotia context, Ian McKay and Rusty Bittermann have argued that the Scottish Highland Clearances "were deftly written out of official public memory" because they did not fit with the controlling interests that were shaping identities in Canada.[8] Yet that subversive memory of the Clearances persisted in the minds of some of those affected. The subversive memory, among the settlers, can produce myths to justify or explain later individual decisions, good or bad, after the results become apparent. Coupled with a deflection of blame, these memories may attempt to come to terms with an unresolved traumatic event or tensions. They can take on feelings of exile and brand migrants as victims of displacement and banishment – "more sinned against, than sinning, and thus exempt from responsibility."[9] This notion of exile as "involuntary movement" also contributes to the notion of a diaspora, which in its early twentieth-century sense was "saturated with the meanings of exile, loss, dislocation, [and] powerlessness." While the term diaspora has been used to describe the exile of Jews from their historic homeland, Paul Basu reminds us that recent interpretations of memory and diaspora have returned "instead to the etymological [Greek] roots of the word ... 'to sow over' or 'scatter' ... referring to expansionism, not forced exile."[10]

Until the 1970s, most scholarship in Canada and the United States overlooked the memories and experiences of immigrant groups. Previous historical writing in Canada was bound up with notions of the nation-state as an entity best studied archivally and on a national scale, and dominated by men with professional academic skills and classical training. Authority in the field was derived from a strict regime of reading, examinations, and publishing in an academic setting. When it did happen, the integration of immigration history into the national narrative tended to come from a nation-building perspective.[11] A somewhat different work, which nonetheless took a similar perspective, was the minister and social reformer James Woodsworth's 1909 book, *Strangers Within Our Gates*. Seeing the foreigner as a problem to be solved via assimilation, reformers "became interested in the spiritual salvation and the social well being of the foreign born."[12] Though it was directed to the Poles in the Prairies rather than the original group of settlers in Ontario, Woodsworth's publication remains one of the earliest writings to describe the Polish group in Canada. Similarly, William Thomas and Florian Znaniecki's 1918 publication, *The Polish Peasant in Europe and North America*, promoted the idea that immigration meant disruption. Because the social bonds of the peasantry had been loosened, the country needed to be concerned about the effects that modernization might have on immigrant groups.[13] At the time, there was little opportunity for those wishing to study the internal history of an ethnic group.

Meanwhile, as in other distinct ethnic groups in Canada, the Poles were left out of the developing national narrative unless their efforts were part of a national network. Feeding into this idea, beginning in the 1930s several articles and books were published that analyzed the colonization roads created by the government to promote the expansion of the country into previously wild regions. Paul Gates's 1934 article, "Official Encouragement to Immigration by the Province of Canada," which appeared in the *Canadian Historical Review*, as well as John Hodgetts's 1955 book, *Pioneer Public Service: An Administrative History of the United Canadas, 1841–1867*, were early examples of the top-down approach to the study of immigration and colonization. Writing in 1957, George Spragge documented the construction of colonization roads to promote settlement and Norman Macdonald's 1968 work, *Canada: Immigration and Colonization 1841–1903*, analyzed the actions of bureaucrats with a more critical eye. Despite their shortcomings when analyzing the histories of ethnic communities, these publications were later used by authors, such as Marilyn Miller,[14] as source material for the settlement part of their narratives for the Polish settlers, providing less scholarly authors insight into the colonization scheme. But apart from these works, there was little published work available for those wishing to write a history of the Polish group in Canada in the 1950s. Although migration to the Wilno and Barry's Bay areas had taken place almost a hundred years before, the record remained silent on the everyday patterns of their lives.

Such an absence was due in part to the divisions in academia at the time. One does not have to look far among immigration historians to see this. As John Beckett writes, for many years there existed a "residual hostile environment among professional historians, for whom 'local' meant parochial, antiquarian, and not 'proper' history."[15] To ensure the professional integrity of the craft, academic historians were to be siloed from other amateur writers. The concern was that those who wrote about the past without formal training would not be equipped to interpret what they found and would mislead readers. Writing in the *Canadian Historical Review* in 1932, D.C. Harvey placed the general and professional historian at the top of the hierarchy and the local historian at the bottom. The latter was defined as the one who worked "more or less spasmodically, spurred on by family interest or tradition," producing genealogical trees of their family (or kin group) from sources such as marriage licenses, deeds, baptismal registers, and death certificates. The general attitude was that local history was "cluttered up by meaningless details" and needed the trained eye of the professional to alleviate the attendant noise and disorganization. The perceived role of the local historian, therefore, was to provide the professional with "verified and verifiable facts about [the] smaller fields" so that he or she could weave them into a proper synthesized and contextualized narrative.[16] And what remained of the storehouses of information gathered by antiquarians or local historians? They remained outside the scholarly record. There was no place for them.

The mid-twentieth century, however, saw the emergence of filiopietistic works within ethnic communities, which put successful and notable representatives of the community on a pedestal. Such works "romanticized accounts of the culture and homelands of origin, [and highlighted] culturally determinist characterizations of their people emphasizing their proud, intelligent, and stoic qualities as well as their genius for 'success.'"[17]

The Polish group could turn to *Canada Ethnica IV: The Poles in Canada*, penned by Ludwig Kos-Rabcewicz-Zubkowski in 1967, which endeavoured to "depict the achievements of outstanding individuals"[18] of Polish descent in Canada and examined notables such as Casimir Gzowski, a superintendent of roads in 1841. The book being a product of its time, the notable men are studied in isolation from the group and the Barry's Bay/Wilno settlement is not mentioned at all. Other books were authored by William Bolesław Makowski, a postwar immigrant who became a secondary school teacher in St Catharines, Ontario. In a short paper presented to a Slavic academic audience in 1965, Makowski also documented notable Polish figures, with an emphasis on successful arrivals between 1776 and the 1960s. Makowski references those who immigrated individually or with their families, the settlement of Polish-Kashub peasants, late-nineteenth-century labour migrants, and postwar immigrants. But his reliance on source material was scant and he was unsure about the year of arrival for the first group.[19]

Two years later, Makowski published a much broader study, *History and Integration of Poles in Canada*, which devoted a full chapter to the Polish-Kashubs. Proceeding from the premise that integration into the nation meant progress, Makowski relied on several printed sources, sprinkled with some local knowledge. The first third of the chapter relies on geographical descriptions from a history of Renfrew County,[20] as well as oral accounts from local people. The focus of the chapter is on the religiosity of the settlers. Makowski draws on a diocesan history by O'Dwyer to outline the various priests and parishes that served the settlers.[21] Adding his own observations, Makowski highlights the generosity of the Polish people and concludes the chapter with an interview with a local physician. The extent of his local knowledge was questionable: locals noticed that he incorrectly captioned an interior photo of St Hedwig's church in Barry's Bay as "Interior of St. Mary's Shrine, Wilno, Ontario, 1967." The correction was visible in the Barry's Bay Public Library's copy of the book for many years. Makowski concludes the chapter with this observation: "Strongly nationalistic and deeply adherent to the Catholic religion, the Polish Kashoubs [sic] have nevertheless integrated well into the general life of their new country."[22] The book reflects the contemporary mindset, which was to study Polish immigrants with respect to how successfully they had integrated into Canadian society. At the time, as Makowski notes, there was no concrete model for examining the integration of immigrant groups into mainstream society. But in the wake of the Royal Commission on Bilingualism and Biculturalism in 1965, and the multiculturalism policies that were subsequently introduced, ethnic histories were firmly entrenched in the writing of Canadian history, no longer bracketed off as mere adornments.

Broadening the Spectrum of Knowledge: Multicultural and Grassroots Movements

Sociologists in the Chicago School in the United States were known for their early scholarly approaches to the study of migration, looking at immigration, modernization, and assimilation, mainly in urban areas, using a behaviouralist approach. Ethnic Turnerians, such as Theodore Blegen and George Stephenson, branching off from the work of Frederick Jackson Turner, on the other hand, used the frontier as the subject of their investigations. But each school held to a one-dimensional framework of migration from Europe to the United States and tended to look at immigrants only after they had set foot in the US.[23] Such an approach was denounced in 1960 by Frank Thistlewaite, who implored immigration historians to be "sensitive to the politics, economics, and social forces of the individual countries with which the migrant under study is associated." In addition to widening the research field to other receiving areas – namely Canada, Australia, and South America – Thistlewaite encouraged American scholars to study the environment and conditions the emigrants had left behind. Further, by adopting a "grassroots" approach to migration history, as encouraged by Turnerian Theodore Blegen, the field proliferated, casting earlier investigations in a new light.[24]

In Canada, studies of ethnic groups analyzed their integration into the nation. Influenced by the work of scholars in the United States, Canadian scholars produced newer works. These were in turn influenced by the natural succession of second- and third-generation immigrants, who entered post-secondary institutions in larger numbers. After the Royal Commission on Bilingualism and Biculturalism produced its preliminary findings, ethnic groups felt empowered. They too were a part of Canadian history! In particular, volume four of the Commission's report, "Cultural Contribution of the Other Ethnic Groups," drew the focus away from the writing of a dualistic French and English history to an ethnically plural or multicultural history[25] and also informed the 1971 multicultural policies of Pierre Trudeau's Liberals. Several areas received attention, including the teaching of languages other than French and English in secondary schools, multicultural and multilingual television, radio programming, and documentary films by the National Film Board. Funding was made available from the three tiers of government for these projects. At the provincial level, Robert Harney, a professor of history at the University of Toronto, received a large grant to form the Multicultural History Society of Ontario.[26] The MHSO published *Polyphony*, a periodical designed to address multicultural history in Canada. The Polish group benefitted from the periodical, with articles by Anna Reczynska and Izabela Jost. Also, an NFB production, *Kaszuby*, looked at Canada's first Polish settlement through interviews with group members.[27]

Thus, traditional authority figures acknowledged new forms of knowledge as meaningful. These initiatives in the 1970s and 1980s allowed the complete sequence of the migration to be analyzed in greater depth and at a grassroots level. The historiography on the Polish group also increased in the 1970s, although it was focused on the communities based in urban Ontario and the Prairies.

In 1976, University of Toronto sociologist Henry Radecki and writer Benedykt Heydenkorn published *A Member of a Distinguished Family: The Polish Group in Canada*. Funded by the Multiculturalism Program, the monograph was introduced by the former minister, later senator, Stanley Haidasz. The authors' scope was broad and their approach was developed to facilitate a macro-scale evaluation of the various pre- and postwar waves of immigrations. Although the Polish-Kashub settlers were mentioned, they were considered a particular linguistic enclave within the Polish group and not much attention was given to the Wilno/Barry's Bay settlement. As with Makowski, the authors' local knowledge was limited and they incorrectly identified a township where several Kashubs settled.[28] Yet the original group that settled was still given little attention in the narrative.

Radecki produced another book, in 1979, entitled *Ethnic Organization Dynamics: The Polish Group in Canada*. Again it mentioned the "the Kashubs, [who were] ethnically close to the Poles," but made the same incorrect township reference. Citing many statistics and using records to which he was privy because of his parents' involvement in Polish organizations, Radecki tabulated the efforts of organizations trying to preserve Polish culture. However, rather than discussing the dynamics of the Polish group nationwide, Radecki analyzed organizations in the greater Toronto area, which he designated the "Polish Capital" of Canada.[29] His aim was to highlight the promotional efforts of leaders and successful migrants to preserve their culture. Overall, however, the book's tone hints at a doomed future for the organizations, whose aging members were living in the past. And despite the growing knowledge of Canada's migration and ethnic history that was now available, again the original group of Polish settlers was left out of Radecki's narrative.

But they would soon be consulted for their empirical knowledge. In that era of ethnic euphoria in Canada, writers often, as Roberto Perin writes, "marveled at the persistence of ethnicity even though they were not quite sure what was persisting."[30] Interdisciplinary approaches that combined history, linguistics, sociology, and literature resulted in various models for analyzing ethnic communities, including those of institutional completeness (Raymond Breton) and identity retention (Wsevolod Isajiw).[31] The explosion of work in social history, especially in the fields of labour, family, and community, opened up new avenues for historians to pursue alongside the new immigration history.[32] Scholars attempted to keep a record of the past before it was lost among second- and third-generation descendants. Their efforts hearkened back to comments from the ethnic Turnerian Marcus Hansen: the grandson wishes to remember what the son wants to forget.[33] Writing the history of these ethnic groups meant that oral history became "a critical research device [and] if some [relied] too heavily on the oral recollections of their informants in an effort to give them an 'authentic' voice, their impulse was decidedly democratic."[34] Those who had traditionally been silenced in the national narratives now found an audience among those who were interested in recording what they knew.

Some authors in the realms of folk culture, including Jan Perkowski and John Glofcheskie, concentrated on the social and cultural aspects of the descendants of the first Polish group in Canada. Finally, the local store of knowledge was going to be used. Perkowski, a young Harvard-educated linguist, received funding from the Museum of Man to carry out research around Wilno in 1968 and 1969. Following up on rumours he had heard, Perkowski interviewed locals about their beliefs in the occult, which were published in a book called *Vampires, Dwarves, and Witches among the Ontario Kashubs*. Outlining many of the practices of the Kashub linguistic group, citing O'Dwyer and Makowski, and quoting Lorentz and Fischer's *The Cassubian Civilization*,[35] Perkowski arrived at conclusions about the demonology of the Kashubs from the anonymous oral testimony of fifteen local residents. He declared the Kashubs to be a Slavic people closely related to the Poles in language and lineage, but incorrectly stated that they had departed from Lubawa, Starogard, Gdynia, and other cities. While he was the first to solicit the widespread social and religious knowledge that locals possessed, and give voice to those who had not previously been consulted, his publication came under critical scrutiny by those very people.

After it was published in 1972, there was considerable outrage in Wilno as well as condemnation from the floor of the House of Commons. Not long after, the publication was listed as out of print.[36] Perkowski transcribed tales of inexplicable occurrences in the community as legitimate and painted them as interior and communal esoteric beliefs in the occult. Associating the deaths of fourteen people, over the course of several years, as the workings of a vampire is one of many non-contextualized narratives in Perkowski's work. Instead of pondering the settlers' incomprehension of illnesses, or contextualizing mysterious bite and scratch marks as byproducts of farming, he suggested that this had been and remained a system of beliefs of the larger community.[37] A local priest responded in 1973, saying: "I was amazed that such a thing would be printed ... They are like stories my grandmother would tell to scare us ... It is possible that one or two nuts have those beliefs but the implication is that all of us do ... We get a big laugh out of it, we know the people who have manufactured the story just by reading it ... That nonsense of driving nails [into dead bodies of supposed vampires]. My impression is that he probably stuck a microphone under their noses and to get rid of him they'd made up these tales."[38] Another local, Margina, told a reporter: "This anthropologist [Perkowski], he was not a sincere man ... He was not what he claimed. He sat here. Here, with me in my kitchen. I told him the old wives' tales, things my grandmother told me, but we don't believe these things any more. He wrote terrible things. He caused the people around here a lot of pain."[39]

Ultimately, it appears that Perkowski did not recognize that the informants' remarks were ironic or jocular. For example, when asked about witches, one informant replied, "Witch – there's so many of them. My dear, I will tell you ... my brother is married to one."[40] The fact that the subjects' answers were laced with sarcasm and hyperbole escaped the outsider, who seemed to have been unaware that locals were feeding him tales. Many descendants can attest to the fact that humorous aphorisms about the supernatural exist. I can remember a popular one from my grandmother, Frances (Shulist) Blank: "Don't whistle at night; the devil dances on the stove!" However, Perkowski could have verified the apocryphal character of some of the stories.[41]

Unknown to most in the Ottawa Valley, Perkowski reissued his original publication in 2006 but it would have been a richer text had he re-examined and contextualized the stories.⁴²

Perkowksi's project reveals the divisions that often exist between external and internal community members. It is an excellent example of what Johannes Fabian warns against: that ethnographers and scholars are capable of creating the very thing they discover.⁴³ Although he was trying to hear new voices and to tap sources of knowledge, the project went awry because Perkowski was not aware of the interior dynamics of the community, local historical memory, and embedded local ways of reciting oral history. Returning to the idea that knowledge is the perception by the senses, it appears that in the transition between the passive viewing, listening, reporting, transcribing, and publishing stages, the local knowledge Petrowski had accumulated became distorted from its original form. Encounters and interactions with oral history can sometimes be problematic as audiences often shape their interpretations based on their own concerns.⁴⁴ One wonders if some of Perkowski's claims were shaped by the desire of his employer at the time, as he was quoted as saying that the Museum of Man publishes "these dry things on Eskimo stone carvings ... and they thought they'd have a slightly jazzier thing. So I went along with them ... everybody likes to be frightened a little bit by the Dracula legend."⁴⁵

The publication of Perkowski's work also raised another issue regarding the production of knowledge: how one is positioned, as insider or outsider, in relation to the community. Reflecting on Iacovetta's writings on insider versus outsider knowledge, it becomes apparent that academic outsiders sometimes impose "an artificial order on their research. In doing so they masked complexities, ignored divergent practices, and silenced alternative and resistant voices" – if they even knew where or how to find them. John Walsh and Steven High likewise argue that communities have power relationships. Who is interviewed influences the knowledge passed along.⁴⁶ *Vampires, Dwarves, and Witches among the Ontario Kashubs* shook the local community and its trust of outsiders, while still leaving a large untapped storehouse of empirical knowledge in the area.

The work of a local author, hired by the Museum of Man amid the controversy, sought to document the community in a different light. John Glofcheskie, a student from Barry's Bay in the music program at the University of Western Ontario, was awarded a grant to study the community's folk music, and he interviewed and recorded locals in and around the area in 1973. According to local reporter Gerald Tracey, many locals were willing to share their songs (sometimes with "shady lyrics") and personal stories with Glofcheskie because he was "part of the community and a direct descendant of Kashubian immigrants ... [He] was able to gain their trust and confidence where an outsider would have difficulty." Glofcheskie went on to study musicology in Cambridge University's PhD program and studied Polish language and culture at Jagiellonian University in Kraków.[47] His book, *Folk Music of Canada's Oldest Polish Community*, was eventually published by the Museum of Man in 1980 and Glofcheskie's recordings were deposited in the museum's archives. (Glofcheskie claims that the book, acclaimed by many as an excellent analytical work, was published from the draft copy without his knowledge.)[48] The book looks at the integration of music into wedding and wake ceremonies in the community, and explores the melodic variants of Polish hymns and textual variants of the *frantówka* (short humorous songs). Describing the *pusta noc* (empty night) wake ritual, Glofcheskie echoes the same notions of migrant hardiness and religiosity that had been emphasized in earlier publications. In 2006, a joint reissue of his analysis and recordings on compact disc by the Canadian Museum of Civilization, Library and Archives Canada, and Glofcheskie completed the compendium.[49] Glofcheskie's publications proved that historical knowledge is a shared social discourse. Overall, however, little scholarship on the Polish group in the 1980s relied on local stores of knowledge.

Stories from a Distance and German Migration

While Glofcheskie compiled his work, several academics external to the Polish group in the Ottawa Valley wrote about the community from a distance, drawing from traditional archival and secondary sources. The same year that Makowski published his first book on the Polish group, a British immigrant living in Deep River, Ontario, Brenda Lee-Whiting, published an article entitled "The Opeongo Road – An Early Colonization Scheme." After completing her doctorate in botany at the University of Bristol, and working with Atomic Energy of Canada Limited in Chalk River, Lee-Whiting became interested in local history.

In the article she gives a general history of the creation of the road and supplements it with some statistics from the brochure that French had published for settlers in 1857. This was an important work, as it was the first time a sizable portion of a publication had been devoted to the first Polish settlement. Lee-Whiting also wrote a second article, "First Polish Settlement in Canada," which documented the existence of the settlement along with the persistence of language in the area. These two publications were an important starting point for the exploration of the community's history.[50]

In response to Lee-Whiting's research, a Polish-born student named Izabela Jost published an article with new information in 1974. Jost placed the Polish group in the narrative of the Opeongo by extracting information from some of French's letters at the Archives of Ontario, along with census material and some secondary literature. The first to use a soil survey (several others would follow her lead), Jost puts forth the claim that the land was inferior for cultivation by using a 1966 soil survey in her argument. Although Jost mentions that "hundreds of years ago farming methods and land evaluations were different,"[51] her work does not analyze the technology of the time to qualify the claim.

Nine years later, Jost published portions of her doctoral dissertation (in Polish), from Katolicki Uniwersytet Lubelski, but few in the Ottawa Valley were able to read it in Polish and copies were not readily available. *Osadnictwo Kaszubskie W Ontario* looks at the history of Polish migration in the Ottawa Valley and features several maps showing ethnic concentrations in the area. A year later, Jost wrote an article in *Polyphony*, outlining the general history of the Wilno/Barry's Bay area and the religiosity of the settlers. Jost reiterates the resolve of the settlers along the same lines as the other authors of filiopietist works.[52] In the same decade, Makowski published another book, *The Polish People in Canada: A Visual History* (1987), in which he integrated photos with his previous research.[53] His reissue contains new writings on the more recent waves of immigration, and an abundance of photographs on the themes of strength, success, and resiliency. The half-chapter on the "Polish-Kashoub" group was recycled from his 1967 publication, with minor changes.

Those of Polish descent in the region who wished to learn more about their community's history in the 1980s could only consult the works written from a distance by external authors. During this time, the Poles were also included in publications about German migration to Canada. This was due to the fact that the Polish settlers embarked on their transatlantic journey from German ports at Hamburg and Bremerhaven and were grouped as "Prussian" in early census returns and sessional reports due to the political boundaries of the time. These books mentioned the Polish immigrants but were also penned by authors external to both the local Polish and German groups.

In 1984, Peter Hessel, a retired public servant, translator, and postwar German immigrant, published his investigation into the German settlement in Renfrew County after consulting archival material in Canada and Germany. He outlined the travels and methods of recruiting that two Crown agents, William Wagner and William Sinn, had used in several Prussian provinces. Hessel notes that in Pomerania a "different" German was spoken, "Low German" or *Plattdeutsch*, and mentioned the existence of two sub-groups: Kashubs and Wends.[54] Much of Hessel's publication, six of nine chapters, focuses on activity in the land of departure and the voyage to the Ottawa Valley. By being sensitive to the conditions in the land of departure and devoting efforts to documenting it, Hessel broadened the information available to the Polish and German communities and bolstered the notion that settlers were recruited to come to Canada, thus helping to solidify and expand knowledge of this segment of the migration in locals' historical memory.

A year after Hessel's work appeared, Lee-Whiting published her first book, *Harvest of Stones*, which documents the same settlers as Hessel but with greater detail on the post-arrival period. The book was the culmination of two decades of collecting, documenting, and interviewing. Lee-Whiting reiterates, in less detail, several of the same recruiting activities outlined by Hessel. Her chapter "Bismarck's Legacy," tiptoed toward establishing Bismarck as the instigating cause for migration but did not analyze many of the pre-migration conditions in the land of departure. Instead, Lee-Whiting quickly shifts to a tone she felt comfortable with and drew upon the oral history of descendants in the German-Canadian community. By doing so, she found that the migrants "came to obtain land, or to get away from the wars, or because they were persuaded by letters from a relative already settled in Eastern Upper Canada."[55] Lee-Whiting also writes about the Polish settlers' land selection, quoting a publication written in Poland by Kazmierz Ickiewicz and newspaper articles by Rekowski,[56] reiterating the idea that the Polish settlers chose their worthless land in the hills deliberately – to be isolated. Lee-Whiting also supports this idea with testimony, not from locals, but from the government agent, William Sinn, who wrote that the settlers went too far up the line for employment.

The rest of Lee-Whiting's book highlighted the social history of the settlers on the land, documentation that was unprecedented at the time. She could have deepened her analysis by examining broader trends or comparisons, for example, in the areas of education and religion or in relations with other ethnic groups, like the Irish or Polish-Kashubs. Similarly, Lee-Whiting writes about German, Polish, and Kashubian furniture styles, but does not explore their origins or how much is shared by all settlers in the area. Nonetheless, the work was pioneering.

Despite the shortcomings of *Harvest of Stones*, one can imagine the value of a publication that combines Hessel's analysis of the land of departure with Lee-Whiting's studies into the lives of the descendants. The study of the German group in the Ottawa Valley has languished since these books appeared. These outside authors did not inspire and involve direct descendants, as Rekowski would later do with the Polish group, in rediscovering their ancestry and their emigration experience.

Almost a decade after Glofcheskie's work appeared, the next significant book about the local Polish group was published in 1991. Anna Zurakowski, a postwar immigrant who settled south of Barry's Bay with her husband Jan, secured funding, under the label "Polish Heritage Institute – Kaszuby," from the Ontario Ministry of Culture for the book, which was edited with the help of several people from the broader Polish postwar community. These included a retired National Research Council (NRC) cartographer, Dr Teodor Blachut (1914–2004), Igor Oleszkiewicz, an NRC researcher, and a local priest, Bernard Prince, who was secretary general for the Vatican's Pontifical Society for the Propagation of Faith. The result, Zurakowski's *The Proud Inheritance: Ontario's Kaszuby*, documents the settlement period and glorifies the strength of the Kashubian pioneers throughout the decades. The editors enlisted a local reporter, Ray Stamplecoskie, to give a current socioeconomic overview of the local area and its inhabitants. The publication's outline of the group's history and its rich photography sought to inform locals, tourists, and interested readers about the Polish and Kashubian culture and heritage in the area.[57]

Zurakowski's book represents both the demise of a thread of historiography and a socializing influence. *The Proud Inheritance* marks the last significant publication written by a non-descendant of Canada's first Polish community. It also draws attention to an unresolved tension between ethnic identity and external Polish methods of inculcating culture to local descendants. Evidence of this appears in the seventh and final chapter, "Youth – The Future." Zurakowski draws attention to cultural movements initiated by the external Polish community and former army chaplain and postwar migrant Fr Rafał Grzondziel in the 1950s, crediting Grzondziel with "discovering" the land for Polish youth centres near Barry's Bay in the Wadsworth Lake area in 1953. Indeed, several scouting camps, such as "Karpaty," were set up by postwar Poles in the 1950s. These camps were heavily influenced by the postwar Polish officer and intelligentsia class, and activities, such as pseudo-military marches and nationalist celebrations, were designed by this group for Polish youth from Canada and the US.[58] Zurakowski rightly claims that many Polish youth from Toronto, Montreal, and Ottawa have ties to the Kaszuby camps. However, she somewhat hastily concludes that "close ties of friendship and cooperation arose between the local inhabitants and the newly-arrived Poles."[59] If she were to study the attendance figures – if that is possible – she would likely have found that, for language and socio-economic reasons, very few local, permanent residents enrolled their children in the centres. When the scouting jamboree, "Kaszuby 1976" was held, around 1,400 scouts from across the world arrived at the camps near Barry's Bay. Only four local children were visibly active in the Polish scouting camp at the time.[60]

Between the 1970s and 1990s, many of the studies that were published about the community were written by outsiders such as Perkowski, Hessel, and Zurakowski. These works may be called "regimes of knowledge"[61] in that the authors' professional credentials and the authority and permanence of the printed word influenced the shape of local history. More important, these works repeatedly drew attention to the fact that the settlers spoke a "different" Polish – yet without the group itself admitting this. Commenting on these tensions between language and ethnic identity, Zurakowski correctly writes that "Canadian Kaszubs have always stressed their Polish origins."[62] The thought, on the part of postwar Poles and Hessel, was that these original settlers spoke a vernacular and should be identified as Kaszubian. But this claim was largely ignored by locals, who thought that they spoke low Polish, and that the postwar Polish residents, tourists, and priests spoke high Polish.[63] The reason postwar Poles dismissed the idea was due to the fact that locals had been socialized to think this way for over a century. The production of knowledge in their spheres dictated who they were. They participated in Polish masses, events, and ceremonies organized by traditional authority figures – their Polish parish priests – who were regarded as knowledgeable and charismatic. Locals thought they were Polish.

Socialized Knowledge and Regimes in the Construction of Polishness

Whether they realized it or not, local descendants' production of knowledge relating to their ethnic consciousness, as well as their narratives of migration, were shaped mostly from the outside. These regimes governed the narratives for over a century. Such a construction of "Polishness," or "Polonia," by local descendants was influenced by current events in the homeland, the influence of the social and cultural community, and the influence of the ethno-religion of Poland – Roman Catholicism. The main agents of socialization for families in the Wilno and Barry's Bay areas throughout the latter half of the nineteenth century and in the twentieth century were church, family, school, and, later, the cottaging community of postwar Poles. Via these forces, ideas of Polishness were constructed and reciprocally endorsed, and contributed to the community's sense of identity. It is also important to study the discursive spaces in which these narratives were dictated. In church, school, and in social exchanges with external, educated postwar Poles, the space did not allow for disagreement to be expressed due to the governing mores of the regimes and spaces themselves. Body, mind, and spirit were – to some degree – disciplined and socialized.

The church was a powerful agent of socialization, one that created, bolstered, and buttressed historical memory and ethnic consciousness in the Barry's Bay/Wilno area. As Frances Swyripa reminds us, when faith and a national identity are linked, sacred space, "through its visual images and rituals, becomes a crucial meeting place where the two interact." In order to "cultivate and reinforce people's sense of belonging ... churches turn to history; at the same time they accept custodianship of the 'imagined' past around which that sense of belonging is constructed. Moreover, by providing the setting for and participating in the rites of state occasions or landmark moments in the life of the nation, churches themselves become active partners in making history and inventing tradition."[64] As chapter 2 documents, the ethnoreligious connection has deep roots in Poland and was brought by migrants. Priests, as powerful authority figures, mediated between the temporal and spiritual worlds, and disciplined ways of thinking.

From 1859 to 1876, Polish settlers along the Opeongo attended an English-speaking church in Brudenell until St Stanislaus Kostka was built in Wilno. Between 1876 and 1892, the settlers received a litany of peripatetic Polish-speaking priests, including Fr Specht, Fr Michanowski, Fr Korbutowicz, and Fr Ladislaus Dembski. From 1892 to 1928, Msgr Jankowski ministered to the local Polish settlers and their families and instructed their children in the tenets of catechism.[65] But the promotion of Polishness from the pulpit increased dramatically with the arrival of Fr Edward Wilowski in 1928. Wilowski was a "staunch supporter" of annual 3 May (Polish Day) celebrations until 1961, which he helped orchestrate at St Stanislaus's and St Mary's. For these promotions of Polish culture, Wilowski was awarded the Order of Poland in 1946. Fr Stan Kadziolka, a Kraków-born priest who was imprisoned by the Nazis in Auschwitz, Belsen, and Orienburg, arrived at the parish in 1961 and kept the Polish Day celebrations alive until his resignation in 1985. On the occasion of the 300th anniversary of Catholicism in Poland, Kadziolka helped to coordinate the events of 3 May. The St Hedwig's choir from Barry's Bay was enlisted to sing hymns and Polish songs. A display of Polish costumes was added with the help of Mira Jaworska – a member of the external Polish community. Kadziolka also coordinated the writing and presentation of a booklet about the Polishness of Wilno for Karol Wojtyła – Pope John Paul II – in 1984. Several kilometres west of Wilno in Barry's Bay, Polish Day celebrations also promoted Polishness and were organized by Msgr Peter Biernacki, a descendant of original settlers who was educated in a Polish seminary in Michigan. Wilowski always extended his help to events in Barry's Bay, too.[66] At Biernacki's famed and successful parish picnics, the per-

1.1 The St Hedwig's White Eagles, 1936. Back, left to right: Zita Shalla, Catherine Vitkuskie, Monica Coulas, Ursula Maika. Seated, left to right: Rita Beanish, Christina Coulas, Eleanor Maika, Tessie Dombroskie and Doreen Vitkuskie. Missing are: Teresita Chippure, Pat Cybulski, Josephine Maika, and Rita Cybulski. The team played several exhibition tilts at parish picnics in the Ottawa Valley and were coached by Msgrs Maika and Biernacki. It is ironic that the editor of the *BBR* extolled their "true sports*man*ship" when playing out of town games and games at the Orangeman's Picnic in Maynooth.

formance of Polish culture often appeared in the picnic schedule. Advertisements in newspapers announced that Polish national songs and dances, performed by local Polish musicians and singers, were continually scheduled. The St Hedwig's female softball team, run by Biernacki and Fr Maika, paid tribute to a Polish national symbol and was named the White Eagles (see figure 1.1).[67]

The celebrations surrounding 3 May were popular not only because they provided a day of leisure away from the farm or because they were a celebration of culture. They were also a celebration of a national identity and faith, which had been repressed in the homeland, and for an ethnic group were a powerful connection. As Swyripa argues, such celebrations "symbolize a vision of the nation" and are an "opposition or counter movement, anathema to the ruling regime."⁶⁸ For those who had experienced hardships, such as the pre- and post-Bismarckian groups and the postwar Polish priests, these celebrations reaffirmed their Polish identity and united parishioners and authority figures (both pre- and postwar immigrants) in thanksgiving and protest, solidifying knowledge of their ethnic identity.

Closely linked to the Church was the promotion of Catholicism and Polishness in education. In the 1940s and 1950s, instruction in the Polish language and catechism was given to area students in the summer by the Felician Sisters, an order of Polish nuns from Toronto. The Felician Sisters taught at St Stanislaus Kostka in Toronto as early as 1937, after moving from the United States. Along with Wilowski, they were administering to around 250 students by 1950.Wilowski also ran a series of Polish-language plays and comedies using local talent, such as "Wyrodna Córka" (The Prodigal Daughter) and "Świstak" (The Groundhog) during his tenure.⁶⁹ In conjunction with local schools, Christmas and Polish Day concerts were often held at St Mary's in Wilno and St Hedwig's in Barry's Bay. The performance of culture and ethnicity, buttressed by the traditional and professional knowledge of priests and lay postwar Poles, cemented the notion of Polishness among the descendants of original settlers in the vicinity of the Opeongo. In 1973, Fr Calik, a visiting priest from Calgary, continued similar courses on Saturdays at St Joseph's School in Barry's Bay. He taught more than fifty regular students the Polish language, as well as folk and church songs, to ensure that they did not lose their Polish heritage.⁷⁰

Other educational opportunities for teenagers emerged with the 1971 formation of a Polish studies club at Madawaska Valley District High School (MVDHS) in Barry's Bay. Its aim was to make "its members proficient in dancing, [the] Polish language, the culture of Poland and its literature." Various Polish dances, such as the Polonaise, the Mazurka, and Kujawiak were taught by Mira Jaworska, assisted by Joan Petrzalek, both non-local Poles whose families had immigrated well after the original group. Accordion music was supplied by Barney McCaffrey, a recent American resident with Polish roots. Their efforts were showcased at events throughout the area with the help of the Zurakowskis, Fr Calik, Mr and Mrs T. Wisniewski, Mr K. Rudzinski, and Aldon Kosinski, all from the external Polish community. One of these occasions was the production of the Polish play "Jaselka Polka"

1.2   Polish dance group at St Hedwig's Church in Barry's Bay (c. 1966).

on 29 December 1973, which attracted more than 500 people, and the singing of Polish Christmas carols (*kolędy*).[71]

Such courses and activities were offered by laypersons who had a professional knowledge of Polish culture through a combination of lived experience, knowledge of the outside world, knowledge of contemporary Poland, and the experience of higher education. As a result, local teachers Elizabeth Shalla and her sister, Sr Genevieve, enlisted Jaworska's skills for other Polish events and recitals at St Hedwig's in Barry's Bay (see figure 1.2).[72]

After-school Polish language and culture classes continued into the 1990s in local elementary schools and were taught by external Polish community members Peter Niedojadlo and Wanda Zalewska. Reinforcing what their predecessors had done in earlier decades, they schooled local pupils in the Polish language, culture, and dances. Pupils recited prayers in Polish, practised hymns and songs, and performed dances such as the Krakowiak.[73] These were performed again during Polish Day celebrations.

Local groups could also draw inspiration from several ensembles that toured the area in the 1970s. Ottawa's Paderewski Choir and

Dance Ensemble performed at MVDHS in May 1975 and were led by Dr J. Dobrowolski and Dr R. Pelinski. In July 1975, the Melodia Choir from St Casimir's Church in Toronto sang Polish folk songs in Wilno that were complemented by dances from a Montreal group at the parish's centennial celebration.[74]

The ethnic and national exercises inculcated by the church and schools permeated the public and private lives of those descendants in the Wilno and Barry's Bay area. They connected the lives of families who enrolled their children in out-of-school programs and bolstered a sense of Polishness. This strong sense of ethnocultural identity was also displayed by local residents in public ceremonies and exhibited at sites of memory. One such outlet was the Polish Canadian Pioneer Centre, which was formed in 1965 to "commemorate the Polish ancestors." An endeavour by locals, with the exception of help from Jan Zurakowski, its president was Martin Shulist. Other original members included Alex Shulist, Zigmund Bloski, Frank J. Ritza, Adolph Pecoskie, Bronis Cybulski, Anthony Prince, and Nick Lepinski. According to *Barry's Bay This Week* (*BBTW*), the members planned a museum to showcase the region's "Polish history in pictures and literature" and antiques.[75] In 1972, a ceremonial unveiling of a provincial plaque designating the Wilno area as Canada's first Polish settlement inspired pomp and pageantry. Local youths dressed in Polish costumes showcased their heritage to dignitaries such as Sydney Wise, the president of the Ontario Historical Society, G. Masedson, the warden of Renfrew County, local MPP John Yakabuski, MP Len Hopkins, and Frs Shulist and Prince, local priests of Polish descent (see figure 1.3).

In August 1974, a plaque marking the site of the first Polish church in the Bay (the mission church of the Assumption on Siberia Road), donated by Don Etmanskie, was unveiled in a ceremony. The centennial year for Wilno, 1975, saw numerous visible signs of Polishness as well. The centennial stamp was designed by Frank Ritza and displayed a Polish eagle with a red maple leaf in the centre. A centennial quilt was created that also displayed symbols of Poland: a white Polish eagle on a background of red.[76] Notions of Polishness were passed on from external Poles and traditional authority figures and embraced by locals.

While claims that locals were Kashubian Poles had been made as early as the 1950s, locals often dismissed them for various reasons. Zurakowski, a postwar immigrant herself, echoes this, saying that

1.3 The 1972 provincial plaque ceremony in Wilno.

in "later years many of their descendants did not clearly understand the meaning of the term 'Kaszub.' Some of them even considered it an insult, a reference to their supposedly 'lower' origins."[77] This dismissal of the Kashubian nomenclature had much to do with the elitism that underlaid the thoughts and comments of the postwar Polish-Canadians, including the tourists and visitors who occupied cottages in the Wadsworth Lake area. Locals believed they were Polish. But because the first Polish-Kashub migrants were of peasant origins, or as Roberto Perin quips, "not members of a distinguished family," their lack of education was thought to account for their improper use of the Polish language in Canada.[78] This feeling resonated throughout the local community as their linguistic shortcomings, marked with idioms from English or peasant-based Polish, became apparent, something Rekowski and David Shulist discovered when talking with postwar Poles. One does not have to look far to find such elitism: Zurakowski herself critiques the minor inconsistencies in spelling on the gravestones of local settlers and compares it to proper "literary Polish."[79] Being told they were different – by postwar Polish immigrants who were more closely connected to the homeland on account of their recent arrival, and gave the impression that their lived experience made them more authoritative – promoted a sense of ethnic inferiority among locals. Their culture and that of the mother country did not fit. The politics of exclusion and inclusion are very powerful, especially when they concern one's identity.

No one has investigated why the postwar group would inculcate such histories and identities into the original group. But a broader study into the postwar group reveals the presence of a certain nationalist worldview. The first Polish communities in Canada and the United States were usually organized parochially and few intellectual leaders came before the Second World War.[80] This allowed for internal stability and order and meant that traditional authority figures, such as the parish priest, guided activity. The subsequent introduction of the postwar group of Polish immigrants meant that more professional and managerial classes with nationalistic causes were added to the mix. These emigrants, or exiles, according to Anna Jaroszyńska-Kirchmann, "felt particularly responsible for the protection and nurture of Polish high culture: the literary language, artistic expression, as well as intellectual thought and scientific achievement."[81] In the words of Sheila Patterson, the majority of these Poles were "an army in exile with an almost messianic duty to keep alive certain ideas and cultural values that would otherwise be destroyed." As Jan Karski mentions, due to the absence of education for Polish youth during the Second World War, many Poles felt their youth could fall prey to Nazi temptations if they did not pass on their knowledge. Knowledge of Polish history and a sense of historical memory, to this group, according to Jaroszyńska-Kirchmann, "has always been vital to the Polish experience. The memory of past glories helped the nation endure the partitions" and all their children in exile were expected to know Polish history, language, and culture in preparation for a return to the homeland. These refugees and exiles felt it was their "exile mission" to maintain a pure Polishness and instill it where the forces of assimilation started to take hold. Higher-paying occupations, due to their education and experience as part of the intelligentsia in Poland, a working knowledge of English, and increased leisure time allowed this group to go about their mission.[82]

It becomes more evident how the postwar group looked upon the original group when we analyze an individual's ethnic awareness using three categories delineated by Victor Greene, and envisioned as lying on a spectrum: ethnic naiveté; cultural or polycentric nationalism; and nationalism. Many descendants of the nineteenth-century Poles would most likely be in the first stage. Although they possessed and recognized certain cultural characteristics, they had little or no feeling of membership in the greater ethnic group. With the exception of local priests and a teacher (Elizabeth Shalla), very few from the original pre-1900 group could be placed in the second category, in which individuals exhibit ethnic consciousness and make a point of continuing "traditional" customs. Greene's final category, "nationalism," represents the elite segment of refugees, intellectuals who found "pride and satisfaction in feeling and broadcasting that identity." These immigrants "worked enthusiastically to perpetuate their nation's name."[83] A postwar Pole might, accordingly, classify one of the descendants in the Barry's Bay/Wilno area as naive and attempt to bridge the gap to the nationalist stage by offering lectures, cultural events, concerts, theatre performances, exhibits, and ethnic celebrations. On the other hand, locals who knew who they came from and were content with that knowledge were often skeptical of the foreign high culture and folk arts that the educated class foisted upon them. In the Barry's Bay area, as elsewhere in North America, some locals also resented the newer wave of Poles on economic grounds as they had more disposable income and easier access to modern goods.[84] While original descendants laboured on their marginal farms, many postwar Poles could purchase what they wanted for their cottages in the Madawaska Valley. Roy MacGregor's comments surrounding the tensions between locals and tourists near Algonquin Park also provide insight into the issue. "The defence mechanism is to look down on those who come, before they can look down – as surely they are doing – on those already there ... It is a strange, ritualistic, symbiotic relationship ... both visitor and local laugh at each other behind the other's back ... [but] neither could exist without the other."[85]

In the late 1970s, some postwar Poles in Canada began to suggest more openly that those settled in the Barry's Bay/Wilno area were Kaszubian Poles. They pointed to "traditional" Kaszubian embroidery as proof that another culture existed in the land of departure. They also tried to enlist the support of some local residents and settled postwar Poles in their promotions. By this time, the ethnicity known as

"Kaszubian" was more broadly developed in Poland (see chapter 6) and educated postwar Poles were more familiar with it. In 1976, the Polish New Horizons Club of Toronto made and donated ten Kaszubian embroidered panels to the Polish Canadian Pioneer Centre. A letter from Genowefa Staron, the craft instructor for the group, stated that these historical folk designs were "ready to be hung in the Museum for the inspiration to those of local Polish Kaszubian descent."[86] Two years later, in 1978, Tony Yantha, of the Barry's Bay and Sherwood Jones and Burns Recreation Committee, appointed university students George and John Wisniewski to carry out a program promoting Polish culture in Barry's Bay. Continuing the theme of professional authority imported by educated Poles from outside, the Wisniewskis, who attended high school in the Barry's Bay area but had roots elsewhere in the Polish community, attempted to educate locals about Polish history. Their last presentation acquainted local people with the traditional dress and arts of the Kaszubian region in Poland. Pottery and embroidery for the event were supplied by Eugene and Jadwiga Chruscicki, postwar migrants living in Toronto. Besides working for the CBC, Eugene was recognized as a professional authority by the greater Polish community and was regarded as "one of the best known and respected Polish-Canadian painters."[87] A picture from the event was also featured in the *BBTW* newspaper. When compared with the earlier costumes displayed in local Polish performative events, however, the costumes introduced by postwar Poles to locals as Polish national costumes resembled the regional costume of the Kraków region. The embroidered black bodices of the female costumes and the long black coats of the male costumes are similar to those described elsewhere as Krakówian.[88] This Krakówian-inspired performative costume continued as a mainstay in cultural and performative events for another decade and a half.[89] Similarly, the promotion of the Krakowiak as a national dance, which was only danced by the nobility but had achieved status as a national folk dance in Poland by the 1950s,[90] permeated the Polishness that locals had previously practised.

In an effort to share authority with locals, postwar Polish officials at the scouting camps at Kaszuby formed an alliance worthy of Martin Shulist's bureaucratic endorsement (as president of a local history museum and an "authority" figure) and held a two-week summer day camp for young children for a dollar a day.[91] The 1980 version of the camp reached out to locals for leadership in the promotion of Kaszubianism, naming two local residents, Gordon Lorbetski and Donna Smaglinski, as directors. To cement ties, a priest from the Kaszuby region of Poland attended, "a Kaszubian design was painted on one of the local barns, and a new folk song the 'Kaszub Sewing Song'" was taught. That same year, in response to letters requesting language classes endorsed by multicultural policies, scoutmaster Francis Bahyrycz and another Pole from outside the community, Marek Milan, taught both "high and low Polish words and expressions" in an effort to bridge the two types of spoken Polish. Three years later, Polish heritage classes in Combermere also attempted to instill the Żukowo embroidery and colour guide to locals.[92]

In the face of all this, descendants of the original settlers in the Wilno and Barry's Bay area still resisted the new Kaszub designation and continued to affirm their ethnic allegiance as Polish. Frank Ritza declared: "We are unique. We're so Polish here – that's what makes us so unique." In 1984, a group of nine students wrote a letter to the editor of the local newspaper supporting Polish cultural activities. They claimed: "We are Canadian children of Polish background ... We are Polish class students."[93] A year later, the Madawaska Valley Tourist Association made bumper stickers declaring Barry's Bay the "Polish Capital of Canada." In 1988, Martin Shulist created the winning design for a cancellation postal stamp at the soon-to-be-closed Wilno post office. It displayed a Polish eagle with a maple leaf. Even into the 1990s, some local residents felt stronger about notions of Polishness than Kaszubianness. Mary (Smaglinski) Burant noted that "Church was in Polish. But school was in English. The people are all Polish. But we talk English and Polish, both." Rose Chapeskie had similar thoughts about being Polish: "I was born Rose Burchat. A real Polish name." Frank Ritza, in an interview, again affirmed his insistence that his family was Polish.[94] When *The Proud Inheritance* was released, Ray Stamplecoskie, a local contributing writer to the project, proclaimed that "there are still children here who speak Polish in the home."[95] Reflecting on that era in a 2009 interview, a retired local midwife, the late Helen Dombroskie, claimed that "none of the Kashubian stuff seemed to us like our history. We were Polish."[96]

While many locals resisted the claims of external Poles, perhaps due to the inadequate knowledge of each other's history, the constant promotion of "Kaszubianism" did produce a period of identity crisis decades after the initial mention of difference. To take root and grow, however, the cultural re-creations needed the blessing and involvement of a local descendant and traditional authority figure.

The Surge in Polish-Kashub Historical Knowledge and the Concept of Shared Authority

If we accept that historical knowledge is a social discourse, much of the knowledge record of the first Polish community in Canada, into the 1990s, was created without the benefit of much tacit, local knowledge from the descendants themselves, but dictated to the descendants by external authorities and knowledge regimes. Locals were rarely active participants.

When Rekowski began writing his "Home Ties" articles in the *BBTW* in the 1980s, he bridged several gaps in historical memory and the production of knowledge. As a Redemptorist missionary priest, Rekowski was educated and had travelled the world, including several trips to Poland during his school years. As a local, and one who could read and translate Polish, he was not only an authority figure, but one with professional credentials. His self-published book on the history of the Kashub people in Poland and North America, released in 1997, tackled several themes, including the origins of the Kashubs, their reasons for emigrating to North America, and the documentation of their life along the Opeongo. His research drew on local historical knowledge in addition to some other sources, including parish records and inscriptions on gravestones.

To the academic eye, there are many instances where Rekowski did not adequately answer the questions he posed, such as those about the causes of emigration and colonization policy in the Canadas. Nor does he capitalize on the avenues of research into emigration agents that Hessel had opened up. The book is written in a somewhat sensationalistic tone, with occasional grammatical errors, and a couple of anachronisms render some sections problematic.[97] But Rekowski's book has become the standard work to which many local authors turn before embarking on their own investigations in family history. To this day, Rekowski's work is influential for several reasons. His discourse privileged local knowledge over scholarly findings, and in doing so, he cut away the more elevated, and sometimes condescending, discourse that characterized the works of most external authors. Moreover, his status as a priest (in the eyes of the community) lent his findings and writings a natural authority and credibility. Despite the scarcity of source material used in his publications, Rekowski's version of the discourse instilled local and ethnic pride.

Inspired by the efforts of Rekowski, some locals, beginning in the 1980s, became more interested in their past, although they did not have any formal training to carry out the research or writing necessary to compile a publication. One descendant, Shirley Mask-Connolly, who left her job as an art teacher in 1982 to raise her children in Ottawa, has since pursued researching and publishing family histories.[98] Local inhabitants have looked to her to reconstruct their past and proudly consider her a local historian. By searching parish registers here and in Poland, Mask-Connolly has pieced together details of several waves of settlers. As the curator of the Wilno Heritage Society's museum and the editor of its newsletter, she has cooperated with other locals who have provided pictures and oral testimony. Indeed, it is due to her efforts that a large written record of previously undocumented settlers exists. With the publication of *Kashubia to Canada: Crossing on the Agda*, Mask-Connolly reworked her genealogical information into a book that focuses on a ship that transported around 200 Kashubs to Canada in 1872. She aimed to write a story "of strength and survival" for those who had lost their "connection to those displaced persons who were our ancestors." After a brief description of conditions in the homeland, she describes the voyage and the passengers on the *Agda* by matching the ships' lists with census material.[99] She explains the intent of the quarantine station at Grosse Ile and outlines the sojourn the settlers had to make in Renfrew before proceeding along the Opeongo – a topic not previously looked at. Particularly interesting is a chapter that looks at the "Battle of Brudenell" – the controversial 1872 South Renfrew federal election that the migrants were caught up in while travelling up the Opeongo. Reminiscent of the work produced by Lee-Whiting, Mask-Connolly also outlines the building styles and furniture of the Polish-Kashub community in a chapter entitled "Adapting to Life in the New World."

In 2014, Mask-Connolly released *Marriage Matters in Canada's First Polish Settlement and Kashubian Community*, which looks at marriage practices and customs in the area and includes over 350 photographs.

Particularly valuable is the listing of the names and marriages of those who emigrated from Austrian-occupied Poland (around Poznań) to Canada in the late nineteenth century as well as those coming from the Kociewie region (southeast of Gdańsk). In this book, Mask-Connolly acknowledges and navigates issues of marriage, break-up, divorce, abandonment, the unofficial fostering of "illegitimate" children, consanguinity, death, remarriage, and the Catholic moral codes of the time while remaining sensitive to families' histories.

Through her position with the WHS, and after self-publishing microhistories and related genealogical resources, Mask-Connolly gained professional authority among residents for her historical knowledge. Her efforts have also brought her several awards,[100] which has more firmly established her as the authority on Polish-Kashubs in the Ottawa Valley. Many descendants consult her on a regular basis when trying to expand their own historical memory. But Mask-Connolly's works peer very little into conditions in the migrants' homelands (Prussian- and Austrian-occupied Poland) or the causes of emigration. Her section on Prussian-occupied Poland in *Kashubia to Canada: Crossing on the Agda* relies on a historical dictionary. From a scholarly standpoint, her range of content is wide but her depth is uneven, since she didn't use a wide range of secondary material on the history of migration and settlement from Europe to North America. Although Mask-Connolly documents many families, their arrival dates, and settlement locations, she has not filled in the larger historical narrative.

These critiques help to illustrate the perceived gap between work produced by the amateur, the genealogist, or local historian, and the academic. In many ways, Harvey's words from 1932 still resonate. Some genealogists, too, long ago recognized the limitations of their field. Charles Bolton, an American genealogist, asks, "Are we genealogists writing the lives of people or are we copying records?" Others offer reminders. As Carol Kammen remarks in *On Doing Local History*, local historians "need to know that history bleeds across borders and that there is much to learn even outside a designated place ... this sort of reading not only informs them but also poses questions that might be asked ... [and] introduces topics that may not be otherwise thought of." To be considered as a polished piece of work, local history needs to have a multidisciplinary approach.[101] Recycling old sources without challenging and broadening the scope of research or asking critical questions can limit the narrative. Even though nowadays many academics integrate local knowledge and oral history into their work, those writing on the Polish group in Canada have not.

Despite the fact that local writers may not be classically trained historians, they are, as Michael Batinski writes, pastkeepers in their own sphere and still have valuable contributions to make. Whether scientific, local, *a posteriori*, or *a priori*, knowledge comes from somewhere. The views of locals are also influential, since "what is remembered about the past depends on the way it is represented ... [It often] has more to do with the power of groups to fashion its image than with the ability of historians to evoke its memory."[102] By using word-processing technology and for-hire mass-market printing presses, Rekowski, Mask-Connolly, Prince, and other locals have circumvented traditional gatekeepers in the publishing industry to finally have their voices heard and their accounts circulated. Even though trained social scientists might not regard their works as sufficiently scholarly, their publications represent voices and stories that have been marginalized for a long time.

As Steven High writes, however, much has changed in academia since the days when authority was developed from a distance. Nowadays, the desire to incorporate and include communities as active participants in research is growing. Such a concept of shared authority between the academic and the local, the external and the internal, presents many possibilities for community building and for tackling contested narratives. Collaboration is key, but the relationship is about more than speaking to new sources, as Perkowski attempted to do. According to High, it "requires the cultivation of trust, the development of collaborative relationships, and shared decision-making."[103] It is a beginning, not an end.

Despite High's encouragement to share authority, there are many difficulties when investigating topics such as historical memory, ethnicity, or identity in specific communities, such as the Polish-Kashub one. In the period since the trust in outsiders was broken with Perkowski's project, confidence in another main agent of community socialization has been shaken – the Church. A decade after Zurakowski enlisted the help of Bernard Prince to publish *The Proud Inheritance*, accusations of sexual abuse surfaced in the region. In 2008, Prince was convicted of sexual misconduct for having repeatedly sexually abused thirteen boys from the Wilno area between 1964 and 1984, and in 2009 he was dismissed from the Catholic Church by Pope Benedict XVI. The victims sued the Diocese of Pembroke, claiming it had knowledge of the abuse and did nothing, and the diocese settled several cases.[104] The investigations and resulting shock means that gaining trust in the community is more difficult and access to parish records for research has virtually ended. If locals cannot rely on one of their own – a priest, an authority figure, and a supposed pastkeeper and servant of God – who can they trust?

Community insiders also encounter difficulties. It can be difficult for insiders to pose hard questions, because, as High points out, for some, "community is a romantic discourse that suffers from being an unequivocal good." To ask questions may be perceived as doubting one's neighbours, or attempting to destroy the harmonious past. Yet a historian cannot remain distant. Even though they may use methods that enlarge the experience and can determine the significance of events and experiences, they need to ask the hard questions and probe into tacit knowledge. To strike a balance between the two, however, presents many challenges.[105]

Conclusion

Although the publications mentioned in this chapter are not the only ones that contain references to the Polish settlers, they are the key ones that have produced knowledge about, and helped to shape, local historical memory of the migration and settlement processes in the Barry's Bay/Wilno area. Makowski's works, alongside those of Radecki and Heydenkorn, have analyzed broader, macro trends about the many migrations from Poland and dipped into some local history, it is local authors and local historians who have done the most to keep the field alive. Many of the aforementioned authors wrote for particular audiences. Some publications, like those by Makowski, Jost, Hessel, and Lee-Whiting, were meant to inform. Others, like those by Perkowski and Glofcheskie, were intended primarily to analyze the population's social and cultural aspects. Their contributions, however, have had the advantage of being published and endorsed by a federally funded museum. Finally, other (self-published) texts that looked at ancestors in the attic, such as those written by Rekowski and Mask-Connolly, were written to forge ancestral links with the past and build a community of descendants. As we will see in the following chapters, their narratives of displacement, exile, hardship, and filiopiety help to illustrate how knowledge is able to move from the macro level to the micro and finally to a wider, international audience. As a result, Rekowski and Mask-Connolly, as well as Theresa Prince, have crossed the threshold into knowledge-making territory.

These publications have also all relied upon, and contributed to, historical memory, equally shaping it by highlighting shared themes of the migration experience. Although certain narratives have been repeated in local historical memory, such as the idea that the settlers were packed together on overcrowded ships and given poor land when they arrived in Canada West, they have not previously been examined. What has been written by several local authors on the reasons for leaving the homeland, and the emigration and settlement process, is analyzed and contextualized in chapters 2 through 5. Chapters 6 and 7 broaden historical memory and analyze the emergence of contemporary ethnic consciousness in the Kaszubian region of Poland and the Wilno and Barry's Bay area.

These chapters also bring forth several new perspectives. As scholars in the field have long argued, the writing of migration history needs to incorporate a variety of sources and approaches. The works of Bruno Ramirez and Bruce Elliott have shown that it is not enough to gloss over micro-trends, nor should micro-level or single community histories neglect the wider systems of which they are a part.[106] These historians argue that migration does not begin only when the migrants set foot in the new world, nor does it end when they settle, build homes, and bear children. Further, as Livingstone argues, ideas must be "disarticulated from their social environments to permit them to reshape the very settings they emerged from." If we are to appreciate the ideas, imaginings, and conjectures that have affected the narrative, we need to be aware of how each work was influenced, created, and appropriated.[107] To that end, the broader contexts and circumstances surrounding the migrations need to be considered, and the formation of identity and ethnicity in the new land needs to be examined with the knowledge at hand. Certainly a gap in the record exists when reflecting on the ethnic euphoria in the Wilno and Barry's Bay area after the establishment of the WHS and their *lieux de mémoire*. Though people see the persistence of ethnicity, they may not know how to chronicle or address it. By using shared authority to analyze the reimagination of ethnicity and its transnational exchanges, I thus aim to further advance historical memory and the ethnic experience for descendants and readers alike. At the same time, it is undeniable that ethnic consciousness and the historical record in Canada's first Polish community continue to evolve.

Harvey was right in saying that "Many local historians must have lived and died before one general historian could undertake to write an adequate general history."[108] That has been proven by those who have attempted to write the history of Canada's first Polish community. Although I intend to analyze and offer new perspectives on the history of the Polish-Kashub group, my writings would not have been possible without the writings of those who came before me.

2

Poverty, Piety, and Political Persecution

As Frank Thistlewaite argues, the arrival in the new world was often the starting point for early works on immigration. In many cases, the authors knew little about the homeland and constructed it as the other, the opposite of America. Bruno Ramirez has shown that studying the premigration phase often dispels the notion that the old-world rural communities were static and tranquil. Instead we see how many of these assumptions are mistaken because they were often "viewed through the lens of a static folk-society theory instead of through an historical analysis of a multivariate agrarian universe marked with more volatility than immobility." Quite often, even though the web of relationships in the peasant village offered a sense of stability, the notion of a tranquil past in the village is misleading. Similarly, when considering the narratives that survive in local works we should be conscious of Benedict Anderson's point: that all "profound changes ... bring with them characteristic amnesias ... [and] out of such oblivions spring narratives."[1]

The little that does persist in local historical memory forms the basis, in some cases, of an emigrant identity in a new world. It can provide a point of comparison and help to establish an admixture of culture and folkways. Some authors also use it to ground an identity in upheaval and economic or political displacement. This happens in the current world of mobile strangers because people often feel the need to continually inform others of their group and individual history and origins.[2] As mentioned in chapter 1, most histories of the first Polish settlement have provided a glimpse of these upheavals in Poland. This is undoubtedly due to a number of factors: how knowledge was produced in the area, unfamiliarity with other sources in libraries and archives around the world, language barriers, and a lack of exposure to contemporary or revisionist works. What knowledge has been produced has been reprinted in several publications. However, Thistlewaite's advice should be acted upon and the conditions in the land of departure should be re-evaluated by marrying oral history with further research.

The causes of emigration given in local publications have permeated local historical memory and have been engrained in the settlers' descendants for generations. Since many of the original settlers could not read or write, oral history has enabled simplified categorical injustices to be passed along through succeeding generations. The following excerpts from oral history, arranged chronologically by date of publication were recorded and reused by authors, and have been the key stories shaping local historical memory:

> In 1871 Prussia won a resounding victory over France in the Franco-Prussian war. In the same year William the first ... was proclaimed emperor of all the Germany Bismarck had created. A more formidable crew never existed for the advancement of sinister exploits in history ... It was while John [Pick] was serving his 3 year hitch in the Prussian army which held his country in it's [sic] iron grip that he observed this Prussian militaristic attitude and arrogance. The victory over France instilled ... a lust for power which knew no restraint. John could see it leading to no good and it didn't. It led eventually to the first world war [sic]. Before it happened, however, John Pick ... resolved he would not serve the tyrants in any aggressive wars against peaceful nations ... With a far-away look he saw escape, hope and America. (Ritza, 1961)

> Their group and many others were the victims of the worst act of aggression and the greatest political crime, ever perpetrated on a nation, the portioning of Poland ... After the conquest, the final blow of Bismarck's rule of "blood and iron" fell on these God-fearing and patriotic people. For centuries, with military prowess and the zeal of crusaders, they had defended their altars and hearths and now they were told that they must renounce their faith, speak the language of the conqueror, or get out of their native land. The naked sword of the tyrant flashed above the

heads of these hapless people as the sentence was pronounced. (O'Dwyer, 1964)

The large-scale immigration of the early 1860's ... was prompted by economic factors and the oppressive measures of the occupying powers ... Under the rule of Bismarck, the peasants ... were ordered to renounce the Roman Catholic Church and speak the language of the conquerors who had taken up the best farming land. (Lee-Whiting, 1967 and 1972)

It was during the 1860's and 1890's that Bismark's [sic] power was especially harsh in Poland. The people were not accepting the Prussian rule. (Unknown, 1976)[3]

Their country had been overrun and occupied by an oppressor who set out to exterminate the culture of the Poles. The use of the Polish language was forbidden and a foreign language was ordered to be taught in the schools. The Polish people who would not accept foreign citizenship were ordered removed and their lands confiscated. (Unknown, 1979)

The Prussian rule in their land was becoming intolerable: their farms were expropriated, their language was forbidden and, above all, their Catholic religion was to be renounced. (Glofcheskie, 1980)

Some were slaves in Poland on the huge farms of the rich land owners ... others were soldiers who fought with Bismarck. (former MPP Tom P. Murray, 1980)

Apart from land to work and live on, they were seeking freedom – especially freedom of language and religion – denied to them in their homeland then under foreign occupation. (Jost, 1984)

Many settlers gratefully accepted back-breaking labour on poor, but free, land because the alternative was penury, starvation or persecution. (Shaw, 1994)

The main reason for their decision to leave their homeland, a decision which must have been agonizing indeed to take, was POVERTY – hard grinding, dire poverty – BIEDA! ... Dissatisfied with living conditions under Prussian domination and the extreme poverty of their land, the only hope they saw of ever improving their lot was to emigrate to the United States or Canada. (Rekowski, 1997)

Under Prussian occupation, these people were impoverished farm labourers with little chance of owning their own farms or of economic advancement ... Another compelling reason for emigration was to escape the political situation at home. Life in West Prussia under foreign occupation was always difficult for the Kashubs, but it became intolerable in 1871 when Reich Chancellor Otto von Bismarck ruthlessly initiated his *Kulturkampf* campaign, designed to impose the German culture on the Prussian (Polish and Kashubian) people and eliminate all elements of their ethnicity ... Bismarck was determined to fight them. (Mask-Connolly, 2003)

It is generally conceded that the first Kashubs were enticed to leave their small village farms in West Prussia, where they faced a bleak future of poverty, oppression, and religious persecution, by German shipping agents who promised free lands in Canada, a country of "milk and honey." (Finnigan, 2004)[4]

Of particular note in the above excerpts are Mask-Connolly's observations. Her writings are highly influential in the construction of local historical memory due to her role as museum curator for the Wilno Heritage Society (WHS).[5] What the WHS displays in its museum is also influential. In 2010, a framed picture was put in the museum that furthers a notion of exile. Entitled "The Prussian Eviction," the frame reads: "Following the failed revolution of 1848, Prussian rule over east Pomeria [sic] (Kashubia) became even more harsh. Germanification of schools, churches, and local government accelerated. Farmers were forced and evicted off their land leaving them destitute landless labourers. So an offer of free land in Canada was eagerly but cautiously considered and with great trepidation many families emigrated."

The notion of departure due to poverty and political and religious persecution is more succinctly summarized in the oral histories of local residents: "My parents were two of those wonderful people who made their way to America from Poland searching for the freedom of life which was denied to them under German, Austrian, and Russian occupation of their mother country" (Elizabeth Shalla, 1970s). "[In Poland] they were oppressed under the blood and iron of Bismarck" (Frank Ritza, 1975). "My father told me this story many times – the Germans owned Poland and my father had to go for conscription ... He didn't want to go to conscription" (John Mintha, second-generation settler, 1991). "My grandfather fled Poland because he was called to serve in the Prussian army ... The Germans were trying to make them like themselves, in faith and language and culture. Their schools were taken over and some of the churches were closed" (Msgr Ambrose Pick, 1991). "They were poor and persecuted, unable to get ahead. Their land was confiscated, others were pressed into the army" (Fr Rafał Grzondziel, 1997). "How come they left? It was the Germans. They had to leave because the Germans were on their backs" (Joseph Peplinskie, second-generation settler, 1997).[6] Yet, to the analytical eye, this simplified cause and effect equation of "persecution therefore out-migration" leaves much to be desired.

Questions should be asked about the origins of these alleged instigating factors. Although Mask-Connolly has most recently given greater context for the out-migration movement – devoting a twelve-page chapter to it – there is a wealth of other secondary literature beyond recycled sources and the community history booklet from a Polish settlement in Minnesota that she used to compose her chapter. Her work, though valuable on a genealogical and local micro-study level, is limited when it comes to larger narratives. Unless authors consult a broad net of secondary literature on the subject, community histories, as Ramirez points out, can often "force their authors into a narrative logic and into an organization of data" that does not benefit from the broader temporal and geographical studies of the period in question. Perin echoes these same thoughts, as most of these studies begin with "an outline of the political history of the Mother Country, devoid of historiographical references" and thus "the inevitable genuflections to ethnic ancestors occur." Iacovetta also voices concern over these types of histories, saying that the work of the genealogists is often "valuable because of the often meticulous record-keeping ... but problematic because of the myth-making ... that underscores that activity."[7]

The aim, however, is to revisit the avenues opened by local historical memory and marry them with more research and contextualization to open up new perspectives in the back story. We need to confront the simplified narrative of departure and analyze the perceived push factors and the political and social conditions that helped motivate the potential migrants. This involves a journey into the centrifugal forces at work in Prussian-occupied Poland, and a further study, which uses additional primary, secondary and revisionist publications that analyze serfdom and emancipation. While this analysis expands the written record, like numerous previous publications, it is limited to an extent by the fact that publications on the topic are written in many languages and not always translated. This book does not pretend to be a complete chronicle of the events in Polish history that influenced out-migration to Canada West; rather, it uses certain publications to form comparative points and foils that prompt new perspectives.

Until now, most of the knowledge produced by local authors and historical memory conflates two periods of migration and settlement, with different instigating causes, into one. Also, the persecutory factors of the second period (1871–87) have been pushed back into the first period (1858–c. 1870). Thus, the early part of this chapter explains the economic causes of the pre-1871 departures. The latter part recasts *Kulturkampf*, the assault on Polish religion and culture from 1871–87 and an instigating factor for the second wave of migration, as a response by the Prussian liberal parliamentarians to ultramontanism, the Catholic infallibility doctrine, the Polish nationalism of the lower clergy, and a reactionary crusade by religious orders against rationalist and secular philosophies.

Anatomy of Rule: Szlachta and the Catholic Church

Anna Porter recently wrote that "it is still impossible to escape the Poles' sense of victimhood. Memories of past wrongs invade conversations ... [Poland] is a land of lost battles and persistent dreams" and the years 1772 and 1795 are "iconic dates in Poland that serve as communication shorthand."[8] Indeed, as many Polish historians passionately insist, the history of Poland has been marred by conquest and partition at the

2.1   Partitioned Poland at the turn of the nineteenth century.

hands of neighbouring foreign powers. Most notable is the tripartite partition between Prussia, Austria-Hungary, and Russia in 1772, which was revised in 1793 and 1795 (see figure 2.1).[9]

Many Polish historians, fed by generations of influence by the patriotic intelligentsia, view the partition as one of the most significant atrocities perpetrated against their country and nation. This was echoed most recently by the Speaker of the Senate of the Republic of Poland, Bogdan Borusewicz, who told the Senate of Canada on 5 May 2010: "when the first settlers arrived [here] in 1858, my homeland was occupied by enemy forces. Weakened internally, Poland was erased from Europe's political map for 123 years and divided among the neighbouring powers. Resolute attempts at state reform, based on the ratification of Europe's first and the world's second constitution on May 3, 1791, had failed. Thus began a time of repression, in spite of which Poles managed to maintain their language, culture and the wealth of their traditions."[10] Those who forget Polish history, according to a former United Nations advisor, Daniel Rotfeld, are regarded as having "contempt for ... or [are falsifying], their past."[11] However, the seeds of discontent and disorganization in Poland were sown long before the partition and the two world wars. In the words of Jan Fedorowicz: "At its height, Poland came very close to establishing itself permanently as a European ... power, only to lose that position and plunge into an abyss which threatened the nation's irrevocable extinction. It is this oscillation between extremes which has weighed heavily on the national psyche and has made the influence of history a unique element in Polish consciousness."[12] Thus, in order to understand contemporary events, it is necessary to look at how Poland was divided up among its neighbours, due to the backwardness of its feudal economy and the weakness of its governmental institutions.

At the time, the population was unevenly divided into peasants (*chłopy*), nobility (*szlachta*), and clergy (*kler*). Approximately 9 per cent of the population at the time of the partitions were nobles. Owning land and serfs was a source of wealth and although not all nobles owned land, most did. The nobility's wealth was measured by the number of estates they held. If a noble possessed two or three properties "and he had the serfs to work it, he owed his living to no one. He was ... propertied ... [and a] lord unto himself."[13] But only about a dozen nobles had great wealth. The intelligentsia, made up of writers and academics, although active and fervent, was small and limited to the urban areas of Kraków and Warsaw before the nineteenth century. There were about 50,000 clergy who comprised about 0.6 per cent of the population. Peasants comprised most of the population.[14] Within the ranks of the peasantry there were several categories – those with large holdings, serfs who worked small plots for the estate or the church, and serfs who were landless and worked for sustenance and survival. After nineteenth-century emancipations, the term *chłop* was still synonymous with serfdom, even though the peasant might be a landless labourer or a middling land-holder. This mentality of centuries of subjugation helped to separate Polish social strata up to today.

Typically, the peasant who worked a large holding of 35 to 60 acres needed two servants and several horses and had to cultivate and work the land five to six days of the week. Serfs who worked small plots for an estate, on the other hand, worked only for their sustenance. By the seventeenth century, nobles with holdings paid poll-taxes of 16 grosz to 2 złoty, and serfs paid from 0.5 to 4 grosz.[15] The social and economic disparity between the magnates and the illiterate, the impoverished, or the landless, as Fedorowicz argues, was colossal. The peasants' chance at upward mobility through pastoral success was limited, because, as Jacek Kochanowicz declares, "only the estates belonging to the magnates, the church, and the crown were major exporters." Since investment opportunities such as trade, banking, and manufacturing were not available as they were in the West, holding sizeable tracts of land, supplying regions, and exporting were key foundations of economic success.[16]

Labour requirements for these peasants were put in place long before partition. After 1520, serfs were required to work at least fifty-two days per annum to pay their rent, and after 1611 they were not permitted to buy estates. The landed noble, unlike his many landowning European counterparts, "was free from arbitrary arrest and need not fear confiscation of his land."[17] After the Union of Lublin (1569), the szlachta were given extensive rights and privileges over mere peasants – the "Golden Freedom." They also controlled the *Sejm*, or parliamentary body of the state.[18] The nobles' freedoms were many. According to Jerzy Lukowski, there was "no taxation without consent ... virtual exemption from customs duties; [a] virtual monopoly of land ownership," the right to elect all senior ecclesiastical positions, and "the right to participate in the election of the monarch." The peasant had no freedom, was attached to the soil he worked, was dependent upon the szlachta, and remained without a right to the plot he cultivated. Zamoyski and Kieniewicz also argue that landowners were in complete control over the peasants. Yet, how far the szlachta abused this right depended upon the morality of the master rather than the determination or hard work of the peasant.[19]

While most of the population did not have a political voice, those in the seats of government were also manacled by feudal and constitutional disorganization. A score of families often controlled important state and senate offices and possessed both great wealth and great influence, and membership in the senate was determined by possession.[20] But the magnatial oligarchy and the nobility that ran the country were powerless to repair a number of grave weaknesses in the country because of constitutional gridlock and the unanimity rule of the *liberum veto*.[21] Every vote in the *Sejm* resulted in widespread disagreement between its members and unanimity was needed to pass a bill or attempted reform. Thus, the real enemy was apathy and self-interest. Structural reform, argues Norman Davies, was impossible to introduce as the "most a sensitive man could do was to reflect on the discrepancy between the world around him and Christian religion ... and to pour cold water on the idyllic fantasies which so many cherished." Jean-Jacques Rousseau quipped that the "Polish nation consists of three estates: the nobles who are everything, the townspeople who are nothing, and the peasants who are less than nothing." Lukowski also describes the ruling nobility as "patriots who mythologised themselves into legislators" and added another drawback: the lack of administrative infrastructure necessary to run an up-to-date army."[22]

Also, the Polish army was weak since the nobles did not want to pay taxes. In 1775, the average equivalent nobility tax for the army was 1 shilling in Poland, 6 in Prussia, 6 in Russia, and 20 in Austria. More important, though, the problem for Poland was its social and political structure.[23] The nobility and the magnates disliked the idea of a strong state, fearing restrictions against their liberty and a reduction of their wealth.[24] Fedorowicz argues further along these lines, saying that, "whenever one class or group in a society is given or acquires absolutely everything, any subsequent change in the system must perforce diminish the prerogatives of the elite group, and therefore a political monopoly of any sort is simply a recipe for sterile conservatism. By the end of the seventeenth century, the Polish nobility had achieved ... total control over the system, whereupon it was no longer interested in or willing to allow any change whatsoever, despite the warning of those who could see that the Sejm had legislated itself into a dead end from which escape was only possible at the expense of the legislators themselves."[25] This apathy and inability to govern was exploited by neighbouring powers and was used to justify their partitioning of the land in the late eighteenth century.

Before partition, a cohort of Polish people held economic and political power. Many bishops were, or became, magnates, amassing fortunes in property and monetary capital, after Duke Mieszko adopted Catholicism in 966. Several, including the Bishop of Gniezno and Kraków, owned hundreds of towns and villages. In addition to the canonical staff who managed the diocese, the bishop also employed clerks as landlords to manage the monastic estates and manors. As most szlachta were Catholic, the Church wielded a large amount of power, in concert with the lords.[26] The affairs in Poland were thus so feudal at the time of partition that it is not surprising that the country was swallowed up by neighbouring states, and given the moniker "The Republic of Anarchy." Vorontsov, the Russian chancellor, remarked in 1763 that "Poland is constantly plunged into disorder; as long as she keeps her present constitution, she does not deserve to be considered among the European powers." In the words of Stanisław Staszic, "Poland is barely in the fifteenth century ... [when] all of Europe is already finishing the eighteenth."[27]

But the Church clearly benefitted from the disorganization. Centrally run from the Vatican, it was a thread of continuity. Kingdoms, dynasties, republics, and regimes came and went but the Church continued to operate. In these times of upheaval, the Catholic Church was a beacon for Polish-speaking people who were searching for meaning and identity.[28] Thus, churches were the gathering place for direction and advice. Drawing upon Michel Foucault's definitions of pastoral power as "salvation-oriented (as opposed to political power)," we are able to see how the Church remained strong.[29] Unlike the political system or the lords, the clergy held the keys to the gates beyond earthly life. As a result, their power was very real to followers.

The local Polish clergy also knew the privations of the local people and the inner thoughts of the peasants, another key to pastoral power. The Church "preached that the poor were beloved of God and that the rich were redeemed" only by charity. As a result, local clergy became not only "God's deputy" but counsellors and aldermen of understanding to the peasants. peasants expected representatives of the Church, as the only stable and reliable institution in rural areas, to issue pronouncements on both public and private matters.[30] Since the clergy were able to mediate between earth and heaven, they were seldom questioned. They ministered to the many followers who were denied freedom in their worldly lives. The Church was thus the other powerful institution in Poland and had an enormous number of followers. In addition to the critiques of Staszic, Jan Baudoin de Courtenay, a Pole of French lineage, accused the clergy of wielding such power to "put out the light of reason among the people, because the 'unenlightened' were easier to deceive and oppress."[31] Pastoral power provided priests and "endowed the Church hierarchy with secular authority not usually enjoyed by religious leaders in other countries."[32] To complicate matters, the Vatican was beyond the ruling governments' borders of control.

As most szlachta were Catholic, the Church wielded a large amount of power in concert with the lords.[33] The Church also argued, after 1718, that religious minorities, mainly Orthodox and Protestant, should not have political rights. A year earlier, parliament "ordered all Protestant churches erected in Poland since 1632 to be razed." Although this had been decreed, it was carried out sporadically. Forms of raising revenue for the Church were also imposed upon the Protestant populations with some success.[34] Catholics were also told to give portions of their meagre earnings for Church coffers. For example, Jozef Borzyszkowski mentions that in Brusy, the Mass donations from peasants to the priest and organist were often large and diversified. They paid around 80 groschen per year in addition to special calls for donations, which were often in the form of oats and rye for the priest and organist.[35] These collection models made the Church in Poland a powerful spiritual and economic force and it worried neighbouring states. For Prussia, the Church's power and rules were antithetical to their intended colonial political model.[36] At this point, however, the focus will shift to the exploration of Prussian-occupied Poland since it was the site of future cultural conflict and the region from which the first group came to Canada.

One of the first sections to be partitioned was the area south and west of Gdańsk, newly proclaimed as West Prussia. This territory was brought into the authoritarian Prussian state in 1772. Heavily invested in a militaristic way of governance, Prussian forces were "not only the best drilled in Europe; [they were] the best led, the best fed, and the best armed," and the Prussian administration viewed the szlachta with contempt.[37] In the words of William Hagen, the Prussians viewed the annexed territory as a "commonwealth [that] seethed with anarchy, [whose] peasants were brutish slaves of backwoods squires, [whose] Catholic religion was benighted and fanatical, what urban civilization it possessed it owed to the Germans."[38] One might think, in light of this, that the Prussian system would reform rural Poland. It did, as we will see, but the era was also marked with ideological clashes that heightened during Bismarck's rule. Prussian (or German) domination is often cited as an instigating factor for emigration in the memory of migrants who ventured out of Prussian-occupied Poland to Canada sixty years later. Before jumping to the migration itself, it would be imprudent not to examine exactly what local historical memory says on this topic. Thus, an examination of both sides of the Polish and Prussian/German social, cultural, religious, and political viewpoints is necessary.

Local Memory and Pre-Bismarckian Push Factors

Digging further into local historical memory, we see that the causes of emigration before Bismarck and Prussia's assault on the Roman Catholic Church between 1871 and 1887, known as Kulturkampf, have not been explored. If authors do address the causes for departure pre-1871, they simply say that it was because of poverty. Makowski does not address this question. Zurakowski addressed it and wrote two sentences on the period, saying "after the partition of Poland, the Prussian rulers oppressed the Kaszub population both politically and economically. Under those circumstances, the Kaszubs felt their future was threatened and, due to the rapid increase in population, poverty was also spreading." Yet she gives no further exploration or quantification. Rekowski recognized that Kulturkampf factors were misappropriated for the earliest wave and surmised that the potential migrants were living in poverty, and were lured overseas by shipping agents. More recently, Mask-Connolly writes that the emigrants "had little or no land of their own in Kashubia. Under Prussian occupation, these people were impoverished farm labourers with little chance of either owning their own farms or of economic advancement."[39]

If we turn to writers from Poland who publish on the Canadian Polish/Kashub group, it becomes evident that they do not adequately document the political, religious, or social instigations for the out-migration. Only one author, Borzyszkowski, hinted at changing conditions. Unfortunately, he does not unpack the conditions of Prussian-occupied Poland between the nineteenth and twentieth centuries. Content with a rather anti-Prussian and filiopietistic stance, Borzyszkowski states that "under Prussian domination, Kashubia underwent deep social changes. The local nobility and landed gentry survived only fragmentarily ... as a result of agrarian reforms, land was granted to peasants. From this class descended many representatives of the native intelligentsia." Though he hints at the era of Prussian occupation as the "formation of a modern society," Borzyszkowski dismisses the change as negative since the peasants were becoming "a part of the huge organism of the Prussian and later all-German state." Ickiewicz, another Polish author, largely ignores this group and devotes little space to the economic conditions[40] Again, the record is silent when trying to qualify or quantify the conditions in West Prussia leading up to the first migration to Canada. Moving into the period closer to migration, the following sections will attempt to unearth the pre-Bismarckian conditions that contributed to the desire to leave Prussian-occupied Poland.

Prussian Land Reform Targets Polish Lords and the Catholic Church

Starting in the 1780s, Frederick II of Prussia initiated land reforms in the newly acquired territory. He confiscated many private lands in the region and appropriated many belongings for the Church. The profits of Polish owners were taxed at twice the rate German owners were required to pay (10 per cent) in a move designed to limit the power of the szlachta. Frederick II kept the legal system of the region, Polish law – heavily influenced by canon law – until 1797.[41] Since the Church's wealth and dominance in Poland was antithetical to the Prussian model, the early taxation and legal manoeuvres were attempts to wrest power from it as well as from the nobility.

The szlachta faced economic difficulties as a result and grew increasingly desperate financially. According to Piotr Wandycz and Stefan Kieniewicz, the lords in several areas tried to pass the burden onto their peasants by converting obligatory labour to money rents. Other szlachta mortgaged their fate through easily secured Prussian loans. As a result, many were swallowed up in debt, which, according to Wandycz, caused the loss of one-sixth of estates in 1815,[42] a downward spiral that continued into the 1840s. By the 1850s, many Polish landowners had "sold out" in great numbers to Germans.[43] In 1800 in West Prussia, 65 per cent of manors (364) were in Polish hands. By 1858, that number had dropped to 217. One decade later, only 134 manors, about 27 per cent, were left in Polish hands.[44] Peasants and serfs suffered from the uncertainty of ownership and the uncertainty of knowing who or what system they were under.

The emancipation of the serfs and the reform of the serf-based system took much longer to accomplish. These reforms, argues Takenori Inoki, were an exercise in liberalism and social justice for Prussian reformers.[45] The first edict in 1807 gave personal freedom along class lines.[46] It annulled the "difference between noble and non-noble lands, so that these lands could be bought, sold, borrowed and mortgaged by all citizens regardless of class." At the same time, however, the lord was also freed from the feudal obligation to provide lodging or economic support for his serfs during bad times. Another edict in 1816 codified the criteria for emancipation rights. If serfs did not fit the criteria, they had to continue to pay labour or rents. This continued through 1821, when peasants were able to acquire rights to the property they cultivated but had to compensate lords through ceded land or extended periods of payments. If, after the reduction of their piece of land, it was too small to earn a living from, many peasants were forced to become hired labourers.[47]

After emancipation, in various years, about 40 per cent of the peasants were able to obtain a medium-size freehold within a few years through labour, land, and money. The majority of peasants, however, emerged from this process with very small holdings,[48] and thus were tenants-at-will, obliged to work on estate land. By the 1850s, emancipation was not complete in some areas and many serfs were living without adequate tracts of land to survive. West Prussia was one of these regions, because the szlachta were less liberal than in other areas of Prussian-occupied Poland or Austrian-occupied Galicia.[49] Although emancipation was an exercise in liberalism and social justice, it created another problem – the landless proletariat. During 1860 in Silesia, there were 200,000 peasant owners and about 117,000 of the owners owned less than three acres. Another 300,000 were labourers (proletariat) without land. The situation in Pomerania was equally precarious. These wage workers, *einlieger* (in German), received day wages that amounted to between 175 and 215 thalers per year c. 1872, depending on economic and seasonal fluctuations. Yet we may never know the true number of landless peasants since many do not appear in documents in any systematic way.[50] But, as Wandycz, Kiniewicz, Inoki, Behrens, Groniowski, and Wagner all note, this landless population could not be absorbed by local industry, and so a steady emigration began.[51]

The notion of poverty, mentioned by Rekowski and Mask-Connolly, thus holds true as an instigating factor for the pre-1871 migration. The confiscation of land hinted at by Glofcheskie and Pick can be attributed to the fact that Polish landlords mortgaged their future through debt and mismanagement. Though in-depth primary documents that record or analyze peasant holdings around Lipusz, Leśno, and Wiele have not been unearthed – if they do indeed exist[52] – secondary literature supports local memory and permits a glimpse into the dire land tenure conditions faced by peasants in Prussian Poland.

Population and Climactic Pressures

According to several sources, the population in the partitioned zones was increasing in the early part of the nineteenth century.[53] In the Kingdom of Prussia, the Province of Pomerania grew from 744,298 in 1820 to 1,288,964 in 1855, an increase of 73 per cent. The Province of West Prussia grew from 649,627 to 1,094,332 or 68 per cent. In 1820, Pomerania's density was 25 persons per square kilometre as was West Prussia's. By 1855, this density had changed significantly, when both provinces had, on average, 43 persons per square kilometre.[54] Within 35 years, 18 more persons were occupying the same "rural" square kilometre in West Prussia. This point is more telling when we consider that at the time of partition (c. 1790), the density ranged from 14–19 persons per square kilometre.[55] In the counties of Chojnice and Kościerzyna, the population swelled too. From 1821 to 1861, the increase in the former was 225 per cent and 188 per cent in the latter (see figure 2.2 and tables 2.1 and 2.2).

Baptisms in the parish of Lipusz increased from approximately 95 per year in 1813–20 to 110–20 during the 1830s and 1840s, 135 in the 1850s, around 150 in the 1860s, and 165 in 1872.[56] Yet, while the population was growing steadily, land remained static. The division of land through inheritance – for those who possessed it – further complicated the situation.[57] The amount of cleared land in the area around

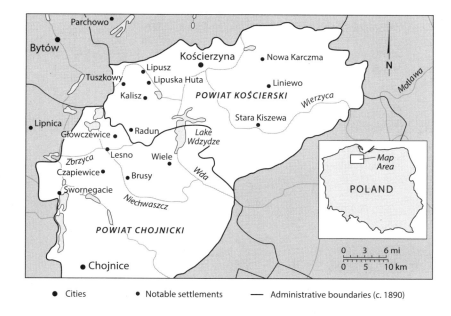

2.2 The Opeongo Road migrants originated primarily from these counties.

Table 2.1: Population statistics, Powiat Kościerzyna, 1821–1890

Year	County population	Increase from last census	Average increase per yr
1821	19,634	–	–
1825	21,072	1,438	360
1828	22,573	1,501	500
1831	23,120	547	182
1834	24,215	1,095	365
1837	24,540	325	108
1849	31,212	6,672	556
1852	32,808	1,596	532
1855	34,718	1,910	637
1858	36,918	2,200	733
1861	38,676	1,758	586
1864	40,863	2,187	729
1867	43,056	2,193	731
1871	43,777	721	240
1890	45,947	2,170	114

Source: L. Belzyt, *Sprachliche Minderhciten im polnische Staat 1815–1914: Die preußische Sprachenstatistik in Bearbeitung und Kommentar* (Herder-Institut: Marburg, 1998), 93–107.

Table 2.2: Population statistics, Powiat Chojnicki, 1821–1871

Year	County population	Increase from last census	Average increase per yr
1821	26,433	–	–
1825	30,632	4,199	1,050
1828	34,121	3,489	1,163
1831	35,050	929	310
1834	36,879	1,829	610
1837	39,331	2,452	817
1846	49,364	10,033	1,115
1849	50,659	1,295	432
1852	54,344	3,685	1,228
1855	56,188	1,844	615
1858	59,465	3,277	1,092
1861	62,083	2,618	873
1864	65,913	3,830	1,277
1867	67,981	2,068	689
1871	70,817	2,836	945

Source: L. Belzyt, *Sprachliche Minderhciten im polnische Staat 1815–1914: Die preußische Sprachenstatistik in Bearbeitung und Kommentar* (Herder-Institut: Marburg, 1998), 93–107.

Table 2.3: Locality densities, c. 1870s

Locality	Area (morgs)	Area (km²)	Residents	Houses	Persons per house	Buildings	Density (km²)	Parish population
Głowczewice	2,825	6.97	223	23	10	52	31.9	
Kalisz	7,425	18.33	690				37.6	
Karsin	10,549	26.04	1,265	157	8	334	48.6	
Kaszuba	3,876	9.57	117	9	13	17	12.2	
Kliczkowy	1,267	3.13	60	5	12	20	19.2	
Leśno	8,579	21.18	312	26	12	72	14.7	2,748
Lipusz	8,334	20.57	664	55	12		32.3	3,569
Lipuska Huta	1,101	2.72	108	12	9	7	39.7	
Parchowo			722					2,569
Wiele	9,607	24.95	954				38.2	2,034 (in 1780)

Source: Entries in volumes 2–13 of the *Słownik Geograficzny Królestwa Polskiego*, edited by Sulimierskiego, Chlebowskiego, and Walewskiego.

Lipusz, Wiele, and Leśno had not increased over the past few centuries. The increases in population meant that, structurally, there was a shortage of land for farming, and rarely did the emancipated peasants have the capital to purchase. If they were able to secure a small plot for their growing families, they were pressed into smaller quarters, as evidenced by the population density figures by 1880 (see table 2.3). This contributed to the emigration of 663,000 people out of the Gdańsk region between 1840 and 1910.[58]

In addition to the poverty mentioned in local historical memory, climate conditions in the 1850s may also have, indirectly, been an influencing factor in emigration. According to Leszek Kilma and Kazmierz Mróz, who published a history of the county of Chojnice ("Konitz" during the time of the Prussian partition), the 1850s were abnormally dry. During an average year, about 527 mm of precipitation fell. However, some of the driest years on record occurred in the 1850s. In 1854 and 1858, 305 mm and 370 mm, respectively, fell. Such conditions may have damaged the crops that were planted and affected the employment hired hands could gain. As populations rose, the need to feed larger numbers of people in drier conditions would surely prompt them to look elsewhere. In the 1880s – when migration to Canada virtually ended – the area received as many as 794 mm of rain per year.[59] Thus, while many of the peasants may not have been able to quantify the poverty in a detailed way, it is possible that the dry conditions indirectly induced poverty and led to migration – a topic that has not been considered before.

The Enlightenment and Prussian Colonialism in Western Poland

It is also important to consider the resonance of religious, political, and cultural persecution in historical memory, passed on from those migrants who left. In doing so, it becomes apparent that local historical memory and local authors do not address the greater liberating, or "enlightened," colonialization processes happening in Prussian-occupied Poland before and during Bismarck's administration. Local authors do not explain the Germans' or Prussians' reasons for enacting laws that persecuted the Polish people religiously, politically, and culturally. In lieu of exploring the causes, the authors who have shaped local memory simply dismissed the colonizing power as "evil." Similarly, those parochial writers who have approached the migration solely from a religious point of view, as Stanisław Salmonowicz argues, "look at the matter through the narrow prism of a religious struggle."[60] By trying to reform the feudal Polish territory, enlightened Prussians were attempting to transform the territory and its people into a disciplined, structured, and measurable society.

As previously mentioned, Prussia looked at Poland, on the eve of partition, as a backward society. Hagen commented on the extent of their rudimentary lives during the partition: at best, the peasants "lived a life of rude sufficiency and traditional amusement sanctified by religion and folk custom and watched over paternalistically from the manor house."[61] As German wayfarers toured the land in the early 1800s, they found incredible poverty (see figures 2.3a and 2.3b). Otto Wenkstern recorded the plight of those poverty-stricken people on the rural "Pomeranian frontier," saying that his witness

> beheld hovels covered with musty straw, mere molehills on a treeless and gardenless plain. The hovel, made of wattled clay, had but one room and no chimney; stoves and candles were unknown ... The principal article of furniture was a tin crucifix, with its appendant basin of holy water. The dirty and half savage people fed on gruel of rye-flour, and in many instances on herbs only, stewed into soup, on herrings and spirits ... If they kept bees ... they sold the honey in the towns; they also carved wooden spoons for sale at the fairs, where they bought long coats of coarse blue cloth, black fur caps and the bright red kerchiefs of the women ... all the farm-buildings were dilapidated and past service. The sick had to take their chance with the nostrums of some village-crone, for apothecaries were not to be found ... There was no administration of justice; some of the larger towns had courts whose decisions there was no means of enforcing. The gentry dealt with the common people according to the pleasure or whim of the moment.[62]

According to Hagen, action was needed if Poland, or a remnant of its people, was to remain. The Prussian intentions for reforms were laudable from an enlightened paradigm, or so they believed.

2.3a and 2.3b   Photos of late-nineteenth-century peasant hovels near the community of Liniewo, Poland. The photo area is approximately 20 kilometres east of the area where the Opeongo Road settlers lived. The family of John J. Glofcheskie, one of the last families from the area to emigrate to the Barry's Bay area, moved from Głowczewice to Liniewo before emigrating to Canada in 1907. Whether they met economic hardship or not is unknown.

The Prussian state, fueled by the Enlightenment, sought to reform the staunchly Catholic and impoverished rural Polish state.[63] It believed that emancipation and agrarian reform were necessary for the salvation of Poland.

Hagen argues that Frederick's motivation "arose from his aversion, as the enlightened, disciplined, and autocratic ruler of ... [a] well-organized state" to the "commonwealth's aristocratic constitution, to its inability to defend itself, and to the wealth and cultural dominance within it of the Polish Catholic Church."[64] The more that German-speaking people embraced the secular rationalism brought on by the enlightenment, the more they opposed the Polish Commonwealth.[65] Many leaders thought that exposure to Prussian and German society would result in better economic behaviour, discipline, and education, along with the Kantian belief that the maturing of man involved the challenge to use reason. The Prussian view, that the Polish economy was underdeveloped because of the remnants of the feudal system, was also influenced by Poland's social structure.[66]

The Prussian state's approach was an appeal to the nobility's humanism and common sense. Giving rights to serfs and peasants, it was thought, was necessary to improve agriculture. This spreading of light and reason by Prussians, according to Wandycz, was a "crusade against prejudice, irrational tradition ... and oppression." Furthermore, "skepticism towards metaphysical speculation and religious dogmatism combined with an abhorrence of fanaticism" generated an anti-clerical stance toward the old-regime Church rule. Needless to say, the conditions in Poland matched these indicators of an unenlightened nation, especially when Voltaire's belief in freedom based on law is compared with the szlachta's so-called Golden Freedom.[67] However, in order to reform the territory, the enlightened Prussian regime had to unseat the two institutions that held control: the landlords and the Church.

Taxation, discussed earlier, was one way to weaken the control of the szlachta. Another way was to forbid them from holding office, especially in the *Landrat* – the lowest tier of Prussian bureaucracy in the countryside, which maintained order in each county, collected taxes, and drafted recruits.[68] In turn, the szlachta spread their dislike for the German bureaucracy in Polish circles. But this period represented the transformation of administration in the territory from feudal to modern and secular. The General Code of 1794, which wrested political control away from the landlords and the Church, was a constitution that bridged the transition between feudal and modern rule.[69] The result meant that secular rationalism became the basis for the administration of the territory.

This form of governance was bound to annoy the other major institution in the area: the Church. Though someone living in Prussian-controlled Poland would see the confiscation of Church lands as a clear indication of German hatred for their faith, from a Prussian stance, it was done to mitigate the administrative power and capital of the Church. The western influence of reason and law was opposed by the Church, which had, according to Bideleux and Jeffries, steadfastly invoked Counter-Reformation measures in monasteries and clerical schools for a century. The Jesuits set the stage for future conflict through their insistence that "to be Polish was to be Catholic," and viewing colonialization as a parochial conflict fought strictly on the grounds of faith.[70] Furthermore, the Church capitalized on the confusion (or non-existence) of ethnic and national identities among the illiterate peasants by promoting the Polish label in rural areas. As a result, the non-secular (Polish) versus secular (Prussian) dichotomy used to describe the conflict was instilled in the minds of peasants. Any exercises of Polish nationalism were rebranded by priests as Polish Catholicism rather than as cultural nationalism or self-determination, which they feared would promote a distinctive citizenship in a future Polish state.[71] As a result, a national identity based on religion rather than state was formed.

But Catholics were promised by Frederick in 1772 that "true and obedient subjects" would be offered protection and that he would "administer them in their possessions and right, in the spiritual and secular realm, and in particular grant the adherents of the Roman Catholic religion free exercise of their faith."[72] While the clergy and upper echelons of the Church were hampered by measures such as clerical travel restrictions, lay followers were treated differently. Until the 1870s, when Bismarck came into power, Davies says, "the obstacles placed in their path ... were, at most, informal."[73] However, the clergy were the ones who preached, spread, and controlled anti-Prussian sentiments from the pulpit in well-attended churches.

Once the two controlling institutions were subdued, the modernizing and colonizing plan of the Prussian government could take effect.

In order for Prussia to cultivate the new territory, a modern state had to be planted and instituted the *Landrat*. Each district was given its own court of justice, postal communications, and police; townships were created and made responsible for law;[74] and state registration was begun. In 1772, the regime started documenting the landed nobility.[75] It also sent surveyors across the land to map the territory for which they were now responsible. These efforts resulted in the detailed Schroetter-Karte maps produced in 1802. Since the Prussians producing these documents spoke German, many localities previously known by vernaculars were supplied with Germanized names. Several years later, in 1813, Frederick William III introduced the system of passports to document those travelling into or out of Prussian territory and to ensure that foreigners would not penetrate their territory illegally.[76] The passports also served to consolidate power and more closely monitored the movements of their people within the new territory.

While authors such as Mask-Connolly have pointed out that acts of recording were ways of Germanizing, which may be true, her work does not discuss the larger system at work. We are reminded of Gaddis's comments on maps and space – that the former reduces the "infinitely complex to a finite, manageable frame of reference." Indeed, the thoughts of James Scott also show the purpose in giving the vernacular a comprehensible label: "For the insider who grows up using these naming practices, they are both legible and classifying. Each name and the contents of its use convey important social knowledge. For an outsider, however, this byzantine complexity of names is a formidable obstacle to understanding local society." Thus, this act of renaming can be considered a part of an ongoing project of legibility,[77] to understand the imperial territory that the state now controls.

Implementing the notion that Polish people should follow the disciplined regime of the Prussians, a system of conscription was put in place for the occupied region based on the Kanton Reglement of 1733. By the 1850s, garrisons for these recruits existed mainly in the northern area of the occupied territory in cities such as Gdańsk, Lębork, and Słupsk, as well as Wejherowo and Chojnice. These centres sought to enroll those with higher levels of education,[78] and Prussian military training was targeted at the nobility. It was thought that conscription, combined with the desire for educated soldiers in cadet academies, would produce an informed nobleman. Such was the intent with the academy that opened at Chełmno in 1776. The academy housed around sixty students, most of noble stock.[79]

One of the difficulties that the Prussian regime encountered when forming the new bureaucracy was a paucity of potential bureaucrats for the new system. Since many Polish people were not well-educated, mainly German-speaking peoples were employed in the beginning.[80] As Wenkstern comments, Polish residents were able to take a state examination to test their efficiency for the public service but many did not fare well. In some areas, as early as 1815, sums of money were set aside to attract Polish university graduates to the service, without success. One might question the bias of the tests, the bureaucratic body, or the education system. Several authors, including Wenkstern, Hagen, Trzeciakowski, and Wandycz, maintain that Polish was taught alongside German in the Prussian-controlled elementary school system.[81] Wenkstern also comments on the fact that both languages were used simultaneously in judicial courts, laws, decrees, and at the district and provincial assemblies. Furthermore, "the regulations made by the Government provide that a Pole who addresses a communication in the Polish language to any of the authorities, is entitled to a reply in the same language" But the clergy, in their civic functions and when acting as school inspectors, were to keep their registers in German.[82] This change is evident in parish records from the Lipusz, Leśno, and Wiele areas: most of the entries are in Latin into the 1820s but then in German thereafter.

Thus, it appears that the regime targeted the literate clergy and nobility more than the common peasants. The "guaranteed" administrative reply in Polish hinged on the ability of the plaintiff to address the state in written Polish, which was impossible for many of the peasants. Many Polish citizens chose not to work for the Prussian regime for a host of reasons: some hoped for a return of the Kingdom of Poland, some szlachta were incensed at losing their titles and retreated into the background, and others, fed by the belief that the Germans were inherently evil, refused to work out of fear that it would mean endorsing the German way.

The prospect of reforming the almost non-existent education system in Prussian-occupied Poland proved to be a more lengthy process. While higher schools did exist, they were confined to certain areas, such as Poznań and Wilno, and were designed to cater to the upper echelons of Polish society.[83] Frederick II was interested in educating Polish people in the administrative language of German, but also, at the elementary level, in their mother tongue. The Prussian minister of education, von Altenstein, in 1822, echoed Frederick's original soft reforms in the realm of language and religion, saying that those who were Germanized, as opposed to being bilingual, would not contribute to the "cultural development of the Polish nation."[84] Since few higher schools existed – or Polish teachers to fill the roles[85] – the influence of German in schools attempted to perfect Polish people's command of the administrative language.

According to several authors, Polish was recognized alongside German as the official state language until Bismarck's era.[86] Once West Prussia came into being in 1772, "the monarchy took special pains to expand primary education … [and by] 1778, a total of 125 schools had been established" in the region.[87] On a more micro scale, a list of school texts from 1845 in Czyczkowy contains several Polish and German readers and affirms the fact that the educational system was at least somewhat bilingual.[88] Catholic teachers' seminaries were also allowed to continue in the territory and were almost exclusively Polish in character. Many schools were allowed to instruct in Polish, including schools in Ostrowo, Trzemeszno, and Poznań. By the 1850s, there were approximately 1,200 small schools in the Poznań region, around 600 of which used Polish as the language of instruction.[89] Specific to the area of the Opeongo Road migrants, only a few schools existed by the 1850s. These included the smaller Catholic schools in Kościerzyna, Lipusz, Kalisz, Leśno, Wiele, Czyczkowy, and the secondary school in Chojnice.[90] The success of these schools, however, is difficult to measure since the greater part of the literature on this era is focused heavily on political manoeuvres rather than the social ramifications or internalizations of those enrolled in the schools.

It is difficult to determine how the reforms affected the rank and file Poles. They tend to be left out of the narrative because of a multitude of factors, including the long-practised top-down approach to writing Polish history and the fact that few documents have survived. The extent to which we can quantify their impact on those living in the West Prussian region is also difficult. While pupils could attend school for free in subsidized schools, attendance in West Prussia did not im-

Table 2.4: Language and religion statistics in West Prussian counties

County	German	Polish	Bilingual
BERENT (KOŚCIERZYNA) 1855			
Urban population	2,119	1,355	1,560
Rural population	10,364	12,456	6,819
CONITZ (CHOJNICE) 1855			
Urban population	6,636	528	N/A
Rural population	19,285	29,739	N/A

County	Protestant	Catholic	Jewish
CARTHAUS (KARTUZY) 1852			
Rural population	121,011	30,213	1
BERENT (KOŚCIERZYNA) 1852			
Urban population	1,860	2,357	601
Rural population	12,149	15,849	21
CONITZ (CHOJNICE) 1853			
Urban population	3,355	2,189	1,217
Rural population	8,827	38,066	680
CONITZ (CHOJNICE) 1861			
Urban population	4,044	2,926	1,322
Rural population	9,959	42,976	860

Source: Böhning, *Die Nationalpolnische Bewedung in Westpreussen 1815–1871*, 216–19.

prove as it was only between 25–50 per cent and there are also stories about skipping school and bribing the teacher to ignore truancy. Marjorie Lamberti also mentions that even though school hours were reduced to accommodate farm labour, attendance was often undermined by hostile attitudes from frugal parents who could not contribute funds and landowners who pined for cheap labour. As a result, many children heavily employed in agriculture left school as semi-literates. By 1871, 89.1 per cent of male and 83.5 per cent of female pupils born before 1861 in Prussia could read and write German. In Polish-speaking areas, like Posen, the literacy rate in German was lower (68.2 per cent for males and 59 per cent for females). In West Prussia, according to Walser Smith, the peasants were considerably more rural, Catholic, and disproportionately more pious and illiterate than in other regions and in many areas.[91] Table 2.4, while pointing out that a certain level of bilingualism existed in West Prussia, also helps to illustrate the divide between languages and denominations in the area.

It is thus no surprise that the migrants who came to Canada from the Lipusz, Wiele, and Leśno region also managed to evade the educational reforms of the Prussian regime.[92] Nonetheless, these reforms appear as instigators of migration in local historical memory. Although illiteracy will be discussed in greater detail in the following chapter, it is possible that these impoverished peasants concentrated their efforts on a pragmatic solution to their plight. In other words, their efforts were better served trying to cultivate the land – or trying to secure some through work – as opposed to becoming an educated citizen, especially one educated by foreigners. The fact that German was taught in school could very well have been a factor in non-compliance as well.[93]

Persecution on the basis of language and religion as an instigating factor, as surmised by Jost, Pick, Grzondziel,[94] and others, was not likely in the pre-Bismarckian era. If it did appear as a factor, it occurred in isolation. If we are to believe, from the peasants' standpoint, that there were widespread language and religious encroachments, we must remember to situate ourselves in the time and remember how unknown and modern these enlightened ideals propounded by Prussia must have appeared. If educational encroachments did prompt outmigration in the pre-Bismarckian migrants, the discontent might have originated in the peasant belief that an education, in Polish or German, was an unwelcome frivolity. Although schools were state-subsidized in West Prussia, regular attendance was poor. We must also remind ourselves that, at the time, the only other option to revert to – if Prussia exited – was feudalism. Nor should we deny that some measures instituted by the Prussian regime proved beneficial to the beleaguered Polish people, including agricultural reforms outlined by Kieniewicz and Wandycz, whether they left or stayed. For example, the traditional three-field system was discouraged in favour of crop rotation, and the cultivation of potatoes became more widespread among peasants, who primarily produced grain for their lords. Wenkstern also mentioned the introduction of the potato, and that the shift to fruit farming proved to be beneficial.[95]

At the macro level, the efforts of the Prussians in Poland seem to point toward a scheme of colonialism. As Salmonowicz points out, we cannot focus solely on the religious aspect since it would render only a parochial – implying both a narrow-minded and a non-secular definition of the term – view of history. However, if we take into account the acts and thoughts of the Prussian regime we see a greater force at work. The Prussian actions were products of the social structure in which they were imbedded. Through their "enlightened" ways, the Prussian administration was trying to transform the docile and servile peasant into a functioning citizen of the state. This transformation was not unique to Poland since many other lands experienced similar changes.[96] That it came at the hands of a foreign power has incensed Polish nationalists to this day. But the measures that were implemented by the Prussian regime point toward the notion that "the standardization of administration and law within it, and ... state education, transformed people into citizens of a specific country."[97] Everything, from the Prussian overseas passport of Jacob Czyrson to the military record book of Andrew Erdmannczyk, points toward the production of knowledge, resulting in the creation of a body of information about its previously anonymous citizens. In essence, they echo Scott's observations: by making territories and societies legible and measurable, the government was able to maintain authority.[98] Yet, as we see through the Polish people's refusal to become "enlightened" educated citizens, as demonstrated by the phenomenon of out-migration and internal bureaucratic difficulties, the colonizing state often faces problems in establishing and/or maintaining obedience, loyalty, and co-operation among its subjects.

The Bismarckian Wave in Local Memory

Unfortunately, when sifting through local historical memory, it is impossible to measure to what extent memory of the post-1871 Bismarckian migrations transposed a later set of circumstances into the historical memory of the first pre-1871 wave. What can be isolated are the differing conditions that drove the post-1871 migrations to Canada since different push factors entered the equation. Although the language is at times sensationalist and the sources are cited only sporadically, local authors do discuss Bismarckian social and political conditions in their publications. Ritza states that with the combination of Wilhelm I and Bismarck, "[a] more formidable crew never existed for the advancement of sinister exploits in history ... [they and] the Prussian army ... held [Poland] ... in it's [sic] iron grip." In his epic narrative, O'Dwyer writes that the "naked sword of the tyrant flashed above the heads of these hapless people." Glofcheskie did not specifically mention Bismarck's laws but he does mention the suppression of the Polish language and Catholic religion.[99] Makowski touched on some encroachments, but without providing dates or sources. He contends that:

> Bismarck's Germany energetically promoted a national policy to exterminate the Polish element ... by creating economic conditions so severe that they would be forced to leave the country. A well-planned and ruthlessly executed action of appropriation of Polish farmers left many of them homeless or penniless. As a result, approximately 130,000 Kashoubs [sic], or roughly a third of the population of Kashoubia, emigrated in that period ... The Prussians soon realized that the struggle with the Kashoubs would be long and difficult and began to forbid the use of Polish in schools, offices and churches. German teachers were sent to instruct and indoctrinate Polish children. All Kashoubs who refused to accept Prussian citizenship were expropriated and removed. Special edicts were proclaimed, aimed at taking land away from the Poles ... When the Prussians, hoping to force them to sell, forbade them to build houses on their own land, they lived in barns, gypsy wagons and underground caves.
> One of them, Frank Peplinski, lived for years in a gypsy wagon, refusing to leave his land.[100]

Rekowski recognized that the inhabitants left because of Bismarck's Kulturkampf but did not provide specific details in his account.[101] Recently, Mask-Connolly has further expanded on these antecedent conditions. However, she recycles many of Makowski and Rekowski's claims:

> Life in West Prussia under foreign occupation was always difficult ... but it became intolerable in 1871 when Reich Chancellor Otto von Bismarck ruthlessly initiated his *Kulturkampf* campaign, designed to impose the German culture on the Prussian (Polish and Kashubian) people and eliminate all elements of their

ethnicity. These oppressive regulations were aimed primarily at the Catholic church and the Catholic population. Bismarck was determined to fight them. All Prussians were restricted in their rights of ownership, in the use of language other than German and in their religious practices. All services including their church masses were held in the German language; no Polish language training was permitted and all classes were taught in German; Poles and Kashubs were not allowed to build homes (although they could build barns). The elimination of their ethnicity extended to the mandatory Germanization of their surnames and village names. Under *Kulturkampf* policies, the fervently Catholic and culturally proud Kashub developed a hatred for the German overlords. It proved to be the "final straw" for some of these people who for generations had lived no better than slaves.[102]

Her additions from a historical dictionary are, unfortunately, buried in an endnote:

> *Kulturkampf* ... originated in a struggle over the clerical control of education. The first move was the abolition of the Catholic department in the Prussian Ministry of Culture on July 8, 1871, followed by the *School Supervision Law*. Penal measures against the clergy included the *Pulpit Clause* and *Jesuit Law*, and culminated in the *May Laws of 1873*, which were supplemented by the introduction of civil marriage (Registry Offices) in Prussia. Papal protest against these laws was countered by the *Expatriation Act of 1874*. In 1886–87 Bismarck made his peace with the Roman Curia and by 1891 much of the *Kulturkampf* legislation was suspended, although some (state school supervision, pulpit clause, obligatory civil marriage) remained in force. Many Kashubs fled Prussia during the *Kulturkampf* years while emigration dropped off dramatically after 1891.[103]

Theresa Prince, a local genealogist and historian, also attempted to contextualize the cultural causes in a recent publication but fell short of providing specific references or quantifying the conditions.[104] Since the knowledge of this area of the migration has not been influenced by parallel studies into the systemic issues of the period, readers and descendants are presented with the opinion that Kulturkampf was a knee-jerk reaction on Bismarck's part to a hatred for a specific cultural group, the Poles. In fact, a plethora of historians argue much to the contrary, that the previous viewpoint is only a part taken for the whole in the greater record.

The Origins of Kulturkampf

Over the past several decades, Kulturkampf has been misunderstood by many writers. This is rooted in the tendency of authors to approach the struggle "from the point of view of the Catholic victim, not from that of the Prussian or German state and its administrative capability." As a result, the focus has been on the hardships faced by bishops or clergy, and, as Trzeciakowski points out, Kulturkampf has "become the symbol of animosity toward everything Polish."[105] Other authors, however, wrote about the period quite differently. In addition to the Bishop of Mainz, who admitted that Bismarck was not simply a sectarian fanatic, several authors, such as Otto Pflanze, highlight the necessity of Bismarck's measures from an international political standpoint and point out that the opposition to the Polish cause was political, not cultural or racial (see figure 2.4).[106]

Richard Blanke and Polish authors such as Trzeciakowski, Wandycz, and Benjamin Murdzek do not take the face-value approach either and argue otherwise, stating that Kulturkampf was an attack on the Catholic hierarchy and the landed nobility.[107] Contemporary authors Ronald Ross and Michael Gross approach it more methodically. They contend that the Kulturkampf was a struggle between nineteenth-century Prussian liberalism (arising from the utopian project of the Enlightenment) and the Counter-Enlightenment and ultramontane ideologies of the Roman Catholic Church. Unfortunately, the ones who were most affected in the end were the Polish-speaking Catholic peasants. Helmut Walser Smith reminds us that similar struggles were being waged across Europe in Catholic and Protestant countries. Austria, Spain, Switzerland, Belgium, the Netherlands, and France all passed Kulturkampf-like legislation.[108] Working from the paradigm that Prussia was trying to transform land into territory, the implementation of a colonial scheme added to the intensity of conflict between the Church

2.4 Bismarck is Coming!

and the Prussian liberal elites, of whom Prussian Chancellor Otto von Bismarck was one. Furthermore, Kulturkampf measures are, in a sense, part of how elites maintain control in a colonized land.

Once in power, Bismarck's intention was to unite the collection of provinces and denominations under strong leadership. In the beginning, according to Lukowski and Zawadski, he "considered Polish-speaking peasants capable of loyal service to the Prussian state." But, as Murdzek argues, Bismarck's maintenance of control in Prussia meant tackling the same two groups that were targeted in the era of the partitions: the nobility and the Church.[109] Both were still present in the Polish provinces: the former assisting in the Posen uprisings in 1848, and the latter as the guardians of Polish nationalism. Although the szlachta were beleaguered by the reforms earlier in the century, some managed to stay alive and, alongside literary exiles, articulated their romanticized yearning for a Polish state from Paris.[110] Bismarck's view of the utopian and romantic thought of the Polish intelligentsia was summarized in an interview conducted by Hans Kleser in 1892.

Bismarck said that the Polish noble is "an intriguer, hypocritical, untruthful and unreliable, quite incapable of maintaining a state organization – today he overflows with *Jescze Polska*, tomorrow it is *Waschlapski* and *Krapulinski*" – meaning that they shifted their fight from one imposing power to the other. In his memoirs, Bismarck stated that he was not anti-Catholic, but rather against Polish nationalism.[111] The Church in Poland, on the other hand, maintained its stance as the custodian of Polish nationalism from the time of partition through the revolutionary upheavals of 1848 and into the Bismarckian era.

After the November 1830 uprisings in the Russian-controlled, previously semi-autonomous Congress of Poland, it became known that the Polish clergy had fostered the movements' sentiments and were involved.[112] Even though Pope Gregory XIV issued the *Cum primum* in 1832, instructing bishops to remain loyal to princes and to stay away from the liberal tricksters of revolution, the Polish clergy, away from the shadow of the Vatican, continued to promote nationalism in their zones of influence.[113] The Polish-speaking clergy, in the mid-nineteenth century, adopted what Brian Porter terms national messianism.[114] The Polish "nation," under the influence of the lower clergy, was compared to Jesus. Just as He died, was crucified, and rose again, Poland's fate, at the hands of the evil powers, would be the same. Fuelled by the writings of literary figures living abroad, exiles like Adam Mickiewicz, Julius Słowacki, and Zygmunt Krasiński built upon this notion. An excellent example of the Jesus analogy is reflected in a poem written by Kazmierz Brodziński: "Hail O Christ, Thou Lord of Men! / Poland, in Thy footsteps treading / Like Thee suffers, at Thy bidding; / Like Thee, too, shall rise again."[115] Comparisons from the Book of Genesis, which pointed to a time when no laws existed and God was supreme, also propounded the notion that the Polish-speaking people did not need a governing foreign power.[116] People cringed at a future where Poles were forced to serve Russians, Prussians, or Austrians and pondered the question, "Why has Providence allowed such a crime to be perpetrated?" Such thoughts are again summed up by the dramatic pen of Morelowski, who wrote: "O God, although you justly punished us, / Less virtuous sons of our fathers, / But are our enemies better than us? / Is the cruel Muscovite better than us?"[117]

The lower clergy's efforts were aided by the fact that there were many venues for their work. In West Prussia, around 120 churches provided possible venues to preserve a vaguely constructed, but omnipresent, Polish nationalism.[118] It could also be argued that the survival of the Church, to an extent, was predicated on the existence of a Polish nation – not as a real political entity, but as an abstract and utopian belief in the minds of Polish-speaking individuals. For believing Catholics in the Province of West Prussia, of which there were many, God became a player in modern nationalist politics.

After the failure of the numerous nationalist and liberal revolutions of 1848 across Europe, the bishops of the Catholic Church in the Prussian state believed that the roots of the conflicts were due to factors other than nationalism. The bishops believed that "the people had been 'blinded' and 'bewildered,' 'bewitched' and 'bedazzled' by modern and fashionable philosophies: materialism, rationalism, liberalism, and democracy, all propagated, church leaders claimed, by an endless number of anti-Christian and antisocial newspapers." Thus, after a conference in Würzburg in late 1848, missionaries from several denominations, from the Rhineland to Gdańsk, preached an anti-Enlightenment campaign against these very philosophies. Among these were the Franciscans, Redemptorists, Dominicans, and Jesuits.[119]

During their missions, they often stopped in rural and urban areas for days and weeks. Work in the fields and at home was suspended. Often sermons were conducted three times daily: at dawn, in the afternoon, and in the evening. Topics included the origins of man, judgment after death, the sacraments, and the incarnation of Jesus. Trying to curtail popular culture in the Gdańsk regions, the missionaries "ranted against alcohol consumption and tavern life, dancing, playing cards, gambling, reading novels, foul language and sexual license."[120] In response to the missionary efforts, Brotherhood of Sobriety societies were formed in many parishes, including Wiele, Lipusz, and Leśno in 1852, 1855, and 1861.[121] The missionaries also condemned the uprisings of 1848 as sins and the work of Satan.

However, the missionaries and their message through the 1850s and the 1860s became increasingly ultramontane. Rural parish priests, "with their closer ties to peasant sensibility ... encouraged the missionaries to give ... powerful, forceful sermons emphasizing sin and repentance. Missionaries therefore adopted a theatrical style that looked like a tantrum. They screamed, pounded the pulpit, stomped their feet, jumped up and down, and thrashed about."[122]

In trying to keep the peasants away from the evils of knowledge, the missionaries and clergy kept them subservient to the Church and away from enlightened ideas in schools and a society run by Prussian (German) officials. In West Prussia, since villagers were disproportionately rural, illiterate, and extremely pious, it is no surprise that parishioners from Lipusz, Leśno, and Wiele stood by their Church against the Prussians. If we take into consideration the old Polish saying, "Germans are dissenters," we see the divisiveness that the church built to counter ideologies.[123]

In the 1860s, the liberals and Bismarck resented the Catholic hierarchy since they meddled in the political field beyond their realm and used their influence in West Prussia to keep the peasant population from integrating into or co-existing with the enlightened German way of life. In the words of Bismarck:

> In religious matters, my toleration has at all times been restricted only by the boundaries which the necessity of various denominations co-existing in the same body politic imposes on the claims of each particular creed. The therapeutic treatment of the Catholic Church in a temporal state, is, however, difficult by the fact that the Catholic clergy, if they desire to properly discharge what is theoretically their duty, must claim a share in the secular government extending beyond their ecclesiastical domain ... [The clergy] transmits ... their own conviction that ... the Church, wherever she does not rule, is justified in complaining of Diocletian-like persecution.[124]

Soon enough, this resentment would turn into a full-fledged conflict between competing ideologies and result in the creation of policies against the Church hierarchy. One of the main instigators of this conflict dividing the Prussian liberal elite and the church was the missionaries' preaching about the Vatican. Although the Vatican had "abandoned" Polish people earlier, the Franciscans, Redemptorists, Dominicans, and Jesuits became more ultramontane and advocated "an unwavering dedication to the absolute incontestable authority of the pope in Rome."[125] This set off alarms in the minds of liberals and Protestants. While Catholic lower clergy propagated nationalism in the face of "discrimination," the hierarchy and its missionary foot soldiers feared these rationalist philosophies and propagated an ultramontane agenda. These were equally obnoxious to Prussian liberals and Protestants, who feared the allegiance of Catholics (Polish or German) to a figure and institution outside Prussian territory.[126]

The Implementation and Results of Kulturkampf

This ultramontane line of thinking resulted in a wave of anti-modern decrees from the Catholic Church. The 1864 *Syllabus of Errors*, which anathematized modernism, liberalism, and rationalism, combined with the formal declaration of papal infallibility in 1870 by the Vatican Council, astounded Bismarck and the Prussian elites. In their minds, the doctrine of infallibility "was sanctioned by neither scripture or tradition."[127] The measure was seen as hypocritical and demonstrating a backward sense of logic and provincialism. Frustrated by the Church's indoctrination of the people in West Prussia, Bismarck and the Prussian elites embarked on a campaign after Rome issued the doctrine of infallibility to mitigate (again) the influence of the Church and take control of their territorial gains among the Prussian peasants.[128]

The need to act swiftly against the Church was a product of the enlightened schema. A citizen of the enlightened Prussian state was supposed to act with reason, not blind allegiance, according to several of the leading Prussian thinkers of the time. Liberal thinkers, such as Eduard Zeller, thought "the church [now] threatened the most basic freedom of conscience and independence of the individual."[129] The new papal doctrine was a play for control initiated by the Church. Leading up to 1870 in Prussia, the Church did not advocate for freedom of faith or conscience, but rather the specific recognition of their conservative doctrine. Thus, the liberals were convinced that these recent measures confirmed that the Catholics of West Prussia were out of touch with modern society and that their beliefs were overlaid with a hysterical sense of piety and newly invented superstitions. Aligning with the modern age over primitive medieval times, Prussian liberals believed that the state must strive for its own secular independence as ultramontanism vitiated the growth of the nation.[130] Kulturkampf was thus initiated.

Adding to the belief that Catholics in Prussian-occupied territory were irrational in their extreme piety, other acts in the nineteenth century left Prussians with a conviction that Catholics' ultramontane beliefs were "inimical to Germany's ... social modernization," civic emancipation, and moral improvement. Cloisters practised obscurantism, the "servility of their religious adherents" were endless, and their practices were concealed beneath shrouds of self-imposed secrecy.[131] Pilgrimages, like the 1844 one to Trier where, allegedly, the robe of Christ was on display, frightened Prussian officials – perhaps because of this group's revolutionary potential. In 1854, the Church introduced the dogma of immaculate conception. Ten years later in Marpingen, the appearance of the newly refashioned Virgin Mary to three eight-year-old girls and a subsequent pilgrimage in 1876 contributed to the Prussian belief in the "irrationality" of Catholics as "credence to apparitions bathed in celestial light was perceived by their Protestant fellow countrymen as the willful abnegation of critical intelligence."[132] None of the four supposed appearances ever received episcopal sanction.[133] To the thinking Prussian, who undoubtedly had pre-existing negative views of the peasant Poles, these conditions marked the era as one ripe for ideological conflict.

Measures were put in place as early as 1871 to try to turn the tide of the ultramontane Catholic Church in Prussian-occupied Poland. A series of policies were enacted under the umbrella that came to be known as the May Laws in Bismarck's Kulturkampf. Bismarck supported the acts and was the figurehead at the helm of the regime, but the policies had widespread support from liberal elites in the government. What many local authors also fail to mention, due to their Polish-centric lens, is the fact that many of the measures were also enacted against the many German-speaking Catholics.[134]

The first measure, enacted in July of 1871, was the dissolution of the Catholic Section of the Ministry of Educational and Ecclesiastical Affairs in Prussia.[135] Although Pope Pius IX condemned this policy as "reminiscent of anti-Christian outrages ... in ancient Rome," several policies were enacted not to exterminate Catholicism but to place specific limitations upon it in the enlightened state. In December, the criminal code was amended to prevent clerics from using the pulpit for their own anti-political propaganda. A year later, in March 1872, the Catholic clergy's ability to inculcate beliefs through their supervision of the schooling system was eliminated. The new law required that lay persons be appointed instead. To a Catholic reader, such an act, at face value, would seem drastic; however, over the years, many priests who supervised schools disliked the burden of inspecting and reports. As a result, this may have been more of a minute point than it seems. James Van Horn Melton points out that entrusting education to the clergy was often a risky venture as most clergy only taught the peasantry "little more than formulaic phrases and superficial devotional forms." Lamberti also remarks that many priests' concerns were narrow and they often turned a blind eye to truancy and innovations in the classroom.[136] The Jesuits (who taught catechism), Redemptorists, and Lazarists were also banned. These were attempts to limit the revolutionary potential that such ultramontane missionaries could spread to rural Polish populations. The Cloister Laws attempted to accomplish the same end. These enactments of May 1875 banished all orders in debt to the state, except those devoted to hospital work and those who would accept the Prussian teaching prerequisites. These last laws prompted the closure of 296 religious establishments, such as convents and monasteries, displacing 1,181 male and 1,776 female conventuals. In 1873, additional legislation again weakened the teaching capacity of the Catholic Church after the *Landtag*'s adoption of the May Laws. Aspiring clergymen who wanted to teach would now have to attend university and pass examinations in philosophy, history, and German literature.[137]

By 1875, the effects of these changes were being felt and more legislation to deal with the final remnants of church control was enacted. This led the Vatican to retaliate. In the *Quod Nunquam* of 5 February 1875, Pope Pius IX declared all the Prussian legislation invalid "as they totally oppose the divine order of the Church [and bishops] cannot be deprived of the episcopal office by any lofty power of the world." wielding divine authority, Pius IX threatened those who followed Prussian orders with excommunication.[138] To show the Vatican that the Church's success hinged on material and worldly goods, the 1875 Breadbasket Law cut off the state subsidy for Catholic churches unless their bishops submitted, in writing, to the requirements of the previous legislation.[139] Priests who violated the laws were subject to prosecution. Convictions resulted in fines up to 100 thalers and those unable, or unwilling, to settle their accounts were taken into custody for one day or for several months. Laymen were punished if they were summoned and refused to appear in court to testify against members of the clergy. In West Prussia, 62 people were charged and 39 convicted under this law in 1876. The liberal elites and Bismarck, in the face of papal infallibility, brought the clergy under civil law and away from their previous position of divine power. These laws were designed to separate church and state in Prussia and its dependencies.[140]

The results of these laws became evident in 1875 and 1876 when, out of 12 Prussian dioceses, 5 bishops were judicially removed, and 4 who had passed away were not replaced. On the micro scale, about 1,400 of 4,600 Catholic parishes in Prussia did not have a priest.[141] The impact of the volleys of power between enlightened Prussia and the Catholic hierarchy was felt by German and Polish-speaking peasants, who were now not able to receive their sacraments and practise their faith. For example, "Last Rites often could not be administered to the dying, marriage ceremonies were inconvenienced, burials sometimes became the focus of unseemly quarrels and the regularity of sacramental observance became increasingly difficult."[142] In the district of Marienwerder, 116 clergymen were relieved of their school inspection duties and replaced by 23 laymen who traversed West Prussia. By the 1880s, 112 Catholic and 69 Protestant full-time inspectors had been appointed and 2,204 priests had been relieved of their duties across schools in Prussia. Priests, however, could still attend religious lessons to see that the correct instruction was being given and, if needed, complain to the state. Nonetheless, this removal left some priests aggrieved at losing their positions and politicized them.[143] Despite the fact that, in the words of Murdzek, the average Polish peasant "cared little who occupied the office of Archbishop of Gniezo-Poznań, the inflamed press and his equally impassioned parish pastor gave him the belief that their cause was his." The Church branded the laws, in Polish-speaking areas, as a specific attack on the Polish Church hierarchy and all Polish people. Just as the Church promoted the equation of Polish as Catholic, many accounts of Kulturkampf, including those by local authors, continued to present it as an attack on all Polish life.[144]

Yet, while the Church was left beleaguered, it was not entirely exterminated.[145] It was Bismarck's intention, argues Ross, to reduce the role of the Church in the land and not, as many of Bismarck's liberal colleagues advocated, to expunge all traces of Polishness from the land. Murdzek also writes that there were "no concerted efforts at forcing lingual and cultural assimilation. These latter were never regarded as a threat to the security of the Prussian state."[146] Ross argues that until the

1880s, Bismarck's "aims were restorative, not innovative." They were meant to restore control over the two aspects of Polish life that held it back. Bismarck commented on these laws after the fact and admitted that Minister Adalbert Falk's legal apparatus, which was created to pursue and harass priests using Prussian gendarmes, did not help them achieve their goal. Neither did it address the separation between Church and state.[147] Bismarck himself thought that "the fear of the law's application will have a beneficial effect."[148] But it is also significant to note that during the clergy's fight for freedom, they did not advocate for widespread equal rights, just their own, and unfortunately, some succumbed to anti-Semitic prejudice.[149] In 1878, when the German Liberal Party split, the main thrust of Kulturkampf was over, according to Gross, until the Colonization Commission was set up in 1886, forcing the colonization of German-speaking peoples in Polish territory.[150] Those topics, however, are beyond the scope of this study.

The Legacy of Conscription and Bismarck

As evidenced by the words of several local residents, such as John Pick and John Mintha, the militarized Prussian state, especially in Bismarck's era, has left its imprint on local historical memory. Not only do several oral accounts attest to this but it is also mentioned by Mask-Connolly: "There was also the fear that the Kashubs might have to fight yet another war for their German oppressors. This fear was not ungrounded. After all, they had borne the brunt of three German wars in seven years: 1) the *War of 1864* (against Denmark when the Prussians acquired Schleswig), 2) the War of 1866 (the *Seven Weeks War* against Austria when they acquired Holstein), 3) the *Franco Prussian War* of 1870–1871 ... Many feared the possibility of further mandatory, military service and of conscription for themselves and/or their sons – so they fled. Such was the case for 18-year-old Frank Cybulski, who was living in the parish of Lipusz when he and his family decided to emigrate."[151] Although Mask-Connolly does not quantify how widespread this notion of militarism extended in the minds of people beyond Frank Cybulski or Andrew Etmanski (if that is even possible), it is a fear that has nonetheless survived. Yet readers are left wondering why such measures might – all of a sudden – promote thoughts of out-migration. To arrive at a plausible answer to this question, several watershed moments in the administration of the Prussian army need to be considered.

As stated earlier, the introduction of the canton system in Prussian-occupied Poland early in the nineteenth century imposed the Prussian sense of order and militarism on the peasant population. Between 1815 and 1860, 40,000 recruits were called up to the Prussian army every year for two-year stints. The Army Bill of 1860 increased this number to 63,000 and the length of the term to three years, plus an additional four or five in the reserves. It also doubled the infantry battalions and increased the artillery by 25 per cent.[152] According to Gordon Craig, "all young males in the district were enrolled upon the regimental recruiting list; and when the quotas could not be filled by voluntary enlistment, the difference was made up from the eligibles on the rolls."[153] These eligibles were considered to be able-bodied men between the ages of 18 and 40. In times of danger, William I believed a strong military to be the main prop of the monarch.[154] This became more important after conflict broke out in 1859 between neighbouring France and Austria, not long after the Crimean War of 1854–55 frayed relations between European powers. The canton system was designed to ensure that a large trained reserve was readily available should they need to be mobilized quickly.[155] After the 1860 army bill was defeated, Wilhelm nonetheless implemented these changes since the liberals agreed that the military needed to be reformed.

Although these changes did not come until later in 1860, once the news of it filtered out piecemeal across the land, they were sure to worry peasants. This was undoubtedly compounded by the military service bill of 1862–63 which gave a concession – a two-year term – that was offset by re-enlisters and payment. The peacetime strength of the army was fixed at 1 to 1.2 per cent of the population and was designed to grow incrementally with population growth. Although the two-year concession allowed some to buy out of their third year, for most of the rural peasantry could not afford to do that. Recently, however, Dennis Showalter has argued that life as a soldier was not always "one of unrelieved misery in an alien environment. After his initial training the cantonist spent as much as ten months of every year at home on furlough."[156]

Again, it is unclear how many fellow parishioners from the Lipusz, Wiele, and Leśno areas were conscripted into the Prussian army between 1815 and 1862, or after 1862, and to what extent those who were conscripted migrated away from Prussian-occupied territory. Frank

Cybulski, John Mintha's father, and John Pick are only a few of these parishioners. Michael Gutowski might be another[157] but the passage of time prevents us from querying these migrants. However, if we combine the rumour of increased conscription with the fact that Bismarck became the prime minister of Prussia in 1862, the resonance of the triumvirate of Bismarck, militarism, and military conscription becomes even more potent in the minds of potential conscripts. Despite the resonance of militarism as an out-migration factor in the writings of local historians, those writing about the Polish-Kashubs should broaden their scope to include information from books written about Polish immigration to the US and German immigration to Ontario. Albert Sanford writes that the Polish immigrants in Portage County, Wisconsin left their homeland not only for economic betterment but to escape army service. According to Richard Zeitlin, three Silesian males, Andrew and Lawrence Bautch and Peter Sura, were afraid that the three-year term in the Prussian army would be increased. Fearing this, they left with their families for Trempealeau County, Wisconsin, c. 1853. The record also needs to show that this same factor has been claimed to propel German emigration to Ontario. A quick look at the findings of Lee-Whiting and Finnigan reveals the comparison. The oral histories of the Ziebarth, Luloff, and Haas families also attest that their German ancestors left because of militarism and the threat of conscription.[158]

Conclusion: Economic and Religious Factors

Although many writing on the Polish-Kashubs did not (or were not able to, for a variety of reasons) research the deep-seated ideological struggles before 1871, without a doubt these struggles left their mark in the minds of those who emigrated and those who stayed. For those socialized in the Catholic, ultramontane milieu, the Prussian changes assaulted their entire world. In a secular age it is difficult to imagine the extent of the political power and influence exerted by the Church on both individuals and groups at that time. However, a thorough examination of the social, economic, and political forces at work in the nineteenth century can place the out-migration of the Polish-Kashub group in its proper context. Such an approach yields a greater understanding of the economic conditions in which peasants found themselves during the emancipation era. Parallel migration narratives from the German group also suggest that some Bismarckian measures promoted both German and Polish emigration.

By dividing the migration of Polish-Kashub settlers into two waves – something not done before – it is easier to examine the out-migration factors for the small but continuous flow of people from Prussian-occupied Poland to Canada. In doing so, it is possible to better contextualize the experience of those peasants who left before 1871. The migrants who left West Prussia before 1871 did so mainly due to their economic situation: they lacked enough land and capital to survive and their harvests were hampered by poor weather. If they left during the Bismarckian era, they also became subject to an entirely different set of persecutory factors. Of course, even if they left then, we cannot discount the fact that their incentive to leave might have been compounded by their pitiable economic situation. Unfortunately, in the midst of an ideological struggle between the enlightened Prussians and the Catholic Church, the peasants, including those in West Prussia, were caught up in that whirlwind and affected individually. What was known, passed on, and disseminated about militarism and conscription in Bismarckian Prussia, as evidenced in the words of Mintha and Pick, also instilled fear in those who left.

After this examination, we have a better insight into the prominence, at the local level, of rural parishes, and more important, priests. As one of the few literate and educated persons in a community of peasants, priests acted as missionaries, counsellors, and spiritual leaders and were expected to make prominent pronouncements on disagreements in their parish. This was evident in West Prussia where the local priest held a position of special authority due to the disproportionately illiterate and extremely pious peasants who made up the majority of the parishes. The literary trend of the priest as a pastkeeper continued in whatever land the Polish-Kashubian migrants settled. Just as the missionaries (re)fashioned the 1848 narrative of modernity, so priests in Canada also fashioned an impassioned narrative of migration, exile, and settlement. Furthermore, Polish-Kashubs who left Prussian-occupied Poland for Canada West were, ironically, not only caught in the colonial reforms of the Prussian state but also found themselves in the midst of another colonial scheme at the end of their journey.

3

Migration Memories

> What gives value to travel is fear. It is the fact that, at a certain moment, when we are so far from our own country ... we are seized by a vague fear, and an instinctive desire to go back to the protection of old habits.
>
> Albert Camus, *Notebooks 1935–1951*

Over the last fifty years, several narratives have been produced and attached to the migration of Polish-Kashubs to Canada via oral and written history. Some were uncorroborated literary constructions that took on a life of their own and have survived to the present day. Many passages in these narratives highlight a mournful uprooting from the homeland. This chapter identifies several of the narratives that, over time, have been attached to the Polish-Kashub migration. Although many of the claims are unsourced – thus making it hard to decipher the origins – and poorly researched, it becomes apparent that several local authors have not been able to move away from mournful, Handlinesque language.[1] Many have chosen to depict the migrants as exiled, poor, naive, and deceived, even though this clashes with their insistence that the migrants were strong and hardy. These depictions have inadvertently backed authors into a corner. Adopting such a lens has prevented authors from analyzing the conditions surrounding the actual migration. After bringing these narratives to the fore, this chapter resituates the journey as an impelled migration and examines why that metanarrative survived after the arrival of Galician Poles to the Ottawa Valley. It also examines which factors, like passports and transportation networks, were involved in facilitating the Polish-Kashubs' journey and how they may have affected the decision to migrate.

The Poor and Hapless Exiles

The first publication to devote several pages to the migration of the Polish-Kashubs along the Opeongo set a precedent followed by many publications. Fr O'Dwyer, an Irish priest, gave a history of three local Polish churches in his 1964 diocesan history. Starting with a fictional story of two emigrants, John and Mary, O'Dwyer presented a story that he dramatized for the reading public. He incorporated several details gleaned from actual migrations – including the fact that the emigrants left from Hamburg and sailed into Quebec – but his account added several elements. Using sensationalist rhetoric, he painted the migrants as hapless, naive, and exiled from their homeland because of Prussia and Bismarck[2] (even though Kulturkampf only started in 1871).

Lacking contextual or documentary evidence, O'Dwyer embarked on his discourse, which wove fictional narratives, often laden with religious symbolism, between the general details of the story. For example, he inserted a story that the emigrants, with "many a stifled sob, all on deck began to sing the Polish national anthem. (Sure, wasn't it one of their own patriots, Josef Wybicki, from Pomerania, who, in earlier times, had composed it.) 'Jeszsze Polska, nie zginela' ... 'For the last time my comrads' shouted a leader in the band; as they began to repeat the chorus to the last stanza ... Into this chanting, these poor exiles put their very souls." Commenting in a mournful tone on the emigrants' last memories, O'Dwyer writes that they fondly remembered the parish, the broken-hearted pastor, and the last procession at church. But he contrasted these with the lasting image of "the menacing shadow of the armed Prussian guard" who brought up the rear to "prod the straggler on."

Another memory that O'Dwyer related is the claim that "like the Irish Immigrant of 1848 and afterwards, many of these Polish refugees, too, carried with them a 'Handful of Earth' as a souvenir. This would be placed in their graves in a foreign land ... some of the soil from the heart of the land they loved would mingle with their own bodies when they would crumble in death." Continuing with his dramatic prose, O'Dwyer writes of the "misery of the violent wrench from their homes, the seasickness, the incredible hardships of overcrowding, and the unsanitary appointments of a windjammer. Eleven weeks at sea, however, served but to cement the ties and attachments of their happy childhood."[3] This was followed by a description of a burial at sea. Although it is doubtful that a Polish band was aboard, its inclusion added literary flair. The anthem *"Dąbrowski Mazurka,"* written by Wybicki, was published in Italy in 1799, and not adopted as the Polish anthem until 1927. Its popularity before 1927 is uncertain but its inclusion adds nationalist and regionalist sentiment.[4] Similarly, the inclusion of the "handful of earth," borrowed from the Irish migration narrative,[5] gave literary flair to the religious metaphor "dust unto dust." These inclusions shaped written historical memory and have been repeated by other local authors.

In the 1990s, Rekowski also used the heroic rendition of the national anthem and the mournful tone. Rekowski wrote that "leaving their families, friends and homes was the most painful experience of their lives. It is related that the departure was accompanied by crying and sobs of despair. Those leaving for Canada around 1858 sang 'Jeszcze Polska nie zginęła' (Poland is not Yet Lost)." Describing the transatlantic journey, O'Dwyer made sure to mention, without giving any specific examples, that deaths at sea were commonplace and emphasized crowding and disease: "Packed together like sardines, sickness and disease broke out among them. The weaker, especially young children were not able to stand the rigours of the journey and died. Their bodies were then thrown overboard into the ocean. When they arrived in the new world and had to disembark, there were many reports of people being so weakened and so stiff that at first they could hardly stand on their feet and start walking again."[6]

Several years later, in 2003, Mask-Connolly used similar language when she embarked on her own history. Statements such as "the local parishes mourned their loss. Mothers prayed for children to come home so they might see them at least one more time before they died" exemplify this.[7] She adds other ominous passages into her discourse, expanding on O'Dwyer's last-memories theme, writing that

> Most were scared – some more than others. Some may have changed their minds at the last minute. Others might have had family fights that tore them permanently apart; a few may have said things that they would forever regret for they would never again hear the voices of the ones they left behind ... In all likelihood, these departing Kashubs visited the graves of their loved

ones and planted flowers on them ... They may have pleaded with relatives and friends to care for these graves and to remember them and their deceased ones in their prayers. They probably visited their parish churches and might have wept that they would never again petition God from the worn kneelers. They looked at the backs of the pews where as children they had scratched their mark. They lit candles on the graves and in the church and they begged God to keep them safe on their journey ... Many lost their funds before they ever left Europe as they were charged inflated prices for board and lodging and sold unnecessary gear for the voyage. Rates of exchange were confusing and passengers were readily duped.[8]

Although she uses modal verbs such as "may" and "might," as opposed to O'Dwyer or Rekowski's narratives, which were laden with definitive past tense claims, Mask-Connolly also dramatizes the story with fictional situations.[9]

O'Dwyer's inclusion of the "handful of earth" rhyme (from the Irish famine migrations) has since been brought into the historical memory of the Polish-Kashub group. Rekowski writes that "it was a custom for the emigrants to take with them a handful of their native soil ... the soil would be handed on to their children to be cast into their graves when they would die and be buried in a foreign country!" Unfortunately, he did not legitimize his claim by sourcing it or incorporating oral testimony (if it exists), nor did he contextualize its Irish origins. Yet because Rekowski wielded pastoral power and was a descendant of original settlers, the claim had an air of legitimacy among the local population and was replicated in other works.

The perpetuation of the "handful of earth" trope was furthered in historical memory by its inclusion in a 1997 film, *Kaszuby Canada: Part One*.[10] It was recounted as part of the narrative by Michael D. O'Brien, an Ottawa-born author of Catholic fiction.[11] Although O'Brien's involvement in local history was non-existent at the time of the film, his recounting of the "handful of earth" story confirmed the place it held in historical memory among external authors. Mask-Connolly also included the story and added it to her discourse of the migration – also without corroborating it.[12] Most recently, Peter (the current WHS president) and Michael Glofcheskie brought a handful of earth from Głowczewice, Poland and sprinkled it on the graves of their ancestors in St Hedwig's Cemetery in Barry's Bay at the start of the 2011 Glofcheskie family reunion. The inclusion of these elements, the Polish anthem, and the "handful of earth," fictional or otherwise, solidified their place in local historical memory. The tale passed from a priestly Irish pastkeeper, to external authors, local authors, and a documentary film, and has now been picked up by locals in a symbolic and metaphorical act meant to stimulate ancestral connections. Despite its origins, this organic metaphor of uprootedness has become part of local memory and has taken on a life of its own.

Another dimension of the migration narrative that has evolved over time relates to the poor settlers being lured by emigration or immigration agents. O'Dwyer did not comment on agents but other authors did. After Hessel sifted through official correspondence, he devoted a chapter[13] to the dubious recruiting tactics and shoddy reporting of two German-speaking government agents.[14] Afterwards, these agents were added into the written narrative of the Polish-Kashub group as a catalyst and cause of migration.

Rekowski added the overseas agents into his discourse and assigned them the role of luring emigrants.[15] Mask-Connolly then picked up this statement and inserted it into her discourse in 2002. She also added a biblical reference to the narrative from Exodus, claiming that the "first Kashubs ... were lured to Canada by German shipping agents who painted a picture of a land of milk and honey." Mask-Connolly corroborates this through an 1860 government report that read, "They said the agent at home had deceived them, in telling them the cost of removal from Prussian Poland to Quebec was a great deal less than they afterwards found out."[16] She expands this insertion into the narrative a year later by copying the same quote but inserts an unsourced claim that others were also duped. She added that "the first Kashubs who were convinced to emigrate to Canada and who found themselves on the *Heinrich*, were easy victims to an unethical agent."[17] Continuing her claims against this supposed unethical agent, Mask-Connolly paints the migrants as victims, saying that "these Kashubs wanted to go to Quebec and the agent promised to provide the service requested even though none of the company's regular packet ships made runs to Canada." Continuing the notion that the unsuspecting settlers were lured, she concludes that the *Agda*, which sailed in 1872, was not a regular passenger ship. In trying to situate it, she compares it to an Irish coffin ship. She also makes an unsourced claim that the emigrants on the *Agda* "saw the ship the day of boarding and by that time, it was too late to make a change."[18]

Whether cognizant of the effects of their discourses or not, O'Dwyer, Rekowski, O'Brien, and Mask-Connolly have all contributed to the theme of mournful exile. Their uprooted versions have reiterated the pain of migration though historical fiction rather than oral anecdote or a researched history. Mask-Connolly attempted to give context to the notion of being left behind by using the example of Elizabeth von Orlowski but she still embarks on mournful literary tangents. O'Dwyer, Rekowski, and Mask-Connolly used such language, perhaps, because they were unable or ill-equipped to dissect the migration analytically and look at it as a multifaceted process. Such a task involves situated knowledge and source material from numerous institutions, libraries, and archives. Since these authors had no access to the original migrants, they attempted to portray the experience using literary license. Its resonance can be explained when we consider the researchers' distance from the pioneers and their localized net of literature. Instead of conducting in-depth research into the systems and avenues through which the emigrants left, these authors, in the words of Northrop Frye, relied on "the language of imagination ... [which] begins with the world we construct, not with the world we see. It starts with the imagination, and then works towards ordinary experience: that is, it tries to make itself as convincing and recognizable as it can."[19] The authors' intended audience, also, may have affected the tone of their works. As Stephen Maracle points out, in "mainstream culture, we no longer care to distinguish between fiction and non-fiction, so long as we get a good story." Not all authors bank on a scrupulous historical whistleblower to point out irregularities.[20] Considering the time, place, and audience of their works, the authors' comparisons and portrayals served their purpose – that the migrants were exiles and their journey was one fraught with difficulties and uncertainties. However, several of these authors also portrayed the migrants in another light. Whether aware or not of the conflicting portrayals, they depicted the migrants as strong and hardy in the face of upheaval.

Hardy or Handlinesque? The Resilient Emigrants

As outlined in chapter 2, in the face of land shortages, economic hardships, and perceived religious struggles, the Polish-Kashubs were portrayed as strong and resilient. After writing a sensationalistic passage about the "iron grip" rule of Prussia, Frank J. Ritza gave John Pick, an emigrant, many strong qualities. For example: "John Pick, a man of high ideals and strong will, resolved he would not serve the tyrants in any aggressive wars against peaceful nations. At once he set about with plans. With a far-away look he saw escape, hope and America."[21] Rekowski praised the peasants and wrote that the Kashubs "simply refused, at a terrible cost to their own evolution, to be assimilated by the Prussian juggernaut." He also writes that they were "young and strong and unafraid of hard work."[22] But another of Rekowski's claims conflicts with his earlier depiction of weak travellers. Writing to acknowledge the resilience and hardiness of the travelers, he claims that: "Adolph Pecoskie of Combermere told the writer I. Jost, that his grandfather was born (and survived) in 1867 or 1870 on the 'high seas.' The authoress, Jost, reports that such happenings are cited in the original archives more than once, testifying to the basic physical strength, health and vitality of the emigrants."[23] A year later, Mask-Connolly wrote that they were "strong-willed and determined people, forced out of their homeland." In another publication, she praises their strong and keen initiative, also saying that they were "fervently Catholic and culturally proud." As such, they were prepared to leave for a better life in Canada.[24] Yet the picture of the peasants refusing to be conquered spiritually in Prussian Poland and being young and strong contrasts strikingly with the mournful depictions of the migrants as hapless and weak. While such a lengthy, confined nineteenth-century journey across the Atlantic would test the health of any migrant, several authors express the notion that, on the one hand, they were strong for leaving but, on the other hand, were poor, hapless, and to be pitied because they had been swept out of their homeland.

Several claims that have made their way into historical memory are not quantified and some are hyperbole. While many descendants may have carried with them tales of the voyage similar to those described by O'Dwyer and Rekowski, those have not been recorded. Elizabeth Shalla's memoirs – perhaps the earliest ones recorded by a descendant[25] – illuminate the trip. Shalla described the voyage of her mother, Mary (Kiedrowski) Etmanski, as "one of danger and anxiety as the winds blew the sail ship hither and thither causing much sea sickness and illness among the passengers. It was only after seven weeks of this perilous voyage that the ship landed on the shores of 'The New World.' During the voyage some of the sick died and were buried at sea."[26] Leon Hetmanski recounted a similar horror passed on by his father. The Dombroski family told "of storms at seas which prolonged their journey ... to eighteen weeks," and Max Rekowski of Wilno said that his ancestors spent "thirteen Sundays on the high seas." Agnes (Cybulskie) Glofcheskie recalls that when her grandparents came in 1881 "they were nine and eleven years old ... Both had excellent memories and they told me many times of their journey across the ocean. They came in a sailing ship and the trip had taken three months to cross the seas. Many people didn't survive and many, old and young, were buried at sea."[27] Günter Moltmann was able to contextualize such recollections of death. He found that the mortality rate on ships departing from Hamburg between 1854 and 1858 was 1.8 per cent.[28] In the latter year, according to the *Journals of the Legislative Assembly*, of the 12,834 people who were supposed to land at Quebec, 22 died on route.[29] Later on, Mask-Connolly writes that there were 14 deaths on the *Agda* in 1872, but the comment was tucked away in an endnote and rates for the 1870s were not contextualized.[30] What may help account for the perpetuated narrative of widespread death and sickness on a ship is the story of the *Leipzig*. By the time the ship arrived in New York in January 1868, nearly one-fifth of its passengers had perished due to sickness. Outrage prompted the owner to change the name of the ship to *Liebig*.[31] Later that May, the Paul Yakubowski and Joseph Yantha families sailed from Hamburg to Quebec on the same ship. Whether its reputation travelled with the ship, though, is unclear. Though stipulations of "many deaths" cannot be quantified in oral histories, the impact of such a traumatic experience can only be imagined, hence its repetition over time in the narrative.

Reference to settlers departing on crowded ships,[32] however, have not been quantified in local literature. Rekowski reported an unnamed ship that carried 900 passengers. Mask-Connolly listed several ships and the number of passengers, but did not connect them to the crowded-ship myth. Further, Rekowski claimed that the "ocean jour-

Table 3.1: Ships that brought Polish-Kashub emigrants to Canada

Ship name	Departure date	Port	Arrival date	Port	No. of passengers	Identified Polish-Kashubs on board
Heinrich	4 June 1858	Bremen	28 July 1858	Quebec	170	18 families, 83 people
Elbe	14 May 1859	Hamburg		Quebec	274	18 names
Franklin	2 June 1859	Hamburg		Quebec	122	4 names
Amelia	15 June 1859	Hamburg		Quebec		4 families to Renfrew Co., 4 to Portage Co. (Wisconsin)
Donau	8 July 1859	Hamburg		New York	276	22 names
Main	3 Sept 1859	Hamburg		New York	290	1 family
Oder	19 May 1860	Hamburg		Quebec	214	44 names
Elbe	1 June 1861	Hamburg		Quebec	330	4 names
Golden Light	15 May 1868	Hamburg	8 July 1868	Quebec	167	10 families
Franz de Paul Armesen	1 May 1868	Hamburg	16 July 1868	Quebec	173	5 families
Leibig	4 May 1868	Hamburg	2 July 1868	Quebec		2 families

Sources: *Deutsche Auswanderungs-Zeitung* (4 June 1858); Mask-Connolly, *Polish Pioneer Families*; and *News from the Wilno Heritage Society* 7, no. 1 (Spring/Summer 2008), 7.

ney sometimes lasted three months or more."[33] Such hyperbole and unsourced claims are partly a result of the lack of documents. Many nineteenth-century ships' lists from the port of Bremen were discarded in 1907, and lists were not archived in Quebec until 1865.[34] Based on Mask-Connolly's findings, coupled with other sources, we see that the ships often carried large numbers of passengers. It is possible to contextualize and quantify the length of some journeys by looking at the voyages. In 1868, it took approximately two months to cross the Atlantic and this had much to do with ship technology. Into the 1860s, most of the ships used sail, including the ones that carried migrants to Quebec (see tables 3.1 and 3.2).

In the 1870s, advances in technology allowed for faster travel. The average run from Hamburg to New York now took 11 or 12 days by

Table 3.2: Hamburg departures by ship type, 1859–1869

Year	Sail	Steamer	Total	Percentage by sail	Percentage by steam	Trips to Quebec
1859	59	19	78	76	24	6 sail
1866	58	39	97	60	40	8 sail
1867	47	46	93	51	49	6 sail
1868	55	56	111	50	50	8 sail
1869	42	69	111	38	62	2 sail

Source: Compiled from *AAZ* (1859–1869).

Table 3.3: Nineteenth-century Hamburg ship types, captains, and owners

Ship Name	Captain	Company	Type	Tonnage
Elbe	Winzen until Sept. 1857 and then Boll	August Bolten	barque	513
Franklin	Johannsen until 1858 then Benzin	Louis Knorr und Co.	barque	300
Donau	F. Meyer	August Bolten	schiff	711
Main	Haack	August Bolten	brig	291
Oder	Meier until Sept. 1858 then Winzen	August Bolten	schiff	828

Source: Compiled from *AAZ* (1855–1870).

steamer. Although no steamships left from Germany to Quebec in 1858, the average trip from Ireland was 14 days.[35] By consulting several emigrant newspapers and advertisements in Germany during the 1850s, it is possible to further contextualize the types of ships as well as the number of passengers they carried. The *Elbe* and *Franklin* were barques, the *Donau*[36] and the *Oder* were schiffs, and the *Main* was a brig (see table 3.3). All five were different types of ships, but their sizes and types have never been explained in a publication on Polish-Kashub emigration. According to Lucille Campey, an ocean-going brig was a "two masted vessel with square rigging on both sides," a barque was a "three-masted vessel, square rigged on the fore and main and fore-and-aft rigged on the third aftermost mast." Similarly, a schiff (or ship) was a "three-masted vessel, square-rigged on all three masts."[37]

Based on Campey's findings, the tonnage of the ships that carried the Polish-Kashub migrants can be converted to approximate ship sizes. The closest comparison to the *Elbe* is the *Alexander Hall*, a 404-tonne barque, whose dimensions were 34 m × 7 m × 5.5 m (111' × 23' × 18'). The *Franklin*'s closest comparison is the *Berbice*, a 240-tonne barque that was 33 m × 8 m × 5 m (107' × 27' × 17'). The *Donau* and the *Oder* were considerably bigger. Mask-Connolly wrote that the *Oder* was 44.8 m × 8.6 m (147' × 28') with a capacity for 319 passengers.[38] The *Donau*'s closest comparison is the *Aurora*, a 709-tonne ship, which measured 44 m × 8.8 m × 6.5 m (144' × 29' × 21'). Finally, the *Main*, a 291-tonne brig, and the *Albion*, a 266-tonne brig, measuring 29 m × 8 m × 5 m (94' × 26' × 17'), are similar.[39] Although these comparisons are between ships that sailed out of the port of Aberdeen and ships that sailed out of Bremen and Hamburg, they are not far off since nineteenth-century ship engineering in the North Atlantic shared a common pool of technical knowledge.

As to the claims that the ships were overcrowded, many were, whether they departed from Bremen, Hamburg, Le Havre, Liverpool, or Hull. We cannot experience or describe the voyage that was experienced by the migrants. My intent is not to prove these narratives true or false or discount the notion of overcrowding that has been passed down in local memory. Instead, I want to pull it away from the mournful literary diatribes and quantify the claim with comparative statistics. By looking at the numbers for each ship, we can get a glimpse into how crowded the ships were for the Polish-Kashubs compared with other similar voyages for the same era.

The barque *Elbe*, owned by August Bolten, usually travelled the Hamburg–Quebec and Hamburg–New York routes in the 1850s and 1860s. The *Franklin*, owned by Louis Knorr, ran several routes, including those to New York, Quebec, and San Francisco. The *Donau*, another Bolten vessel, made exclusive return trips to New York. Two other ships owned by Bolten, the *Main* and *Oder*, sailed to various destinations. If we compare the number of passengers on other voyages, we can contextualize how crowded the ships were for the Polish-Kashubs. The charts are created from statistics collected at the port of Hamburg, and the italicized entries – the voyages taken by the Polish-Kashubs – help to illustrate comparisons. In all but two cases, the Polish-Kashubs did not travel on the most crowded voyages. While this may be a moot point

Table 3.4: Voyages on the Barque *Elbe*

Year	Captain	Passengers	Departed	Destination
1857	Winzen	194	1 Mar	New York
1857	Winzen	244	16 Jun	Quebec
1857	Bohl	199	10 Oct	New York
1858	Boll	195	16 May	New York
1859	Boll	149	15 May	Quebec
1859	*Boll*	*109*	*2 Oct*	*New York*
1860	Boll	109	15 Apr	Quebec
1860	Boll	202	16 Aug	New York
1861	*Boll*	*248*	*2 Jun*	*Quebec*
1861	Boll	62	16 Nov	New York

Source: Compiled from *AAZ*.

Table 3.5: Voyages on the Barque *Franklin*

Year	Captain	Passengers	Departed	Destination
1857	Johannsen	209	1 Jun	Quebec
1858	Benzeihn	175	16 May	New York
1859	*Benzin*	*125*	*2 Jun*	*Quebec*
1860	Benzin	196	23 Jun	San Francisco
1861	Benzien	199	25 Apr	San Francisco

Source: Compiled from *AAZ*.

for the descendants, it does contextualize and quantify the density of passengers on the ships. The *Donau* and the *Oder* were able to accommodate more passengers than the midsized *Elbe* or the smaller *Main* and *Franklin* (see tables 3.4 to 3.8).

The density of steerage, on the other hand, cannot be contextualized unless we know the interior dimensions of the ships. However, it is possible to calculate the "persons per tonne of vessel." According to David Eltis, the average number in the early 1850s varied from 0.21 to 0.26 person per tonne. During the Irish famine migrations, the average was 0.65, and for slave ships that landed in the Carribbean in the 1840s, it was 2.72.[40] Using the same calculation, we can compare the ships that brought the Polish-Kashubs. Arranged chronologically, the 1859

Table 3.6: Voyages on the Barque *Main*

Year	Captain	Passengers	Departed	Destination
1857	Haak	352	20 Apr	New York
1857	Haak	348	2 Aug	New York
1858	Haak	362	16 Apr	New Orleans
1858	Haack	99	4 Sept	New York
1859	Haack	180	20 Apr	Quebec
1859	*Haack*	*188*	*3 Sept*	*New York*
1865	Boll	216	16 Apr	Quebec
1866	Boll	381	1 Apr	Quebec

Source: Compiled from *AAZ*.

Table 3.7: Voyages on the Barque *Donau*

Year	Captain	Passengers	Departed	Destination
1857	F. Meyer	295	2 Apr	New York
1857	F. Meyer	289	14 Jul	New York
1857	F. Meyer	120	16 Nov	New York
1858	F. Meyer	306	2 May	New York
1858	F. Meyer	194	2 Oct	New York
1859	F. Meyer	123	3 Apr	New York
1859	*F. Meyer*	*259*	*9 Jul*	*New York*
1859	F. Meyer	141	2 Nov	New York
1860	F. Meyer	290	15 Apr	New York
1860	F. Meyer	240	15 Jul	New York
1861	F. Meyer	248	16 May	New York
1865	F. Meyer	325	16 Jul	New York
1865	F. Meyer	312	16 Apr	New York

Source: Compiled from *AAZ*.

voyages saw ratios of 0.26 (*Elbe*), 0.38 (*Franklin*), 0.33 (*Donau*), 0.60 (*Main*), and 0.22 (*Oder*) persons per tonne. In 1860, the ratio for the *Oder* was 0.12 and in 1861, the ratios were 0.44 (*Elbe*) and 0.38 (*Oder*). Despite the fact that some of the passenger figures do not correspond with Mask-Connolly's numbers from ships' lists, the ships were not as crowded as the Irish coffin ships. Using her numbers, the *Elbe*'s ratio was 0.48 in 1859 and the *Oder*'s was 0.235 in 1860. Thus, the ratios of

Table 3.8: Voyages on the Barque *Oder*

Year	Captain	Passengers	Departed	Destination
1857	E.Meier	267	18 Jun	New York
1857	E.Meier	248	16 Oct	New York
1858	E.Meier	189	16 Jun	New Orleans
1858	Winzen	88	17 Oct	New York
1859	*Winzen*	*202*	*2 May*	*New York*
1859	Winzen	70	8 Nov	New Orleans
1860	*Winzen*	*107*	*28 May*	*Quebec*
1860	Winzen	224	13 Oct	New York
1861	*Winzen*	*345*	*4 May*	*Quebec*
1861	Winzen	180	2 Oct	New York
1865	Winzen	292	16 Sept	New York
1866	Winzen	279	1 Apr	New York
1866	Winzen	269	15 Jul	New York

Source: Compiled from *AAZ*.

the ships that brought the Polish-Kashubs were higher than average but they were not as packed as the famine ships and not nearly as crowded as slave ships.

It is also possible to contextualize the allowable room in steerage quarters by referring to passenger laws. Using data from the chief emigration agent at Quebec, it is apparent that most emigrants in 1857–58 leaving from English, Irish, Norwegian, and German ports did so in steerage. In 1857, 4,957 persons arrived in steerage and 4 in cabins. A year later, 138 sailing and 16 steamships docked in Quebec. Of those arriving from Germany, 922 passengers arrived in steerage, and none via cabin class.[41] Depictions of steerage quarters were often conflicting (see figures 3.1 and 3.2).

The 1852 *British Passenger Act* stipulated that no more than 1 person per 2 tonnes was allowable and that 12 feet of clear superficial deck was needed and at least 6 feet of clearance between decks for one passenger. American regulations in 1855 were similar: 2 persons per 5 tons, 16 feet of deck space, and 6 feet of clearance between decks.[42] Calculations for the deck or clearance space are not possible but comparative tonnage stipulations are. Using figures from the *Allgemeine Auswanderungs-Zeitung* (*AAZ*), all of the above-mentioned voyages that carried Polish-

3.1   A cross-section of an immigrant ship showing ample room in steerage (*zwischendeck*). On many ships, steerage was above the cargo hold or ballast level, but below the cabin or second-class quarters.

3.2   The realities of steerage. A depiction of steerage on the *Samuel Hop*.

Kashubs passed British and American tonnage requirements, except the 1859 and 1861 voyages of the *Main* and *Elbe*.[43] Yet, as Forbes Adams reminds us, the official and recorded numbers aboard vessels can be deceptive. Children were sometimes counted as a half or third of a statute adult.[44]

The nutritional component of the voyage is another area not mentioned by local authors or local historical memory. The only surviving account of food on the ships is buried in an article written by Brenda Lee-Whiting in 1986. Thanks to the generosity of Keith Schleuter, "who provided her with a copy of the ship's contract signed by his ancestor, Mathes Horcun" for their voyage on the *Gellert*, booked through Donati & Company of Hamburg, the document gives us an idea of what contracts were like. The Horcuns' *Schiffs-Contract* reveals that those travelling in steerage set to depart on 1 April 1863 "were supplied with food for the entire voyage, prepared and served by the ship's crew, and had a more generous allowance for luggage, 20 cubic feet per adult and 10 cubic feet per child, than on the steamships of the Allan Line which only permitted half that amount." The passengers were to supply their own utensils and bedding. The ship was to supply the Horcuns, in particular, with tea, coffee, bread, butter, meats, fish, peas, beans, barley, lentils, sauerkraut, baked goods, potatoes, plums, and vinegar. A male would also receive "a glass of brandy every morning."[45] The cost of such a voyage was 28 thaler for adults, 22 thaler for children under ten, and 3 thaler for children under a year. In comparison, the Allan Line, in 1872, charged £6–6s–0d for an adult, £3–3s–0d for a child under eight, and £1–1s–0d for infants under a year. Whether or not they received such a variety of foods throughout the journey is not clear, and local historical memory has not shed any light on it either. If the Horcuns were given these provisions on the ship, they exceeded those required by British law for ships coming to America.[46] In a way, however, the Polish-Kashubs were fortunate to depart from the ports of Bremen and Hamburg, because these cities had enacted protective regulations in the 1830s to ensure that provisions for at least a 90-day voyage were on board. The US did not pass such legislation until 1855 and self-provisioning was common at other European ports.[47] Yet whether those who emigrated from Prussian-occupied Poland received similar menus and their share of the provisions has still not been, and may never be, substantiated.

Literate or Not? A Re-evaluation

In trying to uplift the character of the migrants, Rekowski and another priest, Fr Rafał Grzondziel, went so far as to claim that the pioneers could read and write. The former argues that "many of the early pioneers could read Polish" and Grzondziel claims that "those people who came could read and write. They'd brought to Canada these huge books and hymnals." Mask-Connolly claims that though "many of the emigrants from Poland had received an education under the tutelage of the German occupiers, many of their children living in the Canadian bush never learned to read or write."[48] She also adopts the claims of Rekowski and Grzondziel and writes that the "first comers amongst them were generally educated ... Some children were schooled at home and taught to read Polish prayers and hymns from the missals and books that the parents had brought from Poland."[49] However, this section argues that, contrary to the claims of Rekowski, Grzondziel, and Mask-Connolly, most Polish settlers, into the mid-1870s, were illiterate.

The only corroborating evidence that Rekowski provides was that "the Polish writings of the Kashub poet Derdowski, a contemporary of our forefathers, were very popular among the Kashubs."[50] Therefore, in Rekowski's logic, because Derdowski was popular, the settlers could read. Grzondziel's premise does not hold up analytically since possessing prayer books – a sacred object connecting an individual to faith – does not mean that one had the ability to read and/or write. Mask-Connolly claims that the migrants were taught to read and hints at the fact that they could write, but admits that there is no surviving evidence. Instead, she copies a letter sent from settlers in Winona, Minnesota to Poland in 1891.[51] However, using sources that Rekowski and Grzondziel did not (Mask-Connolly used the same sources, but not to establish literacy) allows the migrants' literacy to be re-evaluated.

If the settlers who arrived from Prussian-occupied Poland were literate, one would expect them to be able to write their names. Harvey Graff reminds us that it is difficult to assess levels of literacy from those who could sign their name on a document. "It has been agreed that the ability to sign lies somewhere between the ability to read and the ability to write and that some degree of fluency in reading (which does not mean comprehension) may correspond to signing."[52] Therefore, if the act of writing one's name is a determinant of a basic level of literacy, the extent to which the settlers were literate is evident through land petitions from the 1860s. In 1864, twenty-seven settlers met with the Reeve of Brudenell, John Watson, and applied for land. Only four of the male settlers could sign their names: Albrecht Omernyk, Mikolaj Prynz, Joseph Shalla, and Paul Zblewski. The rest etched an "X" beside their name.[53] Under the 1868 Free Grants and Homesteads Act, more recent settlers could also petition for land. The petitions, written by Crown Lands Agent James Reeves, or John Watson, a Renfrew County commissioner, attest to the later level of literacy. A sampling of petitions from Hagarty Township between 1864 and the 1890s shows that only about 40 per cent of adult male settlers could print their names – and some could barely scratch out the characters.[54]

Most settlers could not read or write when they arrived. Some, like Walenti Etmanski (between 1864 and 1883) and August Blank (between 1873 and 1883), learned how to write after they landed. In other cases, some children of the original migrants could write, such as Walenti Persic's son, John, who signed his name on an 1875 petition. Francis Libera, the son of widowed Rosalia, is an example of the younger generation who learned how to write. Arriving as a seven-year-old in 1859, Francis, a shoemaker in Renfrew, signed his name on an 1875 petition.[55] However, when acquiring a new language, it is hard to use writing as a measure because many factors influence the process.[56] Although many of the original settlers could not write, such abilities were not crucial for nineteenth-century farmers to survive on the frontier. Practical knowledge of agriculture and a good work ethic were better determinants of success than literacy or formal education.

If literacy is accepted as a crucial determinant of survival in the nineteenth century, it still does not adequately historicize the time and space in which the settlers lived. Reflecting on the fact, as argued in chapter 2, that illiteracy was widespread in northern Poland, most peasants were preoccupied with agriculture and other paid work instead of obtaining an education. An 1803 church document from peasants in Kalisz also attests to the fact that some of the migrants' neighbours and relatives, such as Wojciech Turzynski, Antoni Prync, Maciej Kulas, Pawel Rekowski, Jan Grzenia, Lukasz Bienk, Pawel Knopik, Andrzej Piechowski, Chrusztof Kaszubowski, Jan Cybella, and Wawrzyniec Rekowskie[57] could not sign their names either. Illiteracy was not the stigma in the latter half of the nineteenth century that it is today. However, literacy today "has been invested with immeasurable and indeed almost ineffable qualities, purportedly conferring upon practitioners a predilection toward social order, an elevated moral sense, and a metaphorical 'state of grace.'" Literacy is now represented in popular discourse "as an unqualified good, a marker of progress, and a metaphorical light making clear the pathway to progress and happiness."[58] Using that trope and overlaying it to show hardiness or success for the first settlers does not accurately depict their time and place.

A better measure of strength may be the progress migrants made on their plots. Looking at the time it took a family to turn forest into farmland gives a better glimpse into a crucial aspect of survival and serves as an "index of both economic success and social advancement" on the nineteenth-century frontier.[59] In that time, a pioneer and bush worker's pride was tied up with their ability to work and clear land. However, as Ian Radforth argues, these bush workers were looked at as unskilled even though bush work required skill and specialized knowledge. Although there were no official records of all pioneers or bush workers' clearances, several figures are available from undated ledgers deposited in the Archives of Ontario that shed light on their clearing practices. Judging by the fact that the longest residing settlers had been occupying the land for 4.5 years, the document was probably written c. 1862–63. The calculations also use the rate of clearance calculated by Peter Russell, who found that the average male in the Bathurst-Dalhousie District of Upper Canada cleared around 0.6 acre per year c. 1840.[60]

The data in tables 3.9 and 3.10 and the average calculation is similar to that of non-Polish settlers in the Townships of Radcliffe and Sherwood and lengthier stays by Irish settlers in the Township of Brudenell. A year or two after these figures were recorded, many applied for deeds to their land through John Watson, who was also the Reeve of Brudenell. Fortunately, Watson recorded their progress on the petition. Many of the above fulfilled the requirement to clear 12 acres. All had at least a house and barn, and most had a stable.[61] Tracking their progress – and the progress of newcomers – into the 1870s and 1880s is difficult. Documents in the Township Papers before the 1870s do not record the clearing rates and only some petitions recorded cleared land and the structures that the settlers built.

Of course, the figures cannot be relied upon as the sole barometers of economic and social advancement since the clearing rates for initial clearing and subsequent brushings were affected by many things,

Table 3.9: Forest to farmland clearance rates, c. 1862–1863

Settler name	Cleared land (acres)	Years settled	Clearing rate per year
Albert Omernik	7.25	3.0	2.40
Joseph Lorbelski	7.00	3.0	2.30
Joseph Jezierski	8.50	4.5	1.80
Henry Krushewski	13.50	4.5	3.00
Thomas Shulist	9.00	4.5	2.00
Joseph Suszek	1.25	1.5	0.80
Joseph Szala	5.00	1.5	3.30
Paul Zblowski	4.00	3.0	1.30
August Janta	1.00	3.0	0.30
John Coulassa	3.25	4.0	0.80
Jacob Coulassa	8.00	4.0	2.00
Francis Prince	5.75	4.0	1.40
Michael Prince	5.00	4.0	1.20
Antoine Prince	13.50	4.0	3.40
Adam Dombroski	4.50	3.0	1.50
Paul Trebenski	14.00	3.0	4.60
Albert Kulas	10.00	3.0	3.30
Michael Szycpior	23.00	4.0	5.75
August Flis	15.00	3.0	5.00
Joseph Zblewski	8.00	3.0	2.60
Walenti Perzick	8.50	2.0	4.30
Jacob Norlock	6.00	2.0	3.00
Matthew Pecarsky	7.50	4.0	1.90

Source: Assembled from AO, RG1-VI-3, Vol. 10.

including the number, health, age, and availability of strong workers in the unit, as well as weather, the success of crops, the need for cropland, the terrain, the quality of the soil, the quality of the logging implements, and clearing techniques like girdling (slashing), chopping, and burning. Considering that many six- and seven-pound long-handled, double-bit axes were being used well into the 1880s in the Ottawa Valley even though cross-cut saws, which made felling quicker, were used in other parts of the country, also speaks to the strength of the settlers (see figure 3.3).[62] T.P. French was right when he declared in 1861 that the "Prussians are a hard-working, thrifty and honest people; they are fast acquiring a knowledge of the language and habits of the

Table 3.10: More forest to farmland clearance rates, c. 1874–1890

Settler name and age (if possible)	Cleared land and structures on the plot	Year petitioned for grant	Year of arrival in Canada
John Kaszubek	10 acres	1874	1872
Antoin Lukowich (42)	10 acres	1874	1868
Antoine Czapiewski	10 acres	1877	1872
John Palubiski	15 acres	1877	1872
Frank Blank (35)	25 acres, 18' × 18' house	1883	1868
John Etmanskie (27)	25 acres, house, barn, stable	1883	1859
Walentin Etmanskie (60s)	25 acres, house, barn, stable	1883	1859
Joseph Lorbiesky (the younger)	15 acres	1884	1859
Tomas Laszinski	20 acres, buildings	1884	1871
Stephen Baderski	10 acres, shanty, stable	1886	1884?
Andreas Czira	14 acres, barn	1887	?
Jann Blank (38)	15 acres	1888	1868
Frank Czapiewski	3 acres	1890	1872
Albert Lukovitch (Lechowicz)	40 acres and buildings	1890	?

Sources: Assembled from AO, Township Papers, RG-1, C-IV. Ages and year of arrival are gleaned from a host of other publications.

country."[63] However, by the 1870s and/or the 1880s, some settlers had actually relocated to "better" plots, which affected their clearance figures. One such example is Walentin Etmanski, who moved from the Opeongo to another plot in Sherwood Township. However, by using an identifier such as clearing land instead of literacy, it is possible to better contextualize the time and place in which these pioneers lived. Thus, a more apt comparison is to place their efforts against Russell's average clearing rate. Such a comparison suggests they were hard-working loggers and pastoralists.

Another myth, and a point of contention with settlers' literacy, had to do with the misspelling of the settlers' names. Makowski passionately asserted that "Polish names were often grossly mutilated, or even changed completely, by government agents or other officials." Bringing the complaint into the contemporary and local realm, Rekowski echoes Makowski's complaint, and Mask-Connolly mentions it too.[64]

3.3 The farm of Joseph Hildebrandt and Matilda Gutowski. Their farm in the "Martin Siding" area of Sherwood Township was almost completely cleared of trees by the 1920s. As with many farms in the area, rock piles and fences were created with the many stones that littered the land.

Yet, the origins of this "mutilation" are not as insidious or malicious as Makowski and Rekowski suggest. Once the Polish-Kashub migrants settled on plots of land, agents formally recorded them. Not familiar with their language, they recorded their names phonetically.[65] In 1864, when several settlers met with Watson, a list was compiled by a settler, Mikolaj Prynz, who could write. To the right of the names supplied by Prynz, Watson recorded the settlers' names phonetically in a column entitled "pronounced."[66] Although Prynz's list appears in the Archives of Ontario, it is not dated. Thus, it is difficult to establish whether this list was produced before or after Watson sent the petitions. Since 1859, official records have listed several spellings: French's, Watson's, Reeves's, Prynz's, and mixtures of the four. Although there is no evidence to suggest that French or Watson changed the names with the intent to "civilize them" with English names, Makowski and Rekowski chose to err on the side of suspicion. Their approach was influenced by the discursive influences of the eras in which they were schooled – the 1940s and 1950s, which were characterized by individuals, the state, or the elite, who acted as gatekeepers and aggressively attempted to assimilate new arrivals through immigrant-reforming initiatives.[67] There is little evidence to suggest that French or Watson acted as gatekeepers aggressively attempting to assimilate the settlers.

Why Have These Narratives Survived?

One explanation for such narratives may be found, as Basu wrote, "in the desire to maintain [or create] a positive or moral self-image."[68] Influenced by ancestor worship, this line of thinking dictates that the forced uprooting predetermined the mediocre economic success of the Polish-Kashubs. If the voyage is portrayed as a forced migration or considered as an exile, the migrants bear less responsibility for their destination and outcomes. They were victims, not responsible for their outcomes. Blame for settlers' illiteracy is shifted to Canada, according to Rekowski and Mask-Connolly, since they became illiterate *after* they were directed here.[69] The land of departure was a static and tranquil home (before Bismarck's rule) and their new home, according to Rekowski and Mask-Connolly, forced them to regress.

In the metanarrative of Canadian immigration and settlement, such stories fit well with other groups' exile narratives, especially the migration of Ukrainians, Doukhobors, Mennonites, Jews, and Icelanders to Western Canada. Driven by everything from ideology, economic duress, religious persecution, and volcanic eruptions, these groups were victims cast from their land.[70] As a result, many could identify with the Polish-Kashub experience. Closely related to the nineteenth-century Polish-Kashub exile experience is the Irish narrative. Kerby Miller writes that the Irish, especially Irish Catholics, regarded emigration as involuntary exile, due to English tyranny. Some Irish, like the romantic Polish nationalists, felt they were like the "children of Israel" when they were driven out of Erin. In addition, many practised a peculiar custom, called the "American wake," in the early nineteenth century. Such a leave-taking ceremony, predominant among Irish Catholics but also practised by Irish Protestants, was designed to project sorrow and anger at the English foe, "to impress deep feelings of grief, guilt, and duty on departing emigrants, and to send them forth as unhappy but faithful and vengeful 'exiles' [with] their final, heart-rending moments at home burned indelibly into their memories." Indeed, Miller writes that the self-pitying exile motif and "its underlying causes led Irish emigrants to interpret experience and adapt to

American life in ways which were often alienating and sometimes dysfunctional." In some ways, this is similar to the Polish-Kashub group, because part of the Irish exile motif resulted from the poverty and prejudice that the Irish experienced (or perceived) in America.[71] And although "American wakes" were Irish in nature, one wonders if Legree or Mask-Connolly was influenced – perhaps unwittingly – by these stories from the Irish narrative to such an extent that the tone of their writings about the Polish-Kashubs became more dramatic.

One also wonders why this narrative so resonates and dominates the metanarrative for the Polish group in the Ottawa Valley, considering that a group from Austrian-occupied Poland has long been a part of the settlement. Indeed, sentiments of displacement are not unique to the Polish-Kashub group. Matthew Frye Jacobsen argues that collective emigration "nourishes a political culture based on ideas of injury and displacement"[72] and the social and economic conditions of Galicia, at the time, had numerous similarities with Prussian-occupied Poland.

The social composition of Galicia was similar to that of Prussian-Poland even after emancipation in 1848: 2 to 3 per cent of the population were wealthy aristocrats, 8 to 10 per cent were gentry landholders and upwards of 84 per cent of Galicians, into the 1870s, were involved in agriculture. In 1857, the average landowner had 33.1 acres which produced around 60 krone, but by 1896, landowners had around 2.3 acres which produced an income of 26 krone. Additionally, in 1859, 66 per cent of peasant holdings in Galicia were less than 10 morgs (14 acres) and 20.3 per cent were less than 5 morgs. The countryside, sectioned off lengthwise through parcellation (*parcelacja*) of the property by district courts in inheritance cases, meant that a patchwork of plots covered the land. Galicia's population was dense as well. In the late 1870s, it had an average population density of 69 persons per square kilometre and several *powiati* (counties), including Biala (940 persons per square kilometre), Tarnów (860 persons per square kilometre) and Nisko (434 persons per square kilometre), had very high densities.

Compounding the problem was the fact that the development of agricultural techniques and output, as in northern Prussian-Poland, was stunted. Franciszek Bujak claimed that Galician farmers were using implements "exactly the same as those used in the thirteenth century," nor did they use manure or fertilizers. As a result, it was estimated that Galicia had one of the lowest levels of agricultural productivity in Europe. This translated into frequent malnourishment as the peasants could not grow enough on their measly plots to survive. Compared with French citizens, Hungarians, Germans, or Belgians, the average Galician consumed far less wheat, meat, milk, and sugar but consumed more potatoes and alcohol. As a result, year after year, the undernourished and impoverished peasants were extremely vulnerable to crop failures after famines struck in 1847, 1849, 1855, 1865, 1876, and 1889. Further, the life expectancy of a Galician in the 1880s was 27 years compared with 41 in England. As a result of these factors, between 1875 and 1884, 23,649 peasant holdings were auctioned off over debts of around 40 krone – the equivalent of about 10 bushels of wheat. In contrast, civil servants in Austria earned 400 krone a month c. 1900. Peasants sought a way out, and in the 1870s Galicia started to lose its population due to emigration. In the 1880s, around 82,000 people left and around 341,000 left in the 1890s.

As expected, and as in northern Prussian-Poland, many in Galicia also did not participate in the educational system. In the 1870s, only 15 of every 100 children attended school – possibly since working the land to survive was more of a priority and the szlachta had a vested interest in keeping peasants illiterate. Around 1869, out of 11,373 settlements (6,134 of which were villages or hamlets) there were 4,925 manorial estates. Since the szlachta also held most of the forest lands (fuel) and meadows (grazing land), peasants, like the Prussian-occupied Poles, could deflect blame for their plight against the ruling powers and the socially conservative elite who failed to remedy the structural limitations around them.[73] Thus, the impetus to emigrate for the Galician Poles – lack of land, widespread poverty, a poor future ahead of them, and a lack of freedom – accords well with the experiences of the Prussian Poles. The metanarrative, as a result, was not challenged.

Returning to the conflicting portrayals by the Polish-Kashub group, which uses the contrasting rhetoric of exile and uplifting filiopiety, another question comes to mind. If they were strong, proud, unafraid, and could read and write, how could they have been swept out of their homeland by uncontrollable forces and agents who deceived them with contracts? Whether local authors were aware of this conundrum or not, in their attempt to portray the migrants as uprooted, exiled, and forced out, they have made their framework too narrow to allow for any agency the migrants might have exercised in the process.[74] As a result, these authors attempt to ascribe some positive and uplifting characteristics to their ancestors so as not to promote ethnic disesteem. However, looking at the migrants through the paradigm of impelled migration and facilitating factors shows that migrants did wield some agency.

Navigators of Their Own Voyage

Because the emigration involved travel over one continent, across an ocean, and onto another continent, it was a multifaceted process that involved numerous decisions and actions. O'Dwyer, Rekowski, and Mask-Connolly concentrate on the uprooted paradigm but the integration of broader theoretical scholarship allows us to understand the emigrants as actors in the narrative rather than passive exiles.

The causes of migration comprise a wide array of factors ranging from agricultural crises to overpopulation, the search for employment, the spirit of adventure, excess capital, or war. Several of these conditions and impetuses were analyzed in chapter 2. Yet, as J.J. Mangalam and Harry Schwartzweller argue, "the mere existence of some deprivations does not necessarily induce migration ... it is when the existing social situation fails to satisfy individual needs ... that certain members of the collectivity entertain the notion of moving away." It is the matching of the "hierarchically ordered set of values"[75] held by the potential migrant with their perception of the likelihood of attaining those goals in their present social or political context that determines whether they will migrate. This correlation is expanded upon by William Petersen, who reminds us that "economic hardship, for example, can appropriately be termed a 'cause' of emigration only if there is a positive correlation between hardship, however defined, and the propensity to migrate."[76] There is, however, some diffusion involved. Jerzy Zubryzcki writes that the migrant "ostensibly chooses between going or leaving on the basis of what he/she knows of the advantages and disadvantages of the two alternatives."[77] Nonetheless, the Polish peasants made the choice to leave based on a set of criteria that they had assimilated from the social groups of which they were a part.

To portray these migrations to Canada as forced does make for a mournfully poetic and dramatic narrative. However, the term "forced" implies that the emigrants did not have any power over the decision.[78]

Using information from Mask-Connolly, the fact that Elizabeth von Orlowski stayed behind when her family left in 1872, shows that a choice did exist. In the same decade, Mary Kiedrowski's family stayed behind, too.[79] These may not have been easy choices, but they were choices nonetheless. Also, since the migrants left on different ships in different years, there was also some choice about when to leave the country. Categorizing the migration, using Petersen's typology, as an *impelled* migration, is more apt considering that the migrants did hold some power about when deciding whether or not to emigrate.[80] Despite the fact that no group from the Lipusz, Wiele, Leśno area had departed for Canada before, the desire for land was evidently high enough on their hierarchy of needs to prompt departure. This also means that without prior knowledge of the destination from their social circles, the initial wave chose to believe the agents and depart for an unknown land, rejecting the deprivations they were experiencing in their homeland. This distinction between forced and impelled is analytically clear, but some impassioned descendants of these migrants may disagree since they have been influenced by local pastkeepers and their discourses have been based on forced exile.

Nancy Green's call to examine emigration as a choice embedded "within a series of constraints and regulations that the individual must comply with" opens up new avenues of study.[81] If we move further away from the push/pull dichotomy, since that paradigm implies that migration was *always* an option, we can better situate the migrants among the social and political structures of the time. Peter Moogk also contributes the idea of facilitating factors, which tipped the balance in favour of emigration at a certain point in time. These facilitators could be anything from lax emigration restrictions, to attractive advertisements, subsidized passage, improved transportation infrastructure, and recruitment techniques.[82]

The migrants had to skirt several barricades in their attempt to leave Prussian-occupied Poland. For example, the ability to migrate hinged on state policy. Before the 1830s, taxes were levied on emigrants going to non-German destinations and these prevented many peasants from emigrating. The emigrants also had to prove that their country of destination would admit them before they were granted permission to depart.[83] The legal right to emigrate was not universal until 1848, when the Prussian National Assembly enshrined it in the constitution.

Afterwards, emigration was much easier. According to Mack Walker, German states did regulate emigration but only by region and by family. Those with inadequate finances for the voyage, or debts, or who were avoiding military service were prevented from emigrating. However, migrants could exercise agency and circumvent these restrictions by leaving the continent through Rotterdam.[84] A similar avenue was used by Franz von Klopotek-Glowczewski (1891–1960), who fled occupied Poland and hid in France to avoid conscription. His family, including his father, Jan Pawel, a former German soldier who feared his sons would be conscripted, departed Hamburg on the *Kaiserin Auguste Victoria* on 1 May 1907. When the ship docked in Cherbourg, France, Frank jumped on board and sailed with them to Ellis Island.[85]

Another hurdle to navigate was the emigration pass card. The Pass-Card Treaty (*Passkartenvertag*) of October 1850 was another attempt to regulate who left so as not to deplete the ranks for service. The treaty standardized the information across several states but it also meant that emigrants would have to procure a pass in order to leave.[86] To comply with these restrictions, payment and justification for leaving were necessary. Although this aspect of the migration is not noted in the recorded histories of many families, all migrants had to fulfill these requirements. The first group, which arrived in 1858, needed pass-cards. Only one of these remains to this day – the Szczypior family pass. To obtain the forms and be released from Prussia, it appears that Mathias Szczypior had to make two trips to Danzig (Gdańsk) on 13 March and 24 April, before his family's voyage on 1 May 1858.[87] Some, however, could not navigate this requirement, preventing them from being able to migrate. In the case of the Kiedrowski family, the cost of passports in the 1870s was too much for the family to bear. Thus, only one daughter, Mary, left for North America. Some families, such as Jan Pawel von Klopotek-Głowczewski's, lied in order to obtain pass cards (see figure 3.4). He told the officials that they were going to visit family in America. But, unlike the Szczypiors, Głowzcewski only had to travel to Berent (Kościerzyna)[88] to obtain his family's papers.

In the early part of the nineteenth century, if Polish-Kashub migrants harboured thoughts of emigrating, their task was made difficult by the lack of transportation routes on the continent. At the time, travel in the counties of Konitz (Chojnice) and Berent (Kościerzyna) was done on foot or by wagon.[89] The 1830s and '40s saw great advances in rail-

3.4 A Prussian Pass Card belonging to Jan Pawel von Kłopotek-Głowczewski.

road building. A railway from Danzig (Gdańsk) to Koszalin was completed in 1837. The Berlin to Stettin line was constructed in 1842, Berlin to Hamburg in 1847, and routes from both Bremen and Hamburg to Hanover in 1847. In 1851, the Bytów–Kościerzyna–Gdańsk route was finished. These tracks made it much easier for inland travel to the ports.

For Polish-Kashubs who departed before 1861, the closest train station was still quite far away. Their nearest stations were Chojnice, about 40 to 60 kilometres away, or Gdańsk, about 70 to 80 kilometres away.[90] From Gdańsk, they could take the Bromberg (Bydgoszcz)–Berlin–Hamburg route (or the Hanover to Bremen route) to arrive at port. Alternatively, the Gdańsk to Koszalin route would get them there too. From Chojnice, they could take the train to Deutsche Krone (Walcz) and then on to Stettin and beyond.[91] The cost of such a journey is, unfortunately, not known. Sinn recorded that the Polish-Kashubs claimed that the agent at home deceived them about the cost of leaving.[92] This is the only reference to the cost. Once the migrants arrived in Bremen or Hamburg, depending upon how early the parties were and how much they could afford, they had to pay for food and lodging. Numerous lodging houses advertised in emigrant newspapers, such as Angelus Steinhardt's *Auswandererhaus* in Hamburg, to capitalize on the emigrant traffic. As can be imagined, considerable strength was needed for the long and arduous journey via foot, rail, and sail. Once rails were extended from Chojnice to Kościerzyna in 1861, emigrants had a shorter distance to travel to arrive at the ports but still faced some logistical difficulties.[93]

Migration also hinges on the availability and characteristics of potential destinations. This availability works hand-in-hand with transportation networks. Several areas in the United States were well-established as receiving states for German emigrants, including, by the 1850s, Michigan, Wisconsin, and Missouri. As Jonathan Wagner argues, to attract immigrants, Canada's image needed to compete with America's. This was accomplished through articles written in emigrant newspapers. Canada was portrayed as a welcoming land and the climate was described as moderate.[94] In analyzing the attractiveness of several destinations, Marcus Hansen outlined several criteria that potential emigrants evaluated. These ranged from a moderate climate, personal freedom (no slavery), political conditions, religious toleration, and large amounts of available land. This often meant that the tropical areas, such as the Mosquito Coast, Brazil, Venezuela, and Texas (slavery) were eliminated. However, Canada, along with the United States, fit many of these conditions.[95] Thus, the attractiveness of the receiving country was also a facilitating factor in the process. Vessels departing for the United States were plentiful in the 1840s, so much so that in 1846 New York City could not handle all the emigrant traffic from Bremen and Hamburg. As a result, direct service was offered to Quebec City. Weighing this evolving conjunction of circumstances, some Polish-Kashubs decided to depart for Canada. Some of their brethren from Prussian-occupied Poland, on the other hand, emigrated to other areas such as Australia, Texas, Minnesota, and Wisconsin in the 1840s and 1850s.[96]

The cost of transportation to these destinations was a barrier for emigrants. In many cases, the poorest of the poor were unable to emigrate because they could not afford passage on ships going abroad. However, the poor were still able to depart if they could stash away their savings or quickly and efficiently liquidate their assets. The assets of 499 emigrants who left the district of Berent (Kościerzyna) between 1858 and 1861 (429 of them were to depart for Canada) were valued at 32,622 thaler. Divided evenly, each emigrant had assets of approximately 54 thaler. Regional daily wages at the time were: male (summer) 0.33–0.5 thaler, female (summer) 0.25, male (winter) 0.2–0.33, female (winter) 0.17–0.25, and a potato harvester earned 0.25–0.38. Annual wages for servants topped out at around 25 thaler. Wages for boys were as high as 15 thaler, and maids earned approximately 17 thaler.[97] In 1863, Donati & Company of Hamburg charged 28 thaler for adults, 22 thaler for children under ten, and 3 thaler for children under a year for passage on the *Gellert*. Later in the century, passage to New York or Canada on the Hamburg-America Line amounted to approximately 63 thaler for adults and 31 thaler for children under twelve.[98] Therefore, the *Schiffs-Contract*, plus costs for transportation to and from the ports, took up much of the emigrants' hard-earned money, savings, and profits from the sale of property, crops, and/or livestock. A decade later, in 1872, a group of about 300 emigrants destined for Ontario, including many "Prussians" from the *Agda*, could not afford transportation to their final destination but the government assisted them and emigration agent J.W. Wills arranged for their transportation to Renfrew,[99] accompanied them, and helped them find employment. Although figures for the 1872 group do not exist, William Wagner estimated that in 1860, an emigrant to Canada needed to possess 300 thaler to establish a viable home.[100]

Reflecting on the factors that induce migration, Walter Kamphoefner argues that too much emphasis has been put on emigrant literature (ads, posters, pamphlets, etc.). He suggests that another facilitating factor was recommendations from family and friends. While there is no surviving evidence of this with the Polish-Kashub group in Ontario, the role of emigrant brokers or agents, who "eased" the process, was named as a factor. After all, the first group in 1858 made the choice to leave after putting stock in the words of an agent in Europe. But the effectiveness of agents is debatable. Agnes Bretting argues that although the activities of the agents were decisive in the beginning, their function over time was reduced to a mere brokerage role. Drew Keeling echoes these thoughts, writing that "networks of steamship agents were a facilitating adjunct to the processes of human transfer across the Atlantic." But, as Kristian Hvidt suggests, agents "could to a certain degree raise the level of emigration beyond normal 'push and pull' [numbers]."[101]

Conclusion

Although several narratives produced by what was known or perceived at the time and attached to the migrations from Prussian-occupied Poland are questionable, they survive for a variety of reasons. Hearkening back to the words of Gaddis, some stories take on a life of their own.[102] This is the case with several narratives in the Polish-Kashub community. Some of the details, such as the notion of overcrowding, are not quantified, but by looking at primary and secondary migration literature, we are able to contextualize these notions.

Although some authors underestimate the agency exercised by the settlers, the adoption of other paradigms, including Petersen's notion of impelled migrations and Moogk's notion of facilitating factors allows us to appreciate that migrants did exercise some agency. Through these paradigms, we see how the migrants had to negotiate their hierarchy of needs and how they were influenced by agents in their decision. Despite the fact that several authors claimed the migrants were duped by agents, the Polish-Kashub migrants still made the choice to sell their small quarters and property – if any – to obtain free land in Canada. They were poor but they had enough assets and savings to allow them to emigrate, and their decision to leave was predicated on their desire to improve their lives. The alternative, to stay and face hardships, was not the better choice in their minds. After all, as Piotr Gorecki argues, if the move was made based on economic grounds, the risk was that they could become landless again.[103] We can be thankful that they took the risk and made the choice to leave. Otherwise, Rekowski, Mask-Connolly, Prince, and others, including me, would not be writing, questioning, and amending such discourses.

In the process, it is possible to step away from literary constructions, such as O'Dwyer's "Prussian guard" who prodded the emigrants on. With the mournful and sensationalist tones removed, the narrative of migration may seem dull. Perhaps this too is why the authors embarked on their epics. Despite the literary license taken by O'Dwyer, Rekowski, and Mask-Connolly, we will never be able to recreate the voyage or what the migrants *may* have done before they left. Try as we might, it will not happen. Susanna Moodie wrote that nineteenth-century emigration was often performed "at the sacrifice of all those local attachments which stamp the scenes in which our childhood grew."[104] Such a voyage involved a strength of mind and body that we can never truly know and never truly recreate. Yet, the voyage should not be discounted simply because it is inaccessible to us. We want to quantify it somehow as such decisions, as Adam Gopnik writes, demand all the courage that one possesses. "And although we know that moral courage is not the same as physical courage [as] many people who have great physical courage have no moral courage at all ... the courage to endure physical hardship is linked in deep and mysterious ways to the courage to be bold, to take risks."[105] Even though we may not comprehend such courage, we know it exists and we attempt to understand it.

This chapter also uses primary documents to re-examine and evaluate the literacy of the first settlers to refute claims of widespread literacy. Although it is difficult to determine the precise level of literacy of each settler in the settlement period, by using the basic act of signing one's name it is possible to determine whether a basic level existed.[106] Rather than literacy, this analysis shows that a more meaningful indicator for success was settlers' ability to clear the land to build a home and a farm. Indeed, the old saying *"gbur to mur"* (the farmer is a rock)[107] carries meaning for pioneers and descendants alike.

4

Intending Settlers: T.P. French and His Guidebook

Although the motto on one of the logos displayed by the Wilno Heritage Society reads "*Wiara I Wolnosc*" (Faith and Freedom), the main reason the first wave of Polish-Kashub settlers came to Canada was to procure and cultivate land. However, the way in which authors and community members approach the question, "How did the Polish peasants know there was free land in Canada?" varies. Some authors do not mention this part of the process at all, approaching it *ex post facto* once the migrants had set foot in Canada. Some credit the Crown's immigration agent William Wagner (though he was sent to Germany only in 1860). Others conclude that it was an 1857 English-language pamphlet of T.P. French that brought the peasants to settle in Canada in 1858.[1]

Most authors do not examine the contents of French's publication and refer to it cursorily (and isolated from other publications) as a "tract," "pamphlet," or an "advertisement." This chapter proposes that potential emigrants were informed earlier than 1857 about free land in Canada. It will also resituate French's publication as an informative emigrant guidebook, an attempt by the state to dictate the behaviour of an ideal settler in a utopian project. By contextualizing this document alongside other similar publications, it becomes apparent that potential emigrants in Prussia were informed about the land available in Canada before French's publication.

T.P. French: Attracting Settlers

Over the decades, local historical memory has implied that French's publication informed the Polish-Kashub peasants in Europe and attracted them to settle in Canada (see figure 4.1). This is evident in the

INFORMATION

FOR

INTENDING SETTLERS

ON THE

Ottawa and Opeongo Road,

And its Vicinity,

BY

T. P. FRENCH,
Crown Land Agent,

PUBLISHED WITH THE APPROVAL OF
THE HONORABLE JOSEPH CAUCHON,
COMMISSIONER OF CROWN LANDS.

AND

THE HONORABLE P. M. VANKOUGHNET,
PRESIDENT EXECUTIVE COUNCIL AND MINISTER OF AGRICULTURE.

OTTAWA, CANADA WEST,
1857.

4.1   The guidebook that reportedly brought Polish settlers to Canada.

---

writings of several authors. Ickiewicz, writing in 1981 and 2008, says that French's publication was "sent to Germany, and the first Kashubian settlers, who French referred to as 'Prussians,' arrived in Renfrew already in 1858." Jost, writing in *Polyphony* in 1984, declares that "in answer to a 1857 advertisement for the distribution of free land grants, Polish immigrants arrived in Canada as early as 1858." Zurakowski arrives at the same conclusion. She writes that, "The decision was then made to include Prussia and Scandinavia in the recruitment of potential settlers. The same agent, Thomas French, published and distributed a brochure ... [as] a result of this campaign the first Kaszubs arrived in Renfrew County as early as 1858."

Rekowski supports this claim and writes that French's leaflets were "distributed in Germany and that is how, before the year 1858 was over, the very first Kashub settlers arrived in Renfrew."[2] Even though Renfrew County was not created until 1861, Mask-Connolly, perhaps unsure of the previous claims, states that in 1858 "Renfrew County was one of the few counties in Upper Canada that was looking for immigrants."[3] Yet none of the authors prove their claim – that it was French's publication that attracted the migrants. Several authors imply that because French was responsible for the Opeongo and wrote a publication to induce settlement in 1857, the settlers, who arrived in 1858, must therefore have been attracted by his publication. This is a fallacy.

On page two of his publication, French noted that free land grants were being given. Since the mention was placed at the front, it can be deduced that its intention was to attract settlement to the road. The pages following were meant to inform potential settlers about the area. As Crown Lands Agent for the Opeongo Road, French was one of the "point-men for the state." He was responsible for providing information about where land was available.[4] In order to attract settlement, government officials, like French, sought to inform potential settlers by issuing guidebooks.

However, the aforementioned authors writing on the Polish-Kashubs do not address the greater content of French's publication. Brenda Lee-Whiting includes a few statistics supplied by French to give some social context but the only one who addresses the material at length is Joan Finnigan. The publication was retyped as a chapter in her last publication, *Life Along the Opeongo Line*. These authors did not place it within the genre of emigrant literature but treated it is an isolated document. They also apply different terms to it, including "report" (Lee-Whiting), "pamphlet" (Miller), "advertisement" (Zurakowski), "leaflet" (Rekowski), and "tract" (Finnigan). None of these terms adequately describes the document, nor its intention. Although it was an advertisement, it was also a report on the land and its prospective yields, and an informative piece providing advice for the voyage. Describing it as a leaflet implies it was a small or brief publication, when in fact it was a detailed

36-page document. Finnigan defines it as a tract, which draws upon the declarative aspect of the document. However, the term "tract" in this sense is a term usually applied to religious or political publications;[5] this is neither. It was a government publication. Describing this document as a guidebook is more accurate as it attempted not only to entice but also to inform. The document is a product of a mid-nineteenth-century colonization scheme in Canada West and should be considered in relation to that initiative. Furthermore, describing the document as a guidebook situates it in the context of similar literature that was produced across North America and Europe with similar intentions.

Resituating French's Guidebook and the Migration in the Colonization Project

Emigrant guidebooks provided an array of information and they were a common form of reference for potential emigrants in the nineteenth century. Produced by individuals, emigrant societies, land companies, states, regions, or countries, they served a dual purpose: to entice the emigrant to settle in the region and to provide information to ease their transition to the area. Guidebooks were also used to "combat stereotypes about colonial and frontier societies and to remove inhibitions about emigrating to or investing in them."[6] Such guidebooks were popular in the United States, especially during the era of resettlement of the frontier and the Oregon land craze in the late 1840s and 1850s.[7] They also appeared earlier in the United Kingdom and in other parts of the British Empire. Emigrant societies in Prussia, such as the one in Breslau, and German travellers who toured the United States between 1815 and 1850, produced around 100 guidebooks for prospective emigrants.[8] Part of the colonizing project in the Canadas involved the production of such guides.[9] As Bruce Curtis and John Walsh note, the main period of production by the colonial government was between 1850 and 1870 and it began in a period of declining immigration.[10] Planning both colonization and the guides was the jurisdiction of two government entities: the Bureau of Agriculture and the Department of Crown Lands.

Under the jurisdiction of the Bureau of Agriculture, emigration agents and agencies to receive newly arrived persons were stationed in Quebec, Montreal, Ottawa, Toronto, Kingston, and Hamilton. These agents were to assist emigrants and direct them to available tracts of land. They also, in the words of John Hodgetts, "kept a parental eye on the general progress of the settlers, and pressed headquarters for the extension of postal services, larger grants for branch roads ... and supplies."[11] The responsibility for the colonization roads, from 1852 to 1862, was shared between the Bureau of Agriculture and the Crown Lands Department. Of the two, the Bureau, according to Walsh, "acted as a fulcrum around which the administration of colonization unfolded."[12] In the 1850s, William Hutton, the Secretary of the Bureau of Agriculture,[13] and A.C. Buchanan, the Chief Emigration Agent at Quebec City, assembled guides that attempted "to promote the welfare of Immigrants thereby [increasing] further immigration."[14] Hutton published guides and delivered lectures in his native Ireland in the early 1850s.[15] Following the publications by Hutton (1854, 1857), Catherine Parr Traill (1855), and Vere Foster (1855),[16] French's guidebook was part of a greater transatlantic network of discourse out of Canada, the northern United States, and England.[17]

Once it was decided, through the Public Lands Act in 1853, to offer 100-acre grants, the colonial government agreed that settlers had to abide by certain rules.[18] These guidebooks, which highlighted features of the land, also constructed what the colonial government envisioned as its "ideal settler." By setting out requirements for the clearance of land, prescribed dwelling sizes, and crop requirements before receiving a deed, the guidebooks expressed the official desire for a "social order predicated on stability and permanence." These guides were a mechanism by which the state sought to make "normal and routine a wide range of practices and aesthetics about family, community, landscape and the self."[19] Their vehicles to deliver these implied codes of the ideal settler were the guidebooks and the statistics and figures provided. That the guidebooks may not have been widely successful, as Norman Macdonald implied,[20] does not negate the intentions of the government in attracting settlement. Yet the disconnect between laissez-faire acts of recruiting well-capitalized "proper settlers" via guidebooks, and the arrival of poor settlers at Quebec City, demonstrates that the project did not proceed as envisioned by the public servants.

In the government's view, if a population of settlers showed commitment to their property, the necessary institutions and landscapes of progress could be implemented. Such a population was desired over one that would be a burden to the country.²¹ But Buchanan himself soon realized that many immigrants coming to Canada could not afford to procure inland transportation. A paradigm shift thus occurred once these groups arrived. Officials had to treat them as recipients of government aid rather than potential customers or profitable traffic.²² In 1858, the Emigration Department spent $3,535.97 in relief in Canada West. One thousand five hundred and eighty-six adult equivalents (2,101 souls) were assisted at an average cost of $3.09. Of these, 734 were Irish, 319.5 were Norwegian, 287.5 were English, and 179 were German. Out of 1,586 adults, 160.5 were forwarded to the Ottawa agency from Quebec, and 726.5 were directed to Montreal.²³ The 76 Poles of 1858 must have been included with the Germans because the German translator at Quebec, William Sinn, "procured free passage for them from the Chief Agent to Renfrew."²⁴ The government wanted young and strong emigrants, but according to the agent in Ottawa, Francis Clemow, the Prussian Poles were too old, too poor, and had large, dependent families with them. Fortunately, the Poles' tenacity and work ethic won over the Ottawa agency two years later. The agency was happy with the Poles' progression from being a "burden" to being stable settlers, as Sinn mentions they were looked upon favourably by the Ottawa agency in 1860.²⁵ They then fit the government's intent as set out in the guidebooks.

But was French's guidebook the medium that informed potential Polish-Kashub emigrants about Canada? Local publications have not shed much light on whether or not it was accessible to the potential migrants in Poland. Lee-Whiting claimed that French's pamphlet was translated into German and 6,000 copies were printed but she did not source the claim or give a year for its translation.²⁶ How likely is it that an English-language publication sent to Europe in 1857 would have attracted a group of Polish-speaking migrants a mere year later? Walsh unearthed testimony from a secretary in the Bureau of Agriculture, Evelyn Campbell, in 1859 that suggested Hutton's and French's guidebook was translated into French, German, Norwegian, and Swedish. Upon closer inspection, it appears that, before 1859, Hutton's guidebook had been translated into German, Norwegian, and French, and that 15,000 copies had been circulated in Europe. In 1857, the Bureau "widely circulated" French's guidebook but there is no mention of its translation until 1859.²⁷ When Hutton mentioned that French's guidebook was "widely circulated," he may have been generous as, in 1857, French was informed that the Bureau would be promoting another guide (Hutton's) and not French's. Further, there is only evidence suggesting that one box of French's English pamphlets were being sold. These cost "6 Sterling" and were available through Mr Stanford at Charing Cross in England.²⁸ It thus appears that the potential Polish-Kashub migrants were informed through another publication or medium.

Networks of Agents and Earlier Emigrant Literature

Investigating how emigrants were encouraged yields several avenues not considered by local Polish-Kashub authors. Although Mask-Connolly has continually cited the 1860 testimony of Sinn in her publications,²⁹ she did not include some crucial parts of his testimony and report dealing with his recruiting ventures. In his testimony, Sinn explained how since 1851 he had helped direct thousands of people from Germany onto tracts of land and to find employment. In his dual role as an agent for the Grand Trunk Railway³⁰ and the colonial government, he stated that he had directed settlement to the Waterloo area and, since 1858, to the Ottawa district. Further, he mentioned that Canada should expect further emigration from Northern Germany – directed to Canada by emigration agent Charles Eisenstein of Berlin. In fact, Sinn testified that of the 47,000 Germans who landed at Quebec between 1846 and 1860, Eisenstein had directed "more than 15,000." Sinn and Eisenstein connected Prussian emigration to Canada. Eisenstein, the independent broker, had, according to Sinn, "Agents throughout the Country" and "at his own expense lately published, and circulated gratis, a small pamphlet on Canada." While officials prodded Sinn with questions about the possible establishment of a colonial agency in Bremen or Hamburg, Sinn encouraged the government to publish departure dates for ships and passage rates in several emigrant newspapers in Hamburg, Bremen, and Rudolstadt. When asked if he had written such articles, Sinn admitted that he had "many times sent correspondence to papers in Germany" but since they yielded little capital for newspaper owners, he discontinued them.³¹ Nor had he circulated Hutton's 1857 pamphlet to German contacts. Eisenstein's personal recruiting activities thus provide us with other avenues through which the first group of Polish-Kashub settlers may have been informed.

A search in two prominent German emigrant newspapers, *Allgemeine Auswanderungs-Zeitung* (*AAZ*) and *Deutsche Auswander-Zeitung* (*DAZ*) reveals a host of articles about Canada as early as 1852.[32] Sinn and his network of contacts favoured publishing in the *DAZ* until 1857. As early as 1853, the *DAZ* promoted Sinn as a reputable and upstanding agent. The newspaper argued that Buchanan had hired Sinn to ensure that fellow Germans would not be swindled in their dealings and that he helped find cheap tickets to North America.[33] Two years later, Sinn, writing in the *DAZ*, commented on German emigrants to Canada and the generous financial support that they were given once they arrived.[34] That same year, an agreement was made between Bremen and the Central Department of Emigration at Quebec. Instructions circulated by the Bremen Information Bureau referred emigrants to "W. Sinn," as he was to provide "free information about the cheapest opportunities for travelling inland, available lands, prospects and employment."[35] The Minister of the Bureau of Agriculture, Malcolm Cameron, also authorized the printing of 2,000 copies and the "publication of a work for distribution in Germany" written by Sinn in 1853.[36]

To further entice potential migrants, more articles were written about Canada. In an 1853 article, "Briefe aus Canada," the freedom of individuals in the Canadas was highlighted. The freedom granted to people in the British system was summarized in another 1853 article. The system of taxes in Canada was explained in 1857. The *AAZ* wrote that taxes could only be enacted with the approval of the municipal residents in the area and had to be spent on their welfare.[37] If conveyed to Prussian serfs and peasants, who had few rights, such claims would appear quite attractive for those who harboured thoughts of emigrating.

The colonial government circulated advertisements for free land along the colonization roads in 1856 in publications such as *The Canadian Agriculturalist*, with paragraphs of information on the roads and the corresponding agents. Information on land west of Ottawa also appeared, in German, in the September edition of the *DAZ*,[38] listing the colonization road agents, including French, who would allocate a free homestead to them. Publication in the *DAZ* evidently solicited a quick response from some readers and agents. A Mr Wichelhauson wrote from Bremen on 5 November 1856 to inquire if the free grant advertisements were indeed true offerings.[39]

Although it is clear that French's guidebook did not induce the first migration of Polish-Kashubs to Canada, we should not discount the fact that after 1859 it may have renewed interest in Canada as a destination. But without French's guidebook as an instigator, there is a void in the history of the Polish-Kashub group. There is no proof that the first migrants arranged their voyage through one of Sinn's or Eisenstein's entrepreneurial connections. The best evidence of this is a letter from Sinn to the Lutheran Pittsburgh Synod in which he claimed that he had started the first settlements of Germans and Prussian Poles in the Ottawa area. Sinn wrote that in the summer of 1858 he decided to establish a settlement on the Ottawa and had directed 900 Northern Germans from the region of Pomerania, Mecklenburg, and from around Danzig in Prussian Poland to that settlement area in Renfrew County. Whether Sinn continued to recruit in Prussia after 1858 is debatable. He stated that he did but since the articles outlining Canada as an eligible destination – with free land – were read by thousands of people in the 1850s,[40] a lesser known agent could also have capitalized on the opportunity.

Certainly emigrants arrived on lines other than the one Sinn is known to have associated with. According to Gerhard Bassler, Sinn promoted one shipping line, the "equally cheap Hamburg shipping line Knorr & Holtermann about whose past six years of direct services to Quebec not a single complaint had been registered."[41] As chapter 3 states, several of the ships that brought the 1860s settlers to Quebec were owned by August Bolten & Co. and only one was a Knorr vessel. However, agents often worked with multiple lines[42] and Sinn may have done so too. Lee-Whiting found the family of a German settler in the Ottawa Valley who had kept a passage contract. Matthew Horcun, his wife, and three children departed Hamburg on the *Gellert* in 1863. Horcun booked his passage through Eisenstein, when he was an agent for Donati & Co. of Hamburg.[43] Donati were agents for Rob M. Sloman's shipping firm which booked passages with Louis Knorr & Co. Indeed, the web of agents in the German states was extensive. In 1853, the following offices, according to Hermann Kellenbenz, were located in Bremen: Karl Pokrantz & Co. (1 *Generalagent*), F.J. Wichelhausen & Co. (1 *Generalagent*), Wilhelm Bodeker (1 *Generalagent* and 4 *Agenten*), Lüderiing & Co. (4 *Agenten*), and Wilhelm Stisser & Co. (1 *Generalagent* and 4 *Agenten*). During the same year, Hapag had 4 *Agenten* and Knorr und

Holtermann had 2 *Agenten* in Hamburg.⁴⁴ Tracing the network of business relationships thus complicates matters and, again, the passage of time does not permit us to query the migrants themselves. However, the Mr Wichelhauson who wrote to the Canadian government in 1856 about free land may have been the general agent in the firm of the similar name. Thus, it is possible that other major firms knew about the initiative before French's document was published.

In the colonial government, emigrant recruiting practices were in a state of flux. Confusion reigned over whether Canadian officials should be dependent on shipping companies to recruit emigrants on an ad hoc basis⁴⁵ or whether colonial offices for emigration should be opened in Europe. The government denied requests by William Wagner of Ottawa in 1857 and P. Christie (of Hamburg) in 1858 to become Canadian emigration agents in the German states but allied with Geo. P. Wilkinson of Berlin to promote migration in 1858.⁴⁶ Finally, in 1860, armed with maps, publications, and his oratorical skills, William Wagner, an immigrant turned land surveyor, was hired by the government to tour Prussia to win over agricultural emigrants.⁴⁷ He was to cross the land in an upstanding and legal fashion⁴⁸ and write home to report on the permissions he had secured to speak and post information in various locations. Other Canadian agents were sent abroad, including Reverend Henry Hope to London, John Donaldson to Londonderry, and Alexander McLachlan to Scotland. Taking over from A.B. Hawke, who was sent to Liverpool in 1859, Buchanan himself tried to attract emigrants, starting in 1861. Although the government offered Donaldson a salary of $1,200 in 1860, it only allotted a daily per diem of $6 for Wagner – but covered his expenses. By 1862, Wagner reported that he had advertised in papers read by 400,000 people and that he had distributed 3,500 guides and displayed 222 maps of Canada. However, he only received 178 letters of inquiry, and his expenditures, of more than $6,000, were excessive based on his results.⁴⁹ In April of 1860 he also intended to tour through Berlin and then Pomerania to promote more emigration to Canada. A year later, the Bureau of Agriculture withdrew all foreign agents because it was becoming too expensive and planned an inquiry into recruiting activities.⁵⁰

At home, after several years of questionable emigrant recruiting tactics, Sinn was chastised "for conducting private business in the course of his duties."⁵¹ Over the years Sinn's salary had risen from £60 in 1852

4.2   Caricature of an emigration agent. A woodcut, by Eduard Kretzchmar (1848), shows agents as wolves who preyed on naive emigrants, women, and children. The faceless money counter at the table speaks for itself too.

to £150 in 1857. On the side, he received the equivalent of between $400 to $500 from the Royal Mail Line. Besides his salary and whatever his work for the Grand Trunk Railroad netted, Sinn, on occasion, would also ask the department to reimburse him for expenses to locate settlers in Canada – an added cost not intended by the government as it did not want to fund pauperism. Such a request came in October 1857 when Sinn asked to be reimbursed £21–5s for locating Norwegians in Canada and in 1858 for locating "Swedes" on the Bobcaygeon Road. In 1860, Hutton wrote to Clemow saying that, at $400, the extra expense for the Ottawa agent's office was too high and advised him not to incur a debt like that again. One wonders if this cost was incurred while assisting the Polish emigrants in their winter lodgings for 1858–59 and their travel to their plots in 1859.[52] Bassler also mentions that in 1854, Sinn accepted 88 emigrant vouchers from the Württemberg Ministry for the settlement of at least 210 Germans, netting him 15 to 20 gulden for a family head and 10 gulden for each family member. These practices, ultimately, led to Sinn's dismissal as a government official but mystery and suspicion continue to surround his activities (see figure 4.2).[53]

Conclusion

Although laden with numerous statistics, descriptive claims of the geographical area, and the announcement of free grants along the Opeongo Road, it was not French's publication that informed the first group of Polish-Kashubs about free land along the colonization roads. The publication does tell us how the government tried to entice "ideal" settlers in the period of flux leading up to Confederation. Research into Sinn's entrepreneurial recruitment ventures shows that Canada was portrayed as an eligible and attractive destination before French's publication. Articles such as those from the *DAZ* attest to this and circulated the notion, as early as 1856, that free grants were available along the colonization roads in Canada West. Although this research challenges a narrative in local historical memory, the findings situate the question of recruitment in the maelstrom of nineteenth-century emigrant agent activities and relationships.

What does persist, locally and in the literature, is resentment toward the agents, both foreign and domestic. Local authors, including Rekowski, Mask-Connolly, Finnigan, and Prince, treat them with contempt.[54] Yet it is imperative to acknowledge the emigrants' own agency and their decision to leave, based on the emigrant's hierarchy of needs, rather than dwelling only on the questionable business practices of emigrant agents. The resentment toward Crown agents in Canada, on the other hand, stems from official statements describing the land and its capability, that, according to local authors, were lies. Such claims are not unique to the Polish-Kashub group. John Lehr writes that the Ukrainian population around Stuartburn, Manitoba, also disseminated questionable information from hearsay and handbills, regarding their turn-of-the-century migration to and settlement on the land.[55] However, after taking into consideration Walsh's study into the government's utopian vision for the Ottawa-Huron Tract, a different perspective emerges.

5

Poor Land and Victorian Science

Yi-Fu Tuan wrote that space is a "symbol of freedom in the Western world. Space lies open; it suggests the future and invites action. On the negative side, space and freedom are a threat ... To be open and free is to be exposed and vulnerable."[1] After the Polish-Kashubs' "escape" from occupied Poland, local historical memory marks the settlement period as one of great disappointment. Msgr Pick said that after settling the land a "great poverty" started.[2] The idea that the land had enough rocks to build many walls of China was written by Fr Dembski in Wilno and published in an 1888 edition of Buffalo's *Polak w Ameryce*. It carried on in local historical memory to such an extent that authors Radecki and Heydenkorn, as well as Rekowski, recorded it almost a hundred years later without recording, or possibly knowing, its source.[3] And the notion that the settlers were given poor land by agents and officials was passed down through descendants as a subversive local memory against the official version, which stated that the land was good for settlement.[4] In the most recent attempts to analyze this aspect of the settlement narrative, three authors – Rekowski, Mask-Connolly, and Prince – conclude that the agents knew the land was poor and not fit for settlement.

These conclusions, however, do not entirely represent the situation. Jon Gjerde declares that the responsibility of the historian, among other things, is to historicize the time and space in which the immigrants lived.[5] The record thus far has not benefitted from the application of this paradigm. Unfortunately, to justify their claims Rekowski and Prince use soil surveys – which are only authoritative to an extent – completed in the 1970s. Although they do not realize it, using these surveys renders their argument anachronistic because they have analyzed it using contemporary forms of measurement without considering nineteenth-century ways of thinking. This chapter offers new perspectives. It examines and explicates government officials' beliefs of the time alongside the valorized professional knowledge of Victorian science and the drive for state formation in Canada. As a result, it becomes apparent that officials initially thought the land was fertile and fit for farming. Since the information was produced by men in the "inventory sciences," it was considered legitimate. This chapter does not deny that the soil was poor; but states that the use of the soil survey inflames the narrative and makes the situation seem worse to twentieth-century readers than it was. Last, neither Rekowski, Mask-Connolly, nor Prince take into account the idea that agriculture in the Ottawa-Huron Tract was not intended to be pursued independently of the lumber industry.[6] The two industries acted symbiotically. The additional off-farm income garnered by Polish settlers was important for survival but it was equally part of the economy and their regular livelihood.

Deception from the Crown

As noted in chapter 4, authors looked upon emigration agents and their misleading recruiting tactics with contempt. Upon arrival, similar views were cast onto Crown agents and government officials, who misrepresented the terrain, according to external authors interested in local history. In 1967, Lee-Whiting wrote that "the report written by Crown Lands Agent T.P. French in 1857 was unduly optimistic ... In his description Mr. French must have let his enthusiasm get the better of him." Marilyn Miller writes that "the tone of these publications was unfailingly optimistic." Hessel argues that Wagner's 1860 publication "smacks of misrepresentation" and that his German translation of Sinn's government reports omitted the struggles that settlers endured on the land.[7] Similarly, local authors treated the agents with contempt, but added another subversive level to the narrative – that the agents knew the land was poor.

Taking statements from Miller's *Straight Lines in Curved Space*, which accused agents of deceiving settlers, Rekowski accentuated the claim and argued that "surely even then it must have been evident to government officials that such hilly, stony country had not been designated by God for farming." Mask-Connolly built on this statement in

2001, writing that "T.P. French did everything he could to disprove 'mere assertions of the utter worthlessness of the land along this road for farming purposes.'"[8] Without providing evidence from agents M.P. Hayes or French to corroborate her statement, Finnigan declared in 2004 that "Hayes and T.P. French were equally capable of over optimistic and misleading statements. They disregarded bad conditions and insisted on settling land they knew was poor." Finnigan copied Mask-Connolly's aforementioned quote and placed it in her discourse too.[9] Two years later, Prince replicated the claims saying "land agents tended to distort the true picture, and often presented misleading information concerning the quality of the soil on the free grant lots. Their description of the land's potential often disregarded the poor conditions, and showed their insistence on settling poor land they knew was most rocky."[10]

Yet the function of the poor-land narrative is still unclear. Perhaps it has emerged from the poor exiles and sturdy emigrant dichotomy and now functions to support a "hardship overcome" myth. Perhaps it is also a way to mask a perceived lack of development by inviting a myth of continuous discrimination. Indeed, these latter postulations seem plausible when we consider some of Rekowski's words:

> When they applied for land at French's office [they] received third rate land, officially classified as not fit for farming or even pasturing. Perhaps that is why there is a residue of resentment among the Kashubs in Ontario, the feeling that their evolution and development has been retarded because of initial discrimination and prejudice; that their forefathers escaped from a ghetto in Poland only to be forced by adverse economic conditions to find shelter in another ghetto of poverty in Canada; the reason their fathers were directed to such a poor part of Ontario was because, at that time, Eastern Europeans were considered Bohunks who could and would be satisfied to eke out an existence anywhere.[11]

Although Rekowski also considers the chronology of settlement as a factor in land application, his rants and his tone represent a thread of historiography that has influenced local written historical memory. The more Rekowski painted the Polish-Kashub settlers as persecuted, the more innocent they were. They are, as Basu would argue, exiles "more sinned against than sinning, and thus exempt from responsibility."[12] In Rekowski's logic, because they were "Bohunks" and settled on poor land, this must have been done deliberately. And that must have happened because they were discriminated against. On a broader canvas, such thoughts accord well with the Poles' claims of religious and ethnic persecution in their homeland. In the end, though, one wonders if these claims survive in local historical memory to absolve ancestors for their lack of long-term success in farming.

Supporting Evidence: Soil Surveys

Besides the ghetto hyperbole used by Rekowski,[13] another aspect of his narrative is anachronistic. The inclusion of a soil survey by several authors, including Rekowski, to demonstrate that Crown employees knew the land was poor, is not logical. Jost, writing in 1974, was the first to employ a soil survey to justify her argument that the soil was unfit for cultivation. Although Jost recognizes that "hundreds of years ago farming methods and land evaluations were different,"[14] she did not analyze the technology of the time. Instead she used a soil survey from 1966 to qualify her argument, making the assumption that since the land was unfit for mechanized agriculture in the 1960s, it must also have been unfit in 1860. Hessel, too, corroborated his views on the terrain by consulting an unsourced guide: "Proof of how unsuitable the land was for farming is found in Agriculture Canada's Land Inventory that describes most soils found in the German settlement areas as Class 7: 'Soils in this Class have no capability for arable culture or permanent pasture.'"[15]

Rekowski entered the fray, using what appears to be the same land inventory used by Hessel. He claims that all "the rest of the soil along the Madawaska heights and in the area around Wilno etc. to be settled by the Kashubs was classified as belonging to the seventh (7) category, that is, extremely poor, 'not suitable for cultivation or for permanent pasture land.' Hence, the Kashubs, when they applied for land at French's office, received third-rate land that was officially classified as not fit for farming or even pasturing."[16] In 2006, Prince followed Hessel's and Rekowski's lead, writing that "according to the 'Ontario Ministry of Agriculture and Food Report of 1975,' Renfrew County does not have any class 1 soil, which is highly suitable for cultivation. Most of the soils in the townships of Hagarty, Radcliffe, Sherwood, Jones and Burns, in the western part of Renfrew County, belong to classes 4–7."[17] Yet they did not incorporate and analyze concepts and methods of agriculture practiced in nineteenth-century Canada. They assumed modern farming methods and practices, such as the use of mechanized equipment like combines, when evaluating the soil's capability for farming in a soil survey.[18] However, in the nineteenth century, it was, on the contrary, possible to cultivate smaller zones on land that modern machinery was unable to traverse, such as small valley or creek clearings, with horse ploughs, spades, and cradles.[19] Such surveys clearly do not apply to the space and time in which the settlers farmed.

The soil survey and land inventories cited earlier by local authors have their roots in investigations by pedologists and students, which took place between 1963 and 1975.[20] Of course, when taking soil readings, a certain standardized set of data was required. To suggest that these broad lines on the soil survey and land inventory maps are more general than specific is to point out the obvious.[21] James Scott echoes such cautions, writing that maps that grade soil class use averages that may mask great variation.[22] Nine factors – soil drainage, thickness of unconsolidated material, soil horizons, particle distribution, soil reaction, slope, surface stoniness, crop heat units, and soil location – contribute to generating a soil rating and the categories themselves are skewed by the act of human sampling. For example, the test for "stoniness" required a percentage of stones larger than 15 centimetres and boulders larger than 60 centimetres in diameter to be gauged over an arbitrary tract of land.[23] Since many workers were taking inventory of the land, it is likely that readings varied by researcher. The angle and height of the slope also affected the land inventories. Researchers who compiled the surveys judged whether or not modern machinery could traverse slopes and factored it into their evaluation of the land and soil. However, in the 1860s, much of the farming was done by hand or team, thus more areas were accessible to planting crops – even if the slope was too steep for modern machinery. The measure of each soil horizon is not accurate when we consider the era of research – the 1960s – and the era of comparison – the 1860s. Soil horizons change over time depending on the activities carried out on the land. Since soil is made up of four components – minerals, bacteria and organic material, air, and moisture – it can change depending on how these elements are combined. Depending on the clearance rates and practices that return bacteria and organic material to the soil, the "A" horizon (the horizon closest to the surface), can be left parched and its capability decline over time. Thus, using a recent soil survey and/or land inventory to justify soil capabilities a hundred years ago is anachronistic. Since external and local authors alike have not realized the fallacy in their logic, a detailed examination of the science and knowledge behind the land and settlement in the era in question is needed.

Opening the Land with Ambitious Plans

To say that the colonization scheme in the Ottawa-Huron tract was ambitious seems to be stating the obvious. In the 1850s, development along the St Lawrence and the Great Lakes encircled the Ottawa-Huron Tract. Loyalists and British immigrants were settled along the St Lawrence, Scottish Highlanders in Glengarry, and military settlements along the Rideau River. McNab's colony was settled, the Tipperary Irish were occupying Huntley and March Townships, Peter Robinson's Irish were in Ramsay, Pakenham, and Goulbourn and the townships of Ross, Westmeath, Pembroke, and Stafford received a mixture of Irish, Scottish, American, and French-Canadian settlers from the lumber industry. To the south, Irish settlements near Peterborough such as Cartwright, Manvers, Douro, Cavan, Ops, and Robinson's second group of settlers occupied lands.[24] But until the 1840s, only a few people ventured into the Ottawa-Huron Tract on exploratory excursions, including Samuel de Champlain (1615–16) who traversed the northern tip, Lieutenant Catty (1818) and Lieutenant Walpole (1827) of the Royal Engineers, David Thompson (1835), Alexander Shireff (1839), and Alexander Murray, of the Geological Survey of Canada (GSC) (1853).[25] By 1856, when several colonization roads had penetrated the wilderness in the tract, Vankoughnet, the Minister of Agriculture, declared his expansionist vision and predictions for the land. His oft-quoted comments suggested that "the Ottawa country, lying south of Lake Nipissing, and of the great River Ottawa ... is capable of sustaining a population of eight million people, and it is now attracting attention as the more western portions of Canada are being rapidly filled up."[26]

The Ottawa-Huron Tract was the next frontier for development in "old Ontario." The vast forests that covered the territory were a region of possibility. To comprehend the expansionist thoughts of this mythical space we can turn to the writings of Tuan: "The trees stand behind the other as far as the eye can see, and they encourage the mind to extrapolate infinity ... The forest is a cluttered environment, the antithesis of open space ... At first there is wilderness, undifferentiated space. A clearing is made in the forest and a few houses are built. Immediately differentiation occurs ... To the passerby or visitor, the fields and houses also constitute a well defined place ... With the continual extension of clearings the forest eventually disappears. An entire landscape is humanized." As farmers cleared more space, a governable and manageable territory existed in what otherwise would have been a mythical space – "a fuzzy area of defective knowledge surrounding the empirically known."[27]

In order to create this settlement area, the first step in the process "was the alienation of [First Nations] claims by the Crown. Next came the survey. The division of land into concessions, lots, and townships defined locations that could be quickly transferred to individual settlers. The assignment of legal title followed." The population in the area increased, its spread controlled by the survey.[28]

Catharine Wilson reminds us that "much of Western culture rests on the desire to possess privately held land and the belief that it is the source of independence and power. [Land] was also deemed to be the cornerstone of the capitalist order as markets depended on secure title and the free disposal of property."[29] To attract settlement, therefore, government agents, who had no equipment or geological training, attempted to portray the land as attractive for clearing and settlement. These descriptions are the ones that are contested by local authors. For example, French, previously a teller and a bank clerk in Ireland, stated that "the soil in this part of the Province is a sandy loam, in some places light, but in others deep and rich ... The country presents rather a hilly aspect, but by far the larger portion is composed of gently undulating and flat lands. Few of the highest hills are incapable of cultivation, and it is strange that the best soil is not infrequently found on their summits."[30] Yet, while authors critique French's "exaggeration," a survey of other statements relating to the colonization scheme yields similar results.

Supporters of colonization in the Legislative Assembly wrote that "the fertile loams of the interior ... [and] the rich valley of the Madawaska, and the no less rich valleys that [lay] scattered among the granite ridges [would] teem with life and the bustle of commerce."[31] William Hutton told an Irish audience that "along the entire length of the Ottawa and its numerous tributaries, there are to be found the richest possible lands in the most desirable situations." Not having seen the extent of the land for himself, Hutton relied on the information and reports from "William Logan and Alexander Murray ... and the land surveyor and newspaper publisher Robert Bell [who] had all mapped it, and declared its soils and resources ideal for settlement."[32] If there was any skepticism, argues Graeme Wynn, it was concluded that "patient effort ... would bring the forested 'waste lands' of the Crown to a state of civilization." Further, if the skepticism came from timber interests – who had the most first-hand knowledge of the territory – it was dismissed since the timber trade and its workers were portrayed as self-interested villains who desired a monopoly.[33] But beyond the surveyors' reports, little was known about the Ottawa-Huron Tract.

In 1852, the *Canadian Journal of Science, Industry and Art* said that "little is known of that most interesting section of the country."[34] Two years later, the noted civil and canal engineer Thomas Coltrin Keefer, in a lecture about the Upper Ottawa, declared that the government knew more about foreign countries than that portion of Canada West. This lack of knowledge is confirmed by Hutton, who wrote to French in 1856 that the maps that staff were supplied with lacked sufficient detail.[35] Indeed, argues Walsh, "together the state and science provided the language and legitimacy to establish the Ottawa-Huron Tract as a theoretical space (or 'field') whose colonization was in the national interest."[36] The knowledge created by the surveyors and scientists was deemed "truthful" and was propagated as such by others in the government.

After the 1850s, according to Helen Parson, the land capability came under scrutiny. "Land clearing revealed the rock; crop yields declined after a few years as the fertility of the thin soils was rapidly depleted."[37] This prompted some to re-examine the scheme. Thomas D'Arcy McGee, a former MLA, came to realize the errors of surveyors in 1862, saying that "science, with its hammer and its theodolite, has been for twenty years, at work in these wildernesses." McGee declared that it became evident that, "the granite country between the Ottawa and Lake Huron could never sustain a numerous population."[38] The agent for Hastings Road, M.P. Hayes, also scrutinized the territory he was assigned to govern, saying in 1863 that "we have tracts of good land, but they are separated and cut up by rough tracts of hilly and broken land." Ezra Stevens, a Northumberland farmer, also argued that the land along the Hastings Road was "poor, and the greatest part of it entirely unfit for settlement."[39] Hence, blame fell upon the surveyors and agents[40] because they were blind to, or unaware of, these realities. Yet the question of how the knowledge produced by science initially fooled the officials remains.

Victorian Science: The Production of Knowledge and Governable Spaces

From the comfortable government vantage point, influenced by Victorian science, the Ottawa-Huron Tract was a potential agrarian landscape. Prevalent between the 1830s to the early part of the twentieth century, "Victorian culture attributed increasing importance to science, the rational study of nature, as a dominant mode of thought." It drew its power from two British concerns: the need for resources and the need for colonists to "master their environment."[41] In assessing the potential of the land and nation, "science became the gauge by which Canadians assessed ... [what] they could one day become" and enabled not just a chance for survival – for officials or colonists alike – but increased prosperity. Inherent in the tenets of Victorian science were the influences of Baconianism and Newtonianism, which sought to identify the natural with the rational, especially the former since it "assured that new scientific concepts and theories would arise through the amassing of facts by observation and experiment." Thus, inventory science became popular and was also a key belief in the Victorian notion of utilitarianism. It "encouraged the belief that even social problems were manageable through quantification and the statistical accumulation of facts."[42]

The belief in the worth of such inventory sciences represents what Scott terms a high-modernist ideology, "a strong ... self-confidence about scientific and technical progress, the expansion of production, the growing satisfaction of human needs, the mastery of nature (including human nature), and, above all the rational design of social order commensurate with the scientific understanding of natural laws ... It was, accordingly, uncritical, unskeptical, and thus unscientifically optimistic about the possibilities for the comprehensive planning of human settlement and production."[43] When such a notion of Victorian science and high modernism was applied to the Ottawa-Huron Tract, it sought to understand the territory through calculated findings and measurable results.

The first to peer at the Ottawa Valley as a field of study were the Royal Engineers. Their surveys for potential canals and roads "offered great opportunities to observe the geology of the country." Several of the engineers traversed the tract in the first quarter of the nineteenth century, compiling information as they went. The GSC, funded by the province in 1841, was another state-sponsored institution on the hunt for scientific knowledge and natural resources.[44]

Murray, as a representative of the GSC, traversed the tract in 1853. Based on the scientific findings of these expeditions, the engineers were encouraged to develop the territory. As Arthur Lower points out, surveyors "were sent out to look for agricultural land, and it is not surprising if sometimes they found what they were earnestly instructed to discover."[45] As a result, the Victorian notion of progress produced the statement that such a tract could sustain eight million people.[46]

The rhetoric of progress, initially encouraged by and further entrenched in Victorian science, was prevalent in the minds of officials. In the words of J. David Wood, "the image of progress as armed opposition to nature became deeply embedded in the nineteenth-century psyche." The production of knowledge to conquer the territory was done by surveying and creating numerous townships across the province.[47] Building on Lower's commentary, surveyors were agents of the state who promoted expansionism and the production of knowledge. Their task was to "use calibrations based on compass readings, astronomical observations, trigonometrically deduced angles and measurements, and the baselines provided by previous surveys, to blaze markers and straight property lines that paid little respect to the intrusive forests, rocks, and waters but instead privileged the necessity, logic, and scientific aesthetic of the cadastral grid."[48] Transferring these calculations to a map meant that administrators, living away from the territory, were able to visualize the territory and impose spatial order to an otherwise wild tract.

Expansionist nationalism, galvanized by Victorian science, created colonization roads throughout the tract. It also created small worlds, which were simplified so they could be understood and governed.[49]

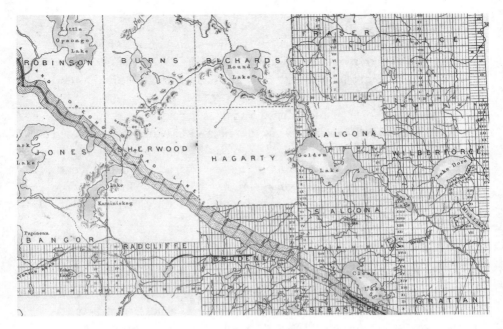

5.1 Devine's 1861 Map of the Ottawa-Huron Tract showing recently created townships surrounding the northwestern section of the Opeongo Road.

Once settlement occurred on the roads, townships needed to be surveyed in order for the space to be governable rather than thin sinews connecting the Ottawa to Lake Huron. Thus, townships like South Algona, Sebastopol, Brudenell (1857), Radcliffe (1859 and 1861), and Griffith (1859)[50] were surveyed, chipped away from the tract, and shaped into a manageable, orderly, and governable settlement-in-the-making (see figure 5.1). The emptiness was filled in through surveys. These lines on the land, or imagined geographies, attempted to impose order and create control.

The creation of knowledge, in the area near the Opeongo Road, was generated by the work of surveyors and the cartography skills of Thomas Devine. When the survey crew led by Robert Bell blazed the Opeongo Road in 1851, it created measurements and brief notations for the terrain. Between 1854 and 1863, "some five million acres – most of them in the newly opened shield districts – were added to the surveyed area of the province."[51] The "split-line method" of surveying, which was used in the Ottawa-Huron Tract, was devised by Devine and by 1856

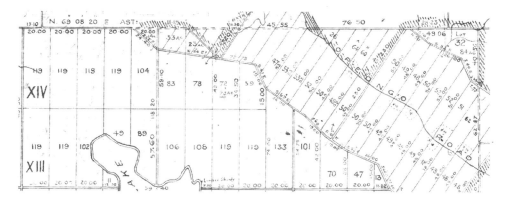

5.2 The 1,000-acre sectional survey of Radcliffe Township surveyed by Edwin Kirkland, Provincial Land Surveyor, in 1860. This system was used c. 1835–1906. It plotted out lots 50 chains by 20 chains. The road allowance was one chain in width after every fifth lot on the concession. On the right, earlier lots surveyed along the Opeongo Road are visible. Archives of Ontario.

was considered standard practice. "It placed a survey line down the middle of the page and placed all intersecting surveyed lines at carefully drawn right angles."[52] In the Ottawa-Huron Tract, the broad strokes of cartographers outlined 1,000-acre townships and lots and concessions on the land (see figure 5.2).

Starting in 1857, Devine produced his map of the tract. Considered to be the authority in depicting the Ottawa-Huron, the map appeared in the Annual Report of the Commissioner of Crown Lands in 1861.[53] Mathematical calculations had created the townships of Sebastopol and Brudenell with plots on the map, but only vague outlines of Hagarty, Lyndoch, Richards, Sherwood, Raglan, Burns, and Jones Townships.[54] One-hundred-acre lots along the Opeongo were surveyed, along with the southern portion of Radcliffe and Bangor Townships (since the Hastings-Opeongo junction road was to follow this route). Thus, although these townships existed on Devine's map, their interiors were not surveyed or methodically catalogued.

As we now know, the surveyors were only plotting the most cursory of boundary surveys to keep up with the demand for land. Such thoughts had been expressed decades earlier, in 1822, by R. Gourlay, who wrote that "such was the haste to get the land surveyed and given away that ignorant and careless men were employed to measure it out, and such a mess did they make."⁵⁵ According to Louis Gentilcore, "a frequent instruction to the early surveyor directed that he should 'survey and mark the front lines' of a township and then carry the side lines back." By 1829, surveyors would only outline the boundaries by "marking out the front corners of the lots along the concession lines. The running of the side lines was left to the settler."⁵⁶ Kirkwood and Murphy mention that the surveyor was instructed to "make posts of the most durable wood he can find, squaring about two feet of the top, and cutting the numbers of the lots, concessions, &c., with a proper marking iron; the posts at the corners of the Township are to be at least six inches square, those at the ends of Concessions five inches, and the lot posts four inches, all planted firmly in the ground ... Where a tree stands in the place for a post, he is to blaze it on four sides, and mark it as he would the post."⁵⁷ Although these techniques sound precise, they would be difficult to find in the thick forests, especially if they were not adhered to. Catherine Parr Traill comments that blazing a line was often "nothing more than notches or slices cut off the bark of the trees to mark out the line ... The boundaries of the different lots are often marked by a blazed tree" and these markers were "of as much use as finger posts [in] a dark night."⁵⁸ As settlement dictated that more territory be surveyed, names were added as well as the Devine map. "Blank space" was devoured by 1,000-acre sections and 100-acre lots.

Although imagined geographies – often ignorant of the topography – were being produced in the upper strata of the government,⁵⁹ emigration and immigration agents were not as well-informed as local authors claim. As early as 1857, timber agent A.J. Russell wrote to Hutton about the need for practical knowledge of the surveys so as not to create a straight road in the wilderness that might be costly. But emigration agents were only armed with "the Devine map and with a number of accounts copied from surveyors notebooks."⁶⁰ Devine published extracts from the surveyors' notebooks but inferior soil was rarely attributed to the entire township and an optimistic trope about progress was often extolled. Excerpts for Hagarty Township, surveyed in 1862 by Provincial Land Surveyor (PLS) Robert Hamilton, illustrate this point. "The soil is rich and generally fertile ... Hagarty is not mountainous ... there are a few rocky declivities ... but, taken as a whole, the surface is not rugged; the slopes are even, or gently undulating ... it is, therefore, well adapted for the construction of roads."⁶¹ A quick look at

5.3   A settlers' hut along the Opeongo in 1901. The residents harvested a crop of potatoes on this rugged land.

surveys created after the initial settlement of Polish-Kashubs, such as those used by local authors, proves otherwise.

However, Devine, consistent with a proper believer in progress and Victorian science, believed that swamps and marshes in the townships "could be brought along by settlers."[62] The authenticity of surveying was supported by the power of the surveyor and the veneer of Victorian science. In the words of McGee, the Bureau of Agriculture relied on the land surveyors when selecting an area "considered most suitable for settlement."[63] This belief was then passed on to the agents, who believed – or were led to believe – similar sentiments. For example, in 1859, French wrote to P.M. Vankoughnet claiming that the land beyond Brennan's Creek was of very inferior quality. However, French had little familiarity with the land beyond (this will be discussed later) and this claim was intended to push the agenda of free grants as opposed to the sale of lands for capital. French felt that such land far in the interior could not be sold. If it was instead given away, settlement plans could continue.[64] In this sense, French, too, was a believer in Victorian

5.4 Settlers toiled with their hands and with animals to clear land for farming. Oxen could pull heavier loads, live on coarse feed, and be slaughtered for meat. Horses, however, moved faster, were easier to handle, and ate less. This photo was taken near Madawaska, Ontario, c. 1900.

science. If given land free of charge, a group of settlers could shape the land from wilderness into settlements.[65]

James W. Bridgland, a surveyor who was put in charge of maintenance of the roads for the Department of Crown Lands, also endorsed the inventory sciences' conclusions about whether the land was good. He wrote in 1861 that the measure of good land was gauged by whether crops could grow. "Indisputable proofs" of good soil existed if crops of wheat, peas, potatoes, and turnips were growing (see figures 5.3 and 5.4). Since there were many farms, and more land past Lake Clear was being cleared, Bridgland also believed that the land was arable and considered it "prosperous and progressive."[66]

If the plots of land did not produce, the fault, in the nineteenth century, lay with the farmer, not the surveyor. An 1880 letter to the editor of the *Renfrew Mercury* entitled, "Why go West? Is the Ottawa Valley too poor for farming, or is it too poorly farmed?" illustrates this point. The author, "Progress," argued that failed farms were the result of poor knowledge of crops, poor care of stock in the winter, and "too little capital" for the purchase of new machinery, the "mistake ... by many of our farmers ... in allowing the low land to remain uncleared, while they devote all their time to cultivating the high lands."[67] Robert Jones also argues this sentiment. According to a government report, settlers were often to blame for the poorer soil on account of their poor agricultural methods as "the clearance ... of everything most likely to maintain its productiveness ... [left] a gradual drain upon and reduction of the quality of land."[68]

Over time, the legitimacy and limits of Victorian science have been exposed. Gentilcore mentions the difficulties in surveying such a territory, saying that "the first surveys could only be carried out superficially. The surveyor was confronted with a host of difficulties including rugged or swampy terrain, largely forest covered, and the lack of experience help and proper equipment."[69] When making the decision to open the Opeongo, the Bureau of Agriculture put its trust in the inventory sciences of PLS Bell. Accordingly, the Bureau wrote that "Mr. Bell's line crosses the red pine section where it presents most fertile land; he has selected the location with much care and judgment."[70] But the practices of the surveyors were not as rigorous as once thought. In fact, the inventories taken by Bell and his team are quite dubious.

According to the diary of assistant surveyor Hamlet Burritt, Bell himself was absent from the survey from 23 April 1851 to 5 February 1852. By that time, the crew had hacked its way past "Barries Bay" and returned back past Lake Clear, almost returning to Renfrew.[71] A.H. Sims – who the Bureau described as "a civil engineer of much experience in road making"[72] – was also often a week behind in his notes, according to Burritt. To complicate matters, Sims, a comical character, often broke his instruments, as was the case on 10 August 1851, became ill, and was generally lazy. While blazing through the wilderness, Bell's hired hands often got lost and injured. According to Burritt, this was expected of a crew that had "never [been] on a survey before."[73] Devine's own 1861 map was not entirely accurate either. His measurements of Kamaniskeg Lake hardly resemble the detailed measurements and sketch supplied by Murray, the GSC geologist, in 1853.[74] In 1862, French wrote to the Commissioner of Crown Lands that there was a dispute among settlers as to where the boundaries between the townships of Hagarty and Brudenell were. Bell also wrote to Devine in 1863 asking him to clarify several items because he had found that several lines in Radcliffe and Hagarty had not been run and the plans supplied by the office for the latter township had not solved the problem. More errors were found in the late 1860s. Russell found discrepancies and errors between townships and timber surveys as long as two miles.[75]

The route that the surveyors took to create a road through to Opeongo Lake also ignored the terrain. After turning northwest in the vicinity of the present-day settlement of Dacre, the survey of the road proceeded in a diagonal line (without significant diversions of more than a couple of hundred metres) toward the supposed end-point of the road. While such terrain was passable for the surveyors, who were on foot, a portion of the road between Hopefield and Barry's Bay (lots 223 to 197 Range B) was deemed too steep for team traffic and closed in 1886. Now called the "missing link," the road blazed by the survey crew rose from approximately 366 metres above sea level, to a peak of around 472 metres, and down to around 304 metres in less than 5 kilometres.[76] While this may function as after-the-fact proof of shoddy surveying work, because these 1850s observations and notations were made by men of the inventory sciences, they were considered truthful and dictated future development.

The Chronology of Progress and Settlement along the Opeongo

Even though the information supplied by the surveyors was often misleading, the progress of surveying did not match the progress of settlement and the demands for land. Theoretically, proper road allowances and lot lines should be in place before settlement. Although the road was cut all the way to Opeongo Lake by Bell's (aka Burritt's) crew, proper road construction and documentation was far behind. In 1856, French asked (again) to be given a list of lots available and their acreage since he was unaware of both. He wrote firmly that he could not hand out property "in ignorance of the contents of the lot." In the meantime, he attempted to travel the first 50 miles of the road "for the purpose of ascertaining its condition." Unfortunately, the road was not passable past Brennan's Creek (the western branch, just outside Brudenell) and, as a result, French was not familiar with the territory beyond.[77]

French remarked that by 1858 the Opeongo Road was still only a good road for the first 50 miles. He asked his department to make it passable the entire way to Lake Opeongo to induce settlement. That summer, the new section to Lake Opeongo was still unfinished. French granted almost all of the lots up to Brennan's Creek and again asked that the territory beyond be cleared and opened for settlement traffic. "Had it been even partially made for some twenty miles further settlement would have extended westward."[78] Thus, to suggest that French knew precisely the capability of the lands when he started assigning lots past Brennan's Creek to the Poles in 1859 is problematic. This is the reason why French, in 1860, stated to Vankoughnet that "scarcely a lot is unoccupied" where the road has been completed and "a few have been granted beyond the point to which it has been made." He also stated that more townships needed to be surveyed so settlement did not precede the survey.[79] Little did he know that the elevation beyond was much steeper.

As a result, by the time groups of Poles had been located on the Opeongo as far west as Barry's Bay, other "blank" spaces needed to be filled in. Surveys were ordered and initiated to devour several spaces on the map, namely the Townships of Hagarty, Richards, Burns, and Sherwood, which had been calculated by PLS Hamilton in 1860. PLS Forrest did the same for Jones Township in 1862. Unfortunately, Hamilton was only instructed to survey the boundaries for the aforementioned townships. As a result, Forrest was hired in June 1861 to subdivide Sherwood Township into lots.[80] In the meantime, the demands of settlement meant that lots were being granted that were beyond French's store of knowledge. Thus, the combination of poor information derived from surveyors and the slow development of the Opeongo hardly rendered road agents in a position to knowingly deceive settlers. Gentilcore wrote that there "is little indication that survey information was used by writers of emigrant guides,"[81] such as French and others. Once concerns about the quality of land came to light in the 1860s, it was perhaps a different story – one beyond the scope of this study.[82]

Yet, it is doubtful that the settlers' words of protest would have changed the minds of officials in the 1850s and early 1860s, anyway. Knowledge from the modern policy sciences was privileged over the knowledge of ordinary farmers. The settlers' knowledge was often ignored, as was evident in the protests of farmers, like Ezra Stevens. After all, they were the ones who were supposed to reshape the land – not complain about it. In the words of Walsh, the colonization of the Ottawa-Huron Tract was fraught with problems "buried in behind the veneer of professionalism and scientism that surrounded the Provincial Land Surveyor and his new rigorous practices by the late 1860s."[83]

The Agro-Forest Economy in the Ottawa-Huron Tract

The creation of clearings and farms along the Opeongo was itself an agent of change; however, there was another agent of change in the territory in the early part of the nineteenth century – forestry. When Champlain travelled across the land in 1615, he was not impressed with the forest's potential. "Any pines he saw as suitable for naval masts and spars were too distant from saltwater ports to be of any use." Champlain intended to form settlements based on agriculture alone.[84] A source of pristine virgin pine and oak, the Ottawa Valley later supplied timber for the British navy during the Napoleonic Wars. As David Lee writes, "few residents of the Valley lived lives untouched by the pursuit of pine." Around 1820, adventurous loggers started harvesting along the Madawaska River and in 1849 John Egan opened two mills along the Bonnechere River. By 1847, timber licenses were granted for about 2,000 square miles around the Madawaska River. By the 1850s, 10,000 men were working in shanties in the Ottawa Valley and along the Madawaska.[85] However, as loggers pushed further and further into the interior, their supply lines grew further and further away from populated areas. As a result, there were potential market benefits if agricultural settlements were founded.[86] Timber baron John Egan – "the dominant square-timber producer in all of Canada" – became an MLA in 1851[87] and continually advocated for infrastructure to transport timber from the interior and agriculture to supply the camps.[88] Part of the expansionist beliefs of Victorian science included symbiotically balancing two industries, agriculture and forestry. Few of the local authors address intersecting policies for colonization and forestry,[89] but it is a subject of great importance because it attempted to formulate a balance between the two to transform the wilderness into a productive space.

The nineteenth-century relationship between agriculture and forestry was traditionally a controversial one. When lumbering was first in an area, settlement was seen as a nuisance. Where settlement preceded forestry, it was a "distracting and malignant influence."[90] Lumber companies often blamed the destruction of the forests, through ignorant clearance or burning, on settlers.[91] Once the Opeongo Road was cut, it was frequently used by lumberjacks to freight supplies into the interior. As a result, it has been argued that the two industries were meant to cooperate for mutual commercial benefit.[92] Since the time of Champlain, argues Lee, thinking had changed and a mutually dependent formula was considered.[93] The agro-forest economy had been practised unsuccessfully in other areas, such as New Brunswick, but it was still tried in the Ottawa Valley.[94] When Egan made the request for the creation of the Opeongo, the government saw it as an opportunity to find the balance between the two industries.[95] They had colonization in mind and the lumberjacks needed transportation routes. The business elite also favoured agricultural colonization. The idea was that the farmer would harvest and sell his crops to the lumber camps, thus profiting from the venture. French also believed this, writing that continued progress of the survey and settlement would benefit the lumber industry. These developments, alongside the increased supply traffic along the road, in his mind, were "calculated to promote the interests of the county" and were made in the name of progress.[96] Forestry existed in the area before settlement, though, and there was a de facto agro-forest economy before it became government policy. Needless to say, the "image of the yeoman farmer and a great deal of agrarian rhetoric were in the air."[97]

In order for this balance to work, agriculture and forestry could not be too close geographically. After all, the economy of the Ottawa Valley was dictated by the investments in and the development of the timber industry. As Lower concludes, the economy initially succeeded in the Ottawa Valley, compared with other areas, because there was more space between the farmer and logger. On the other hand, its "success" may have had more to do with the chronology of development in the tract. According to J.I. Little, many clashes were caused in the St Francis district because timber licenses were being issued at the same time that colonization roads were being developed.[98] This was not the case in the Ottawa-Huron Tract where timber licenses were granted before colonization. If located close enough to logging roads or shanties, local farmers could supply their goods at a profit as they "enjoyed a near-monopoly in items such as hay, oats, and livestock."[99] Chad Gaffield argues similarly, saying that it was too costly to transport some desired products, such as potatoes, hay, and oats, so they had to be obtained from local farmers.[100]

In the Ottawa-Huron Tract, before the colonization roads were in place, lumber barons needed supplies for the camps. In 1836, Peter Aylen advertised for 40 head of oxen to be slaughtered on arrival at his shanties in the Madawaska, Bonnechere, and Gatineau, as well as for 1,700 bushels of oats. A few years into the colonization scheme, John Robertson wrote that the area represented "cash markets for all produce," and Albert Smallfield, the editor of the *Renfrew Mercury*, wrote that the early settlers found a market for their goods.[101] In the 1870s, the symbiotic relationship was still working as "the lumber shanties afford a certain and profitable market for all the settler's surplus produce of Beef, Pork, Flour, Peas, Potatoes, Oats and Hay." Evidence of the relationship was seen in an 1872 publication that claimed that settlers in the tract "are generally poor ... but in the vicinity of lumbering operations they get the advantage of all the roads and bridges used in taking off the timber ... were it not for these advantages, the pioneer settlers would be shut up in the bush and isolated from all markets; whereas the lumberer provides a market almost at his door for everything the settler can raise."[102]

Supplemental income could be earned in the process as part of the symbiotic relationship. "In the wintertime, when [farmers] and their horses were underemployed, farmers could take cash-paying jobs in the shanties."[103] John Robertson, in 1855, reported that "any farmer who can spare time in Winter, for himself or team, either can have employment from the lumberers at high wages, paid in money. A man and a pair of horses get from 6s. 3d. upwards to 10s and fed per day, for drawing timber and supplies; which enables a man with a small clearance to keep good horses, and to pay a hired man, which he could not do otherwise." Indeed, farmers in the Upper Ottawa River were fetching £4 per ton of hay (a high price to begin with) and those near the headwaters of the Madawaska were receiving £10 per ton, according to Jones.[104] This seasonal economy seemed to work, especially considering that Bytown prices were acknowledged to be the highest in Upper Canada.[105] After all, the boom months in the lumber industry occurred when farmers could not grow crops – between November and March. This, says Little, was also one of the benefits for lumber companies who sided with the agro-forestry scheme. By the 1880s, about 8,000 shantymen were employed in Ontario.[106] Seasonal participation in the forestry industry, however, produced other economic benefits and, as in the St Francis district and Prescott County, the farmer-lumberjack was quite common.

However, as time went on, several issues surfaced. Bruce Elliott argues that timber contracting "facilitated investment in agriculture to an extent that would not otherwise have been possible in a region where the natural endowments of land and climate were limited. Though these farms took sustenance from the infusion of mercantile and timber capital, they remained susceptible to sudden changes of fortune if the businessmen aimed to run [farms] ... as adjuncts to their commercial enterprises."[107] Thus, farmers were tied to the rise and fall of the lumber industry. J.R. Booth is one example of a lumberer who operated an adjunct farm. To cut costs, he opened his own farm at the Opeongo River depot, raising pigs, cows, and over 100 chickens.[108] This brings into perspective another issue, as Normand Seguin shows, via examples from the agro-forestry economy in the Saguenay region. In a Marxist sense, the long-term dominance of large corporations, often founded by the bourgeoisie, and agriculture, pursued by family-run farms, led to the underdevelopment of a region.[109] In this manner, the market created by the corporations lasted only as long as the corporations, and the timber, would permit. Once the timber frontier moved on, the work and market declined rapidly, "leaving behind an underdeveloped poverty pocket devoid of both."[110]

The pioneer farmers were affected differently by the balancing equation that was the agro-forest economy. In the words of R. Cole Harris, "some pioneer families were defeated by the forest; for them pioneering was simply too hard. Some pioneers by vocation, sold and moved. Another option was to find off-farm work, which many men and some young women did."[111] On a local scale, several Polish pioneers fit into these categories. The families of Joseph Grzenia and Peter Kaldunski abandoned their Opeongo attempt and moved to Portage County and Pine Creek, Wisconsin, in the 1850s and 1860s. Paul Libera and his wife Antonina Dolna left and relocated to Winona, Minnesota, in 1860. John Rogala's family did the same. Albert Omernik and August Flis left for the Polonia/Stevens Point, Wisconsin, area c. 1866. John Lica and his wife Mary Suszek moved to Pontiac County, Quebec, with their family in the 1860s. Jacob Grzenia and his wife Antonina moved their family from Hagarty Township to Minneapolis, Minnesota, in January 1879. John Szala moved in 1881 and later settled in Perham, Minnesota. His brother August moved to Seattle, Washington, in 1891. Michael Grudnowski's family, after arriving in 1858, left for Minnesota in the 1880s. The Jezierskis left for Oregon during this time as well. Francis Kubik left for Hennepin County, Minnesota, around 1890. Several other families relocated to lots in the surrounding area. Joseph Szala moved from 191-2 Range B North to 215-6 Range B North in 1862. The Waldochs moved from 201-3 Range B North to Renfrew before the 1871 census. Tomas Szulist moved from 221-2 Range B North to lot 29, concession 3, Hagarty Township, in 1873 and Walenti Etmanski abandoned his lots at 222-3 Range B South and moved to Sherwood Township, lots 7 and 8, concession 9, in 1882.[112]

French also mentioned that the Poles hired out themselves or their children as servants whenever they could. Through this employment, they learned some English.[113] In the Renfrew area especially, such employment was plentiful. According to an 1871 edition of the *Renfrew Mercury*, labour "of all kinds is in great demand at present and the supply is scarce ... Active young men, industrious and willing to work will find that Renfrew offers, at present, as good chances of employment as any part of Canada ... Servant girls, especially, are very much wanted all round this neighbourhood, and quite a good number could obtain good situations immediately." Several females "worked out" (of the home) as servants, such as Margaret Szulist, who worked for the Walsh family in the 1860s; Mary Szulist, who worked for the Coltons in the 1860s; and Mary Kiedrowski, who found employment with the McCarthy family of Brudenell after arriving in the early 1870s. For those who moved to Portage County, Wisconsin, agriculture or off-farm labour was not in demand as it was in Renfrew County and prospects were not always better. Cradling lumber in Portage County netted 50 cents a day; digging potatoes paid 25 cents a day. Women earned one loaf of bread per day. A teenage girl could earn $15 and board for one year of employment, though working in a lumber camp, sawmill, or on the river run near Polonia, Rosholt, or Holt, Wisconsin, could net $15–20 a month.[114]

Others, and their progeny, remained and participated in the agroforest economy in the Ottawa Valley. Although monetary amounts are not recorded, it is said that an original settler, Adam Prince, supplied "the lumber camps with beef and pork ... and hay and oates [*sic*] for the horses" and was extolled by the *Renfrew Mercury* for his "shrewdness."

John Etmanski, the son of Walenti, was a "jobber" for the Campbell and McNab lumber companies. He capitalized on the seasonal market, employed men to go into the forest in the winter, and housed them at his own quarters to save money.[115] Another second-generation farmer, Antoine Ritza, became a foreman near the turn of the century. The trend of families participating in the agro-forest economy also continued beyond the turn of the century. A Barry's Bay reporter, writing about two lumberjacks, Adolph Etmanski and Nelson Olsheskie, and their jobs with J.R. Booth's company, stated that "most of the men that worked in the bush got their first experience lumbering from working on their own farms at home. After they reached an age where they had to go out and work, they would use their experience and get a job in the lumber camps."[116] Before the First World War, Alex Shalla worked as a labourer for the Omanique Lumber Company for a wage of $1.50 per day.[117] Around 1917, when he was still young, John Mintha went to work in the lumber camps in the winter. Ambrose Pick also came from a farming family, yet went into the camps to work when he was fifteen. Joe Luckasavitch's experience was similar: he worked for J.R. Booth and McRae. Others ventured further afield for work when the lumber companies moved into Northwestern Ontario. In 1916, Angus Prince, John Luckasavitch, Frank Etmanski, Edward Luckasavitch, Angus Chapeskie, and Joe Chapeskie worked for Swader's Lumber Company in the Parry Sound area. Across the area, wages c. 1900 for general hands ranged from $18–$25 a month (including board), middle-range shantymen received $25–$40, cooks earned $40–$45, hewers took in $45–$60, and foremen brought home $50–$75. But by the 1930s, locals were lucky to earn 50 cents a day working closer to home for McCrae Lumber.[118]

Little also argues that although they did not have timber rights, some settlers in the St Francis district "supplied the lumber companies with logs not as wage earners but independent farmers."[119] There are no records to show that the Polish settlers participated in such sales since the timber rights on their plots were also the property of the Crown and its timber licenses. When applying for land under the Free Grants and Homesteads Act (1868), part of the petition stipulated that settlers not harvest or sell the pine beyond what was needed for building, fencing, or fuel – until a patent deed was obtained. Earlier legislation, the 1849 Timber Act, also limited timbermen and companies from cutting anywhere outside their timber berths or licensed areas. However, there were disputes where berths and the right to deeded property overlapped or where there were species other than pine. Such overlaps occurred between McLaughlin Bros. Lumber Company and Opeongo settlers Anthony Prinz (Range B South 226 and 227), Anthony Zybert (Range B South 232 and 233), Mattias Szczypior (Range B North 212 and 213), and Matthias Piekarski (Range B North 223 and 224). This was the cause of some angst among Valley settlers as shown by an 1872 article in the *Renfrew Mercury*. The Free Grants policy, whereby settlers had to be on the land for five years before they could apply for and be granted a deed, was "a flagrant defect" considering that lumbermen with berths could "take off the timber even after the settler has entered upon the land, and indeed, right up to the very day upon which he receives his deed."[120] Nonetheless, even after obtaining a deed, so their plots could provide some income multiple settlers sold the timber on their property to McLaughlin, such as Prinz, Zybert (1870), John Szala, Matthias and Michael Szczypior, Matthias Piekarski, John Blaszkowski (1872), and August Flis (1878). In the process of clearing, it is also possible that pine or other timber may have been sold, which benefitted both the settler and the timber baron. An old trick of timbermen was to claim that the timber came from private property rather than Crown land and was therefore exempt from duties. Whether or not these settlers faced the strong arm of the law is unknown.[121] Like the French-Canadians in the St Francis area, the Poles participated in the forestry industry as a way to survive since the miserly land-granting system denied them access to all the valuable timber that grew on their property.

Others supplemented their income, which helped them survive, by procuring employment on road building crews (see figure 5.5). Several of the original settlers earned extra wages when the roads were in need of repair due to wear from settlement and forestry traffic – a topic not addressed in local historical literature. Once the contracts were tendered, several local pioneers sought work as labourers. August Flis, John Pershick, Matthew Chippure, August Yantha, Paul Shalla, and Francis Prince all worked on the road in the summer of 1866. That same fall, Flis, Pershick, Chippure, Yantha, Shalla, Prince, Francis Bloskie, Joseph Sadowski, Thomas Dombroski, and Paul Shalla Jr gained

5.5 Road and rail cutting crews relied on brute strength and the assistance of horses and wagons. The work was tough but any money helped a family in need. This photo was taken by John Walter Le Breton Ross near Algonquin Park in 1894.

up to a month's employment. These labourers earned about $1 per day and were required to be away with the road team for several weeks.[122]

Yet even though many descendants of the original settlers participated in the agro-forest economy, whose added income helped them survive, local authors have not analyzed it as an integral part of the colonization plan for the Ottawa-Huron Tract. Coming back to the notion that the interaction between large corporations and family farms can leave areas vulnerable to decline and underdevelopment, we turn to the arguments of Smallfield, Miller, and Rekowski. Unwittingly, they illustrate Seguin and Elliott's points when applied to the Opeongo: that the decline in the timber industry negatively affected the region and led to a period of decline. As early as 1881, Smallfield claimed that some settlers worked too much for lumbering companies, which "led to their farms being neglected ... This embarrassed the owners and as the lumbering districts receded ... many of the farms were sold in order to realize the means of settling [elsewhere]." Miller writes that when the timber market disappeared in the 1890s, poorer farming areas were abandoned and farms clustered in "better" soil areas. Rekowski agrees, but argued that residents of Wilno, Barry's Bay, and Madawaska were able to survive due to their proximity to the interior forests, until a further decline in the 1930s and 1940s.[123]

Gaffield reminds us that in Prescott County, land was "required as a basis for family economies." This land could be relied upon in times of economic duress.[124] However, if we combine the notion that a few years after settlement the sandy and sloping terrain near the Opeongo was losing its agricultural capability with the fact that the supplemental income from the shanties was declining, farmers in the area were left in dire straits. Jones echoes these conclusions and wrote that when lumbermen paid high prices and hired farmers in the winter, times were good. But when the shanties hired less and moved further away, settlers found that "after a few crops of grain, and perhaps several of hay, the thin vegetable mould of their sandy clearances would be exhausted."[125] According to Miller, this happened along the Opeongo as the timber barons moved into Northwestern Ontario and "a smaller, more localized lumber industry took [their] place."[126]

Looking at the Ottawa Valley's output of pine timber from Crown land and its share of total output for the Province of Canada provides a glimpse into this period of decline. According to Lee, the valley's output was 11,578,554 cubic feet which accounted for 93 per cent of total Canadian output in 1856. By 1889, it had dropped to 2,715,180 cubic feet and only accounted for 50 per cent of the total output for Ontario and Quebec. The proportion of Ottawa Valley pine sawlogs cut on Crown land relative to the proportion cut in the Provinces of Ontario and Quebec had also started to decline by the 1890s. Between 1856 and 1890, the proportion varied between 50 per cent and 61 per cent but by 1891 it had dipped to 42.3 per cent and by 1893 only accounted for 39.7 per cent of cut pine sawlogs. Lee also argues that one of the reasons the barons moved further away to Northwestern Ontario was because of the shortage of large trees. Although it was uncommon to have logs as large as 100 cubic feet, by the twentieth century it was difficult to find one of even 40 cubic feet. In fact, in 1889, sawlog cutting in Northwestern Ontario surpassed that of the Ottawa Valley.[127]

Ironically, Jones also argues that having a good road, after a decade or two of settlement, actually lowered local market prices and helped to produce declines because supplies could be carted in from larger centres like Ottawa.[128] This point is more marked when we consider that J.R. Booth built a company railway through the tract in 1893–94 – at the same time as Miller's "period of decline."[129] Booth also started to saw lumber year-round at this time because he no longer had to rely on ground conditions to transport it.[130] As a result of the disappearance of the shanty market and the struggle to survive, many farmers in the Ottawa-Huron Tract were left with lingering doubts about the success of the settlement and the free grant schemes. To combat these, as well as claims that their own actions had also led to their demise, settlers were prompted to question the foresight of the officials who had promoted these ventures.

Although Rekowski argues that the Wilno and Barry's Bay area began to decline in the 1930s and 1940s, it appears that the localized timber industry that took over after the barons left did provide some reliable employment for locals during the Great Depression until the Second World War. Unfortunately, decades later, the region is still feeling the effects of the declining lumber industry because employment has been affected by US softwood lumber taxes from the 1980s and 1990s. Murray Brothers Lumber Company Ltd., one of the region's largest employers, and a mainstay since the era of J.R. Booth, has even had to halt sawing at times.[131] This leaves many residents wondering about the status of the industry that supported the region for over 150 years. However, a new industry – tourism – has emerged. As chapter 7 will outline, the area has benefitted from regional, ethnic, and international tourism.

Conclusion

In the nineteenth-century migration of Polish-Kashubs from an overcrowded space to a land with ample space, local memory has continued several narratives about the land. In several instances, local authors have accused Crown agents of deliberately deceiving the Polish settlers by giving them land they knew was poor. Several of these authors provide other concluding thoughts, too. Rekowski lifts a statement from Miller, without citing it, and contrasts his previous arguments by writing that "the agents were neither villains nor fools, but hard working men caught up in a vision of the future for the Shield, the settlers and themselves."[132] Unfortunately, Rekowski did not expand on this idea. Prince, like Rekowski, unwittingly contrasts her earlier comment that the agents knew the land was rocky by stating, without sourcing archival material, that the lots the Polish-Kashubs received were "officially classified as not suitable for farming, but [agents] were initially unaware of this."[133] Though these concluding statements point vaguely to a greater force at work (the knowledge produced by Victorian science), local authors have not situated and compared any nineteenth-century paradigms of colonization, science, agriculture, and forestry. It is only by doing so that alternative perspectives can be brought to the fore.

The sophistry that elevated the surveyor and his scientific knowledge was deceptive. Although advocates of colonization and the inventory sciences brought a "sense of spatial order to the tract," agents were influenced by the "rigorous" practices of these sciences and their counterparts in the surveying branch who promoted the idea that the land was productive. If the terrain was thought to be rougher than agents claimed it to be, the paradigms of the time, influenced by expansionist nationalism and Victorian ideas of progress, dictated that man could overcome the land and make it productive. As a result, Walsh concludes that even though "some local agents displayed much empathy and often sympathy for the struggles of settlers, these agents were unable to meet the settlers' needs. They were, however, required to satisfy the needs of their political masters."[134]

Since local interests were often ignored, because more weight was placed on the knowledge produced by literate and educated bureaucrats, the written record of the Polish-Kashub community exhibits disdain toward these employees. However, when the influence of the agro-forest economy in the creation of the colonization roads is considered, it is parochial to evaluate the colonization scheme as solely an agricultural venture. In this paradigm, since forestry was practised in the Ottawa-Huron Tract first, agriculture was meant to supplement the industry, provide a market for farmers, and establish civilized, governable spaces in the wilderness. Even if the intentions of this symbiotic relationship are dismissed, "environmental limitations to agricultural commercialization, dictated that a mixed agri-forest economy was essential to the long-term survival of the settler community."[135] Indeed, geographical determinism holds that the "physical environment shaped the nature of the new society through its ordering of the economic activity that sustained the community." What began as patches of brushed land linked by bush roads became a landscape, both physical and cultural. Just like the Ukrainians' experience in an area of Manitoba that some believed "should never have been opened for homestead settlement," the area developed an economy and a "dynamic set of intra- and inter-ethnic social relations."[136] In the end, the limits of Victorian science were exposed because it did not factor human observation and error into the equation. In trying to experiment with the balance between forestry and agriculture in the Ottawa-Huron Tract, believers in Victorian science forgot to include the territory itself as a variable.

The question remains as to why there are still such negative sentiments toward the agents. After considering the circumstances under which the Polish settlers emigrated, Rekowski's idea that they received poor land because they were unwanted fits well with the narrative of exile and continuous discrimination. Combined with the consequences of the decline in the lumber industry and its effect on the local population, one might wonder if the functions of such narratives are to portray the settlers as, in the words of Basu, "more sinned against than sinning."[137] In this subversive narrative, notions of Victorian science (that settlers could transform the land) are struck down and culpability is removed from the settlers. They can feel solace in the fact that their ancestors were deceived when they look at the homestead and see the abandoned, rotting log buildings.

As the opening quote from Tuan says, to be free and open is to be vulnerable. Thus, with freedom, a certain responsibility in attaining "success" rests upon the individual settler. But today, even if some responsibility for the outcome is placed on settlers due to their choice of plot (likely what was left along the road) and because they did not practise "proper" farming techniques,[138] believers in the "exiled and sinned against" paradigm are provided with another defensive narrative from Rekowski. This other narrative absolves settlers from culpability, since Rekowski also claims that the "Kashubs [had] a tendency, a penchant, to choose 'second best' and to prefer 'isolation' ... [because] they had historically been so beaten down, [and] impoverished" in their homeland.[139] Their naiveté is not present in this narrative. Instead, blame for the choice is deflected back to their German conquerors, continuing the cycle of "sinned against."

Yet the resonance of government deception is not unique to the Polish group. According to Little, French-Canadians ascribe blame toward agents of colonization – French-Canadian elites and Roman

Catholic priests – who encouraged peasants to settle on marginal rural land in Eastern Quebec. Orest Martynowych and John Lehr argue that groups of Ukrainians in Western Canada created subversive narratives after facing hardships in a less fertile area. These subversive narratives are similar to those constructed by the Polish-Kashubs. With the Ukrainian narrative in mind, it appears that such narratives may survive because the settlers' expectations of agricultural prosperity in Canada were not met. However, as John Lehr writes, historians and historical geographers have argued, from other philosophical standpoints, that Ukrainian settlement on marginal land was due to a variety of causes such as "ignorance of alternative opportunities; lack of better lands open to settlement; erroneous evaluation of land capability; and an overwhelming determination to secure timber on their homestead." Lehr also argues that there is no documentary evidence to suggest that the government directed them, on purpose, to inferior land.[140] The same appears to be true for the Polish-Kashub group.

As the colonization scheme turned wilderness into governable spaces-in-the-making, it is evident that communities, histories, and memories were also created. In top-down studies of colonization roads, many of these histories and memories were ignored or written out of the narrative. Whereas the previous pages have outlined the often subversive histories and memories of one group along the Opeongo, others, such as the Irish and German groups, have their own set of histories. Their views may be similar or different, depending on their place and time along the line.[141]

We should also remember that at the time, settlers could not comprehend such narratives and their function, because, in the words of Jane Errington, "Generally uneducated, most did not have the time or the inclination, other than perhaps in times of crisis, to reflect on anything which did not directly impinge on their daily struggle for survival." Roy MacGregor echoes this idea: most were so busy with "survival that they had little or no time to intellectualize the experience."[142] However, today we are able to analyze such themes and the resonance of such narratives. Now that more knowledge about this narrative has been produced, the debate continues ...

PART II
CULTURAL REDEFINITION

6

The Origins and Development of the Kashubian Label

As argued in chapter 1, local residents thought their ethnicity was Polish. Their churches, schools, and some postwar migrants from the homeland reinforced this. However, a second invention of ethnicity has happened more recently because of a body of knowledge that crossed the Atlantic. Despite the fact that several Polish postwar migrants attempted to educate locals about their Kashubian heritage, the second invention started when a local priest, Fr Rekowski, claimed in the 1980s and 1990s that the locals were not Polish. Building on his ideas, the Wilno Heritage Society was established in 1998. As a result, local authors, genealogists, community boosters, and descendants have looked to the homeland for connections. In doing so, they stumbled upon Kaszubian cultural movements promoted by the Zrzeszenie Kaszubsko-Pomorskie (Kashubian Pomerania Association or KPA). Following the KPA's descriptions, the WHS rebranded the settlers in the Wilno and Barry's Bay area with new, essentialist cultural descriptions separate from Polish.

However, in the process, the literature produced on the group in Canada has not explored the origins, the diffusion, the creation, and the promotion of the Kaszubian identity in Poland.[1] Several explanations for this lack of attention come to mind. Not much literature has been written on the topic in the land of departure and the language divide has prevented the exchange of knowledge via in-depth conversations and analysis.[2] Many KPA members cannot speak fluent English and many WHS members cannot speak fluent Polish. In fact, the two contemporary publications that peer into the creation of the Kaszubian identity accessible to English-language readers were translated and published only a few years ago.[3] It can also be argued that for some descendants in Canada the homeland identity is simply of ancient and uncomplicated provenance and thus does not need further analysis. But before analyzing the functions of the celebrations and cultural redefinition in Canada's first Polish community in part II, we need to investigate its origins in the homeland. While this investigation seeks the roots of certain practices and symbols, it also seeks to establish their acceptance as cohesive and continuous with a suitable historic past. The undertaking of such a venture also accomplishes another goal set out at the beginning of this study: expanding on the avenues opened by historical memory in the area of settlement.

Tracing and Constructing the Folk

Research into the origins and self-determination of collectivities, ethnicities, and identities in Europe is not an easy endeavour. As Miroslav Hroch argues, one of the common errors committed in poorly researched histories is the confusion between the ideology of "nationalism" and the existence of the social group or "nation." Though both are constructed concepts, the latter's application among the folk has received much attention since the Enlightenment.[4]

Subsequently, the rise of Romanticism during the seventeenth and eighteenth centuries brought about Johan Gottfried Herder's consolidation and popularization of the concept of the *volk* (folk).[5] As illustrated in chapter 2, the Enlightenment critiqued tradition and religion as ignorant and fanatic. Herder critiqued "modern" beliefs, separated the aristocracy and learned class from the common population, and argued that the practices of the folk were legitimate areas of study. Furthermore, he argued that the culture of the folk held a certain "natural core" before being corrupted by society. Evolving into "one of the great abstractions of Romanticism, 'the Folk' came to be regarded as the epitome of simple truth, work, and virtue, the antithesis of all that was overcivilized" and modern. The folk is also a construct that does not, but is often thought to, coincide with biological ideas of blood or race. In this sense, it was, perhaps, the essence of a "national" identity. According to Ian McKay, belief in the concept of the folk opposed class divisions, the progress of the "urban, industrial world – that *Gesellschaft* of modernity, of contracts and class divisions, and of that scourge of the oral culture of the folk, the printed word."[6] Accordingly, the concept of the folk is often defined as embodied in an informal or subversive mentality in a region, passed on through oral tradition, and lacking certain forms of structural organization[7] – compared with the delineations of a formally recognized state or monarchy. Tracing the emergence of a social or folk group as a distinctive cluster by using printed documents is thus inherently problematic. Despite the backward-looking qualities of "the folk" and their lack of written history, their existence continues to affect the construction of many identities and politics into the twenty-first century.

The emergence of the Kaszubian identity, as a mentality and as a formally recognized folk collectivity, was far from linear and emerged in fits and starts with socio-political developments. Originating either from a vernacular term for a peasant's garment or a ducal Latin title that implied a people called the Cassubs, the concept of being Kaszubian existed in the minds of a few intellectuals in the nineteenth century, was solidified through material culture, museums, and the craft revival at the turn of the twentieth century, and inspired research attention because of interwar political boundary disputes. It was an elite-driven movement of the intelligentsia after the Second World War but attempted to cross class boundaries and reach out to the local populations after the fall of the Soviet Union – just in time to be picked up by Canadians.

The origins of the term "Cassub" and its subsequent variations and applications have been discussed by several authors. As the Polish historian Gerard Labuda remarks, it is important to examine its origins to see whether the group of people adopted the topographical name of the area or vice versa.[8] The answer to that question, however, is buried in the European past.

Early Origins of the Inhabitants of the Vistula River Valley

Writing in *The Slavonic Review* in 1933, Vladimir Polyakov traced the movement of Slavic people into the Vistula River Valley by examining the writings of the father of Russian chronology, a monk named Nestor. According to Nestor, these Slavs called themselves *Lechi* (see figure 6.1). Similarly, Alexander Majkowski, in *Historia Kaszubów*, declared the Slavic people of the Vistula valley to be *Wieletami* (or *Veleti*). Labuda also wrote that an early Ruthenian chronicler considered the

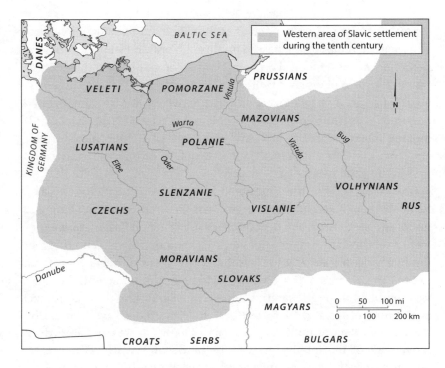

6.1 Slavic peoples in Central Europe during the tenth century.

Veleti a group of the *Lechi*.[9] Nonetheless, the *Lechi* evolved into two groups of people based on "circumstances of environment." They were the men of the fields – *poljane* (or Poles) – and the men of the seaboard – *pomorjane* or (Pomeranians) – whom Polyakov labelled "Kashubs."[10] These labels were also recorded by the German chronicler, Helmond, in the twelfth century. The thirteenth-century Polish chronicler, Vincent Kadłubek, called them *maritime* (coastal peoples) and Danish chronicles describe the river valley people as *polonia*. Friedrich Lorentz, a linguist and ethnographer from Mecklenburg, corroborated the use of the name *pomorani* in thirteenth-century German charters and found that with the advent of the Teutonic Knights in the fourteenth century, the label was changed to *pommern*.[11]

Although these Slavs were classified into two main groups, coastal and inland, documents from the eleventh-century Bremen chronicler, Adam, and the fourteenth-century writings of Archdeacon Mattias of Płock, claimed that these people spoke the same language – Polish.[12]

Politically, these groups were considered one, as evidenced through lawsuits filed in Rome against the Teutonic order for territorial violations in 1422. In these suits, the strong and rooted kinship between the peoples of Pomerania and Poland was argued by Polish plenipotentiaries and acknowledged in the Second Treaty of Toruń in 1466. As a result, the lands of Pomerania, Chełmno, and Michalow were recognized as Polish territory until the Prussian partition in 1772.[13]

The Origins of the Titles "Cassubia" and "Kashubia"

However, the labels ascribed to the early Slavic groups living in Pomerania and Poland and the terms "Cassub" and "Kaszub" have a history separate from the people in the Vistula valley. Lorentz concluded that in the thirteenth century, "the territorial name 'Cassubia' and the tribal name 'Cassubia' ... were applied to Western Pomerania and even to Mecklenburg." When Lorentz's findings are coupled with Labuda's we are given a more complete political history of the appellation. According to Labuda, between the tenth and thirteenth centuries, the West Pomeranian duchy run by the Gryf dynasty "called itself the Kashubian duchy" and Barnim I (1228–1278) gave himself the title around 1250.[14] Afterwards, the term remained attached to the ranks of Pomeranian dukes as Georg I, Duke of Pomerania-Wolgast, was referred to as the ruler of "*Stettinensis, Pomeranie, Cassubie, Gozkoviensis.*" The title was used until the end of the dynasty in 1637 and "through succession" was applied to the titles of Prussian kings until 1918.[15]

While several authors have pointed out that the title Cassub or Kaszub was employed in a ducal title as the ruler of a territory or people, Adam Fischer, a professor of ethnography at the University of Lwów writes of another origin of the term. Fischer found that the term's origin may be explained in the Chronicle of Bogufał (c. 1250 AD). In the words of Fischer, "the name is explained as derived from the long wide garments worn by the people, which fell into folds ... from the Slavonic expression *kasaćhuby*, i.e., to fold one's dress." He attested that the Polish historian, Jan Długosz (1415–1480), repeated the same explanation, as did Benedykt Chmielowski's encyclopaedias from 1754–58.[16] Numerous other writers also recorded similar variations on the history of the name. In his 1837 dictionary, C.C. Mrongovius recorded that the group called themselves that because of the long sheepskin furs or coats (*koża* or *kożuch*) that they wore in the countryside – they were people of the fur. According to Izydor Gulgowski and Lorentz, a W. Czajewski wrote that *koz* (goat fur) and *szuba* (jacket) when said together – *koziaszuba* – later became Kaszuba.[17]

Other claims as to the root of the word have been speculated upon as well. Franz Tetzner writes that there is a word in Lithuanian, "*kuzabas*," that describes a millstone hole where grain is moved. Other meanings, such as the "little Russian" word *kozub*, meaning basket, and the German word for basket, *kütze*, are close to the current word Kaszub, as is *kuzeb*, a Lithuanian holding vessel made from tree products.[18] While these root terms may be related, both Lorentz and Gulgowski, widely acclaimed ethnographers of the Kaszubs, side with the garment origins.

The most recent attempt to synthesize the origins of the Kashubs was written in 2005 by Borzyszkowski and translated into English. Writing as a member of the Instytut Kaszubski (IK), he did not include any of the findings unearthed by Polyakov, Fischer, Lorentz, Macdonald, or Labuda in his book. Instead, he mentioned that "the etymology of the name of Kashubia (in Kashubian *Kaszëbë*, in Latin *Cassubia*) has not been explained to the present day; linguists and historians carry on their dispute concerning both its origin, incipient territory, and the its [sic] range." Vaguely alluding to the territorial claims of Labuda – the "honorary lead" for the book supposed to "present the history … of the Kashubs" – Borzyszkowki states that "since the early Middle Ages until 1945 a process of voluntary or forced Germanization of all Slavs along the Baltic coast had continued from the west." Borzyszkowski also did not acknowledge or examine the origins of the early people in the Vistula Valley, stating that the label "Cassubia" was used by Barnim I in 1238 and in several papal documents afterwards.[19] The KPA, the IK's partner, makes a claim similar to Borszyzkowski's in its 2008 English brochure. In the mass-produced brochure, the KPA ignores the claims of previous authors – perhaps electing to promote a more distinguished and noble origin of the term as opposed to it being derived from a peasant's garment. The KPA writes instead that the origin of the title is from a papal bull of Pope Gregory IX.[20] The brochure also acknowledges that the term "Kashubia was used in the Middle Ages in reference to West Pomerania and not Gdańsk Pomerania which today is inhabited by Kashubian people."²¹ Unfortunately, the KPA does not provide an explanation as to why the term was appropriated.

Both Labuda and Borzsyzkowski claim that the Cassubian ducal label referred to the West Pomeranian lineage. However, the area ruled by Barnim I and his successors around Wolgast, Szczecin, and Colberg did not extend to the territory where most *pomorjane* or *polajne* people lived near Gdańsk nor does it correspond to the territory where the Kashubs live now. This raises several other important questions: how, when, and why was the ducal label moved to denote the Slavic people living further east?

Unfortunately, no historian or researcher has answered this question. However, Barnim I held the title *dux Cassubie dux Slavorum* and Labuda argues that *Cassub* also meant *Slav*.²² Barnim I also ruled both the previously co-ruled Duchy of Pomerania-Demmin and the Duchy of Pomerania-Stettin by himself. After his death in 1295, the two duchies were split into the Duchy of Pomerania-Wolgast and the Duchy of Pomerania-Stettin, with two separate rulers.²³ The territory encompassed by the Duchy of Pomerania-Stettin at the time only stretched to Köslin/Koszalin, in the east. By the time several prominent seventeenth-century mapmakers released maps showing the territory labelled "Cassubiæ," the land controlled by the Duchy of Pomerania-Stettin had expanded to include the land leading up to Lake Leba and southwest to Bytów.²⁴

During the seventeenth and eighteenth centuries, several maps added conflicting labels to an area called Cassubiæ. Three Dutch mapmakers, Jan Blaeu (1645), Jan Janssonius (c. 1645–1660), and Carolo Allard (1683), placed the label in the far eastern portion of the Duchy of Pomerania-Stettin (see figure 6.2). A few years later, cartographers, such as Frederick de Wit (1688), Carolus Gustavus (1696), and Matthaeus Seutter (c. 1725–1740),²⁵ showed Cassubiæ as southeast of Colberg/Kołobrzeg. By the late eighteenth century, the label had disappeared as Prussia, after the first partition, reorganized administrative districts. While scholars have yet to answer these conflicting claims, perhaps Labuda's equation of Cassubian with Slav points toward an answer. They are areas, after all, with high concentrations of Slavic people. The fact that Lorentz found that several Gdańsk chronicles written around 1500 applied the name "to the lower strata of the rural population of

6.2   Jannsonius's map (c. 1645–60) showing Cassubia depicts Cassubia farther east than previous maps.

Northern Pomerania"[26] suggests the term was used to describe Slavic people in Pomerania. This hypothesis makes sense when we consider Fischer's findings about the term being derived from the Slavic terms for peasant's clothing.

The geographical gap between the two areas labelled as Cassubiæ may have been affected by the slow movement of German people into the territory between the Odra and Słupia Rivers, which diluted certain Slavic populations.[27] Regardless of how precisely we can ascertain the shift of the label from the territory southeast of Colberg/Kölberg/

Kołobrzeg to the present-day territory west and southwest of Gdańsk/ Danzig – claimed by Macdonald as "unhistorical"[28] – the period represents something more marked: a term that was first applied to a group of people becoming an official, recorded ducal title.

The Kashubian Label as a Language and as a Folk

This shift to the label of Cassubiæ being applied to denote a language, and a sense of being, came at the hands of several people in the nineteenth century. During the era of the Teutonic Knights, claims were made that the Pomeranian peoples (Cassubians) spoke Polish, the same language as the rest of the inhabitants. By the sixteenth century, the vernacular known as "Polish" had been accepted and formally codified.[29] Yet while the upper strata spoke Polish from 1466 to 1772, other institutions used different languages. In the Middle Ages, owing to the influence of the Holy Roman Empire, Latin was the official language and was used as a bureaucratic language within the Church and among cartographers. With a significant German population in the Cassubian area, the language of many towns, beginning in the fourteenth century and again from 1772 to 1920 in the era of the partitions, was German.[30] Yet, as Lorentz, Labuda, and Polyakoff remark, the Pomeranian vernacular never became an official language owing to the fact that the area lacked an educated population who could codify it.[31] This claim hinges on the idea that the vernacular spoken by the Pomeranian peoples was in fact a separate one from "Polish," which was codified in the sixteenth century and evolved through diffusion after being codified. In the absence of direct proof of either paradigm in the seventeenth and eighteenth centuries,[32] Florjan Stanisław Cenôva tried to preserve (or create) the Cassubian "folk" using a coded lexicon.

After almost eighty years of "Germanization" in partitioned Poland, and the failed uprisings of 1848, several educated Poles looked elsewhere in their refusal to become Germanized. One option was to migrate to another country or continent. Another was to ally with a neighbouring political entity that might lend its political support. The latter option is what Cenôva, a participant in the failed uprisings, chose. Born the son of free peasants on 4 May 1817 in Sławosyn, Cenôva attended school in Chojnice and moved to Breslau, where he studied medicine. In 1843, he travelled to Königsberg to fulfill his mandatory military service as an assistant surgeon, where he came into contact with the ideology of slavophilism and joined the Slav Literary Society, alongside émigré leftists, insurrectionists, Czechs, and Lusatian Serbs.[33] Impressed with what he heard, Cenôva joined the Polish Democratic Society, which later revolted against the partitioning powers. Assigned the role of attacking the West Prussian garrison town of Starogard, Cenôva was arrested and jailed after the failed attack in 1846, but was spared death.

Moving to the small village of Bukowiec, Cenôva became a country doctor, often administering his services free of charge to the peasantry. It was during his tenure in Bukowiec that Cenôva started writing and publishing poetry as well as several pamphlets dealing with local problems. Since, at the time, "the main characteristic distinguishing [oral] Kashub from Polish [was] its pronunciation," Cenôva attempted to write his letters using phonetics from Kashubian speech. "Locally he gained the reputation of being somewhat ... eccentric. In scholarly circles, he was most frequently regarded as a pioneer in a field long neglected [but] ... an amateur ... and something of a maverick."[34] In the Polish press, Cenôva was critiqued as a panslavist, a separatist, and one who ignored the Polish cause, and was chastised by people until his death in 1881.

As a believer in slavophilism, Cenôva echoed the belief that the existing Slav languages were related by the linguistic common denominator, "Slav Q." Thus, he set about to codify the language of his *volk* to prove the existence of the Slavic "Cassubian" nation within a certain territory.[35] In hindsight, the fact that he set about to do this during a period of foreign occupation makes his slavophilism appear even more romantic. More important, it is Cenôva's efforts in orthography that "created" Kashubian as a written language. For this, Cenôva has been proclaimed by Kashubian-identity seekers as, in Borzyszkowski's words, the "father of Kashubian movement and regionalism."[36]

After his death, Cenôva became a legendary character. Labuda praises him and mentions that Cenôva defended "the Kashubian ethnic community through the *awakening of its own ethnic consciousness* on the basis of *its own language and its own culture*."[37] But Labuda ignored Cenôva's panslavic beliefs. As mentioned, Borzyszkowski proclaims him the awakener of the movement *and* the father of regionalism. Yet, while he was alive, Cenôva was not known to his generation as a popular regionalist who argued for regional strength in Poland. The negative sentiments toward Cenôva were also expressed in a poem written by Hieronim Derdowski, "the most famous nineteenth-century Kashubian poet."[38]

> People, as usually people, were shaking their heads a bit
> And you wandered and looked for a heart among the Slavs
> One shrugged their shoulders; another scolded: fool!
> Third smelled a betrayal:
> You were carried by your faith!
> When the son of fame kneels on your grave, shed tears;
> Your faith and hope will lighten his heart,
> And the Aeolian harp will sound in your soul:
> There is no Kashubia without Poland, and no Poland without Kashubia.[39]

Cenôva's publications were also not widely accepted in the region. He even gave them away free of charge and they still failed to circulate.[40]

Another point that many current Kashubian writers, such as Borzsyzkowski, do not address is that Cenôva planned to establish a Kashubian alphabet as a transitional stage before implementing, like a good slavophile, a modified Cyrillic alphabet.[41] They also ignore Lorentz's comment that "when the vocabulary of the vernacular proved insufficient for his purposes, [Cenôva] unhesitatingly created new words or, if this was impossible, borrowed the necessary words from Polish."[42] The "Kashubian father" was quite outlandish in many of his claims. He falsely claimed that his folk had ancient written records that were "systematically destroyed after the forcible introduction of Christianity – because ... the pagan priests ... alone had knowledge of this script."[43] However, his effect on later waves of Kashubian identity seekers was profound.

Up to the twentieth century, the Kashubian name was accepted only sporadically at best. Its development was affected by several occurrences that characterized the period. Most of the Slav-centric and nation-building work that Cenôva attempted, including the desire to have a Cyrillic alphabet, died with him. As argued in chapter 2, many emancipated peasants were struggling to survive as the population increased dramatically in the nineteenth century. Taking into consideration the residents' perceived religious infringements from 1871 onwards, because of Kulturkampf and its subsequent nation-building processes, the period was marked by religious, economic, and political upheaval. Hence, residents of partitioned Poland embarked on many inter-European and intercontinental migrations for economic reasons.[44] Developing a sense of ethnic identity or of regionalism took a back seat to the everyday struggles of the period.

Some gains, however, were made in the linguistic realm by a young scholar, Stefan Ramułt, to whom Cenôva wrote of his intentions to forge a Cyrillic alphabet. Over the course of several years, Ramułt (1859–1913) collected statistics in northern Poland and attempted to create a dictionary. With the 1893 release of *Słownik języka pomorskiego, czyli kaszubskiego* (The Dictionary of the Pomeranian language, or Kashubian), and the 1899 release of *Statystyka ludności kaszubskiej* (Statistics of the Kashubian People), Ramułt tried to rewrite and quantify some of Cenôva's claims, perhaps to give them more credibility.[45] One of these was the estimate that 300,000 people spoke Kashubian during the mid-nineteenth century. Ramułt's more conservative (but still overestimated) numbers said that 200,000 Kashubs lived in partitioned Poland, 130,000 in America, and 182,000 in Germany.[46] Another major criticism of Ramułt's was that Cenôva adopted the argot of "his native village Sławoszyn in the extreme north of the Kashub country"[47] and ignored all other regional variants in southern Kashubia. Ramułt's biggest claim can be found in the title of his dictionary. Whereas Cenôva believed Kashubian to be a Slavic dialect, Ramułt proclaimed it a language and the Kashubs an ethnic group. His statistical research also provided the wider community of the Kashubian folk with territorial boundaries demarcated through language (see figure 6.3).

Ramułt was part of a wider movement. By the twentieth century, many of the rural regions in partitioned Poland were affected by the policies of the partitioning powers. To a group of scholars, the use of non-folk languages meant the corruption or loss of "the mythic" and "the pure folk" at the hands of modern society.[48] The Kashubian-Pomeranian Association argues that this loss of folk identity, in the case of the Kashubians, was caused by Prussia. "Kashubians ... were forced to oppose a perfectly organized Prussian (German) country in their fight for identity. For instance, all of Prussian citizen [sic] were subject to compulsory schooling, which indeed eliminated illiteracy, but simultaneously fostered Germanisation of local people."[49] The

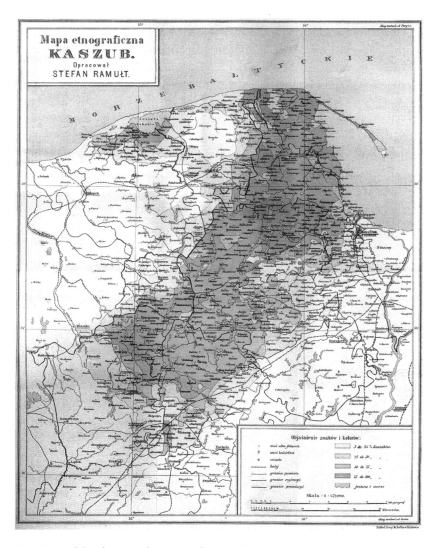

6.3 Ramułt's ethnographic map of areas where Kaszubian was spoken.

emerging field of anthropology also contributed to the emergence of the folk in Europe, with ideas of the primitive alongside emerging regional identities as part of national ones.[50] Locally, however, Rekowski does not consider the aforementioned movements in his writings, and was offended by the use of the word "archaic" when describing the Kashubs. He wrote: "I have seen the word 'archaic' used several times by Kashub writers in Poland when referring to the dialect of Ontario Kashubs and I think I detect a slightly patronizing, pejorative tone in it. Meaning: that our Ontario Kashub is rather old fashioned, out of date, not of pure quality. My reaction to that is: the only claim to honour and prestige the Kashub type of Polish retains is precisely its 'archaicism,' namely: the fact that it is an ancient or archaic old Slavonic tongue. And so the more archaic, the better!"[51] But further investigation reveals that the anthropologists and ethnographers at the turn of the twentieth century understood the notion of the archaic and primitive to connote survival. In the words of Robert Dorson, the study of the folk "as a discipline was past-minded and peasant-minded … [It] was a matter of survivals, antiquities, bygones, throwbacks, and relics."[52]

In Central Europe, folk study echoed the same methodology. We see this through the words of Edward Manouelian, who defines the turn of the century movement in Poland as "the outgrowth of nativist primitivism, one that consciously redefined the periphery as a site of cultural resistance." The theoretical conundrum in documenting and articulating primitivism is evident in the 1906 writings of Polish author Jan Karłowicz: "A people certain of its own existence may calmly study its own folklore from a purely scientific point of view. Tribes deprived of their independence and living in endless fear of suppression and decay, however, must, while reflecting upon the nature and conditions of folkloric tradition, consider practical questions as part of such inquiries. For whenever reference is made to national peculiarities and attributes, there constantly arises the question: to be or not to be."[53] This search for connection and identity meant that, as a result, the connection between the practices of a folk, the material goods of the folk, and the speech of the folk needed to be solidified.[54] In the words of Homi Bhabha: "People are not simply historical events or parts of a patriotic body politic. They are also a complex rhetorical strategy of social reference: their claim to be representative provokes a crisis within the process of signification and discursive address … The scraps, patches, and rags of daily life must be repeatedly turned into the signs of a coherent … culture."[55] In other words, to understand the changes of the present, researchers sought to document the past of the folk and create, or invent, the folk's culture through ethnography and the physical creation of sites of memory to ensure its permanence as a nation or as a group for the future.

One of the ways to ensure the folk's permanence was to incorporate physically what Pierre Nora calls a "site of memory." The first significant site to open in Poland was in the small southern village of Zakopane, in the Tatra Mountains. Built through the interest of several Polish artists, writers, and scholars,[56] the Muzeum Tatrzańskie opened in 1889 to portray the *Górale* (highland) culture. It opened through the efforts of art historian Stanisław Witkiewicz, who believed the Podhale region still had traces of an indigenous folk. He romantically believed that these people, cut off from the outside world, had preserved an ancient, specific folkway. By 1900, he had designed and constructed several buildings that were inspired by the arts and crafts movement but drew on local ethnographic research and woodcarving practices.[57] In essence, the "scraps, patches, and rags" collected from the area were incorporated into the interiors and argued to be the style of the mountain folk – the *Górale*.

Further north, in the Kaszubian region, a movement to solidify another folk culture was taking shape. In the 1890s, a continuing stream of cheap and industrially produced goods from Germany resulted in fewer of the folk's handmade implements. This meant that the primitive and self-sufficient Cassubian, "who made everything he required," from tools to clothes and a home, became a memory. This changed in the 1890s, when an artist, Teodora (Fethke) Gulgowska, and her husband, Izydor Gulgowski, a schoolmaster, moved to the Lake Wdzdyze area near Kościerzyna.[58] In order to preserve the ways of the folk from being "corrupted and lost" by modernization, the Gulgowskis created an ethnographic museum. It opened in 1906 in a house purchased from Michał Hinc; the grounds also functioned as an open air museum.[59] The act of collecting and displaying furniture, farm tools, art, and crafts, meant that, as at Zakopane, the regional folk was preserved as a physical site of memory.

The Gulgowskis also attempted to combat the corruption of the folk by rescuing, appropriating, (and inventing) several kinesthetic folk practices. According to Lorentz, the Cassubian practice of plaiting roots, using stripped tree roots to make potato baskets, flour measures, cans, and buckets, "was nearly extinct ... when it was revived in the first decade" of the 1900s by Izydor. The revived basket-making industry produced earnings for locals and the folk items were exported.[60] Embroidery and home weaving, as mentioned, had declined significantly due to the mechanization of the industry and the import of cheaper goods. To combat this, Teodora introduced stitch embroidery to several women in the area around Wdzydze as an activity during the idle winter months. It quickly became a popular industry, as the market for folk products in Europe was increasing, and the samples were sent to exhibitions in Gdańsk, Kalisz, and Berlin where they were purchased, producing earnings for several local women.[61] The folk industry of embroidery, still prominent up to the present day,[62] was successful because it did not involve much specialized apparatus and it provided some income for women in an economically depressed area.

The Influence of Associations and the Preservation of the Kashubian Identity

The printing of Majkowski's newspaper, *Gryf*, signalled another change in the Kashubian folk movement. It became an ethnic movement spurred on by organizations of the intelligentsia. In the early part of the 1900s, a student association, the Circle of Kashubian Studies, was formed at the Seminary of Pelplin under the direction of Jan Karnowski, which started, secretly at first, to examine local history. After establishing contacts with Majkowski, the Young Kashubs (YK) movement started and in 1908 the *Gryf* became its vehicle. The first issue laid the groundwork for the organization and built on the work of the Gulgowskis: "We believe in the revival of Kashubia and intend to continue a construction on those modest manifestations of local culture. Having realized that the old forms of life must be replaced by new ones, we want to preserve the treasures accumulated by our forefathers for the next generations, and to link the former with the latter by ties of tradition."[63] A year later, the YKs amended their program. The movement located itself within the Polish nation as opposed to a panslavic movement. In this passage we also see, hearkening back to the romantic comparisons outlined in chapter 2, the Christ-like nature of the victimized Kashubs: "This is the program of objectives specified by a handful of younger native Kashubian intelligentsia, who set themselves a task to introduce the Kashubian tribal elements into the all-Polish culture under the motto: 'everything Kashubian is Polish' ... The primary goals of the Young-Kashubian movement are nowadays of cultural nature, as it is the field, where most of the sins against Kashubs have been committed ... [since] under the rule of the Teutonic Knights." Yet, at the time, the threat of increased Germanization and the lack of a connection to Polish worried some of the movement's members, including Karnowski. In 1911, he thought that

> the Polish identity of Kashubia is still very superficial, political and too little internal and ideological. It is commonly known, that up to now any Kashub has not borne any romantic ideal of a future Poland ... that he overestimates the power and value of the German culture. The national consciousness of the Kashubs is not at all subtle, as proven by the voluntary Germanization of the learning of Kashubian youth, e.g. in the secondary school at Wejherowo; we can observe the same phenomenon at the candidates in teachers colleges and seminars, 50 percent of which become Germanized, not to speak about the individuals directly dependent on the government.[64]

Perhaps the lack of interest in the group's message was because most peasants still resented the szlachta and saw the intelligentsia as an extension of the nobility.[65] However, working with the likes of the Gulgowskis and Lorentz, the group's program took shape in 1912 when they moved their operations to Gdańsk – closer to the revered graves of the ancient Pomeranian dukes in Oliwa. The group's objective was to "upgrade the Kashubian population in the cultural, economic and political sense." Makowski became their secretary and worked alongside Fr Ignacy Cyra, of the Bytów area.[66] Unfortunately, their efforts were interrupted by war.

The Interwar Development of Kashubian alongside the Polish Nation

After the First World War devastated many parts of Poland, the peace brought about a renewed interest in the Kashubian appellation. Woodrow Wilson's Fourteen Points attempted to change several conditions and situations. To the dismay of Germany, the thirteenth point dictated the restoration of the Polish state, which had been under foreign rule since 1772. More important, it implied that the "indisputable Polish populations" be included in such a territory.[67] Combined with the Allied belief in "self-determination,"[68] this period saw scholarly attention devoted to the Kashubian identity.

In attempting to define the western boundaries of Poland, where mixed populations lived, questions of identity were raised, such as "Is identity religious or linguistic?"[69] Flowing from this theoretical base, the "Kashub Question" became important. In the words of Peter Brock, "The Kashub 'question' resolves itself into a twofold query. Can the Kashub tongue be considered a separate language and consequently can the Kashubs be regarded as a separate nationality, or are they to be counted simply as speakers of a Polish dialect and members of a Polish nation?"[70] Supplementing the Polish delegation at the peace talks were two Kashubian activists, Antoni Abraham and Tomasz Rogala, who argued the bond between the groups. The Polish delegation argued that the Kashubs were to be grouped into the nation for three reasons: they had lived within pre-partition Poland, Poland needed access to the sea, and they needed to promote ethnographic connections.[71] Refuting claims that Kashubs and Poles could not understand one another, M. Smogorzewski argued that "the Kashubs speak a Polish dialect, and the mountaineers of Zakopane speak another; but an educated man in Warsaw can easily understand both." Plus, he argued, "the Kashubs have never manifested the least desire for separation from the Poles."[72]

The German perspective, based on geopolitical and strategic reasons, argued that the Kashubian people were a separate group from the Poles and portrayed that distinctiveness in several areas of their way of life as a group separate from the Polish. These arguments stated that the Kashubs were Eastern Pomeranians who were half Slav and spoke "a language of their own, which is of Slavic origin, but which cannot be considered a Polish dialect." The French perspective raised several other questions. It was their understanding that the Kashub tongue "contains a number of words and ... constructions which are directly taken from German."[73]

To combat German claims, many residents in Kashubian areas affirmed their regional identity as part of the Polish nation. For example, the resolution of a rally in Kościerzyna on 12 April 1919 stated:

> We, the Kashubs of the Kashubian town of Kościerzyna and vicinities, gathered in number of one thousand at the meeting of the People's Council, solemnly announce to the entire

civilized world that our forefathers, grandfathers and fathers and ourselves are Poles to the core with all heart and soul. Our Kashubian land is Polish, unless Brandenburg is not German! Our Kashubian language is the Polish language, unless the speakers of Low German are not Germans. We are and will remain Poles, like our brothers in Greater Poland, the Kingdom, Galicia, Silesia, and Mazuria. No German historian or politician, no socialist ... shall pull out our Kashubian-Polish heart. Germans! Don't you dare classify us, our mothers, wives, and children as a different, foreign tribe! Hands off! Us, Kashubs, are and will remain Poles in our land! We shall not perish! The Kashubs shall never be doomed.[74]

Demographic data at the time revealed a Kashubian element in the north, as evident in the 1910 Prussian census. Over 85 per cent of the population in the districts of Putzig (Puck), Neustadt (Wejherowo), and Karthaus (Kartuzy) claimed to be Kashubian. Other districts contained a large number of Kashubs too, such as Berent (Kościerzyna) and Konitz (Chojnice).[75] In the end, the American and European experts at the conferences "after an exhaustive study of German official documents and maps, were unanimous in their conclusion that the Pomorze ... always had an undisputable Polish population. This territory, therefore, was awarded to the Polish Republic."[76] As Labuda argues, the rebirth of the Polish state at this time was crucial to the development of the Kashubian movement: "The Kashubs became citizens enjoying equal rights in the new state, although they were a specific part of the Polish national community."[77] Yet the question of identity, couched within the Polish nation, continued after the Treaty of Versailles.

Throughout the interwar period, a large amount of research was conducted that looked into the origins of the Kashubian folk. In 1929, K. Tymienicki, a professor at the University of Poznań, published his findings in an English language monograph, *History of Polish Pomerania*.[78] Two articles authored by Macdonald and Polyakov, used extensively throughout this chapter, are two other examples produced in the 1930s. The research of Lorentz was also prolific during this period.[79] According to Stanisław Gogolewski, Lorentz made "the greatest contribution to [the] scientific examination of Pomeranian"[80] peoples. Culminating in the 1935 compendium, Lorentz's work alongside Fischer and Lehr-Spławiński's appeared in *The Cassubian Civilization*. In this, Lorentz classified the Kashubian speech into three different dialects. On his own, Fischer also produced numerous ethnographic pieces from his post at the University of Lwów.[81] The writings of these leading scholars were, however, not the only contributions. The *Gryf*, organized by Majkowski and based out of Kościerzyna, continued to be a forum for Kashubian and Pomeranian issues and history.

Certain members of the Young Kashubs played important roles in the interwar period. Its secretary, Majkowski, acted as the vice-chairman for the commission that looked at the western portion of the German-Polish border. In the new Pomerania Vovoide, Karnowski was put in charge of the department of Police and Public Security. But morale in the organization during the interwar period was disappointing. Majkowski voiced this concern and claimed that the free city designation of Gdańsk was opposed by the YKs. It was their capital that the rest of Kashubia would look toward, again drawing inspiration from the dukes buried in Oliwa. In the meantime, gains were made toward the promotion of Kashubianism by the creation of the Theatre of Kashubia in Wejherowo in 1930. Majkowski continued to print *Gryf* and Karnowski helped to edit the paper *Zabory* in Chojnice. In 1938, Majkowski, trying to encourage literary output in the Kashubian language, published an epic novel in Kashubian, *The Life and Adventures of Remus*.[82] But the ravages of another war would interrupt their efforts.

Even though the Polish state appeared on the world map again after the Second World War, the restrictions resulting from the "iron curtain" meant that certain activities of Kashubian organizations were put under scrutiny. Nonetheless, several literary activists, like Lech Bądkwoski, in the tri-city region of Gdańsk, Sopot, and Gdynia, kept the Kashubian spirit alive. After a brief thaw in relations with the Soviet Union in 1956, the Kashubian Association was founded and published the biweekly paper *Kaszëbë* until the "popular–scholarly" *Pomerania* was created in 1962. Two years later, the association was reorganized and renamed itself the Zrzeszenie Kaszubsko-Pomorskie (the KPA). With Bądkwoski at the helm, the association promoted Kashubian culture among scholarly circles in Warsaw, Toruń, Łódź, Poznań, and the University of Gdańsk.[83] According to the KPA, the association "is responsible for initiatives supporting a multifaceted socio-cultural and economic development ... for the preservation and development of cultural uniqueness of the entire region; as well as for the popularization of knowledge about Kashubian and Pomeranian tradition." The General Council of the KPA established a student branch of the association called Pomerania in 1962. "It gathers students interested in Kashubian and Pomeranian issues (mainly from local universities) … [and is] often referred to as 'an officer cadet school'" of the KPA.[84] The movement was thus still one of the learned and upper strata, but it gained even more momentum after the collapse of the Soviet Union.

After 1990, the KPA was able to promote its self-governance ideals. These were spurred on by the words of Pope John Paul II in 1987: "My Dear Kashubian Brothers and Sisters! Protect your values and your heritage that prove your identity!"[85] Assisting and strengthening the position of local authorities, many of the KPA's members became commune leaders, mayors, and councillors in the rural areas. In 1992, the 2nd Kashubian Congress was set up by the KPA to discuss the "Future of Kashubianness" in the newly democratic state of Poland. It was decided that developing the literary sphere (by scholarly academics) was crucial. The KPA also realized that Kashubian could only spread if it was taught in schools, so it created language classes in elementary and secondary schools to reach younger audiences. As the post-communist Polish state started to take shape, the KPA saw the necessity of promoting Kashubianness in the media and the Church. This was achieved, after restrictions in post-communist Poland were relaxed, through radio broadcasts on Radio Gdańsk and a television program. In 2004, the KPA created a radio station, Radio Kaszëbë, which broadcasts in Polish and Kashubian.[86]

Although the KPA tried to reach many people through schooling and the liturgy, in the 1990s it was still an upper strata movement centred in the tri-city area. According to the KPA, "since 1999, Gdańsk has been the capital of Pomorskie voivodeship that contains and unites the entire Kashubia." The 1996 creation of the Instytut Kaszubski (IK) in Gdańsk, the scholarly research wing of the KPA, and the publication of the journal *Acta Cassubiana* in 1999 continued the tradition of the movement as a learned one. Cofounded by Borzyszkowski, the IK organized conferences and, in conjunction with the KPA, produced over 400 titles. In 2007, with more than 90 local units, the KPA had around 5,000 members.[87] However, though most of the Kashubian population is rural, throughout my travels in many villages outside Gdańsk in

2009, I saw few visible symbols, such as flags or griffins. This raises the question: how do locals define their ethnicity?

The Legacy of Promotion and Invented Traditions

Nowadays, when people promote the Kashubian identity in Poland and Canada, they do so with a certain distinctive catalogue of items. They wear yellow and black clothing or display yellow and black flags with the black griffin.[88] They proudly wear, stitch, or buy Kashubian embroidery and they speak to one another in a language that is not Polish but Kashubian. As alluded to in the introduction, many of the practices that now define ethnic groups are inventions. This is also the case with the Kashubian group. Borrowing the words of Hugh Trevor-Roper, the Kashubian cultural apparatus, "to which they ascribe great antiquity, is in fact largely modern."[89] It has been developed and invented only over the last century. In the process, several figures have been symbolically honoured and several practices overtly or tacitly controlled so as to solidify continuity with the past – thus fitting one of Hobsbawm's definitions of invented tradition.[90] This section aims to unearth these changes, solidifications, and invented traditions couched as Kashubian. My goal is not to determine "authenticity," since that is a human construct too, but rather to set the stage for chapter 7, which examines the function and importance of these activities and practices in the symbolic and ritualistic interaction of past and present in Renfrew County.

Since the Kashubian appellation was applied to a folk, the transition to a formal language and a sense of being have defined what it means to be Kashubian. Some of the movement's key figures have become icons. One such individual was Florjan Cenôva, now known as the "father" of the Kashubian awakening and heralded as such by the KPA, who created an award named after him: the Awakening Kashubian award.[91] However, his popularity was not always so strong, as we saw earlier in the chapter. Cenôva's transition into a twentieth-century icon is perhaps best explained by Brock, who wrote that "Kashub writers forgave him his political and linguistic separatism ... in view of the great services he rendered in promoting the Kashub dialect." Revisionists ignored his eccentricity and, in the early twentieth century, painted him as an individual who despised the shackles of peasantry and class egotism.[92] He has become known as the inventor of the Kashubian literary

6.4 The Kaszubian coat of arms.

language – even though, as discussed earlier, he thought it was a dialect of the Slav Q – and an acclaimed figure in books and in the Muzeum Kaszubski in Kartuzy, Poland. In this museum, Cenôva's painting sits alongside those of other Kashubian heroes, such as the poet Hieronim Derdowski and the activist Aleksander Majkowski.

In recent years, the KPA has promoted two clearly recognizable signs of the Kashubian movement: the flag and coat of arms. The coat of arms design has been invented and branded as a traditional link to the past. The KPA has promoted it because "it has been customarily accepted" that the black griffin on a yellow background is the coat of arms of the Kashubs (see figure 6.4). The corresponding flag contains two horizontal bands of yellow and black.[93] However, the KPA has not been able to entirely substantiate the connection between these symbols and the Kashubian people. The mythic griffin, which can be traced back to Greek mythology, was a symbol of the Gryf dynasty of rulers until the seventeenth century. It was also used on formal seals in several non-Polish areas. For example, in the thirteenth century, the seal of the city of Stavenhagen in Mecklenburg contained a griffin on a shield and the seal of the State of Demmin in 1265 contained a shield and griffin.[94] In the twentieth century, the symbol was popularized through

6.5 The Pomeranian coat of arms, c. 1530. The black griffin on yellow (top, right corner) in the coat of arms represented the Cassubia but this change was made in 1530. Previously it represented the Pomeranian Duchy territory of Wolgast-Barth.

Majkowski's newspaper, and a connection between the Kashubian people and the griffin was made.

But the connection with the yellow and black griffin is not as clear. Borzyszkowski says that the griffin "has represented the most important symbol and coat-of-arms of the Kashubs and the entire Pomerania for a long time."[95] Yet readers are left to wonder how long "a long time" is. The KPA affirms the connection to the present writing that "a black griffin on a golden background appeared for the first time in the XV century in the heraldry of West Pomeranian dukes. This grand Pomeranian coat of arms represented the sign of Kashubian duchy since the unification of Western Pomerania by Bogusław X (1454–1523). Most probably, Kashubians have adopted it for their present emblem."[96] Upon further research, we find that the Kashubian coat of arms is indeed rooted in the past, but its connection to the Kashubian people before the reign of Bogusław X is not clear – or has not yet been unearthed. During the reign of Bogusław X (1474–1523), the coat of arms for the Duchy of Pomerania only had five emblems. Indeed, the black griffin on yellow, "Gryf #3" in the coat of arms (see figure 6.5), represented the Cassubian area but this change was made in 1530[97] and Boguslaw X's reign was from 1474–1523. The change was made under Georg I.[98] The origins of the "Cassubian" griffin, or "Gryf #3," are not as linear as the KPA presents.

During the reign of Joachim I (1434–1451), five fields comprised the coat of arms for the Duchy of Pomerania, and the term "Cassuben" was not ascribed to any of them.[99] Through 1465, when Erich II ruled, the black griffin on yellow did not represent the "Cassubes." It represented the Pomeranian Duchy territory of Wolgast-Barth.[100] The Wolgast-Barth area is west of the area known to be inhabited by the Cassubs and is closer to the Mecklenburg area where larger portions of German-speaking peoples lived. By 1530, *after* the reign of Bogusław X, the coat of arms was enlarged and reorganized. On 26 July 1530, at the Diet of Augsburg, the coat of arms was multiplied to ten fields. The westward-looking black griffin on yellow (Gryf #3) was switched to represent Cassubia, Barth was represented by a similar black griffin on yellow, looking eastward (Gryf #7), and Wolgast was represented by Gryf #9. In 1609, Gryf #1 was ascribed to Pommern, Gryf #2 represented Stettin, Gryf #3 was switched back to Wolgast, Gryf #7 still represented Barth, and the red- and green-striped Gryf, similar to Gryf #4 (the Wendengryf), represented Cassuben.[101]

No clear connection can be found cross-referencing the territories represented by the maps with coats of arms. The territory of Cassubia outlined by de Wit in 1688 (even taking into account that he may have based his map on Lubin's 1610 findings) corresponds to the Duchy of Pomerania-Stettin, which is represented by Gryf #1 and #2. In Gustavus's map of 1696, the black griffin on yellow was designated as Cassubian and placed with a territory outside "Hinter Pommern."[102] Why Georg I made the switch in 1530 (or Phillip-Julius in 1609) is not known. Thus, to suggest that Gryf #3 initially or consistently represented "Cassuben" or the area outlined as "Cassubia" by Gustavus, is questionable.

Although the attribution of the Kaszubian coat of arms is not as unilinear and unique to the Cassubian people as the KPA argues, it is an invented symbol imbued with meaning. That is, it was a real symbol, but its specific connection to the Kaszubian people is a construction. Having evolved from its fifteenth-century origins as the coat of arms for Wolgast-Barth, it now represents the Kaszubian people in the twenty-first century. And even though it is an invented connection, it still implies continuity with the past for the KPA and its followers.

Similarly, Kaszubian embroidery has been promoted and solidified in recent years by the KPA as one of the prominent Kaszubian folk arts but it becomes apparent that this tradition was also invented in the twentieth century. Since its renaissance, its promoter, Teodora Gulgowska, has been praised and congratulated. Yet the language used by the KPA to promote the embroidery suggests that the practice, in its current form, has been around since the seventeenth century: "Motifs identified as Kashubian were present on altar cloths and other church fabrics as well as on coifs already in the XVII and XVIII centuries." However, there is no exploration of how the cloths were specifically "Kashubian," only the statement that it was practised long ago and "taught in the monastaries of Żukowo and Żarnowiec to young ladies of aristocratic, bourgeois and rich peasant background."[103] The seven-colour palette that is promoted by the KPA and the Muzeum Kaszubski in Kartuzy has been branded, in recent years, as Kaszubian.[104] Despite having some of its origins in the seventeenth century, the embroidery was encouraged by Gulgowska and standardized by Maximilian Lewandowski in the early 1900s.

According to the art historian Aleksander Błachowski, the original designs of Gulgowska were not authentically "Kashubian" and he refers to them as the "new Wdzydze embroidery."

Gulgowska intended to encourage needlework as an income source for local women who took her classes in 1906. The impulse for such a project came from a similar movement in Sweden. Gulgowska adapted several patterns, which were common in seventeenth- and eighteenth-century religious garments, and modified them into her early designs (see figure 6.6).

Afterwards, Gulgowska modified several designs – like the flattened rose or the pomegranate and tulip – taken from furniture, woven caps, painted glass, and priests' garments and encouraged locals in her embroidery classes to adopt similar symbols and add artistic elements too. According to Błachowski, because Gulgowska had been educated

6.6   Embroidery patterns adopted by Teodora Gulgowska. Several patterns, like these, were adopted and branded as Kaszubian.

at the University of Berlin, she avoided copying the Baroque designs directly, since German clients or the imperial court might have recognized the plagiarism.[105] She added vines (*pnaczy*) and leaves to make them appear more rural and folk-like and helped employ people in the depressed area since wealthy aristocrats were always on the lookout for folk artistic creations. As a result, the Gulgowskis created a tradition that was later standardized and given the Kashubian label. But the practice of painting flower motifs on furniture was, in fact, popular in Europe in the nineteenth century and was also influenced by southern-European and Turkish techniques. It is not specifically Kaszubian. One only has to turn to other folk art in European countries to see similar floral motifs painted on German and English furniture dating to the early half of the nineteenth century. Chests with a floral decoration were also made in France and Holland in the nineteenth century and Slovakian flower motifs were painted on furniture and other items, like altars and priests' vestments. Vine motifs and stylized adaptations of common plants also occur in Ukrainian furniture. Exhibitions in large European cities, such as Vienna's World Fair, were meeting places for many of these products.[106] The work of the northern Polish women would not have become recognizable if it had not included common, standard elements.

One of the offshoot schools of this newly created embroidery, at Wdzydze, was run in the 1920s and 1930s by a teacher, Maximilian Lewandowski, in Kartuzy. Lewandowski opposed Gulgowska's freeform and somewhat romantic approach to embroidery – that anyone could come up with their own designs based on a few historical connections. Lewandowski created a collection of predictable designs that he thought should become recognizable and created rules about the colours. Unlike Gulgowska, who avoided Baroque designs, Lewandowski incorporated them into his work. Motifs were standardized for reproduction by the hundreds of people who enrolled in the courses.[107] However, the application of the term "Kashubian" to the embroidery raised some questions. Some discontent surrounding reproductions and what is actually Kaszubian was expressed in an article in *Gryf* in 1936.[108] Nonetheless, other schools emerged in Żukowo and in the 1950s in Wejherowo. They too stitched under the Kashubian banner. Many of these standard symbols have their origins in Baroque stitching.

However, the KPA, in 2014, chooses not to expand on the origins of these practices. Although it mentions several schools that have embroidered over the years, it specifically mentions the twentieth-century Żukowo School, started by Lewandowski's students Jadwiga and Zofia Ptach, which relies on a seven-colour guide. In the guide, dark blue represents the sea, medium blue Kaszubian lakes, light blue the Kaszubian sky, black hardship and sorrow, red love and the heart, yellow the sand, and green the forest.[109] But the KPA does not acknowledge the story behind the invention of the guide whereas, according to Błachowski, it was proven, during the early part of the twentieth century, to originate from a supposed legend of one Grandmother Okoniewski.[110] Nonetheless, for the KPA, the embroidery tradition is Kaszubian, centuries old, and all of the schools "allude to the main trends, and above all to the Żukowo tradition."[111] Some are also critical of the recent proliferation of mass-produced items for sale that feature images of Kaszubian embroidery. As any post-modernist would concur, the very term "folk industry" is an oxymoron. No one can ever reproduce the true work of the folk. It has been suggested that the commercialization of such products undermines the objects and the communities that originally produced them.

In addition to embroidery, a distinctly Kaszubian ethnic costume was standardized in the early twentieth century. By the mid- to late nineteenth century, at the same time that basket weaving declined, manufactured fabric replaced most of the hand-made material in peasants' wardrobes. According to Lorentz, "first the dyeing was given up, the homespun was taken to the dye-works, and printed with varicoloured patterns in accordance with the taste of the people. Then industrial enterprise threw cheap and pleasing materials on the market." Because the traditional outfits were adapted and used for work after they were made, it was complicated to reconstruct such a traditional costume. In the early twentieth century, the revival of a costume had to rely on the memory of people, oral recollections, and accounts from written works of the past. After trying to piece the costume together, researchers found that there were a multitude of varied designs and colours over the territory said to be Cassubia.[112] Bożena Stelmachowska came up with three reconstructions: the peasants' dress, the dress of the northern fisherman, and the costume of the Gdańsk resident. The men's outfit was a black lambskin hat, a long dark blue coat (similar to the folded one that some believe the name Cassub came from), yellow trousers made of lambskin, and tall black boots with tops up to the knees. The women's costume consisted of a bonnet with an embroidered crown, a scarf, a shirt of square or rectangular cut, a blue bodice or jacket, green or red skirt, apron, and boots (see figure 6.7). Stelmachowska noted that the men's outfits had some variety, with a Rococo style. They included a red kerchief, a long vest, and short white trousers.[113] Since 1906, however, the influence of the new embroidery practices has been seen on shirts, aprons, and blouses. This is not, however, a reconstructed folk costume but an ornamented dress composed according to the artistic ideas of intellectuals and based upon a model from female cloisters in Żukowo (contrast figure 6.7 with figure 6.8).[114]

A costume combining elements of both mens' outfits, but highlighted with individual and modern embroidery styles, can be found in the Muzeum Kaszubski in Kartuzy, Poland, and has been promoted

6.7 A reconstructed Kaszubian ethnic costume. The man is wearing a long blue coat and golden trousers with a fur hat. The woman is wearing a long green, red, and black dress with a dark bodice and a scarf with floral designs in addition to the hand-woven hat with golden needlework.

by the KPA.[115] Such costumes were adopted by many dance companies and folk groups in Poland in the twentieth century.

Conclusion

Jan Mordawski and Cezary Obracht-Prondzyński estimate that, as of 2005, 566,737 persons have been found to be of partly Kaszubian descent in Poland.[116] The number, when compared with Ramułt's figures from the late nineteenth century, has increased significantly. Similarly, the use and development of the term has increased exponentially.

6.8 The Kaszubian ethnic costume at Muzeum Kaszubskie. The man is wearing a blue coat, a black hat, white pants, and shirt. The woman is wearing a red skirt and a blue bodice.

Whether it originated as a ducal title or a descriptive term, "Cassubiæ" has been modified and adopted – by individuals and associations – to identify a folk, a language, and a set of invented traditions. In the process, dozens of pastkeepers, academics, writers, and scholars have written about its use in a rather fragmented way, while rarely examining its origins. For Canadian authors like Rekowski and Mask-Connolly, the use of the term in their discourses functioned as a reference point in the past. They used it to reference past ways of life that were so distant that they, perhaps, needed no justification. In light of these discourses and presuppositions, this chapter has provided a glimpse into the chronological and thematic timeline of the Kaszubian appellation. Although it does not attempt to address every scholarly mention of the term – or every individual who contributed to its development – it has outlined the major elements.

Yet, referring to the 2005 figures, the very statistics that define ethnic identification are problematic as each individual internalizes identity and ethnicity in different ways. Essentially, as Simon Gunn asks, "How can historians investigate what is largely a private and hidden subject?" Perin argues that "some maintain ... ethnicity is an objective force identified by such tangible markers as language, religion, and custom."[117] Even using language as a marker is problematic as estimates of the number of speakers range from "a few thousand speakers ... [as] reports of over 100,000 speakers are false," according to a UNESCO publication, to 250,000–300,000 speakers, according to former KPA Chairman Brunon Synak.[118] But many scholars, including Perin, have acknowledged that the concept of culture is a fluid process that develops among different people through time.[119] If we do not acknowledge this fluidity, we run the danger of rendering ethnic labels anachronistic instead of seeing them as an active process. Along these lines, the label "Cassubiæ" has evolved to become Kaszubian or Kashubian, depending upon which continent settlers live. Similarly, the cultural constructions of what it means to be Kashubian have evolved, and have been invented and re-invented since being Kashubian was territorialized and separated from the abstract notion of the folk in the nineteenth century. In the process of identity formation, as evidenced in chapter 2 and this chapter, several binary oppositions have appeared between the eighteenth and twentieth centuries. In the words of Zuzanna Topolińska, "being Kashubian implies being Polish but not vice versa,"[120] and the division between Polish/Kashubian and German has been set along denominational lines. To be Polish or Kashubian is to be Catholic, whereas to be German is to be Protestant[121] even though there were Protestant Cassubians and German Catholics.[122] And finally, if a Pole or a Kashub was to be educated in the German language (solely or partly) it meant that they were losing their connection to the folk and becoming Germanized. The German language (and codified Polish) were the foes of Kashubicity.

Since the early twentieth century, when the KPA attempted to increase awareness of the Kaszubian identity, the surge in ethnic identification in the diaspora, outside the cultural hearth, has heightened, especially in recent years. One of the contemporary questions in these outside areas has been "Can I be considered a Kashub if I cannot speak the language?" While struggling with this question, individuals have developed other signs or exercises to refashion their Kashubian identity. After examining the origins and diffusion of several historically-produced signifiers and practices associated with being "Kashubian," the central concern is not about the validity of these cultural practices. As Werner Sollars writes, "the implications of [such an] approach to the concept of 'invention' ... are both devastating and fruitful."[123] It can be fruitful for research purposes but devastating to some on a personal level. However, the central concerns of part II are how these traditions are imagined, created, and imbedded in exhibitions. The many lenses that individuals in the Ottawa Valley use to imagine their Kashubian identity is a fascinating area of study. Growing from a collection of invented traditions, exercises of symbolic ethnicity in the imagined community have branched out into regional and international realms. Although some of the activities are invented traditions, they represent a continuum of community and a link with the past.

7

Legacies of Promotion: Cultural Recreation and the Wilno Heritage Society

Many organizations, societies, and learned individuals helped to develop the Kaszubian identity, create its language, and shape its culture. It was developed in Poland at the same time as the period of cultural redefinition in the area around Canada's first Polish settlement. Of course, this period could not have been established without the efforts of authority figures and the newfound knowledge that they shared with the greater population. They can be divided into two categories: those with traditional authority (Fr Rekowski) and those with professional authority (Mask-Connolly and Shulist). As noted in chapter 1, notions of internal and external, insider and outsider, jostle in the formation of a new Kashubian community as descendants make use of the knowledge for themselves.

But a bridge was needed to transport these redefinitions in Poland to Canada. Until the 1990s, as shown in chapter 1, most studies on the larger Polish group in Canada, as well as the first Polish settlement, were written by external Polish people, who were not descendants of the original settlers. These authors drew attention to the fact that the settlers spoke a "different" Polish. However, their notion that the settlers spoke a vernacular and should be characterized as "Kaszubian" was largely ignored by locals, who thought they spoke low Polish and that the tourists and priests spoke high Polish.[1] The bridge between these authors' ideas and local descendants was Rekowski. Because the locals felt that the postwar group was elitist, a local authority figure was needed to lend approval or at least proclaim that it was plausible.

Building on this notion of difference, this chapter will chronicle the origins of the cultural awakening, examine the movement that culminated in the Wilno Heritage Society (WHS), and analyze the promotion of Kashubianism through the WHS's activities and festivals. What becomes apparent is that individuals, the community, and the diaspora forged links with the past through the activities and invented traditions of the WHS.

The Realization of Difference

Proclaimed by locals for his discovery of "Kashubian roots," Rekowski's ethnic awakening came after his mother was hospitalized in 1980. He returned to the Barry's Bay area after preaching around the world, and began to look into his family's past by sorting through books and papers at his mother's house. In the process, he rediscovered a copy of Jozef Kisielewski's epic novel *Ziemia Gromadzi Prochy* (The Earth Gathers Dust),[2] which he had read and made notes about in the 1940s. While travelling through interwar Poland, Kisielewski had labelled the group of people along the sea as "*Kaszubi.*" Rekowski, looking into the past during a traumatic time in his life, rediscovered (or refashioned) his mother's identity, and developed a desire to spread the words "Kashubian identity" to other descendants and their families.[3]

In 1983, Rekowski began writing about history and ethnic identity in *Barry's Bay This Week* (*BBTW*), claiming that locals were, indeed, Kashubs. In his writings over the course of several years, Rekowski describes the Kashubs as persecuted by Germans, who called them "*dummer Kashube!*" He then inspired the Kashubs by saying that their perseverance gave Poland claim to the Baltic seacoast after the Second World War. Because of this, he argues, Poland "has been duly grateful and the Kashubs have been duly recognized and have come into their own – finally. To call oneself a Kashub has become a 'badge of honour' instead of one of shame." Rekowski argues that, since the Kashubs have finally "come into their own," they are culturally different from Poles of the other partitions.[4]

Rekowski's book, *The Saga of the Kashub People in Poland, Canada, U.S.A.*, and the interest it garnered signalled a shift in the way locals in the Barry's Bay and Wilno areas thought about themselves. Msgr Pick said that "it was Father Rekowski who found out we were Kashubs." Julian Kulas, a descendant of original settlers, also echoed this, saying that "it was not until Father Al Rekowski's research ... that the Kashub fact was brought to light."[5] As a result, writers, pastkeepers, and community boosters in the area around Canada's first Polish settlement used their writings and activities to discover and create the Kashubian identity. But moving forward with their discovery or rediscovery meant that these descendants had to look into their past and to their ties with Poland to find evidence of Kashub culture.

The Quest for Identity: Reaching Back to Move Forward

Two people in particular, Shirley Mask-Connolly and David Shulist, became interested in spreading the word "Kashubian" after reading the missionary priest's writings. Mask-Connolly became interested on her grandmother's eightieth birthday: "I realized I knew nothing about her." While researching her grandmother's genealogy she found that no one had ever done such research into local families. Since she felt "it should've been done because people didn't know who their ancestors were," she set out to complete the task.[6] In a letter to University of Gdańsk professor Józef Borszkowski, Mask-Connolly articulated her resolve to inspire locals and their new culture: "We need to have confidence in our abilities – we are capable of great things if we stop putting ourselves down. So in fact I go out of my way to boost the ego of the Canadian Kashubs, making them proud of themselves and their heritage. We have to be more assertive."[7]

Shulist's awakening came after returning to Wilno. It happened on his forty-fifth birthday when his father gave him Rekowski's book. In Shulist's words, "when I opened the book and started to read, Father Al opened my eyes to our true culture. Through his journey, I found out about our culture." Afterwards Shulist wrote, "It is hard to believe that one word can make such a big difference ... it has changed my life ... I remember the day I found out about the word ... I got so hooked on our culture that with the help of my father, we started the Wilno Heritage Society. Now I am the president ... Now I am obsessed with our culture."[8] Founded in 1999, the mandate of the WHS and its executive was to "celebrate the accomplishments and traditions of these folk."[9]

Combining their efforts with a few other local supporters, Mask-Connolly and Shulist looked to the homeland and other organizations for connections. Mask-Connolly scoured parish registers in the Kaszuby area of Poland and several parishes in Canada to trace the ancestors of those who settled in Canada. She also liaised with several Kaszubian authors and community boosters in the homeland and in the broader diaspora, such as Borzyszkowski, Blanche Krbechek of the Kashubian Association of North America (KANA), and then-KPA president Artur Jablonski.[10] While in Poland, Shulist met a farmer and former politician, Wojciech Etmanski, "a man that had a true passion for our culture." In the words of Shulist, "he said something that caught my attention. KASHUB is not a dialect of any language, but a language on its own. Wow." Afterwards, Etmanski was invited to speak in Wilno in February 2001. According to Shulist, Etmanski "spoke about the region of Poland that our ancestors left ... He said that our heritage comes from a very special part of Poland where there is a different culture of its own. This culture is called Kashubian. Yes, they are Polish citizens, but their culture is different from Polish culture. They dress differently, they eat differently, their folk art is different. The Embroidery and pottery have their own distinctive design elements. Their emblem is the Griffin ... and not the eagle. The white eagle is for the country of Poland. Their colours are Black and Gold."[11] As president of the WHS at the time, Shulist then set out to refashion the identity of Canada's first Polish settlers.

The WHS's Cultural and Identity Constructions

In celebrating "these folk," the WHS built on Rekowski's idea of difference and separated it from previous notions of Polishness. In doing so, the WHS was now exercising a newfound agency – in the sense that it defied previous power relationships that had been controlled by external Poles in the pursuit of their projects. The WHS created essentialist cultural markers of the Kashubs in Canada based on cultural activities in the homeland. This included overlaying markers of Polish heritage with the Kashubian trope, connecting many everyday practices of their relatives and ancestors, and correlating them under the newly-defined cultural label. For example, the WHS website declares Martin Shulist, David's father, as "one of the earliest promoters of the Kashub culture locally."[12] But this "claim" contrasts Martin Shulist's earlier promotional activities as president of the *Polish* Canadian Pioneer Centre. The WHS also adopted the seven-colour embroidery guide and patterns from the KPA, and embraced the black and gold flag and the griffin. It accepted the KPA's description of the Kaszubian costume, which Shulist often wears during celebrations and events. As recently as March 2015, the organization claimed that "when our ancestors came here in 1858, they brought with them a unique Kashub culture. This culture had its own language, music, dance, food, furniture styles, embroidery and unique churches" and claimed that the language "is on the verge of being lost forever." In the realm of music, "the fiddle was the main instrument that was brought over here by our Polish ancestors and it was the fiddle that entertained at Kashub weddings with guitar as backup."[13] Yet a critical analysis of their claims might question how the music brought over by *Polish* ancestors was specifically Kashubian. In contrast, the WHS claimed that "the Kashubian Dance has been lost ... Our ancestors quickly adapted to the traditional Canadian dance which was mostly from Irish Culture" and also declared that "Kashubian Embroidery was a lost art with the Canadian Kashub Poles."[14] However, the anonymous author of these passages for the WHS does not provide any information to prove that this kind of dance or embroidery even existed among the first settlers' families.

The creation of a small museum and outdoor ethnographic park on the site of the former CN rail station in Wilno have been ongoing projects since the WHS's inception, benefitting greatly from the curatorial work of Mask-Connolly. Starting with a small building, the park now contains several structures and has been beautifully landscaped by dozens of members, who donate their time and efforts. The buildings include a log cabin donated by Ambrose and Martha Chippior and a restored farmhouse donated by the Burchat family. Encircling the stump puller in the centre of the park are "heritage stones" engraved with the names of the first settlers and their plots of land. Each year, more stones and small structures are added as families gather to commemorate, and pay homage to, their ancestors.[15] Since 1998, the museum and park have provided a space for the WHS to house and promote their activities and have become the centre for an annual festival celebrating Polish-Kashub culture.

Starting in 1999, the WHS invited locals to celebrate the traditional Polish holiday in Wilno's heritage park to commemorate the 1791 Polish Constitution. This festival, as previously mentioned, had been celebrated by Polish priests at St Mary's Church in Wilno and St Hedwig's Church in Barry's Bay since the first quarter of the twentieth century. However, in recent decades the parishes had ceased their

7.1   Kashub Day 2008, showing the stage and dance floor in Wilno.

celebrations. According to Corinne Higgins, the owner of the Wilno Tavern, the 1999 "Polish Festival" put on by the WHS attracted around 1,500 visitors, who enjoyed Polish food, music, and dance.[16] However, by 2002 – after Etmanski's words had further developed Shulist's awakening – the event was renamed the "Polish-Kashub festival" and the signs advertising it reflected the change. At the 150th anniversary of the arrival of the settlers from Prussian-occupied Poland, in 2008, the "Polish" label largely disappeared from Shulist's address. Instead, he declared that "the Canadian Kashubs are celebrating their unique Kashubian culture with many special events."[17] A plethora of Kashubian flags and emblems dotted the park, and tables selling yellow and black "Kaszëbë" shirts and sweaters were set up. Even the dance floor was painted in gold and black (see figure 7.1). The first Saturday in May was proclaimed "Kashub Day."[18]

Since 2008, Shulist's claims and initiative have become even more pervasive. In 2006, he organized an annual adult hockey tournament, the Opeongo Heritage Cup, designed to bring together local and regional players and spectators. Each team comprised players who were descendants of Ottawa Valley Polish, Irish, German, (and later Algonquin) ancestors. By 2008, Shulist had renamed the Polish Eagles team the "Kashubian Griffins" and bought new jerseys and flags so the team could compete as the Griffins in Toronto's annual Multicultural Hockey Tournament. The "cultural food" served at the arena in Barry's Bay was also rebranded as Kashubian.[19] The same year, Shulist copied an activity started by Kaszubians in Poland. He started a weekly radio show, "Radio Kaszëbë," through Valley Heritage Radio in Renfrew. Adopting a pseudonym (Johnny Kashub), Shulist and Ray Chapeskie broadcast various genres of music and commented on local happenings on the Saturday morning show. Shulist also lobbied to have Kashubian banners flying from telephone posts.[20]

To spread the word, Shulist sent a letter to Kent Waddington, the editor of *The Combermere Free Press*, with several instructions and requests. The letter reads: "Just to let you know – The language of our ancestors is KASHUB – not Polish. I will teach you how to speak the Kashub language someday. There are only a few of us in the world who can speak this language. I feel good about it ... Kent, from this day on, I want you to use the word '*Kashub*' – out with the word 'Polish' – when you speak of our culture. It is Kashub. We celebrate Kashub Day on the first Saturday of May. Our cook book is Kashub – everything Kashub, Kashub, Kashub, Kashub."[21] Shulist's fervour increased. Is it possible that Shulist sent such a letter to establish a charismatic type of authority for himself, as one of the few people (he claims) who can speak a dying language? After all, those who communicate perceived knowledge can be seen as authorities on a subject.

In 2009, Shulist widened the breadth of his claims and justified them in two newspaper articles. On 7 July 2009, one article appeared in *Barry's Bay This Week*, written by Shulist under the *nom de plume* "Głos Kaszëbsczi/The Kashubian Voice," dictating Kashubian history and traditions to the descendants of the first settlers. Shulist claims that "many things have gone wrong with our history" because the first settlers were oppressed at home and under foreign rule. (It is ironic, however, that Kashubian identity was promoted as a reaction to Prussian rule. Prussian rule could therefore be considered a catalyst rather than a destroyer.) Shulist then criticized the Church, saying that a local priest of Polish descent, Fr Wladyslaw Dembski, made the settlers name the community "Wilno" for his birthplace. Shulist claims that

Wilno should have been called "Kaszuby." He states what he thinks the "true" culture of locals was and provides proof on why locals should believe him. In his words:

> I set a goal to tell my people the true story of our ancestors and their heritage. I knew it was not going to be easy. For 139 years, all they heard from their parents and grandparents was that they were of Polish culture. Here I was with very little education trying to tell them that they were not of Polish culture but Kashubian ... I was driven by my passion, nothing was going to stop me. I got funny looks when I told them that their true cultural colours were Gold & Black and not red and white. That their emblems was [sic] the Kashubian Griffin and not the Polish Eagle ... That the day we celebrate our culture is called Kashub Day and not Polish Day. Our hockey team is called the Kashubian Griffins, and not Polish, our Kashubian embroidery are Kashubian design [sic] and not Polish, never were and never will be. Our radio show is called Radio Kaszebe, the voice of the Kashub people. Our dance costumes are Kashubian ... We were not born in Poland, therefore we are Canadian Kashubs.

He then listed several recent accolades that positioned him as an "authority" and lent legitimacy to advance such claims:

> All my preaching for the last 11 years, was it all bull or was I for real? This past year, I got relief; I got credibility. I won awards from the governments of Poland and Canada for promoting and preserving the Kashubian culture in Canada. I met with Prime Minister Steven Harper [sic] as he acknowledged our 150th anniversary celebrating Canada's Kashub culture. I had lunch with the first lady of Poland in Ottawa where she asked about our project ... This summer I am off to Kaszuby Poland to open the Canadian Kashub log building in a museum at Daniel Czapiewski Szymbark [sic] with Donald Tusk, the first Polish prime minister of Kashubian heritage.[22]

When Shulist received the Governor General's Caring Canadian Award for his volunteer work in the community,[23] he appropriated its prestige and concluded that the award therefore meant that the government was endorsing his viewpoints on culture. Shulist also reworked the prime minister's comments on the 150th celebration and substituted "Kashub" for "Polish." According to the WHS's website, what Prime Minister Harper said was: "These anniversaries remind us how much Polish Canadians – more than 800,000 strong today – have done to build our great country ... Polish Canadians have made their mark in every walk of Canadian life."[24] Since then, Shulist has adopted and promoted the saying: "Wiedno Kaszëbë" (Always Kashub).

Two months later, in September 2009, Shulist wrote a letter about Kashubian cuisine. Since the early part of the twentieth century, St Mary's in Wilno has held an annual parish meal. Other parishes in the area hold similar events, notably the early picnics started in the 1910s by Msgr Biernacki in Barry's Bay to raise funds for the Church.[25] St Hedwig's served sand-baked beans, various meat dishes, and numerous desserts at their events. Over the years, Wilno became known for the chicken that was served at their event. Shulist suggested that because Kashubs (not Poles) attended mass at St Mary's, "the parishioners serve the traditional Kashubian food. Chicken is the number one dish of the Kashubs, followed by pork and fish. When the supper started in 1936, the decision was very easy. We will serve the people our traditional food and the chicken won."[26]

A visible community booster and pastkeeper, Shulist can be found posing for pictures and liaising at numerous formal and informal events wearing his Kashubian hockey jersey. He has received the *Gloria Artis Medal* from the Polish Ministry of Culture for his promotional efforts and the KPA's Florian Ceynowa "Awakening Kashubians" award. More recently, perhaps trying to follow in his father's footsteps, he was elected mayor of the Township of the Madawaska Valley in 2010 until he was voted out in 2014. In his bid to be elected, he cited "his relationship with the European Union and the government of Poland" as an asset.[27] On the website www.kashub.com, which he himself runs, Shulist is described as "a man with a passion for the Kashubian culture that burns deep within him." It also says that "God blessed him with the gift of promotion and a passion for heritage."[28] Using this perceived missionary gift, Shulist continues to promote the "Kashubian culture" on his own time after Peter Glofcheskie became president of the WHS in 2012. Mask-Connolly, another visible booster of the Kashubian community, can be found promoting Kashubianism through the WHS's newsletter, publications, and several small displays which she has constructed in venues such as the Ontario Legislature, the Bytown Museum, and the Royal Ontario Museum.

Cultural Recreation: Analytical Perspectives

Ethnic identities are complex. They can, in some instances, be lost, or be objects "bounded in time and space, as something with clear beginnings and endings, with its own territoriality."[29] Some people believe their ethnic identity is worth fighting and dying for; others find it divisive. In other cases, a person or a group feels a sense of inferiority if they do not have a perceived ethnic identity. Yet many historians are skeptical of the original definition of ethnicity, that is, the belief that historical identities are fixed or innate. Instead, for the most part, they accept that ethnicity is socially constructed and fluid, evolving and changing in response to certain stimuli and to serving certain interests.[30]

The current section and the ensuing ones ask questions and problematize the construction of ethnicity in the area around Barry's Bay and Wilno. Like John Walsh's writings on ethnicity, family, and community, this discussion "is intended to provoke reflection about elements of experience." It also attempts to confront contemporary issues since, as Donna Gabaccia writes, historians must "overcome a deep resistance to the study of the recent past – normally the province of journalists and sociologists."[31]

After determining the differences between Poles and Kashubians, the WHS, headed by Shulist, attempted to carve out a culture separate from Polish. During Shulist's term, the WHS made up a list of the most essential components of Kashubian culture. Unfortunately, he, or they, did not establish how the descriptions, especially those in the dance, music, embroidery, and culinary realms, are specifically Kashub.[32] How can dance have disappeared if the WHS does not present evidence to prove it existed in the first place? How did "Polish" musicians bring over "Kashubian" music? And why is chicken the food of the Kashubs whereas pork and fish are denied status as "official foods?" Can chicken be considered a Polish food if, before the cultural recreation, the parishioners thought of themselves as Polish and chicken was served?

Two of the most visible WHS members, Shulist and Mask-Connolly, have often treated ethnicity as a concept that had been lost or forgotten by previous generations in Canada – yet they do not look deeply into its beginnings or its creation in Poland. Shulist says "the funny thing that happened here was that for some strange reason, our ancestors did not tell us that we were of Kashub heritage. Maybe our grandparents and our parents did not listen very well, or maybe they were ashamed to say they were of Kashub culture."[33] Mask-Connolly echoes this, writing that "over the past century and a half, we the descendants of the Kashub people in Canada lost our connection to our Kashubian cultural homeland. We did not recognize the word 'Kashub,' but knew that our roots were in Poland."[34] Yet neither Shulist nor Mask-Connolly researched the evolution of the labels Cassubia and Kaszuby before arriving at these conclusions, assuming that the awareness, cognition, and body of Kashubian culture were grounded in the ancient past and always present among all classes and all regions in northern Poland.

Believing that it had been forgotten, their quest to revive (or recreate) ethnicity leaves many avenues open for analysis. The WHS has not, until recently, publicly pondered a further duality: that identity can be shaped both from within and without and is filtered and constructed by the subject. Some of the KPA's staff, as expressed in an article in their magazine, *Pomerania*, believe that in order for the Polish-Kashub group to remain culturally viable in Canada, it must forge better ties with the cultural homeland.[35] Believing this is a good idea, the WHS did forge such ties. Taking up the charge, one visible member of the WHS promoted his definitions of ethnicity as determined by descriptions rather than allowing for and emphasizing the individual residents' and members' self-determination or agency. For many years, Shulist declared in his articles that the descendants are Kashub, leaving no room for anyone to adopt hyphenated versions, such as Polish-Kashub, Polish-Canadian, Canadian, Kashubian-Polish-Canadian, Irish-Kashub, German-Kashub, and so forth. His logic, "We were not born in Poland, therefore we are Canadian Kashubs,"[36] is also puzzling. How then are the descendants "Kashub" if they were not born in "Kashubia"? However, when Mayor Shulist, using another *nom de plume* "Johnny Kashub," was asked by reporter Christine Hudder in 2012 if people can identify themselves as "half, say, Polish," he responded by saying that it is purely up to the individual to decide how they want to identify themselves. He also acknowledged that he has "Scottish blood" and Polish too, but that his passion will always be the Kashubian culture, his "true identity."[37]

Mask-Connolly, on the other hand, allows for some negotiation when she includes "Polish-Kashub" in many of her newsletter articles. However, she is prone, in some instances, to ascribing the sole label "Kashubian." For example, after tracing the roots of a local senior, Helen (Lorbetskie) Dombroskie, Mask-Connolly declared, without quoting Dombroskie, "Helen's ancestry is entirely Kashubian." In another case, Mask-Connolly ascribes the Kashubian label to a Canadian Olympian, Vaughn Chipeur, without Chipeur explicitly identifying as such. In her article describing the opening of the Opeongo Heritage Trail, Mask-Connolly wrote that it "was home to Kashubian immigrants." In another publication, she claimed that "unlike some of the other Polish Canadian families in the first Polish settlement, [Julian Kulas's] lineage is completely Kashub in origin."[38] Although there is no evidence to suggest that the original settlers identified themselves as Kashubian, Mask-Connolly imposed a label and rebranded them. Indeed, several prominent boosters of the WHS, via these aforementioned statements, did not publicly reflect on the idea some people have multiple ethnic leanings. Also, although Shulist draws attention to the priests who supposedly imposed the Polish label on the descendants, he seems unaware of the fact that his writings impose another label on them.

Being an "Ethnic": Questions and Influences on Identity

Because we construct memories to make sense of the present, memory can become embroiled in the politics of identity. Since identity, like memory, is both individual and collective, different factors compete with one another as it is being formed. In its nineteenth-century sense, ethnic identity is a given. Clifford Geertz writes that such a definition stems from "assumed givens of social existence: immediate contiguity and kin connections ... the given-ness ... [of] being born into a particular religious community, speaking a particular language ... and following particular practices. These congruities of blood, speech and custom ... are seen to have an ineffable, and at times overpowering coerciveness ... One is bound to one's kinsman ... as the result not merely of personal affection, practical necessity, common interest, or incurred obligation, but at least in great part by virtue of some ... absolute import attributed to the very tie itself."[39] Identities can be described using many terms, such as nation or culture, and can be coupled with traditions, customs, and language to produce ethnicity.[40] Ethnicity is thus a term we invoke to neatly package and/or describe characteristics of our identity. Someone referring to themselves as a member of an ethnic group summons up a certain set of characteristics to which that person *generally* subscribes.[41]

Marcus Hansen's idea of the resurgence of ethnicity along *situational* lines – the grandson wishes to remember what the son wants to forget – is important, as is sociologist Herbert Gans's idea of *symbolic* ethnicity, which allows people to exercise agency when defining their own sense of ethnicity. Similarly, Benedict Anderson opposes the nineteenth-century definition because nations and "communities are to be distinguished, not by their falsity/genuineness, but by the style in which they are imagined."[42] These notions, combined with the idea that many traditions binding groups together are invented, means that the very communities that we identify with are social constructions. As a result, as Johannes Fabian suggests, ethnographers and scholars can create their "discovered" subject. However, even though they are invented, ethnicity and ethnic groups are still, as Timothy Cooley argues, imbued with cultural meaning.[43]

Reflecting also on the words of Iacovetta, social historians approach the study of identity and individuals' experiences of it through the "three-pronged paradigm" of class, gender, and ethnicity, examining how the intersections of these categories influence "the ways in which experiences and identities ... can be shaped by a multiplicity of overlapping and even contradictory influences."[44] As argued earlier, the inculcation of Polishness in churches and schools shaped Polish identity over the course of a century. Since identity and ethnicity are fluid concepts that are "formed through the interplay of the subjective self, individual agency and structural positioning"[45] identities and experiences of ethnicity in the area are shaped and influenced by space, place, time, and encounters within and outside the group.

Unfortunately, when I tried to query notions of identity, many people, including several prominent members of local organizations, were reluctant to respond to such requests, possibly because they have not yet grasped what internal and/or external ethnicity and identity mean. This non-participation might also be due to the fact that their viewpoints could, perhaps, alter the way they are perceived by the small community.[46] I am thankful, however, that some were willing to participate and that there is a great deal of recorded oral history, in various forms, in the Madawaska Valley, making an exploration of identity negotiation possible.

Peter Glofcheskie, the current president of the WHS and a third-generation descendant, grew up in the village of Barry's Bay, the son of two teachers. He was enrolled in Polish classes run by Fr Lewandowski, in Barry's Bay, and Mira Jaworska. In these classes he learned "the high Polish" national songs and dances. At home and at church, however, he picked up "low-Polish" words that are now branded as "Kashubian." Because of this, he shares his sense of ethnic identity between Canadian, Polish, and Kashubian.[47] Clifford Blank, on the other hand, is the son of a farmer and a housewife "in the bush" north of Wilno and a third-generation descendant of settlers. Before attending school, his only language was "Polish," which he speaks to this day. Even though a large portion of his vocabulary might now be regarded as "Kashubian," rather than "Polish," Clifford still maintains that people thought "we were Polish and spoke it. We didn't know of any such term, Kashub." He identifies with "growing up on a farm and speaking Polish," the language of his parents and grandparents.[48] Julian Kulas, who grew up helping out on farms near Wilno, had similar thoughts, writing that "no one in that era knew that we were, in fact, Kashubs." Kulas's early education was from the church liturgy and "in standard Polish."[49] Tony Bleskie, a retired descendant of local settlers, identifies himself as a Canadian-Kashub. Tony states that being a Canadian-Kashub means that he speaks the tongue of his ancestors and is free to practise their faith.[50]

Using the testimony above, it becomes evident that multiple and hyphenated identities do exist in the community. Mask-Connolly, perhaps unknowingly, also shows that multiple identities exist in her family, saying that her children are "half-Irish-Canadian."[51] Unfortunately, when Shulist was president, the WHS did not publicly account for such variants, allegiances, and experiences in its promotions. It seems the WHS was only interested in the Kashubian appellation as the sole ethnic identity. However, with the release of her 2014 publication,

Marriage Matters, Mask-Connolly officially distanced her opinions from Shulist's, writing that, "while a complete rebranding as Kashub, not Polish, is essentially the view promoted by David Shulist (aka *Johnny Kashub*) ... it is not shared by this author, who feels that eliminating the Polish aspect of our self-identification would be a denial of our past history."[52]

Language is another area that interests the WHS. As Benedict Anderson wrote: "Nothing connects us affectively to the dead more than language."[53] Yet, surrounding language is the assumption that it too remains static. Fr Szulist remarked that "the language that they use today [in Canada] is from that time ... 120 to 140 years old." But the Kashub language "here [in Poland] was evolving."[54] Mask-Connolly, also drawing on ethnic triumphalism, writes that although Kashubian in Poland is influenced by German and Polish, in Canada it is a "language that has remained relatively unchanged for generations." However, she contradicts herself in the endnote for that sentence, which reads: "There were no cars when the Kashubs arrived in Canada and so there was no word for them in their vocabulary – hence when cars were invented, they used the English word with a Kashubian twist – 'cara'."[55] That word has remained in locals' vocabulary to such an extent that Natalie Glofcheskie added it into her illustrations for a 2012 children's book, *Ask My Grandpa*, which I wrote and the WHS published. Does the evolution of "cara" thus mean that the language has evolved and changed?

In fact, in the concluding remarks of a dictionary produced jointly by Stan Frymark and the WHS, Ed Chippior writes that as he "prepared the layout for this dictionary I could not help but notice the number of words that we use and assume to be of Kashub original [*sic*] are in fact Polish. This can only spell out one thing – that the influence of the Polish language on our ancestors was quite strong."[56] Yet, whether the "Polish" influence was strong before they left or after they arrived is a question that may never be answered. These comments question Mask-Connolly's claim that the language used by the settlers has changed little.

The claim that the Kashubian spoken here is unchanged might be questioned, but the WHS emphasizes that one of their goals is to maintain and spread the Kashubian language. For several years, the society has encouraged locals to read the illustrated childrens' book *Kaszëbsczë ABECADŁO*, which it has bought and sold. It also encouraged Stan Frymark of Leśno, Poland, and Julian Kulas to produce dictionaries of the Kashubian language for local residents. The WHS and Kulas reached back in order to move forward by encouraging Frymark and by using dictionaries created recently in the Kaszubian region of Poland to craft a local vernacular dictionary.[57] After all, in order for the previously oral "language" to exist, should it not have a dictionary?[58] As shown in chapter 6, Cenôva and Ramułt thought so; perhaps the WHS does too.

Such an emphasis on language means that it is, for some, central in forming and maintaining an ethnic identity. Scholars echo these thoughts. Indeed, the Bilingualism and Bicultural Commission found that language "allows for self-expression and communication according to the unique cultural logic."[59] As Walsh says, "An immigrant who can function fluently in both the languages of their new home as well as their old, [has] an opportunity to (re)construct an ethnic identity in ways which are different from that of the immigrant who is unilingual."[60] This is evident in the words of Aloysius Blank after he went on a trip to Poland with the WHS in 2009. He says that he enjoyed talking with others in Poland and "was impressed with how well we communicated in the Kashubian language. There were words that I had forgotten and they would remind me and I reminded them of some."[61] In his case, he was able to experience, rekindle, and reshape his sense of ethnicity. However, it is not simply the use of oral language that accelerates an individual's ability to function in the public sphere, but literacy. Thus, it is possible that people lacking literacy might not be able to participate in the public sphere.

If an ethnic group loses its mother tongue – or adopts another – does it lose its sense of ethnic identity? In a candid article by Mask-Connolly, she admitted that she felt inferior because she could not speak the language. In her words: "My inability causes me great sadness because language is a big part of our cultural heritage and it is not mine to relish. Last August 2009, I travelled with a group of fellow Canadian Kashubs to Kaszuby/Kaszëbe, Poland, where Kashub was spoken on many occasions and quite fluently by my travel companions ... I felt very inadequate and at times embarrassed by my inability to speak Kashub or Polish."[62] In light of Kulas's statement that the supposed "contamination" of the Kashubian language by others, such as English, "through the years was inevitable but sadly the death knell is tolling,"⁶³ is there still a place for the language of the settlers in the public and private sphere? Although there are still a few members of the WHS, such as Shulist and Chippior, who are able to interact in the Kashubian vernacular in the public sphere in Poland,⁶⁴ does it render those who cannot "less ethnic"? Does this create an elite tier in the ethnic community in Canada and abroad? Do those who are able to speak two languages possess more authority?

The long attachment of the local Polish-Kashubs to the Roman Catholic Church is constantly reiterated throughout many discourses.⁶⁵ Many authors, local and international, allude to this. Before the cultural recreations in the Wilno and Barry's Bay area, the Church was the gathering place for parishioners scattered throughout the neighbouring townships. The Church, and its leaders, put on various events, from bingo to baseball games, plays, and Polish celebrations.⁶⁶ Parish priests also acted as pastkeepers. By creating parish registries, they left an immense archive for genealogists like Mask-Connolly. They socialized people into ways of thinking, including, as shown in the words of Kulas, the idea that the locals were "Polish." Many churches, including Catholic ones, are conservative, reluctant to abandon their traditions. Alan Anderson and James Frideres would agree, but they also state that churches can also bolster ethnic consciousness. G.W. Allport says that the Church can be "the pivot of cultural tradition" for a group.⁶⁷

Since one of the descendants' main reasons for emigrating to Canada was to seek unimpeded religious practice, their allegiance to the Church was strong. A close allegiance to the Church – especially one that was an important part of their everyday life – meant that innovative ways of seeing oneself as "non-Polish" (Kashubian) were limited by the priests, pastkeepers who promoted paradigms of Polishness from the pulpit. Perhaps this is another reason why Rekowski's words – whether corroborated or not – had such a profound effect on locals. Because the people were unwilling to question the word of the priest, it fell to another *local* priest, Rekowski, to cast off the parochial paradigms about ethnicity and classist paradigms between "high" and "low" Polish. Only then could parishioners change their ways of thinking.

To this day, many celebrations of Polish-Kashub or Kashubian culture maintain the link to the Church. To try and further understand this link, Jan Pakulski poignantly argues that for Poles, "participation in religious ceremonies is regarded as a patriotic duty, moral obligation and a political act of defiance in the face of the atheist propaganda" from the communist era. Otherwise, an anti-religious stance "is regarded as so incompatible with the image of the Pole-Catholic and with the national identity, that it sometimes precludes membership in migrant communities" and organizations.[68] Thus, it is no surprise that in Canada, a litany of priests have been involved with WHS activities. Fr Archie Afelskie, a descendant of original settlers and now deceased, was asked to be present at the sod-turning for the park in 1998. Msgr Pick, a descendant of original settlers, was a key pastkeeper interviewed in Barecki's film. Fr Mervin Coulas, a descendant of original settlers, has been asked to say the opening prayers for many WHS events, along with Fr Wojciech Blach. There is also an international link: Fr Wladyslaw Szulist has also been known to say Masses for Kashubian events in Poland.[69] While in years past, masses were conducted in Polish (and Latin until Vatican II) and well attended, the elimination of the Polish mass in 2003, by Bishop Richard Smith at St Hedwig's in Barry's Bay, means that the use of English (and a resurgence of Latin) is widespread. Since priests no longer conduct mass in Polish (or Kashubian), it raises the question, can Kashubianism be promoted and nurtured without the support and language links with the Church?

Mask-Connolly ponders this question. "If only we could find realistic ways to maintain a Polish Kashub element in our Polish parishes. If not, we will risk losing them in the cultural melting pot that will eventually rob us of all uniqueness."[70] It seems that without an alliance with the Church, the Kashubian language and therefore Kashubianism may not survive. But is it still not unique even if a link does not exist? Wojciech Etmanski presents the dichotomy "NO LANGUAGE – NO CULTURE."[71] But can the culture survive outside of Etmanski's dichotomy?

Others question Shulist's ideas about certain foods being ethnic. For some, ethnic food is not a profound marker of ethnicity. Clifford Blank recalls a different feeling of ethnicity when helping to collect food for St Mary's suppers. Polishness, at this event, was exercised not through eating chicken, but by speaking Polish with other community members. Blank views the ethnic food label with chicken as a contemporary construction since chickens were "the food of convenience." They could be raised more quickly and slaughtered close to the event date. Such a claim makes sense in an era without the widespread use of freezers for storing food. Blank also claims that the diet of locals consisted of a large amount of pork because it could be cured, smoked, and salted and eaten at breakfast, lunch, and/or dinner.[72] Newspaper articles around the time the parish supper was started in Wilno mention no such correlation between chicken and being Kashub. In fact, other rural parish suppers, bazaars, and picnics between the 1920s and 1950s featured chicken – perhaps due to the fact that it was the food of convenience.[73] We also see that chicken is not mentioned in Lorentz's writings. He declares that "almost the only meat eaten [in Cassubia] is pork and goose. After the pig is killed in autumn, the largest part of the meat is pickled and made into sausages ... and bacon."[74]

Does this mean that Poles cannot feel ethnic if they eat chicken? Certainly not. Rather, it points to the fact that the WHS's descriptions, constructed during Shulist's term as president, are not the sole ascriptive force in the internalization of ethnicity. In fact, Shulist seems to forget his own similar claim, written in 2000, that pork is a food of the Kashubs.[75] When making distinctions like the WHS has, we should remember that everyone's perceptions of ethnicity are different. We should also carefully heed the words of Northrop Frye, that "assimilating unity to identity produces the kind of provincial isolation which is called separatism."[76]

The Point of Cross-Fertilization: Inconsistencies

After looking at how some have reached into the past to move forward, it is also important to situate the point of fusion between the creation of Kashubianism in Canada and its concurrent point of evolution in northern Poland. Working on the idea that ethnicity and culture evolve, its development in both countries was far from equal. When the WHS was created in 1998, decades had passed since its older partner – the KPA – had been formed in Poland. Similarly, many generations had lived and passed away between the era of settlement and the present era. As argued in chapter 6, the evolution of the Kashubian appellation in Poland went through many phases. Cassubiæ has been modified and adopted – by individuals and associations – to describe a folk, a language, and a set of invented traditions that imply connections with the past. These cultural constructions of what it means to be Kashubian have evolved, and have been invented and reinvented since Kashubia was territorialized and separated from the abstract notion of the folk in nineteenth-century Poland. For some, part of forming "culture" meant a solidification of the language, religion, and folkways of the group. By 2000, Kashubianism was well-established in Poland and grew, with the help of scholars, associations, and individuals, over the course of 150 years. On the other hand, it was only starting to take shape in Canada.

While looking into the past, the WHS adopted many aspects of the Kashubian culture from the KPA. However, since the WHS did not conduct research into its evolution, its claims that these practices were ancestral for the descendants living in Canada are questionable. This becomes evident when comparing the statements made about the Kashubian language and the craft of embroidery. The language used by Shulist and Mask-Connolly faults the descendants for failing to realize they were Kashubian. They imply that the original settlers knew they were Kashubian. But what is Shulist and Mask-Connolly's justification? They have not presented any evidence to suggest that the original settlers identified as Kashubian. French, Watson, and Reeves, working for the Crown, recorded them as Prussian Poles. The oral testimony of Clifford Blank points toward the fact that local populations thought of themselves as Polish. Pick said the same about the Kashub name: "We knew nothing here before [Rekowski]." Kulas, the one encouraged by the WHS to create a Kashubian dictionary, also put forth this claim. Shulist himself noted the evolution of how locals viewed their speech in Canada: Polish, "low Polish," followed by Kashubian (after Rekowski's work was published).[77]

Yes, the Kashubian appellation was written about in Poland during the 1850s, 1860s, and 1870s when the settlers arrived in Canada, yet, as shown in chapter 6, major recognition of the Kashubian folk did not take place until the 1890s and 1900s. The mere fact that Cenôva attempted to create the language and group at the same time as the settlers left for Canada West does not mean that the settlers in Canada identified as Kashubian. If there was a Kashubian movement in the Ottawa Valley, why has documentation not survived? When writing a list of early settlers, why did Mikolai Prynz not label them as "Kaszubi" or a term close to it? Rekowski did not acquire the Kaszubi label from his ancestors. He picked it up from a book produced in the interwar period, long after the original settlers had left Poland. No one has yet suggested that the Church and land agents conspired to destroy all the evidence and remnants of early Kashubianism in Canada. If such a claim were made, it would resemble one of Cenôva's – that early stone writings of Kashubs were destroyed by Christianity. Subversive identities can exist, a thought touched on by Shulist, but without local evidence to suggest it such a claim remains speculative at best.

Similarly, the WHS's claims about the embroidery practised by the early settlers in Canada imply antiquity. Since 2010, when the KPA promoted the seven-colour guide and standardized patterns of embroidery as Kashubian, the WHS has appropriated them as the embroidery of the Kashubian population in Canada. In the WHS's words, "Kashubian Embroidery is a lost art with the Canadian Kashub Poles … [it] was abandoned in the late 1800s and the ladies took to Canadian patterns which they could purchase from the Sears' or Eatons' Catalogues. When the ladies did this, they did not realize that they were losing a part of their Kashubian Culture."[78] These comments, made during Shulist's term as president, reflect an uneasiness or unfamiliarity with cultural hybridity. However, investigations into the evolution and standardization of embroidery and colour patterns in chapter 6 show that although this invented tradition evolved in Poland after the migrants left for Canada, the settlers in the Ottawa Valley did not "lose" the craft by adopting patterns from catalogues – they never knew the standardized patterns or colours to begin with. Further, the WHS shows no evidence of the early patterns, such as the Zukowo designs, that are designated as "official" by the KPA. A blanket box (*skrynia*) displayed in the Burchat house in the park has a painted flower motif on it; however, the motif is not one of the standardized patterns (see figure 7.2). The arched pediments and columns that Wilno wardrobes and cupboards exhibit are Baroque. Thus, there is no continuum between the KPA's official designs and the ones known to Polish-Kashubs in the Barry's Bay and Wilno area before 1998. However, while the floral designs made on furniture by Wilno Poles do not match the standardized designs c. 1900 that emerged in the Kaszubian area in Poland, these surviving pieces keep their value based on the fact that they are small-scale products that were hand-made by pioneers of a small ethnic group that settled in Ontario around 150 years ago. For descendants, they once had a practical purpose. They now have the added nostalgic value of being produced by the hands of relatives or fellow community members.

The WHS, as "custodians of Canada's Polish Kashub History," continues to promote and sell the patterns and guides from Zukowo as

7.2　A Wilno blanket box. The raised base has Baroque elements and mortise and tenon construction was used. The lid is painted dark red. The front panels have dark green flowers and vines with hints of light green.

authentic[79] but they have not considered their origins and the practice has become what is considered an authentic part of locals' heritage.[80] Barbara Kirshenblatt-Gimblett states that heritage is created via exhibition and, in turn, endows heritage with a second life. Through promotion and exhibition, the WHS, as a pastkeeper, creates local heritage or local culture. However, with the commodification of culture, and due to recent increases in ethnic tourism, such products have come to be seen as the quintessential and authentic products of the group's indigenous culture. Despite contrived claims, the promotions achieve a sense of permanence as discourse. Indeed, as Patrick Hutton writes: "What is remembered about the past depends on the way it is represented." But, as Cooley argues: "Ethnographers and tourists alike value what is perceived as authentic rather than what is perceived as spurious." Judging by the popularity of the WHS – which has hundreds of donor-members – we should not negate the fact that, for many, these activities have cultural meaning and a connection to an authentic past – whatever it may be. We should also tread with caution, because, as P.M. Barford argues, when studying a people, the temptation to amalgamate a few scraps of information and come to erroneous conclusions is strong.[81]

Why Has the Cultural Recreation Received Such a Large Following?

Since 1998, in opposition to the history- and peasant-based language label that was "imposed" on local populations by external, educated Poles, the WHS's construction of Kashubian culture has functioned as a bastion of defence and the cornerstone of a unique identity. This seems especially poignant when reflecting on Gans's observations that ethnicity and ethnic organization are used "as a psychological and political defense against the injustices which they suffer in an unequal society."[82] It is a movement that appropriates voice and agency from the previous elite figures who defined locals' culture for them. In the case of the Wilno/Barry's Bay area, the elite were priests or educated postwar Poles – but locals are now leading their own movements. Indeed, the WHS has successfully brought together hundreds of people in their Kashub celebrations. This section investigates how participating in WHS activities establishes a link between past and present in a global society.

In recent decades, writes John Gillis, the proliferation of constructed identities "is becoming evident, particularly in the Western world, where the old bases of national identities are being rapidly undermined by economic globalization and transnational political integration." By delving further into historical constructions, "we are beginning to learn more about those who deploy them and whose interests they serve." In historiography, gone are the paradigms of assimilation or cultural pluralism now that concepts of transnationalism are at the fore.[83] However, ethnicity is still increasingly relevant for multiculturalism. Many need to define themselves to tread atop the sea of cultures. While the ease of modern travel has brought locations separated by great distances closer, globalization has also meant that we are separated from many locations in which we live and work. In some cases, we move to seek employment or to pursue educational opportunities. This, in turn, challenges the durability of ethnic identity, especially for those who venture beyond the cultural hearth. It can cause distanciation, "the spreading out of social relations across time and space."[84] Several people, including Zurakowski and Martin Shulist, acknowledge the effect of these movements on the Polish-Kashubs.[85] It is no wonder then that modernization and globalization are sometimes accused of perpetrating cultural discontinuity.[86]

To combat the metaphysical loss of home, ethnic movements, such as the one initiated by the WHS, have functioned as what Basu calls "homecomings for homeless minds." This "new white ethnic movement" has been described as "the desire of white, suburban, middle-class, assimilated citizens to effectively dissimilate themselves and recover a more distinctive, particular ethnic identity."[87] If, during the course of dissimilation, one finds that one's ancestors were displaced, the desire to return to the home space, or the space believed to be home, is often strong. For some, the desire to return to or to re-establish a "home" finds an outlet in genealogy and the roots phenomenon. Others participate in writing and shaping local history to combat an impending loss as well as a yearning for connection. Genealogists, who read history backwards, attempt to locate continuity with the past. This is done, perhaps, to comprehend the present or the future, or to "assuage their guilt at having given up ancestral practices."[88] In the process, the pre-modern peasants who made the journey long ago are "acknowledged as pioneers in the modernization of consciousness, among the first to adapt to multi-national or 'distanciated' ... space and time in the global economic system."[89]

At times, this longing for connection with the past is described as nostalgia. Its earlier definition described a "pathological illness for which the prescribed cure was 'going home.'" It received a new meaning in the early twentieth century which, according to Walsh, is "an often pejorative sentimentalism that attaches itself to the ephemeral and the prosaic and that, as a result, produces unimportant, false, and inauthentic memories." Mike Featherstone's thoughts are similar. He believes that "successive generations have invested in a form of nostalgia in which the past is viewed as the epitome of coherence and order, something which was more simple and emotionally fulfilling." These childhood memories, images of the past, and ancestors "help foster myths of belonging, warmth and togetherness." They help to describe, recall, or invent the "mythical security of a childhood long relinquished."[90] These comments resemble the feelings that Stella Yarskavitch, a third-generation descendant, recalls about the past. "Times were *good* then," she says, since there was no television or newspapers and people talked together as a group.⁹¹ Such a longing for a simple past can also be described as a yearning for the *volk*. Yet, as Walsh argues, we ought to examine how nostalgia is a vehicle that accelerates present experiences and interactions with understandings of the self and the past.⁹²

Cooley reminds us that the concept of village, or rural life, "has become a metaphor for goodness and purity, the place where tradition thrives."⁹³ The longing to return, for the Polish-Kashub group, has afflicted some who seek a return from the metaphysical and actual loss of home. Martin Shulist observed that locals left for the cities and now "they're coming back ... and buying [the farms] back." Johnny Recoskie is one of those locals who worked for thirty years in "the city" because "it just hasn't paid to work the farm." Now he is back on the land he grew up on and uses it as a garden and for hunting.⁹⁴ It can also be argued that the return to home and the longing for nostalgic connections to the past produced the discourses by Rekowski, Mask-Connolly, Shulist, and Prince. Rekowski started to write after his return to the area because of a longing to know who his mother was. Mask-Connolly, after moving away from the area for school, work, and family, still lives only about 200 kilometres away. Her attempts to reach into the past – evident also in keeping her maiden name – and unearth her grandmother's roots produced mountains of genealogical data. Her lineage exponentially increased the further she reached into the past. David Shulist (re)discovered who he was after he returned to Wilno, and after his forty-fifth birthday. Afterwards, with his father Martin, he attempted, with missionary zeal, to explore who his ancestors were. Theresa Prince entered the field after retiring from her long-time elementary-school teaching position. Her explorations into the past produced several genealogical books. All of these pastkeepers and community boosters have energetically published their findings so that their ancestors will not perish without a trace.

Similarly, Ed Chippior's involvement with the WHS increased after his retirement from the business and computers department at Madawaska Valley District High School. He was first the historical director of the WHS and, as of 2015, the building director. The treasurer, Ursula (Borutski) Jeffrey, retired a few years ago from the MVDHS office.⁹⁵ Secure pensions and free time allow several locals to try and engage with the past and try to disassimilate themselves after being in the English-language workplace for so long. By (re)creating local culture and local history through activities, festivals, and a museum, they are preserving the past and preventing it from being forgotten.

But, one could rightly argue, the motivations and experiences of executive members of the WHS do not necessarily predetermine members' and locals' individual perceptions of ethnicity. To explore these, we need to examine the function of various experiences and activities. Many people participated in the WHS's efforts to open the Opeongo Heritage Trail. For Mary Anne Coghlan, of St Clair, Michigan, her return to the area, in 2009, and her participation in the event was a part of the roots phenomenon. In her words, it meant to "feel where my roots came from and where I started," since her great-great-grandfather, John Brotton, settled in the area in the 1880s. Brian Lorbetskie said that he cleared land and participated in the event as a tribute to his deceased father, who grew up in the Wilno area. It was also done to "help out" his heritage.[96]

The craft of embroidery that the WHS has introduced in local elementary schools is another avenue that locals and members participate in. As seen in chapter 6, the craft was introduced by Gulgowska to supplement women's incomes in early twentieth-century northern Poland.[97] Their designs evolved and were sold for profit. Peasant folk art in late nineteenth- and early twentieth-century Ukrainian communities gave women a similar creative outlet. These "handicrafts were increasingly extolled ... both for their national significance and for their profitability as a cottage industry." Frances Swyripa argued that in their communities, these acts "enhanced women's self-esteem."[98] Similarly, the craft has been adopted by a group of senior women in the Barry's Bay and Wilno region.

Started in 2005, the initiative was organized by Theresa Chapeskie, who "discovered" Kashubian embroidery on a 2004 trip to Poland. She too believes that it is a lost tradition.[99] Joining her to teach are several descendants of original settlers and several postwar migrants: "Bernice Bleskie, Rose Marie Recoskie, Rose Marie Trader, Eva Kulas, Veronica Bialy, Helene Urbanowicz, Sophia Kosinski, Eva Kaczkowski, Leokadia Ziemiak, Bronislawa Mazgaj and Joanna Szymanski,"[100] as well as others, like Theresa Prince. Dozens of students also practise the craft at George Vanier in Combermere, St Casimir's in Round Lake, St Mary's in Wilno, and St John Bosco in Barry's Bay. In 2010, a competition was held at the Kashub Day Festival, and the top design, by Katrina Yantha, remained on display. The work of the other five finalists – Martin Voldock, Raymond Hudder, Sarah McCauley, Rachel Pecoskie, and Justina Sadecki – was placed in the museum in Zukowo, Poland, the so-called "traditional birthplace of Kashubian embroidery." While those participating in embroidery are stitching connections in time, it has a distinct function for one person. Anthony Aide, a thirteen-year-old afflicted with Attention Deficit Hyperactivity Disorder, finds that he is able to focus on the craft and practises it at home.[101] The practice thus also has a function in the present beyond satisfying nostalgic cravings.

In 2010 and 2011, the KPA and WHS helped to foster the resurgence of interest in the Kashubian language. A teacher from Kaszuby, Poland, Karl Rhode, was invited to live in the Madawaska Valley. On Friday nights, local residents eagerly attended classes. Three local elementary schools also participated in the venture and a history lecture was delivered to the broader community at MVDHS in February 2011. According to Rhode, interest in the classes was partially driven by locals' desire to "read and write the language of their ancestors."[102] Regardless of whether or not the alphabet they were learning was standardized after their ancestors left occupied Poland, the participants were still connecting with their past. Another reason for the interest in the vernacular can be found in the writings of J.J. Smolicz and M.J. Secombe, who wrote that in "the case of language-centered cultures ... their survival in a viable form is dependent on the preservation of the mother tongue of its group members."[103] For the adult participants in Rhode's classes, language was evidently a crucial enough component of ethnicity to warrant their interest in preserving it.

Conclusion

This chapter has examined how ideas of difference prompted a group of descendants to embark on a course to reimagine the way other locals and descendants thought of themselves. Through the WHS's claims, we see how a body of culture and invented traditions is formed to contrast the previously hegemonic cultural label imposed on the original settlers and their descendants. Even though the WHS did not often account for multiple identities, it is clear that multiple identities and allegiances have persisted through the period of cultural (re)definition. My intent here is not, in the words of Deborah Anders Silverman, to "imply that one's ethnic identity is primary; it is just one of many identities available" for individuals to choose from. When promoting an essential public or community identity, we need to heed the words of Gillis: "We must take responsibility for [identity's] abuses, recognizing that every assertion of identity involves a choice that affects not just ourselves but others."[104]

Although several claims of the WHS are dubious and have come under scrutiny in this chapter, they are meaningful for many people. This chapter has presented stories of participation in these cultural activities and festivals to show how connections are made with the past. For some, participation may be a way to reconnect with ancestors they knew little about. For others, participation may be a way to honour deceased and/or living relatives. These activities also allow people to reach back across time and space to connect or reconnect with a life, locale, or with the ancestors they left behind. In the Barry's Bay and Wilno area, connecting with the past is accentuated by connecting with the Polish present and bringing the two Kaszubian cultures, with their different histories of evolution, into closer alignment in the present. The question remains, however: can this movement survive?

EPILOGUE

The history of the first Polish settlement in Canada is well-represented in books and other media, with many writings by host-culture and descendant authors. In recent years, the latter group has centred attention on the Polish-Kashub group. In the process of documenting and preserving these works, however, several key questions have been left unexplored, and authors have not critiqued the various migration and settlement narratives. To attend to these gaps in the historiography, this study expands and contextualizes the claims made by local authors, pastkeepers, and community boosters about the history of the community. The study also questions the narrative and recasts parts. Using the concept of the meso level, the study integrates both primary archival and secondary material to marry micro-level movements with the macro-level narrative to produce more knowledge on the subject, expand on the avenues opened by local memory, and address concepts of ethnicity and cultural redefinition.

But with the invention of a new ethnicity today, will the new "Canadian Kashubian" identity fall by the wayside in the coming years? Hints of this have already emerged. Despite the claim that the "Kashubian" culture is in danger of eroding because the language is being lost, ethnic identity can (and does) exist – in the immediate community, in the imagined community, and in the diaspora. When we perceive ethnicity as a fluid concept that is constantly reworked, negotiated, and refashioned on an individual level, we see how it can continue to exist.

No one can know the future of ethnicity in the Polish-Kashub communities of Barry's Bay and Wilno. Wojciech Etmanski and Mask-Connolly feel that the loss of language is directly linked to the loss of ethnicity and impending assimilation. Yet despite the fact that many in the current generation are losing their ethnicity because they are losing the language (or adopting another), they are still participating in local folk activities. Other paradigms look at the subject of ethnic identity and change. Anderson and Frideres's definition of an ethnic identity includes ethnic origin (largely determined by labelling the nation from which one departed or the common mother tongue), mother tongue, ethnic-oriented religion, and group folkways. Jadwiga Kucharska, after researching ethnic retention among the Polish-Kashubs in Ontario during the 1970s and 1980s, concluded that locals identified several categories of ethnicity. Some were similar to conventional definitions, some slightly different. Kucharska determined that locals' ethnic identity could be categorized by attachment to their language (which they knew to be Polish), their religion, their attachment to the soil, and their inherited farms.[1]

Whatever the definition, change results when any of these categories is de-emphasized. Some pastkeepers and members of the WHS emphasize certain keynotes of ethnicity; others emphasize different ones. In the words of W.D. Bourrie, "the degree to which an ethnic group feels that its identity is being eroded is related to the emphasis which the group traditionally places on language, religion, and folkways as the keynote to group identity. In other words, if an ethnic group has tended to emphasize maintenance of its own traditional language, loss of that language will be equated largely with the loss of group identity."[2]

Herbert Gans also reminds us that ethnicity can persist by emphasizing certain categories and symbols and without physically returning "home." The concept of symbolic ethnicity, "a nostalgic allegiance to the culture of an immigrant generation, or that of an old country ... can be felt without having to be incorporated in everyday behaviour." Unlike imposed ethnic identities, symbolic ethnicity is voluntary and expressed in a myriad of ways. This type of ethnicity suits many people today because it can be practised from a distance. In this paradigm, the abstract past and the old country "are particularly useful as identity symbols because they are far away and cannot make arduous demands on ... ethnics; even sending large amounts of money is ultimately an easy way to help." Symbolic ethnicity also "does not require functioning groups or networks; feelings of identity can be developed by allegiances to symbolic groups that never meet, or to collectivities that meet only occasionally."[3] This type is currently practised and evident through the 2007 donations by parishioners of St Hedwig's in Barry's Bay to the Church of St Martin in Borzyszkowy, Poland. Parishioners like Andy Etmanski, Mary (Glofcheskie) Blank, Anna Etmanski, and Fr Chris Shalla sent $5,000 to help with restoration costs even though they never spoke or met with the parishioners in Poland.[4]

Timothy Cooley's analysis of ethnomusicology in southern Poland can also be applied to the Polish-Kashub group. Working from the ideas of symbolic ethnicity, Cooley interprets the folk music festival in Zakopane as a performative, modern-day ritual. Since rituals are "symbolic representations of objects, beliefs, or truths of special significance to a group," the festival acts as a ritual that integrates aspects of the past into a changing *Górale* ethnicity. Because the ritual is so effective, ethnicity is transformed into entertainment, influencing its reception among audiences. As a result, the audience, as passive participants, denotes what they see on display as ethnicity. This experience, in turn, renders them ethnic since they are participating (albeit passively) in an ethnic celebration. "Performed tradition becomes the tradition; the representation becomes the actuality."[5] At the same time, ethnicity on display can be dangerous in the externally-directed capitalist marketplace because it becomes more difficult to distinguish between mere acts for entertainment alone and authentic expressions. David Harvey also worries that a quest for authenticity can lead to artificial "invented traditions and a commercialized heritage culture." Cooley has a similar argument. Because of the festival and performance, the continued survival of the *Górale* "as an ethnic group no longer depends first and foremost on successful crops and healthy livestock." The folk festival promotes tourism and tourism dictates the survival of the distinctive *Górale* "music-culture in the face of increasing globalization."[6]

Cooley's findings can be applied to the annual festival put on by the WHS. Originally called Polish Day, its transformation into Kashub Day, and its popularity, as shown by the large crowds, means that ethnicity can survive the onslaughts of assimilation, acculturation, and globalization. The celebration becomes ritual. Even if they are not born in Kaszuby, Poland, those who perform on stage become "authentically" – if only for a day – Kashubian. The wearing of "Kashubian costumes" and the yellow and black colours, imported from Poland,[7] render the stage Kashubian. The awards presented for embroidery affirm the works and their creators as Kashubian, and those who report on the events become Kashubian.[8] The festival, as ritual, becomes heritage, and its performances, given in the cultural hearth of Canada's first Polish settlement, become authentic experiences for the audience. The practice of opening the festival with a prayer is also transformative. The blessing functions as a symbolic, continuous ritual (or tradition) that connects ancestors, deeply rooted in faith and the land, to the scattered crop of descendants joined together in the present-day festival.[9] Of course, at the end of the day, its symbolic participants return to their locales across the land and those wearing Kashubian costumes don their street clothes.

The Polish-Kashub group and the WHS also rely on ethnic tourism to spread ethnicity. Indeed, without it the festival would not exist. And without the festival, symbolic interactions with ethnicity would not be as plentiful. These commemorative festivals and rituals, to borrow the words of Featherstone, "can be understood as acting like batteries which store and recharge the sense of communality" among the group.[10] These theories make sense when we view ethnicity as a fluid concept that is continually reinvented and negotiated. But, to its credit, the WHS has done more than (re)create or revive ethnicity in the Barry's Bay and Wilno area. It has firmly grounded it within the transatlantic sphere.

The WHS, the Diaspora, and Sites of Memory

Several of the WHS's activities and ventures have created a gathering space and places of memory for the local as well as the broader Kashubian diaspora. The term diaspora, as mentioned in the introduction, has been used to describe the "dispersion and exile of Jews from their historic homeland." Basu, however, reminds us that recent interpretations of memory and diaspora have returned "instead to the etymological [Greek] roots of the word ... 'to sow over' or 'scatter' ... referring to expansionism not forced exile." In recent years, diaspora has been used to describe the broad scattering of ethnic groups, such as the Irish, across several continents.[11]

In the face of globalization and the metaphysical loss of home, many people have adopted symbolic forms of ethnicity and, knowingly or not, are a part of an imagined community. Distance limits but does not extinguish such a concept. In Anderson's words, imagined communities exist even though their members may never meet or communicate, since "in the minds of each lives the image of their communion." But a greater sense of symbolic ethnicity can be felt when it is attached to symbols and sites of culture.[12] By building the park and museum, the WHS, under the curatorship of Mask-Connolly, has transformed a physical space into a "place" where ethnic interactions are centralized on a recurring basis for the North American diaspora of Polish-Kashubs. As Perin argues, "the notion of a space is basic to ethnicity ... An ethnic culture cannot survive simply on memories of a distant space. To maintain its distinctiveness and to flourish, it must interact with a real, immanent space." Moreover, since community museums can focus on minority populations, they can and do draw upon the lure of transnational ethnic tourism. Thus, the creation of the museum can maintain an imagined community.[13]

The original museum is a small, one-storey log building, which was donated by the Chippior family in 1998. The building, considered the "Welcome Centre," houses books, paintings, furniture, and the "Heritage Store," and is able to accommodate about eight persons comfortably. The second building on the site is a log shed, which functions both as a display building and, on Kashub Day, as the stage. It too was donated by the Chippior family and moved to the park. The shed displays lumbering, cabinetmaking, and blacksmith tools, among other items. A third building is a scoop-roofed shelter that houses the iron cross made by Leon Ostrowski. The cross is significant for the local population: it was rescued from the 1936 fire at St Stanislaus Kostka Church in Wilno. The interlocking pattern of hollowed-out logs on the roof made a quick and effective "scooped roof" for many early settlers in the Ottawa Valley. A fourth building, a log farmhouse, was donated by the Burchat family, moved to the site in 2006, and opened in 2008. Among other items, it displays typical pioneer objects including an old stove, blanket box, tables, chairs, spinning wheels, cupboard, and beds. Like the home of the good and fervently pious Polish-Kashub family of yesteryear, the walls are hung with large pictures of the Virgin Mary and Jesus. In 2013, a blacksmith shop featuring Ostrowski's blacksmith tools and John Borutski's workbench, with antique carpentry tools, was opened to the public. The pathways in the park were beautifully landscaped by Andy Borutski and have been maintained by Teenie Mask and Ursula Jeffrey.[14] The centre of the park, as mentioned in chapter 7, is dotted with heritage stones that commemorate and honour the original settlers. Admission is free, although the WHS does appreciate a donation, a membership, or a purchase from the Heritage Store.

As Laura Schneider writes, "a notable quality in Ontario's local community museums is the desire to articulate a local quality or flavour, and to distinguish this from broader characterizations of identity."[15] Operating as the "Wilno Heritage Park & Skansen/Open Air Museum," its myriad of titles distinguishes it among others in the Ottawa Valley.[16] The exteriors ensure that passersby recognize its function as the gathering place for the Kashub community. Embroidery patterns and the word "Kaszëbë" were painted on the front doors of the shed/stage by Mary Bloskie and Sarah Chippior, and Kashubian flags are flown throughout the park. Yet, since the focus of the museum is centred on – and controlled by – a community group with specific cultural intentions, it can be accused of a parochial conception of local identity. Indeed, as Schneider found, the "collecting practices in community museums tend to concentrate on regional archaeology, parochial events, and local heroes such as community founders."[17]

This is not entirely the case with the Wilno Heritage Park. Stepping into the "Welcome Centre," one is bombarded by the sheer volume of items and displays attributed as Kashubian or Polish-Kashubian. This museum building functions as a filiopietistic site for ancestor worship. The walls and ceiling are covered with large pictures and portraits, many from the collection of local artist Frank Ritza. A visual hagiography of community leaders – including priests, of course – meets the visitor's eye. The genuflections to notable ethnic community heroes are equally apparent at the Muzeum Kaszubskie in Kartuzy, Poland (see chapter 6). Stepping into the log shed/stage, the Burchat farmhouse, or the blacksmith shop, one is greeted with a different display. The barn and farmhouse portray a different way of life, and showcase the many donations from locals. These include everything from wooden spoons to cast-iron pots and wooden chairs. The Ostrowski Blacksmith Shop was dismantled, moved to the park, and rebuilt in 2012. Ed Chippior led the initiative with the help of a dozen or so people. The blacksmith shop was completed by including hand-forged tools, used by Leon Ostrowski until his death in 1922.

Other than the small plaques, which give a bit of information about the building or the implements, the character of these buildings seems to point to a pioneer way of life rather than something specifically

Kashubian or Polish-Kashub. The fact that they were adopted and used by Kashubs or Polish-Kashubs may mean that they retain sentimental value as Kashubian or Polish-Kashubian, but to the uninformed twenty-first-century eye, they evoke a way of life that has long since passed. They can also function as a reminder of the tough old days before mechanization and convenience eased the routines of everyday life. It has been remarked that, more often than not, pioneer museums depict an idealized past of displaced objects, as opposed to operating as precise research or educational tools.[18] Visitors step back to a more nostalgic perspective of history (it is doubtful the dirt floors were as clean and bug-free as the new concrete floor). While the Welcome Centre attempts to educate visitors about Kashubs, the barn and farmhouse represent a pioneer past, idealized or not. The reason that these artifacts do not seem Kashubian is because of the extent to which, despite their much-touted geographical isolation, Polish-Kashubs rapidly adopted North American houses and agricultural methods.

As an outdoor pioneer museum, it is targeted to a local audience as well as the casual tourist and ethnic tourist. Like other pioneer museums in North America, it depicts the simplicity of life for the pioneers. It is not a repository of high culture or a place where children must be kept in order. Mary Tivy synthesizes these tropes and their appeal, saying that they are antimodernist, a reaction to present modern conditions, and a nostalgic longing for the past. They also appeal to visitors because of their perceived "loss of a sense of community, alienation from the family, and a lack of personal involvement in the production of primary goods such as food, clothing and furniture." Adopting the words of Schneider, "these sorts of museums seek to extol the perils of settler life in order to inspire visitors' gratitude for modern comforts." In the process, "'The Pioneer' himself (and occasionally, herself) is constructed as a model to emulate (or at least admire)."[19] Visitors can worship their ethnic ancestors, and connect to the past, by going to the museum and digesting its material. They no longer need to feel guilty about forgetting the past.

Lowenthal argues, "Visitors flock to pioneer museums not to reenact their forebears' lives but to … affirm a connection with a heritage." They return visitors to their roots. In this way, the museum/park/skansen functions as a contact zone for ethnics. As such, "their organizing structure as a collection becomes an ongoing historical, political, moral

Table 8.1: Summer visitors to WHS Heritage Park

Year	Visitors	Year	Visitors
2002	1,095	2008	1,858
2004	2,191	2009	1,456
2005	1,497	2010	1,951
2006	1,798	2011	1,905
2007	1,650	2012	1,958

Source: Wilno Heritage Society, 2014.

relationship – a power charged set of exchanges."[20] What is collected and displayed is given a sense of authority that, in turn, prompts the recollection, diffusion, and the reimagining of the past. The popularity of the museum/park/skansen before and after Kashub Day is also significant to the greater Polish, Kashub, and Polish-Kashub diaspora as a contact zone. Many people who have roots in these ethnic groups often make a point of visiting Wilno and the site (see table 8.1). However, the number of actual visits cannot be counted, since the outdoor park can be visited before and after museum hours. Many visitors with family and/or friends in the Canadian diaspora arrive from Poland every year, and members of the North American diaspora also visit.[21]

One visitor from the diaspora was Fr Paul Breza of Winona, Minnesota.[22] He is the founder of two Polish organizations in Winona, the Polish Heritage Society and the Polish Cultural Institute, where several nineteenth-century Poles from the Kashubian and Silesian regions settled. These organizations split for about thirty years, but in the years after Breza's visit to Wilno in 2005, the two have been slowly merging and have forged closer ties with their sister city of Bytów, Poland. Also, in the last couple of years, their website has been taking on a Kashubian trope alongside its Polish past. The "Polish Cultural Institute, Inc. & Museum" now declares itself the "Kashubian Capital of America" according to the "unofficial opinion of the webmaster," Joseph Jan Hughes.[23] The header on its website includes a large yellow and black Kashubian griffin icon that dwarfs the red lettering of the organization and the Polish eagle. Despite these claims by Hughes, many Polish, Irish, and other family-oriented activities take place at the museum or are promoted by the museum – such as the 2009 Vietnamese music festival, St Patrick's Day events, or the annual *Smaczne Jabkla* (tasty apple) Festival. Frances Edstrom, in an article entitled "What Winona Needs," writes that after Stan Frymark, an ally of the WHS, visited Winona, he mentioned a large "Kashubian population near Wilno, Ontario, Canada, where they still speak the language, unlike in Winona, where most people of Kashubian descent don't know much of the language at all, except ... certain pronunciations and words leftover from childhood." As a result of this information and Frymark's Kashub/English dictionary, Edstrom wonders whether locals would be able to decipher the language of their ancestors. One also wonders whether the Heritage Society's dwindling membership (about 280 in 2010, down from about 400 in its heyday) and the 400 or so members of the Cultural Institute[24] will be able to engage and broaden their membership, as the WHS has done, with their recent amalgamations, diasporic connections, and re-ethnicization efforts. Only time will tell.

The persistence of ethnicity in the Barry's Bay and Wilno areas, in the age of globalization, is also dependent on global phenomena. Travelling to the festival adds to the movement's size, popularity, and ability to recharge ethnic identity. As a result of its creation of a place for the diaspora, the WHS has opened up what Gerber labelled transnational social fields.[25] The site, as a contact zone (during Kashub Day or the summer months), has linked members of the imagined community in different ways. Connections and dialogue are now happening in several transnational social fields, including: public organizations or associations (the WHS, the KPA, the museum in Panna Maria, Texas, and Daniel Czapiewski's Museum in Szymbark, Poland); agencies and businesses (the WHS promotes some individuals and businesses in Poland that cater to travellers from Canada); and personal connections to relatives in other locations across the diaspora.[26] Because of the connections that were strengthened, Polish Prime Minister Donald Tusk even visited the park in May of 2012 alongside Polish senator Kazimierz Kleina and the Polish ambassador to Canada, Zenon Kosiniak-Kamysz. While the difficulty of nineteenth- and early twentieth-century travel meant limited meetings for the imagined community, the ease of contemporary travel and technology has made the encounters more frequent and regular. It has meant that a building from Wilno was shipped and set up in Szymbark, Poland, so that the "Canadian Kashubian" diaspora could live in the homeland.[27] Easier travel to other points in the diaspora also means that "diasporic actors nourish their ethnic imaginations and at the same time redefine their positions by assessing the complexity of cultural paths and by transforming the manner of ethnic homecoming into a mobile creative diasporic cosmopolitanism."[28]

The WHS's activities and hard work (especially through Mask-Connolly's efforts) have also produced lieux de memoire and aides-mémoire for the ethnic community. As I wrote in *Ask My Grandpa*, it's a "place, filled with history in one small space." Since Peter Glofcheskie took over as president and Beverly Glofcheskie as secretary and membership chair, the variety and frequency of events at the park has increased. In the spring of 2013, an online platform for telling stories, called *Plesta*, which means "storyteller" in Kashubian, was launched by Glofcheskie to preserve family stories. In July and August, a set of Thursday activities was scheduled, including a wood carving display put on by Don Burchat, a relaxing knitting day with Ephrasine Kutchkoskie, a candlemaking day with Carol Sulpher and Marcella Cybulski, and a one-room-schoolhouse memories day with retired teachers Bernadette Dudack and Shirley Etmanski. Zosia Kosinski's Kashubian embroidery days continued during the summer months as well. Three other events in August filled the park's schedule. On 4 August, Karen Connolly set up a display of vintage Pyrex dishes, common to farmhouses in the area. Four days later, a craft day was held and around fifty visitors decorated ceramic bisque-ware mugs, coasters/tiles, and dessert plates under the direction of Natalie Glofcheskie, using Polish and Kashubian designs. That same month, Peter Glofcheskie and Ed Chippior branched out by giving a "tip of the hat to the Irish from the Wilno Heritage Society" and put a small float in the Irish Gathering in Killaloe. The following year, 2014, saw events such as a Canada Day celebration held at the park with face painting, horseback riding, a family scavenger hunt, and a pioneer hat/moustache photo booth. After the release of *Ask My Grandpa*, Beverly Glofcheskie encouraged visitors to the park to photograph themselves reading the book to their children and grandchildren. Many parents and grandparents, like Dennis and Stasia Hudder, Audrey Bromwich, Teenie Mask, Frank Recoskie, Don Burchat, Ron Lorbetski, Caroline Biernacki, Rita Mask, Ursula Jeffrey, Eddie Etmanski, Agatha Dombroskie, and Terry Recoskie found a quaint spot to read and submitted their pictures for inclusion in a growing display. Beverly also brought a host of new items to the

Heritage Store to rejuvenate its stock, including T-shirts, embroidered museum tote-bags, scarves, golf/fishing towels, and Kashubian leather bracelets.[29] In June 2015, elementary students from St John Bosco (Barry's Bay), St Mary's (Wilno), and St Andrew's (Killaloe) visited four learning centres – a blacksmith's shop, a schoolroom, a farmhouse, and music on the verandah – at the park. The activity was developed by retired teacher and principal Carol Sulphur, who also played the role of Ostroski, Wilno's first blacksmith. Several retired teachers volunteered to run the centres. Students wore pioneer clothing, sang a haying song, and learned how a blacksmith shoed a horse, among other things.

Indeed, the museum/park/skansen acts as a stimulus that rejuvenates and reinvigorates a sense of connection to the past. In the ever-globalizing and modernizing world, it assists people in their quest to remember the past, their ancestors, and their way of life. As Anderson writes, museums help imagine a domain, "the nature of the human beings it ruled, the geography of its domain, and the legitimacy of its ancestry."[30] The diaspora has been given a space to gather and global social networks have opened up. Wilno's Heritage Park also serves as a meeting place. Hundreds mourned, prayed, and held a candlelight vigil for three women who were slain in September 2015. Although the vernacular known as Kashubian may be dying out, new forms of dialogue have transformed what it means to be Kashubian or a Polish-Kashub in Canada's first Polish settlement.

As Jan Fedorowicz wrote in 1982, there really is no precisely defined Polish culture. There are "a host of different Polish cultures, defined by region, by social class, by historical tradition, by the time in which particular groups emigrated from Poland, and even by the foreign models imposed or adopted at different times" by each group. To privilege a fragment as a rigid stereotype is not productive and Federowicz argues that there should be forums of interchange for all of these cultural models. While some conservative groups may be uncomfortable with such exchanges, the interchange and dialogue needs to happen for some organized Polishness to be retained.[31]

Such reimaginations and reinventions of an ethnic identity or label are not unique to the Polish-Kashub community. The community need only look to one of its neighbours to see the transitions in another ethnic community as authors more distant from the original migrations continue to dispel the notion of a meta-narrative or singular pioneer-like identity. In the 1990s, the Ukrainian-Canadian identity evolved to show that it was more diverse than its peasant and pioneer beginnings. Paul Magosci writes that, in the 1990s, many Ukrainians were torn between their identity as Canadians and as Ukrainians. In this struggle, many hung onto some identifiers from the past, such as language, marriage practices, political affiliations, and religious and cultural practices. As such, their symbolic ethnic exercises and their attachment to various identities present a good opportunity for research into the Ukrainian-Canadian experience. As Stella Hryniuk and Lubomyr Luciuk write in their edited collection, *Canada's Ukrainians: Changing Perspectives 1891–1991*, the experiences of descendants born and educated in Canada point toward an evolving and more dynamic ethnic community. One wishes that more contemporary studies of identity and memory akin to Stacey Zembrzycki's dissertation about early nineteenth-century Ukrainian experiences in Sudbury would appear. More recently, however, Rhonda Hinther and Jim Mochoruk write that scholarship on the Ukrainian-Canadian community has branched off into different directions and entirely new fields, depending on descendants' study interests and language abilities (or inabilities), as well as their distance from the organized community. No longer is it a monolithic group with a single shared reality. Newer concepts, methodologies, and theoretical paradigms outside the realm of Ukrainian studies are refashioning what it means to be ethnic. Hinther and Mochoruk write that more recent scholars are interested in notions of intersectionality as well as transnational approaches. Karen Gabert's study, intersecting public history and its impact on ethnic identity in the Ukrainian Village east of Edmonton, Alberta, is one step in the right direction in the study of contemporary ethnic imaginings. But more needs to be done.

As hinted at by several authors, some longstanding and contemporary experiences from ethnic communities are still absent from the record. Gabert writes that certain uncomfortable issues, such as alcoholism and spousal abuse, have not yet been recognized and addressed in the Ukrainian Village "living history" museum. For the Polish group, Benjamin Murdzek mentions that there is evidence to support the claim that the decline of the Galicians in Poland was due to excessive alcoholism. Dennis Koliński, writing about Poland Corners, Wisconsin, in the 1860s, mentions that there were drinking-related problems at nearby taverns outside St Joseph's Church – even during Sunday Mass.[32] In the Wilno/Barry's Bay area, Msgr Jankowski tried to curtail the heavy drinking at weddings in the late nineteenth and early twentieth century by limiting the length of weddings – which could carry on for a week. The liquor that was produced in the area at the time had no regulated alcohol content. Thus, levels of consumption did not always dictate similar levels of intoxication. Some batches were known to make people violently ill and make them unconscious. In the 1920s, several locals were charged and pleaded guilty to liquor violations resulting from the production of "wicked Wilno moonshine."[33] John Lehr also draws attention to similar issues by writing that the isolation and drudgery around the Ukrainian community in Stuartburn "made escape from reality an attractive proposition, and escape for many came through consumption of alcohol or narcotic-laden patent medicines." But these are topics that cross many ethnic and generational lines and require intersectional approaches.[34] Indeed, the study of evolving contemporary ethnic imaginings in the public sphere is promising and their intersections are common enough to be applied to many different ethnic, religious, and community groups.

Again, my intent is not to discount the notion of being Polish or Kashubian but to examine, question, and analyze the origins and function of certain myths and ethnic (re)creations. Since Michel Foucault claims that "present struggles revolve around the question: Who are we?,"[35] my intent is to produce more knowledge of the group to provide descendants with an increased awareness of their past and its invented traditions so they may navigate their ethnicity in an informed way.

After a preliminary version of this book text was read by Mask-Connolly, she changed several of her views on ethnicity and identity in her 2014 release, *Marriage Matters*. She still notes that the loss of the language is a "very real concern." But Mask-Connolly also writes that "an aspect that is reassuring is that ethnic and cultural definition and identification need not necessarily be lost even if the language disappears from usage. This is evidenced in the resurgence of interest ... amongst many descendants who do not know or speak the Kashub language." Later on, when reflecting on identities, she acknowledges and states that the community has a "unique and evolving ethnic/cultural identity ... [and] ethnic identity relates to shared factor ... some factors are tangible, others are not. Identity/self-identity is also subject to change."³⁶

Change is often difficult and moves slowly. However, the record continues to evolve 157 years later as identities and the past are negotiated. Although some of the WHS's activities are invented traditions, they can and do represent both a link with the past and a continuum of community in a globalizing world. The very act of publishing these findings ensures a sense of permanence, too. We reach back to move forward.

APPENDIX

Emigrants from Prussian-Occupied Poland Who Settled on the Opeongo and Surrounding Townships

Emigrant Family	Parish of Origin	Date of Emigration
Etmanski, Walenty and Veronica Turzynska	Lipusz	1858
Flis, Albert and Victoria Pelowski	Kościerzyna	1858
Grudnowski, Michael and Mary Blaskowska	Wiele	1858
Jakubek, Francis	Parchowo	1858
Jezierski, Joseph and Agnes Romlewska	Kościerzyna	1858
Kryszynski, Andrzej and Mary	Kościerzyna	1858
Kulas, Constantine and Anna Kostka	Lipusz and Kościerzyna	1858
Kulas, Jacob and Elizabeth Bryszka	Kościerzyna and Lipusz	1858
Kulas, Joseph and Margaret Kalinowska	Lipusz?	1858
Lorbiecki, Joseph and Maryanna Czapiewska	Lipusz	1858
Omernic, Albert and Victoria Stroik	Lipusz	1858
Prince, Anthony and Magdalena Kinowska	Lipusz	1858
Reca, Casimir and Regina Styp Rekowska	Lipusz	1858
Szczypior, Michael and Marianna Goszkowicz	Sierakowice and Stezyca	1858
Szulist, Thomas and Rosalia Waldoch	Lipusz	1858
Trzebinski, Paul and Marianna Kostka	Lipusz	1858
Zybert, Anthony and Marianna Jereczek	Parchowo	1858
Dombroski, Adam and Marianna Kurszewska	Lipusz	1859
Grzenia, Joseph and Agnes Kolinska	Lipusz and Leśno	1859
Jereczek, Christian and Marianna Wiczorek	Parchowo	1859
Kaldunski, Peter and Constantia Turzynska	Wiele	1859
Libera, Rosalia (Pestka) and children	Wiele	1859
Perszyk, Walenty and Catherine Ostrowska	Leśno	1859
Piekarski, Matthias and Catherine Libera	Wiele	1859

Emigrant Family	Parish of Origin	Date of Emigration
Rekowski, Stanislaus and Catharina	Lipusz	1859
Sadowski, Matthias and Antonina Von Wesierska	Lipusz and Parchowo	1859
Zblewski, Joseph and Magdalena Yakubowski	Leśno	1859
Zblewski, Paul and Magdalena Knopik	Leśno	1859
Zblowski, Albert and Barbara Rekowska	Lipusz	1859
Dota, Albert and mother Bridget and half-brother	Wiele	1860
Lica, John and Mary Suszek	Wiele	1860
Rogalla, John and Mariana Keizer	Wiele	1860
Suszek, John and Victoria Piferke	Wiele	1860
Szala, Joseph and Josephine Libera	Wiele	1860
Yantha, August and Josephina Zblewska	Leśno	1860
Dargas, Joseph and Justina Czapewska	Leśno	1860s
Yantha, Henry	Leśno	1860s
Blaszkowski, John	Parchowo	1861
Narloch, Jacob and Mary Dobeck	Wiele	1861
Reca, Peter and Magdalena Helta	Leśno and Brusy	1861
Waldoch, Jacob and Agnes	Brusy and Leśno	1861
Biernacki, Anthony and Brigitta Lila	Parchowo	1868
Blank, Anthony and Victoria Walk	Lipusz	1868
Burchat, Joseph and Catherine Dobeck	Wiele	1868
Dobeck, Jacob and Marianna Miloch	Wiele	1868
Dombroski, Christian and Mary Boska	Lipusz	1868
Dzieminski, Michael and Marianna Literska	Lipusz	1868
Gutowski, Albert and Mariana Prykowska	Parchowo	1868
Lorbiecki, Jacob and Julianna Czapiewska	Lipusz	1868
Lukaszewicz, Anthony and Dorothy Libera	Wiele	1868
Machut, Valentine and Catherine Szulist	Lipusz	1868
Prince, Adam and Francesca Burant	Lipusz	1868
Prince, Joseph and Brigitta Czapiewska	Lipusz	1868
Skibo, Joseph and Marianna	Leśno	1868
Stoppa, John and Marianna Miszewska	Wiele	1868
Szmaglinski, Michael and Marianna	Wiele	1868
Yakubowski, Paul and Anna Kunda	Leśno	1868
Yantha, Joseph and Paulina Repinska	Leśno	1868
Krizel, John and Cecilia	Leśno	1868?
Romlewski, Frank and Agata Fryda	Kościerzyna	1870
Gutoskie, Joseph and Josephine Pasik	?	1870s–80s?
Trader, Michael	Lipusz	1870s–80s?
Laginski, Thomas	Lipusz?	1871

Emigrant Family	Parish of Origin	Date of Emigration
Lukowicz, Annie, son, daughter	Kościerzyna	1871
Waldoch, Jacob and Agnes	Brusy	1871
Burant, Joseph and Marianna	Lipusz	1872
Cybulski, Andrew and Marianna Knopik	Lipusz	1872
Cybulski, Peter and Magdalena Wrobel	Lipusz	1872
Czapiewski, Michael and Magdalena Popka	Lipusz	1872
Grudniewski, John and Josephine Blaszkowska	Wiele	1872
Heron, Valentine and Marianna	Stezyca?	1872
Kaszubik, John and Marianna Czarnowski	Lipusz and Wiele	1872
Kaszubik, Joseph and Magdalena Baska	Lipusz and Wiele	1872
Kniter, Marciana and Martin (siblings)	Lipusz	1872
Konopacki, Joseph and Rosalia Jazdzewski	Lipusz	1872
Kubiszewski, Stephen and Augustina Peplinski	Lipusz	1872
Kujach, John and Anna Blawat	Lipusz	1872
Kulas, Anthony and Bertha	Lipusz	1872
Literski, John and Julianna Slominski	Lipusz	1872
Mask, Joseph	Lipusz	1872
Myszka, Paul and 5 daughters	Lipusz	1872
Olszewski, Martin and Catherine Rekoskie	Lipusz	1872
Palubiski, John and Marcianna Cybulska	Parchowo and Lipusz	1872
Pastwa, Joseph and John	Wiele	1872
Peplinski, Jacob and Marianna	Leśno	1872
Polczynski, Casimir	Lipusz	1872
Rekowski, Stephen and Marianna	Lipusz	1872
Repinski, Marianna	?	1872
Scuza, Joseph	Lipusz	1872
Szulfer, John	Lipusz	1872
Trawicki, Martin and Catherine Kujach	Parchowo	1872
Trocka, Marianna	Lipusz	1872
Turzynski, August and Josephine Rekowski	Lipusz	1872
Waldoch, Frank and Marianna Eller	Lipusz	1872
Waldoch, Marianna (with children)	Leśno	1872
Witkowski, Anthony and Victoria	Lipusz and Kościerzyna	1872
Wroubel, Joseph and Josephine Czapiewski	Lipusz	1872
Yandernoll, Michael and Theresa	Ugoszcz	1872
Yantha, Michael and Victoria	Lipusz	1872
Maszk, Michael and Magdalena Piechowska	Lipusz	1874

Emigrant Family	Parish of Origin	Date of Emigration
Yandreski, Thadeus and Agnes Zielinski	?	1874
Kiedrowski, Michael and Catherine Burant	Borzyzskowy	1877?
Slominski, Ignatius	Leśno	1881
Golka, Antoine and Dorothy Glofcheskie	Leśno	1882
Omernic, Augustina and Vincent Zblowski	Suleczyno	1882
Laginski, Thomas	Lipusz?	1883?
Ostrowski, Leon	Windorp	1884
Peplinskie, Matthew and Marianna Literskie	?	1884?
Głowczewski, Marianna and John	Leśno	1886
Kasobuski, Andreas and Francisca Jedrewski	Brusy	1886
Kasobuski, Adam and Marianna Kloskowska	Brusy	1887
Stamplecoskie, Joseph and Frances Werra	Lipusz?	1887
Etmanski, Henry and Veronica Skiba	Leśno	1888
Kuczkowski, Joseph	?	1888?
Utronkie, Thomas and Agnes Bembenek	Leśno	1890?
Utronkie, Vincent and Mary Waldoch	Leśno	1890?
Cyra, August and Martha Gutoskie	Ugoszcz	1890s
Pick, John and Anna Lubiecki	Ugoszcz	1892
Buch, John and Marianna Treder	Parchowo	1895
Recoskie, Anthony and Mary Ann Czapewski	?	1904
Głowczewski, Jan Pawel and Julianna Gemba	Swornegacie then Liniewo	1907

Notes: This is not a perfect compilation of everyone who emigrated and settled. For the sake of brevity and presentation, many of the children from the emigrant family were not added. Often, multiple children and their families arrived with the parent family. Once in Canada, several males and females remarried after the death of their spouse. There were also other families from the above parishes who went elsewhere once they landed in North America (such as Renfrew; Pontiac County, Quebec; or Massachusetts and Wisconsin, US) and never set foot on the Opeongo. Some members of families who originally settled in Renfrew or the US married and lived in and around the Opeongo later on. The spelling of names has also changed over the years, so surnames might be slightly different than what is written above.

Sources: Several publications by Mask-Connolly. Also, Blank, Lorbetskie, and Prince, *Sto Lat*.

NOTES

INTRODUCTION

1 The community was incorporated as the Village of Barry's Bay in 1933, but had been known by that name several decades beforehand. The origins of the town hearken back to the reference "Barry's Camp" on the bay, according to the booklet *Village of Barry's Bay 50th Anniversary* (Village of Barry's Bay, 1983), 9; See also the *Eganville Leader* [hereafter EL] 30, no. 43 (16 September 1932). The amalgamated township comprises the former townships of Sherwood, Jones, Burns, Radcliffe, and the Village of Barry's Bay. The hamlet of Wilno is partially in Sherwood Township and Hagarty Township. Hagarty and Richards Townships and the former Village of Killaloe have amalgamated to create the Township of Killaloe, Hagarty, and Richards. See also: Map #1: Townships and Major Roads in the Upper Ottawa Valley; and Blank, "Pitching, Pies, and Piety," 61–85.
2 Fraser, "The Renfrew Region in the Middle Ottawa Valley," 19, 24.
3 Although the Golden Lake Reserve was set up by the government in 1864, after Crown Lands Agent for the Opeongo Road T.P. French petitioned on behalf of the Algonquins, they never surrendered the territory. Hessel, *The Algonkin Tribe*, 69–71.
4 Kennedy, *Ottawa Valley*, 160, 169, 188. See also Lee, *Lumber Kings and Shantymen*, 17, 18; The lumberjack also remarked that "nothing was to be seen but a mass of pine tops; in fact one could imagine that it would never be cut or used up."
5 Spragge, "Colonization Roads in Canada West 1850–1867," 5; Gates, "Official Encouragement to Immigration by the Province of Canada," 22–38; Lee-Whiting, "The Opeongo Road," 76–83; Parker, "Colonization Roads and Commercial Policy," 31–9; also Miller, *Straight Lines in Curved Space*. The Opeongo Road got its name from Lake Opeongo, where surveyors plotted the end of the road. It is believed the name originated from the Algonquin phrase "Ope au wingauk," "sandy at the narrows." Bernard S. Shaw mentions this in *The Opeongo*, 24. Over the years, the common reference term associated with the road has changed to "the Opeongo Line."
6 French, *Information for Intending Settlers*, 1.

7 Walsh, "Performing Public Memory and Re-Placing Home in the Ottawa Valley, 1900–1958," 26. Doug Owram also mentions that after 1870, immigration was looked upon as the solution to populate the western lands, as it had been in the Ottawa Valley. See *Promise of Eden*, 104.
8 Literally translated as "culture struggle," Kulturkampf is a term that summarizes a nation's struggles between the ruling regime, the country's population, and organized religion. It has become most closely associated with the nineteenth-century struggles between the Prussian regime and the Roman Catholic Church. See chapter 2 for a further analysis.
9 Praszalowicz, "Overseas Migration," 63. Traditionally, Galicia comprised the current Polish voivodships of Bielsko-Biała, Kraków, Tarnów, Rzeszów, Przemyśl, Nowy Sącz, and Krosno, and the Ukranian *oblasti* of L'viv, Ternopil, and Ivano-Frankirsk: Drummond and Lubecki, "Reconstructing Galicia," 1314. Rev William O'Dwyer wrote that the parish priest in Wilno, Fr Jankowski, "disguised as a peasant, journeyed through Poland, and over a period brought out a goodly number of families. The good evangelist returned from his native land laden with almost priceless vestments and sacred vessels for the new church in Canada." *Highways of Destiny*, 166. Fr Joseph Legree stated that, in the 1890s, Jankowski "engaged in immigration work from tripartite Poland, and the number of families in Hagarty and Sherwood Townships increased considerably in four years." *Lift up Your Hearts*, 329. None of O'Dwyer's statements have been corroborated, and the numbers from Jankowski's assisted migration of people from Poland and the group from Webster have not been quantified. Unfortunately, the archives of St Hedwig's Parish in Barry's Bay and St Mary's in Wilno are not open for study. Analysis of these topics, however, is long overdue. The list of families has been assembled from multiple publications and the oral histories of several families.
10 Legree, *Lift up Your Hearts*, 345. Legree's claim of forty families may be an overstatement.
11 It is thought that the Webster group immigrated to Canada c. 1894–95. See Blank, Lorbetski, and Prince, *Sto Lat*, 131, 150, 226, 255, 308. The population of Webster is taken from "Table v," *Fourteenth Census of the United States*, Department of the Interior, Census Office, 1890.
12 Avery and Fedorowicz, *The Poles in Canada*, 5–18; also Kelley and Trebilcock, *The Making of the Mosaic*, 120.
13 Zucchi, *Italians in Toronto*, 4.
14 The micro level includes localized knowledge and experiences. The macro level includes broader global systems and international concerns. The meso level refers not only to the regional notion of study but includes study into the interactions and/or the interplay between aspects of the

two aforementioned levels. The meso level addresses important general trends and systems yet uses local specificity.

15 Hoerder, "Changing Paradigms in Migration History," 118. Authors who used these paradigms include Gjerde, *From Peasants to Farmers*; Ramirez, *On the Move*; and Elliott, *Irish Migrants in the Canadas: A New Approach*.

16 Basu, *Highland Homecomings*, 188. Basu writes this in relation to Scottish family history and the Highland Clearances; but it can also be applied to local authors writing about the first Polish migration to Canada.

17 Gaddis, *The Landscape of History*, 136.

18 O'Dwyer, *Highways of Destiny*; Makowski, *History and Integration of Poles in Canada*; Makowski, *The Polish People in Canada*; Radecki and Heydenkorn, *A Member of a Distinguished Family*, 21; Mask-Connolly, *Kashubia to Canada: Crossing on the Agda*, 10; Ickiewicz, *Kaszubi w Kanadzie*, 55, 102; Jost, "Polish Kashub Pioneers in Ontario," 20; Zurakowski, *The Proud Inheritance*, 15; Rekowski, *The Saga of the Kashub People*, 26.

19 Mask-Connolly's comments on a recent television program sum up the notion that settlers were given bad land. "Polish Studio," OMNI-TV Toronto, 2 January 2010.

20 Rekowski, *The Saga of the Kashub People*, 27; Mask-Connolly, *Kashubia to Canada: Crossing on the Agda*; and Prince, *The Kovalskie (Kowalski) Family of Barry's Bay*.

21 Gjerde, "New Growth on Old Vines," 57.

22 This view was expressed most recently by the Canadian ambassador to Poland, Daniel Costello, who mentioned it in a 2009 interview: "Polish Studio," OMNI-TV Toronto, 2 January 2010.

23 Mask-Connolly, "Our 3 Polish Parishes – But For How Much Longer?" *IYDK* 3, no. 1, 13; Schulist, "A Kashubian Treasure on the Top of Our Tongue," 6–8.

24 Iacovetta also acknowledges this in "Post-Modern Ethnography," 292, 295.

25 Livingstone, *Putting Science in its Place*, 7.

CHAPTER ONE

1 "knowledge," *Oxford English Dictionary*, 3rd ed., accessed 21 February 2012; Cruikshank, *Do Glaciers Listen?*, 4, 9.

2 Pace and Hemmings, "Understanding Authority in Classrooms," 5.

3 Weber, *The Theory of Social and Economic Organization*, 341, 358, 359.

4 Climo and Cattell, *Meaning in Social Memory and History*, 1.

5   Green, "Individual Remembering and 'Collective Memory,'" 35–6.
6   Bodnar, *Remaking America*, 15; Nora, "Between Memory and History," 7–8; also Seixas, "What Is Historical Consciousness?," 11; Young, *The Texture of Memory*, viii.
7   Several have encouraged the intersection of individual and collective memory: Green, "Individual Remembering and 'Collective Memory,'" 35–6, 41; Bodnar, *Remaking America*, 13; Gillis, "Memory and Identity," 14–17; and Seixas, "What Is Historical Consciousness?," 15.
8   McKay, "Tartanism Triumphant," 32; Bittermann, "On Remembering and Forgetting," 259.
9   Basu, *Highland Homecomings*, 188.
10 Akenson, *The Irish Diaspora*, 11. See also Basu, *Highland Homecomings*, 192.
11 Berger, *The Writing of Canadian History*, 10–11; and Iacovetta, "Manly Militants," 221; Harvey, "The Importance of Local History in the Writing of General History," 245.
12 Hoerder, "Ethnic Studies in Canada from the 1880s to 1962," 4.
13 Woodsworth, *Strangers Within Our Gates, or, Coming Canadians*, 142. Woodsworth wrote that the Polish are "peasants, the majority illiterate and superstitious, some of them bigoted fanatics, some of them poor, dumb, driven cattle, some intensely patriotic." See also Woodsworth, *My Neighbour*, 305; and Thomas and Znaniecki, *The Polish Peasant in Europe and America*.
14 Gates, "Official Encouragement to Immigration by the Province of Canada," 24–38; Hodgetts, *Pioneer Public Service*; Spragge, "Colonization Roads in Canada West 1850–1867," 1–17; Macdonald, *Canada*. Marilyn Miller used these sources when researching the history of a particular colonization road, the Opeongo, in a 1978 historical essay, *Straight Lines in Curved Space: Colonization Roads in Eastern Ontario*. Most of her research, however, centred on the structures along the road and their potential value for tourism.
15 Beckett, *Writing Local History*, xii. Other works touch on this issue as well. One example appears in the words of Akenson in the preface to Elliott, *Irish Migrants in the Canadas: A 'New Approach,'* 2nd ed., xv. Others include: Ramirez, *On the Move*, 15; Batinski, *Pastkeepers in a Small Place*, xii, 89.
16 Wright, *The Professionalization of History in English Canada*, 4; also, Harvey, "The Importance of Local History in the Writing of General History," 244–7.
17 Iacovetta, *The Writing of English Canadian Immigrant History*, 3.

18 Kos-Rabcewicz-Zubkowski, *Canada Ethnica IV*, 1.
19 Makowski, "Poles in Canada," 19–23. The author lists 1844 as the arrival date, with "(1864?)" beside it.
20 Price and Kennedy, *Notes on the History of Renfrew County*.
21 O'Dwyer, *Highways of Destiny*.
22 Makowski, *History and Integration of Poles in Canada*. The 18-page chapter (51–69) was one of seventeen to appear in the 274-page book. In Appendix D, Makowski also included some early German families in his list of Polish settlers in the Renfrew area because their country of birth was listed in the 1871 census as Prussia. The quote that comments on integration is on page 66.
23 Gjerde, "New Growth on Old Vines," 41; and Hoerder, "Changing Paradigms in Migration History," 105.
24 Thistlewaite, "Migration From Europe Overseas in the 19th and 20th Centuries," 77. See also Gjerde, "New Growth on Old Vines," 41–3; and O'Brien, "New Wine in Old Skins," 221–37.
25 Canada, Minister of Supply and Services. *The Cultural Contribution of Other Ethnic Groups*, Report Book. The Commission started in 1963 and produced its findings, in writing, in 1969.
26 Ibid., 16–19. The Museum of Man is now in the Canadian Museum of Civilization. See also Stolarik, "Multiculturalism in Canada," 123–6. Appropriately, the first appointed Minister of State for Multiculturalism in Canada was a Polish-Canadian, Dr Stanley Haidasz, who manned the post for two years, 1972–74.
27 Reczynska, "Emigration from the Polish Territories to Canada up until World War Two," 11–19; and Jost, "Polish Kashub Pioneers in Ontario," 20–4; also *Kaszuby*.
28 See the authors' preface for the intent of their book: Radecki and Heydenkorn, *A Member of a Distinguished Family*. Also, they write that Kashubs settled in Hogarty, Richards, Sherwood, Jones, and Burns (21). Hogarty should be "Hagarty."
29 Radecki, *Ethnic Organizational Dynamics*, 46, 58.
30 Perin, "Clio as an Ethnic," 441.
31 Breton, "Institutional Completeness," 193–205; Isajiw, "The Process of Maintenance of Ethnic Identity," 129–38; and Isajiw, *Ethnic Identity Retention*.
32 Hoerder, "Towards a History of Canadians," 434; and Iacovetta, *English Canadian Immigrant History*, 1.
33 Hansen, *The Problem of the Third Generation Immigrant*, 9–10.
34 Iacovetta, *English Canadian Immigrant History*, 5.

35 Perkowski, *Vampires, Dwarves, and Witches Among the Ontario Kashubs*. See also Lorentz, Fischer, and Lehr-Spławiński, *The Cassubian Civilization*.
36 Colombo, *Mysteries of Ontario*, 45. Sandra Peredo found out that only 600 copies were printed. "Count Dracula in Canada?," 12. When subsequent publications in the series were issued, Perkowski's was the only one listed as "out of print."
37 Perkowski, *Vampires, Dwarves, and Witches*, 28, 35–6.
38 Peredo, "Count Dracula in Canada?," 12.
39 Evenson, "Vampires: Scholar Unearths More Than Legends," D3. Responding a few days later, a reporter from Barry's Bay, Ray Stamplecoskie, wrote to the *Citizen*: "Vampire Tale Drives Stake Through Wilno," *Ottawa Citizen*, 10 September 1989, A8. A decade later, another reporter interviewed several locals, former reeve Martin Shulist, Wilno Heritage Society president David Shulist, and Fr Rekowski. The most colourful comment came from Martin Shulist who said "It's all crap ... Just pure crap. And underline that I said 'pure crap.'" MacGregor, "Why the Vampires of Wilno Will Not Die," A1.
40 Perkowski, *Vampires, Dwarves, and Witches*, 30.
41 One in particular is the account of how a young priest, Fr Antoni Słominski, from St Hedwig's in Barry's Bay, died. According to one of his sources, a witch was preparing dumplings for a picnic and Słominski ate one: "as soon as he put the first piece in his mouth, he began to choke and the priest had a doctor and immediately began to die and died before reaching the hospital. No one ate those dumplings. They were whispering among themselves that she had implanted his food." Perkowski, *Vampires, Dwarves, and Witches*, 34. However, if one were to look into the cause of death, one would find that Fr Słominski contracted an infection while in Manitoba in 1927 and was transported to St Michael's Hospital in Toronto, where he died of peritonitis. See Felix J. Slominski, "Some Memories – The Slominski Saga," in Rekowski's *The Saga of the Kashub People*, 165.
42 Svitlana Krys also wanted an updated bibliography for the 2006 reissue, "Jan Louis Perkowski," 116–18.
43 Fabian, *Time and the Other*, 1, 80.
44 Cruikshank, *Do Glaciers Listen?*, 10.
45 Peredo, "Count Dracula in Canada?," 12.
46 Iacovetta, "Post-Modern Ethnography," 282; also Walsh and High, "Rethinking the Concept of Community," 257.
47 Tracey, "Music of the Kashubs Becomes Part of the Archives Series," 8. After chairing the Department of Music at Brock University, in 1989, he

moved to British Columbia where he teaches music history and theory at Douglas College.
48 Mask-Connolly, *Marriage Matters*, 137.
49 Glofcheskie, *Folk Music of Canada's Oldest Polish Community*; Glofcheskie, *Folk Music of Canada's Oldest Polish Community* (Audio-CD).
50 Lee-Whiting, "The Opeongo Road," 76–83; Lee-Whiting, "First Polish Settlement in Canada," 108–12.
51 Jost, "New Documentation," 443–52.
52 Jost, *Osadnictwo Kaszubskie W Ontario*. Several errors were also repeated from her dissertation, including a caption that mislabelled St Mary's Church in Wilno as St Hedwig's Church in Barry's Bay. See also Jost, "Polish Kashub Pioneers in Ontario," 20–4.
53 Makowski, *The Polish People in Canada*.
54 Hessel, *Destination: Ottawa Valley*, 7, 17.
55 Lee-Whiting, *Harvest of Stones*. Pages 23–5 chronicle the reasons for emigrating.
56 Ickiewicz, *Kaszubi w Kanadzie*.
57 Zurakowski, *The Proud Inheritance*. Anna's husband, Jan, is best known as a fighter pilot who escaped Poland during the Second World War. He trained pilots in Britain and was hired as the test pilot for the Avro Arrow. The couple settled on the shores of Kamaniskeg Lake, and built Kartuzy Lodge. More recently, Zurakowski claimed that Stamplecoskie stole $6,000 from the Polish Heritage Institute Kaszuby that was destined for a Polish heritage museum. Stamplecoskie was once president of the organization: Zabrovsky, "Virginia Woman Falls in Love with Ottawa Phantom," A1.
58 The links are also evident in their pseudo-military marches and celebrations. For example, the "Dedication and Presentation of the 1st Polish Amoured Division Pennant to the Gen. S. Maczek Polish Sea Scout Troup Kaszuby in Barrys Bay, Ontario" on 15 July 1973 featured many notables from the officer and intelligentsia classes such as "Col. Z.M.L. Szydłowski, PhD, DSO, the former Commander of the 3rd Rifle Brigade in the 1st Polish Amoured Division, the most senior Officer of the Division ... etc." Source: a *Polish Scouts Association* notice from the collection of Elizabeth Shalla. The "Polish World Scouting Jamboree" was held at Kaszuby near Wadsworth Lake in 1976. Zurakowski, *The Proud Inheritance*, 141. In 1994, an elaborate monument to commemorate the 50th anniversary of fallen scouts in the Warsaw Uprising was also built.
59 Zurakowski, *The Proud Inheritance*, 132–5.
60 *BBTW*, 4 August 1976.
61 To quote a term used by Livingstone, *Putting Science in its Place*, 10–11.

62 Zurakowski, *The Proud Inheritance*, 91–2.
63 Rekowski, *The Saga of the Kashub People*, viii. The reference to "low Polish" is also reiterated by Shirley Mask-Connolly in Christinck, "Wilno's Rich Heritage is Brought Vividly to Life by Researcher," A12. John Glofcheskie comments on the usage of language, saying that "standard literary Polish [is the language] which the Kashub recognizes as his Language for writing and reading, for singing hymns, and for all 'official' occasions. His dialect is reserved for the informal daily dealings of life, for his oral literature and for the *frantówka*, that category of short and happy song, so expressive of his good humor." *Folk Music of Canada's Oldest Polish Community*, 3.
64 Swyripa, "The Mother of God Wears a Maple Leaf," 342.
65 O'Dwyer, *Highways of Destiny*, 161–5; Legree, *Lift Up Your Hearts*, 328–30.
66 Corinne Higgins, "Celebrate Polish Day – May 3 – Na Zdrowie," *BBTW*, 29 April 1987, 33; Legree, *Lift Up Your Hearts*, 331, 334, 338; Carol Doran, "Father Stan Kadziolka," *BBTW*, 11 March 1971. Kadziolka died a year later in 1986. See also *EL* 39, no. 27, 9 May 1941.
67 Blank, "Pitching, Pies, and Piety," 61–75.
68 Swyripa, "The Mother of God Wears a Maple Leaf," 347.
69 *EL*, 13 July 1943.
70 Apolonja Kojder, "Polish Schools in Toronto," in Heydenkorn, ed., *A Community in Transition*, 8; Higgins, "Celebrate Polish Day," 33; and Legree, *Lift Up Your Hearts*, 331; "Weekend School Helps Preserve Polish Heritage," *BBTW*, 19 December 1973.
71 *BBTW*, 4 March 1971; 11 March 1971; 3 January 1974; and 16 May 1978, 1, 6; "Polish Play Attracts More Than 500 People," *BBTW*, 3 January 1974.
72 *BBTW*, 27 June 1973. According to her memoirs (LXXX), Elizabeth also taught Polish language classes for 30 minutes a day between 1944 and 1952 at the request of Msgr Biernacki. After looking over some of her writings, it appears that she taught a mixture of Polish and the vernacular passed on to her by her ancestors.
73 Higgins, "Celebrate Polish Day," 33; "Polish Day Concert staged at St. Mary's," *BBTW*, 6 May 1987; "Uczymysiepo Polsku w Wilnie," *BBTW*, 13 April 1988 and the author's own recollections as a student in these classes.
74 "Centennial Celebration at Wilno," *BBTW*, 23 July 1975.
75 *BBTW*, 25 March 1965; and 4 March 1971.
76 *BBTW*, 16 August 1972; "Plaque Marks Site of First Polish Church in Bay," *BBTW*, 21 August 1974; "Wilno Centennial Stamp Designed by Frank Ritza," *BBTW*, 22 January 1975; see also *BBTW*, 23 April 1975.

77 Zurakowski, *The Proud Inheritance*, 91–2.
78 Perin, "Clio as an Ethnic," 450; Radecki and Heydenkorn, *A Member of a Distinguished Family*, 95–9.
79 Rekowski, *The Saga of the Kashub People*, viii; Schulist, "A Kashubian Treasure on the Top of Our Tongue," 6–8. Zurakowski critiques the following words and points out the proper "literary Polish" terms: "spociwa" should be "spoczywa"; "urodzoni" should be "urodzony"; "umar" should be "umarl"; and "proszi" should be "prosi." See Zurakowski, *The Proud Inheritance*, 77.
80 Radecki and Heydenkorn, *A Member of a Distinguished Family*, 98.
81 Jaroszyńska-Kirchmann, *The Exile Mission*, 14.
82 Patterson, "This New Canada," 88; Karski, *Story of a Secret State*, 292; Jaroszyńska-Kirchmann, *The Exile Mission*, 14; and Heydenkorn, ed., *A Community in Transition*, 1.
83 Greene, *For God and Country*, 3–5.
84 For the general North American trend, see Jaroszyńska-Kirchmann, *The Exile Mission*, 163.
85 MacGregor, *The Weekender*, 137–8.
86 The article also mentions that the collected works for the museum have been stored in a two-storey house up until this point and a museum is expected to open next year (1977). Indeed, readers were left to wonder where the supposed "sizeable cash donations that have been received from countries outside of Canada in aid of the museum project" were being used after Shulist's "ten years" of work on it: "116 Years of History in Wilno's Polish Canadian Pioneer Centre," *BBTW*, 25 August 1976. Another article from two years before mentions that the Polish Canadian Pioneer Centre also received a $3,200 grant from the federal government. In that article, Shulist also claimed that he hopes to have the museum open by the following year. See "Wilno Museum is planned to preserve Polish culture," *BBTW*, 17 July 1974.
87 "Polish Culture Program Ends," *BBTW*, 16 August 1978. Zurakowski mentions that Eugene was educated at the Wojciech Gerson School of Fine Art in Warsaw. Jadwiga, a descendant of a Kaszubian family in Poland, had some teaching experience. See *A Proud Inheritance*, 114. Information on Chruscicki is from Andrew Pawłowski, "A Polish Way to Canadian Art: Contemporary Painters and Sculptors in Toronto," in Heydenkorn, ed., *A Community in Transition*, 74.
88 Compared with the patterns of traditional dress of the Kraków region in Piskowz-Branekova, *Polska Stroje ludowe*, 91.
89 "Polish Day Concert Staged at St. Mary's," *BBTW*, 6 May 1987, 23; "Polish Day – May 3rd celebrated in style throughout the valley," *BBTW*, 4 May 1988, 14.

90 Benet, *Song, Dance, and Customs of Peasant Poland*, 141.
91 In 1971, a scouting instructor and postwar emigrant turned local resident and restaurateur wrote the following in the *BBTW*: "It is unfortunate that through a lack of communication a closer relationship has not developed between the local inhabitants and the summer visitors. One group is too busy with their daily chores, the other engrossed in their heavy program of summer activities ... Wouldn't it be great if we could have the descendants, children of these earlier settlers, join in the activities and become part of an organization with a long and proud history." See *BBTW*, 4 March 1971; "Polish Summer Day Camp," *BBTW*, 26 July 1978; "Summer Day Camp Project a Success," *BBTW*, 30 August 1978, 16.
92 "Kaszuby Youth Camp '80," *BBTW*, 10 September 1980; "Polish Heritage Classes in Wilno," *BBTW*, 19 November 1980, 1; "Polish Heritage Class – Combermere," *BBTW*, 30 March 1983, 10.
93 Lynn Griffiths, "Words of Wisdom about Our Precious Past: Frank Ritza," *BBTW*, 13 April 1977, 9. "Is There Lack of Interest?," *BBTW*, 20 March 1984. Note that the names of the class have been omitted by the author so as not to prompt any ethnic rivalry or strife from a letter published many years ago.
94 *BBTW*, 13 February 1985; *BBTW*, 8 June 1988; "Needed at Home," Barry's Bay Public Library Oral History Project (1992/93), 11; "You Have to Do What Comes to Your Hands," Barry's Bay Public Library Oral History Project (1992/93), 1; "Faith and Liberty," Barry's Bay Public Library Oral History Project (1991), 4–5.
95 Ibbitson, "The Last Stronghold of Kaszuby Culture," D1.
96 From an interview conducted with Helen (Lorbetski) Dombroskie at Valley Manor Nursing Home in Barry's Bay, Ontario, 9 February 2009.
97 For example, when trying to analyze the land application process in Canada, he described the settlers' exodus from a "ghetto" in Poland. In fact, they did not escape from an urban ghetto, as many post–Second World War migrants did, but a rural area. Rekowski, *The Saga of the Kashub People*, 27.
98 Finnigan, *The Story of a Canadian Colonization Road*, 192. These findings were released in several self-published works, such as: Mask-Connolly, *Polish Pioneer Families*; *Kashubia to Canada: The Shulist Story*; and *Brudenell Revisited*. In the latter publication, Mask-Connolly included short narratives and expanded her genealogical inventories with photos. In doing so, she provided a visual record of people who had previously only existed as rote entries.
99 Mask-Connolly. *Kashubia to Canada: Crossing on the Agda*, vii, 49–70.
100 Including the Diploma of the Minister of Foreign Affairs for Outstanding Services for the Promotion of Poland and the Kashubian Pomeranian

Association's Florian Ceynowa Awakening Kashubian Award: Paulsen, "Wilno Heritage Society Honoured at Ceremony," B8.
101 Bolton, "The New Genealogy," 127; Kammen, *On Doing Local History*, 144.
102 Batinski, *Pastkeepers in a Small Place*, xii, 89; Livingstone, *Putting Science in its Place*, 1; Hutton, *History as an Art of Memory*, 6.
103 High, "Sharing Authority: An Introduction," 12–14.
104 Ha, "Vatican, Canadian Church Officials Tried to Keep Sex Scandal Secret"; Contenta, "Vatican Knew of Abuse in Ontario"; *Ottawa Citizen*: Seymour, "'Deep Breach of Trust,'" A1, D7; Seymour, "Priest, Church Face Lawsuits," C1; Kennedy, "Earning Contempt," A11.
105 High, "Sharing Authority," 28; See also Kammen, *On Doing Local History*, 67, and Gaddis, *Landscape of History*, 9.
106 Thistlewaite, "Migration From Europe Overseas in the 19th and 20th Centuries," 77; Hoerder, "Changing Paradigms in Migration History," 118; Gjerde, "New Growth on Old Vines," 41–3; Ramirez, *On the Move*; Elliott, *Irish Migrants in the Canadas*.
107 Livingstone, *Putting Science in its Place*, 7, 12.
108 Harvey, "The Importance of Local History in the Writing of General History," 244.

CHAPTER TWO

1 Thistlewaite, "Migration From Europe Overseas in the 19th and 20th Centuries," 77. See also Ramirez, *On the Move*, 14; Anderson, *Imagined Communities*, 204. The migrants in Oscar Handlin's *The Uprooted* are a classic example of the myth-making that can arise after being uprooted from the "quaint" homeland. The language in O'Dwyer's monograph endorses this notion: *Highways of Destiny*. Michael J. Goc's study of the Polish people in Wisconsin assumes the homeland was one of tranquillity: *Native Realm*, 10.
2 Climo and Cattell, "Meaning in Social Memory and History," 15.
3 "Saga of the Polish Pioneer," *Barry's Bay Review* [hereafter *BBR*], 11 May 1961; O'Dwyer, *Highways of Destiny*, 155–6; Lee-Whiting, "First Polish Settlement in Canada," 109; The second sentence was repeated in Lee-Whiting, "The Old Wooden Crosses of Wilno"; "116 Years of History in Wilno's Polish Canadian Pioneer Centre," *BBTW*, 25 August 1976.
4 "Polska, Zabawa: Polish Heritage Night in Renfrew," *BBTW*, 4 July 1979; Glofcheskie, *Folk Music of Canada's Oldest Polish Community*, 1; Finnigan, *Some of the Stories*, 13; Jost, "Polish Kashub Pioneers in Ontario," 20; Shaw, *The Opeongo*, 17; Rekowski, *The Saga of the Kashub People*, 7 (emphasis in original); Mask-Connolly, *Kashubia to Canada: Crossing on*

the *Agda*, 10–11; Finnigan, *The Story of a Canadian Colonization Road*, 191.

5 This was echoed by the Canadian ambassador to Poland, Daniel Costello, in an interview on the program "Polish Studio," Toronto: OMNI-TV, 2 January 2010.

6 See Elizabeth (Etmanski) Shalla (1890–1978), Memoirs; "Wilno Centennial Stamp Designed by Frank Ritza," *BBTW*, 22 January 1975; "Land is the Land: John Mintha," 3; "A Local Pastor: Oral History with Rev. Msgr. J.A. Pick," 5; and *Kaszuby Canada, Part One*, dir. Henryk Bartul.

7 Ramirez, *On the Move*, 15; Roberto Perin, "Clio as an Ethnic," 448; Iacovetta, "Manly Militants, Cohesive Communities, and Defiant Domestics," 223.

8 Porter, *The Ghosts of Europe*, 29, 38, 44.

9 Instead, some local writers focus on the "glorious" battles of Poland, such as the fourteenth- and fifteenth-century defences against the invading Teutonic knights, and fail to look at the internal difficulties that occurred thereafter. For example, Rekowski, *The Saga of the Kashub People*, 2–5; Mask-Connolly, *Kashubia to Canada: Crossing on the Agda*, 3.

10 Hansard of the Senate of Canada, 3rd Session, 40th Parliament, vol. 147, issue 25, 5 May 2010. Online, http://www.parl.gc.ca/40/3/parlbus/chambus/senate/deb-E/025db_2010-05-05-e.htm?Language=E&Parl=40&Ses=3, accessed 10 August 2010.

11 Written in a 2009 article entitled "*Der Spiegel.*" See Porter, *The Ghosts of Europe*, 101.

12 Fedorowicz, *A Republic of Nobles*, 9.

13 Davies outlined the confusion in translation that often happens in English-language publications. Since szlachta is habitually translated as "gentry," it is often misused by historians. Davies maintained that, to be accurate, szlachta should be translated as "nobility." Davies, *God's Playground: A History of Poland: Volume 1*, 160, 170, 386.

14 Lukowski, *The Partitions of Poland 1772, 1793, 1795*, 2; Zamoyski, *The Polish Way*, 237; Davies, *God's Playground: Volume 1*, 386.

15 Stauter-Halsted, *The Nation in the Village*, 10; Hagen, *Germans, Poles and Jews*, 14; Davies, *God's Playground: Volume 1*, 159.

16 Fedorowicz, *A Republic of Nobles*, 6; Kochanowicz, "The Polish Economy and the Evolution of Dependency," 101.

17 Wandycz, *The Lands of Partitioned Poland, 1795–1918*, 4.

18 Also referred to as the Diet or Assembly in some publications. Bideleux and Jeffries, *A History of Eastern Europe: Crisis and Change*, 145.

19 Lukowski, *The Partitions of Poland*, 3; Zamoyski, *The Polish Way*, 213; Kieniewicz, *The Emancipation of the Polish Peasantry*, 4.

20 Davies, *God's Playground: Volume 1*, 170.
21 Lukowski, *The Partitions of Poland*, 3; Davies, *God's Playground: Volume 1*, 150, 386; and Wandycz, *The Lands of Partitioned Poland*, 7. Michener points out the absurdity of the *liberum veto* in his piece of historical fiction, *Poland*, 211.
22 Davies, *God's Playground: Volume 1*, 189; Rousseau's comment appears as cited in Lukowski, *Liberty's Folly*, 9. See also Lukowski, *The Partitions of Poland*, 127–30.
23 Fedorowicz, *A Republic of Nobles*, 2.
24 Kochanowicz, "The Polish Economy and the Evolution of Dependency," 115–16.
25 Fedorowicz, *A Republic of Nobles*, 6–7.
26 Several "made their careers by working ... on behalf of foreign paymasters." These "collaborators" were in the highest political circles. Several bishops, an archbishop, and primate were influenced by Russian pay. Davies, *God's Playground: Volume 1*, 170–3, 386–9. According to Lukowski, eighteen Senate positions were reserved for the bishops, who were "as much politicians as ecclesiastics." In addition, the archbishop of Gniezno was the "second-highest-ranking personage in the kingdom after the monarch. He was the ... acting head of state when the throne fell vacant." Lukowski, *The Partitions of Poland*, 20–1. See also Piekarski, *The Church in Poland*, 32.
27 Vorontsov in Davies, *God's Playground: Volume 1*, 386. Staszic (1755–1826), a writer, as quoted in Wandycz, *The Price of Freedom*, 109.
28 Ögelman, "Ethnicity, Demography, and Migration in the Evolution of the Polish Nation-State," 160.
29 Foucault, "The Subject and Power," 131–2.
30 Behrens, *Society, Government and the Enlightenment*, 59; Piekarski, *The Church in Poland*, 60; Davies, *God's Playground: Volume 2*, 22.
31 Jan Baudoin de Courtenay, *Poparcie uwag nad życiem Jana Zamoyskiego z roztrząsanien pism, które się z ich powodu ziawiły*, 98, as quoted in Butterwick, "What is Enlightenment (Oświecenie)?," 27.
32 Kruszewski, "Nationalism and Politics: Poland," 151. He also writes that this pattern of power continued. In 1939, three quarters "of the Polish people were rural, parochial and deeply affected by the church in its role as the prime agency of socialization," 161.
33 Lukowski, *The Partitions of Poland*, 20–1.
34 Davies, *God's Playground: Volume 1*, 388; Hagen, *Germans, Poles and Jews*, 18–19. The decree did, however, force the closure of many Protestant churches and confined their worship to the private sphere until the partition of 1772.

35 Borzyszkowski, *The Kashubs, Pomerania and Gdańsk*, 35.
36 Alvis, "On Hallowed Ground," 248.
37 Davies, *God's Playground: Volume 2*, 115; Wandycz, *The Lands of Partitioned Poland*, 15.
38 Hagen, "The Partitions of Poland," 120.
39 Makowski, *The Polish People in Canada*. For Zurakowski's quote, see *The Proud Inheritance*, 16. Also see Rekowski, *The Saga of the Kashub People*, 6–7; Mask-Connolly, *Kashubia to Canada: Crossing on the Agda*, 10.
40 Borzyszkowski, *The Kashubs*, 21, 33. Also see pages 34–6 as his writing glossed over political history and vaguely referred to laws without providing any year references or antecedent measures. Ickiewicz, *Kaszubi w Kanadzie*, 11, 12, 14–16. The first version was published in 1981 and small additions and several pictures were added before it was reprinted in 2008.
41 Alvis, "On Hallowed Ground," 248–9; Hagen, *Germans, Poles, and Jews*, 40; Wandycz, *The Lands of Partitioned Poland*, 14.
42 Wandycz, *The Lands of Partitioned Poland*, 9, 16, 70; Kieniewicz, *The Emancipation*, 35.
43 Poliakoff, *Eagles Black and White*, 79.
44 Böhning, *Die Nationalpolnische Bewedung in Westpreussen 1815–1871*, 55–6.
45 Inoki, *Aspects of German Peasant Emigration to the United States, 1815–1914*, 121–2.
46 Kieniewicz, *The Emancipation*, 58; Behrens, *Society, Government and the Enlightenment*, 194.
47 Inoki, *Aspects of German Peasant Emigration*, 122–5.
48 Hagen, *Germans, Poles and Jews*, 81.
49 Böhning, *Die Nationalpolnische Bewedung in Westpreussen 1815–1871*, 25. He remarks that it is not possible to analyze German, Polish, or Kashubian holdings at the time as the records do not contain ethnicities.
50 Kieniewicz, *The Emancipation*, 70–1; Inoki, *Aspects of German Peasant Emigration*, 136; Kochanowicz, "The Polish Economy and the Evolution of Dependency," 109.
51 Wandycz, *The Lands of Partitioned Poland*, 71; Kieniewicz, *The Emancipation*, 192; Behrens, *Society, Government and the Enlightenment*, 196; Groniowski, "The Socio-economic Base of Polish Emigration to North America, 1854–1939," 3; and Wagner, *A History of Migration from Germany to Canada 1850–1939*, 19.
52 Kochanowicz echoes the frustrations when dealing with such topics: "Our knowledge of peasant social and economic life is limited to fragmentary evidence from crown, Church, and magnate estates." See "The Polish Economy and the Evolution of Dependency," 106.

53 For example, Behrens, *Society, Government and the Enlightenment*, 196. Between 1864 and 1913, according to Dutkiewicz, the population in Galicia increased from five to eight million. An over-supply of labour meant migration for many residents. *Main Aspects of the Polish Peasant Immigration to North America*, 65.
54 Extrapolated and calculated from the findings of Köllman and Kraus, *Quellenzur Bevölkerungs-, Sozial-und Wirtschaftsstatistik Deutschlands 1815–1875, Band I*, 160–1.
55 Wandycz, *The Lands of Partitioned Poland*, 3.
56 Mask-Connolly, *Kashubia to Canada: Crossing on the Agda*, 73.
57 Benet, *Song, Dance and Customs of Peasant Poland*, 33.
58 Böhning, *Die Nationalpolnische Bewedung in Westpreussen 1815–1871*, 19.
59 Kilma and Mróz, *Powiat Chojnicki w Świetle Cyfr*, 4.
60 Salmonowicz, "The Culture of Eastern Pomerania," 121. One example of this point of view can be found in the words of Ignacy Wieniewski who claimed that Bismarck's Kulturkampf was specifically "anti-Catholic and anti-Polish." See *Heritage: The Foundations of Polish Culture: An Introductory Outline*, 87.
61 Hagen, *Germans, Poles, and Jews*, 14.
62 Wenkstern, *Prussia and the Poles*, 9–12.
63 The enlightened Frederick also passed these judgments on his own countrymen who seemed to lack enlightened qualities. Hagen, "The Partitions of Poland," 121.
64 Hagen, *Germans, Poles, and Jews*, 37.
65 This is the case when one considers that "since the German Enlightenment was virtually official ideology in late eighteenth-century Prussia, to be a member of the Prussian elite was to be a product and bearer of the Enlightenment as well as a Prussian patriot." Hagen, "The Partitions of Poland," 120.
66 Hagen, "The Partitions of Poland," 121; Wandycz, *The Price of Freedom*, 105. This same approach was taken by Peter the Great and imbued his many reforms, including the edict to wear German clothes. E.V. Ansimov, "Peter I: Birth of the Empire," in *Major Problems in the History of Imperial Russia*, ed. James Cracraft, 91, 110; Davies, *God's Playground: Volume 2*, 226.
67 Kieniewicz, *The Emancipation*, 16; Wandycz, *The Price of Freedom*, 105–7.
68 All edicts were sent to these officials and passed on to landlords and priests to be read to the peasants. Forbidding Polish nobility from these positions was withdrawn after the death of Frederick II (1786) with the hope that it would change their ways. Hagen, "The Partitions of Poland," 119; and *Germans, Poles, and Jews*, 38.

69 Gillis, *The Prussian Bureaucracy in Crisis 1840–1860*, 4. See also Wandycz, *The Lands of Partitioned Poland*, 15.
70 Bideleux and Jeffries, *A History of Eastern Europe*, 150; Porter, "Patriotism, Prophecy, and the Catholic Hierarchy in Nineteenth-Century Poland," 223. The "shock-troops" of this counter-measure, the Jesuits, imbued thousands of nobles who entered their schools "with a ready-made set of religious, social and political principles opposed to the humanism of the fifteenth and early sixteenth centuries." The long-lasting effect of cultural protection under the equation "Polish-Catholic" is evidenced by the fact that Borzyszkowski claims that "the Kashubs of East Pomerania have preserved their identity and language to large degree owing to the Catholic Church and strong affinity to Polishness, which were strengthened since the first half of the 19th century." *The Kashubs, Pomerania and Gdańsk*, 21.
71 Dorota Praszałowicz also notes that this "confusion created an opening for anti-Semites to claim that Polish Jews couldn't be real Poles, a theme that has unfortunately survived to the present day." See "Local Community and Nineteenth Century Migrations," 175–6.
72 Frederick II as quoted and translated by Hagen, *Germans, Poles, and Jews*, 38. James Van Horn Melton also mentions that Frederick granted freedom of worship and faithfully observed the Peace of Berlin (1742), "which guaranteed Silesian Catholics freedom of worship." *Absolutism and the Eighteenth-Century Origins of Compulsory Schooling in Prussia and Austria*, 185.
73 Alvis, "On Hallowed Ground," 249; Davies, *God's Playground: Volume 2*, 117.
74 Kieniewicz, *The Emancipation*, 34; Wenkstern, *Prussia and the Poles*, 13; Borzyszkowski, *The Kashubs*, 37.
75 Hans-Joachim Winzer, "Personen Register Der Grundbesitz des Adels, Westpreussen und Ermland 1772–73," in Mortensen, Mortensen, and Wenskus, *Historisch-geographischer Atlas des Preußenlandes*, 427, 428.
76 Torpey, *The Invention of the Passport*, 59–60.
77 Mask-Connolly, *Kashubia to Canada: Crossing on the Agda*, 11; Gaddis, *The Landscape of History*, 32; Scott, *Seeing Like a State*, 65, 80.
78 Hagen, *Germans, Poles, and Jews*, 38–9; Borzyszkowski, *The Kashubs*, 38.
79 Hagen, *Germans, Poles, and Jews*, 40. This notion of the disciplined and proper political education given by the army was endorsed by many reformers, such as Freiherr von Stein, in the early part of the century. See Ritter, *The Sword and the Scepter*, 166.
80 Hagen, *Germans, Poles, and Jews*, 25.

81 Areas like Posen offered 2,000 thaler in exchange for service. Wenkstern, *Prussia and the Poles*, 36–7, 39; Hagen, *Germans, Poles, and Jews*, 44; Trzeciakowski, *The Kulturkampf in Prussian Poland*, 123, 126; and Wandycz, *The Lands of Partitioned Poland*, 68.
82 Wenkstern, *Prussia and the Poles*, 40. In many areas, school inspectors were members of the clergy. This was due to the fact that priests were educated so people thought they knew what was right and wrong since they held divine power and mediated based on the word of God. For locals, their oversight would also alleviate communal fears of Prussian education.
83 Wandycz, *The Lands of Partitioned Poland*, 68–9; Bideleux and Jeffries, *A History of Eastern Europe*, 167.
84 Hagen, *Germans, Poles, and Jews*, 44, 82.
85 Melton, *Absolutism*, 180; Borzyszkowski, *The Kashubs*, 40.
86 Wandycz, *The Lands of Partitioned Poland*, 68; and Kieniewicz, *The Emancipation*, 195.
87 Melton, *Absolutism*, 157, 180, 190–1.
88 Borzyszkowski, *The Kashubs*, 40.
89 Hagen, *Germans, Poles, and Jews*, 82; Wenkstern, *Prussia and the Poles*, 39, 40.
90 Assembled from many entries in volumes 2–13 of the *Słownik Geograficzny Królestwa Polskiego*, eds. Filipa Sulimierskiego, Bronisława Chlebowskiego, and Władysława Walewskiego (Warszawa, 1880–1884). Also, Borzyszkowski, *The Kashubs*, 40.
91 For the attendance figures, see Melton, *Absolutism*, 180; Łajming, *Czterolistna Koniczyna*, mentions a story about skipping school, 43. See also Lamberti, *State, Society, and the Elementary School*, 18, 24–6; Walser Smith, "Prussia at the Margins," 78.
92 According to an 1803 church document from Lipusz, copied by Edward Breza. Many farmers from Kalisz who could afford to donate to the priest (Fr Lindenblatt) were unable to sign their names and marked their contribution with an "X." Edward Breza, "Mieszkańcywsi Kalisz z początku XIX w," *Pomerania*, no. 7 (1984), 39. This trend continued because many of the migrants along the Opeongo were unable to sign their names (see chapter 3).
93 Rekowski passionately contends that the Kashubs from Pomerania "simply refused, at a terrible cost to their own evolution, to be assimilated by the Prussian juggernaut." *The Saga of the Kashub People*, 61. The stance taken against the Enlightenment by the Redemptorist order (of which Rekowski was a member, although almost a century later) in Prussia advocated ultramontane beliefs.

94 Jost, "Polish Kashub Pioneers in Ontario," 20; "A Local Pastor," 5; *Kaszuby Canada, Part One*, dir. Henryk Bartul.
95 Kieniewicz, *The Emancipation*, 89, 94; Wandycz, *The Lands of Partitioned Poland*, 16; and Wenkstern, *Prussia and the Poles*, 10. James C. Scott also mentions that we should be careful not to jump to the conclusion that all the impacts of the state are detrimental since society depends on some of these extensions of the state: *Seeing Like a State*, 2–3. Paradoxically, as Daniel Chirst argues, it was only after being partitioned and exposed to German and Russian markets that parts of Poland began to progress economically. See "Causes and Consequences of Backwardness," in *The Origins of Backwardness in Eastern Europe*, 8.
96 Hobsbawm, "Mass-Producing Traditions," 264–5.
97 Ibid.
98 Czyrson's passport was featured in a photo, but not analyzed or integrated into the narrative by the editors (Fr Breza and Ben Schultz) in The Polish Cultural Institute, *The Kashubian Polish Community of Southeastern Minnesota*, 14. For the biographical information of the record book see Mask-Connolly, *Kashubia to Canada: Crossing on the Agda*, 11. For Scott's argument, consult *Seeing Like a State*, 2–3.
99 Frank J. Ritza, "Saga of the Polish Pioneer," BBR, 11 May 1961; O'Dwyer, *Highways of Destiny*, 155; Glofcheskie, *Folk Music*, 1.
100 Makowski, *The Polish People in Canada*, 54–5. Presumably, Makowski received the specific reference to Frank Peplinski from a relative recounting the family's oral history.
101 Rekowski, *The Saga of the Kashub People*, 6.
102 Mask-Connolly, *Kashubia to Canada: Crossing on the Agda*, 10–11.
103 Endnote 16 in Mask-Connolly, *Kashubia to Canada: Crossing on the Agda*, 15. Italics in original.
104 Prince, *The Kovalskie (Kowalski) Family of Barry's Bay*, 7.
105 Ross, *The Failure of Bismarck's Kulturkampf*, 10; Trzeciakowski, *The Kulturkampf*, 1.
106 Ross, "The Kulturkampf," 186.
107 Blanke, "The Polish Role in the Origin of the *Kulturkampf* in Prussia," 253; Trzeciakowski, *The Kulturkampf in Prussian Poland*, 1; Wandycz, *The Lands of Partitioned Poland*, 228; and Murdzek, *Emigration in Polish Social-Political Thought, 1870–1914*, 4.
108 Ross, "The Kulturkampf," 173; Gross, *The War Against Catholicism*, 21; and Walser Smith, *German Nationalism and Religious Conflict*, 19.
109 Lukowski and Zawadski, *A Concise History of Poland*, 184; Robinson, ed., *Readings in European History*, vol. 2, 585–6; Murdzek, *Emigration, 1870–1914*, 4–5.

110 Wandycz, *The Price of Freedom*, 162; Lorentz, "An Outline of Cassubian Civilization" in *The Cassubian Civilization*, 19; Snyder, *The Blood and Iron Chancellor*, 349. Also expressed by Porter, "Patriotism, Prophecy, and the Catholic Hierarchy in Nineteenth-Century Poland," 215.

111 The first statement is from a 31 May 1892 interview conducted by Hans Kleser, the editor of *Westdeutsche Allgemeine Zeitung*, and published in Snyder, *The Blood and Iron Chancellor*, 349. For Bismarck's memoirs see Bismarck, *Otto von Bismarck*, 212.

112 Porter, "Patriotism, Prophecy," 214; Reinerman, "Metternich, Pope Gregory XVI, and Revolutionary Poland 1831–1842," 603.

113 This decree implied that the Vatican did not know the privations of the Polish people. Reinerman also argued that although the pillar of faith remained strong among Polish-speaking people, their faith in the workings of the Vatican would not heal until the election of Karol Wojtyła as Pope in 1978: "Metternich, Pope Gregory XVI, and Revolutionary Poland, 1831–1842," 610.

114 Porter, "Patriotism, Prophecy," 215.

115 "Na dzień zmart wychwstania pańskiego r 1831," *Poezje* (Wrocław, 1959), 239–40, as cited in Davies, *God's Playground: Volume 2*, 9. This sentiment is still evident years later. Ignacy Wieniewski wrote that "Poland was the Saviour of nations, for whose redemption she suffered a martyr's death, to be resurrected on the third day." See *Heritage, the Foundations of Polish Culture: An Introductory Outline*, 43.

116 Porter, "Patriotism, Prophecy," 219–21. Mickiewicz's work was also condemned by the Vatican.

117 Czubaty, "'What is to be Done When the Motherland has Died?,'" 96–7.

118 Obtained from a map insert of parishes, c. 1816: Sadkowski, *Drewniana Architektura Sakralna Na Pormorzu Gdańskim w XVII–XX Wieku*.

119 Gross, *The War Against Catholicism*, 31, 35, 43.

120 Ibid., 41.

121 Assembled from many entries in volumes 2–13 of *Słownik Geograficzny Królestwa Polskiego*, eds. Sulimierskiego, Chlebowskiego, and Walewskiego.

122 Gross, *The War Against Catholicism*, 38–42.

123 Walser Smith, "Prussia at the Margins," 78. An old saying "*co niemiec, to odmieniec*," as recorded by Hagen, *Germans, Poles, and Jews*, 27–8. Another one says that the devil wore "German dress" and when he spoke "it was in German." The use of the term is also present in the findings of Lukowski, *The Partitions of Poland*, 34–5.

124 Bismarck, *Reflections and Reminiscences*, 213.

125 Ross, "The Kulturkampf," 173; Gross, *The War Against Catholicism*, 43.

126 Trzeciakowski, *The Kulturkampf*, 119; Gross, *The War Against Catholicism*, 242.
127 Ross, "The Kulturkampf," 173; Trzeciakowski, *The Kulturkampf*, 45.
128 Gross, *The War Against Catholicism*, 242; and Ross, "The Kulturkampf," 173; Murdzek, *Emigration, 1870–1914*, 4; Ross, *Bismarck's Kulturkampf*, 5.
129 Eduard Zeller's words as paraphrased by Gross, *The War Against Catholicism*, 247.
130 Ross, "The Kulturkampf," 185, 190–1; Trzeciakowski, *The Kulturkampf*, 119; Gross, *The War Against Catholicism*, 247; and Walser Smith, *German Nationalism*, 28.
131 Ross, *Bismarck's Kulturkampf*, 5, 23.
132 Trzeciakowski, *The Kulturkampf*, 44; Ross, *Bismarck's Kulturkampf*, 19.
133 Walser Smith, *German Nationalism*, 45.
134 Walser Smith comments that roughly one-third of German parishioners in the Cassubian region were Catholics. See "Prussia at the Margins," 78.
135 Gross, *The War Against Catholicism*, 243, 255.
136 Ross, "The Kulturkampf," 173, 174; and Gross, *The War Against Catholicism*, 255; Melton, *Absolutism*, 165, 197; Lamberti, *State, Society, and the Elementary School*, 15–16.
137 Gross, *The War Against Catholicism*, 61, 257; Ross, "The Kulturkampf," 175; Holborn, *A History of Modern Germany 1840–1945*, 263; Walser Smith, *German Nationalism*, 41.
138 Pope Pius IX, *Quod Nunquam: On the Church in Prussia*, 5 February 1875, http://www.papalencyclicals.net/Pius09/p9quodnu.htm, accessed 5 August 2010. Also expressed in Holborn, *A History of Modern Germany 1840–1945*, 264; Trzeciakowski, *The Kulturkampf*, 59.
139 Trzeciakowski, *The Kulturkampf*, 60; Gross, *The War Against Catholicism*, 257.
140 This paradigm was especially evident in the 1874 law making civil marriages compulsory. Although non-secular marriages are recognized as civil marriages today, at the time the Catholic Church saw this as yet another attack on its divine rule and authority. Ross, "The Kulturkampf," 174–5, 193.
141 Holborn, *A History of Modern Germany 1840–1945*, 263; Gross, *The War Against Catholicism*, 257–8.
142 Ross, *Bismarck's Kulturkampf*, 7.
143 Lamberti, "State, Church, and the Politics of School Reform," 70–80; Lamberti, *State, Society, and the Elementary School*, 48–9.
144 Murdzek, *Emigration in Polish Socio-Political Thought, 1870–1914*, 16.
145 Ross argued that suppression in France during the Third Republic had a greater effect than *Kulturkampf* did and that it was not as violent as New York City's Orange Day massacre in 1871. "The Kulturkampf," 195.

146 Murdzek, *Emigration, 1870–1914*, 5.
147 Bismarck, *Otto von Bismarck*, 217, 221.
148 Lamberti, *State, Society and the Elementary School*, 43.
149 Persecuted Catholics, in some areas, chose to persecute another faith group, Jews, who were deemed "backwards," says Ross, "The Kulturkampf," 190, 193.
150 Gross, *The War Against Catholicism*, 243. Ross, *Bismarck's Kulturkampf*, 182. The Colonization Commission was known after the *Ansiedlungsgesetz* law which required the creation of the *Ansiedlungskommission* to settle Germans in Polish-speaking territory. See Murdzek, *Emigration, 1870–1914*, 5.
151 Italics and formatting in original: Mask-Connolly, *Kashubia to Canada: Crossing on the Agda*, 11–12.
152 Holborn, *A History of Modern Germany*, 139–40.
153 Craig, *The Politics of the Prussian Army*, 9.
154 Showalter, "Prussia's Army: Continuity and Change, 1713–1830," 227; Grenville, *Europe Reshaped*, 139.
155 Craig, *The Politics of the Prussian Army*, 10.
156 Ritter, *The Sword and the Scepter*, 148; also Showalter, "Prussia's Army," 227.
157 The *Eganville Leader* mentions that he came to Canada in 1873 and had previously served a two-year term in the military. It does not mention, however, that he left because he feared being enlisted again. See EL 17, no. 26, 30 April 1920.
158 Sanford, "Polish People of Portage County," 265; Zeitlin, "White Eagles," 81–2; Lee-Whiting, *Harvest of Stones*, 26, 27; Finnigan, *Canadian Colonization Road*, 148; Lee-Whiting, *On Stony Ground*, 19.

CHAPTER THREE

1 Referring to Oscar Handlin's *The Uprooted*, which contains many sensationalized and generalized accounts. Tales of deception, poverty, and disease and plight woven into the narrative captivated many readers.
2 O'Dwyer, *Highways of Destiny*, 155.
3 Ibid., 155–7.
4 See Trencsényi and Kopeček, *Discourses of Collective Identity*, 137–8.
5 O'Dwyer, *Highways*, 157.
6 Rekowski, *The Saga of the Kashub People in Poland, Canada, U.S.A.*, 14.
7 Mask-Connolly, *Kashubia to Canada: Crossing on the Agda*, 16.
8 Ibid., 21, 22, 40, 86. The author also described the voyage of the *Agda* using a Handlinesque tone.

9 After reading portions of the text for this book, Mask-Connolly wrote more critically about O'Dwyer's epic tales in *Marriage Matters* (2014), realizing that O'Dwyer had taken literary license when crafting the narrative. See pp. 133, 135.
10 *Kaszuby Canada, Part One*, dir. Henryk Bartul.
11 He is also a "writer in residence" at a private Catholic college in Barry's Bay (Our Lady Seat of Wisdom Academy). See: "Michael O'Brien Named Artist and Writer in Residence," http://www.seatofwisdom.org/news/latest/michael-obrien-named-artist-and-writer-in-residence.html, accessed 23 June 2010. O'Brien also added that pioneers used to bury the Gospel underground. This statement has not been corroborated and it has not been repeated.
12 Mask-Connolly, *Kashubia to Canada: Crossing on the Agda*, 20.
13 In 1967, Lee-Whiting suggested that it was T.P. French's reports that encouraged settlement, including the Poles, along the Opeongo: "The Opeongo Road," 77, 82. Jost echoed this in 1974 and 1984: "New Documentation," 446; "Polish Kashub Pioneers in Ontario," 20. Parker, writing in 1975, claimed that "extensive governmental advertising brought only a few poverty stricken Poles and Germans into the Ottawa-Huron region." See "Colonization Roads and Commercial Policy," 35. See also Hessel, *Destination*, 32–61.
14 William Sinn was the German translator at Quebec in the late 1850s and William Wagner was employed as an overseas emigration agent from 1860–63. See Gürttler, "William (Wilhelm) Wagner."
15 Rekowski, *The Saga of the Kashub People*, 6 and 14. He did not cite Hessel but Ickiewicz, who, in turn, did not source his claim: *Kaszubi w Kanadzie*, 81.
16 Mask-Connolly, *Brudenell Revisited*, 3. It is also replicated in her article "2008 Special Year for Canada's Polish Community: marking the 150th ANNIVERSARY of the arrival of the first large group of Polish immigrants – the KASHUBS – to Canada in 1858," *NWHS* 7, no. 1 (Spring/Summer 2008), 7. The proper citation and page number is: *Report of the Select Committee to whom was referred the Annual Report of the Chief Emigration Agent and Supplementary Report of the German Assistant at Quebec* (Quebec: Thompson & Co., 1860), 41. A "land of milk and honey" appears several times in the book of Exodus (NRSV). The first reference to it is Exodus 3:8.
17 Mask-Connolly, *Kashubia to Canada: Crossing on the Agda*, 40.
18 Ibid., 35, 44–5.
19 Frye, *The Educated Imagination*, 9.

20 Maracle, "Fudging The Truth: A Tradition As Old As Uncle Tom," F2.
21 "Saga of a Polish Pioneer," *BBR*, 11 May 1961.
22 Rekowski, *The Saga of the Kashub People*, 28, 61.
23 Unfortunately, Rekowski again did not source his claim to any publication authored by Jost. Rekowski, *The Saga of the Kashub People*, 16.
24 Mask-Connolly, *Polish Pioneer Families*, 6; Mask-Connolly, *Kashubia to Canada*, 10–11.
25 Her memoirs also appeared in an article in Poland: Brzeski, "Nauczycielka Ontaryjskich Kaszubów," 66. After tracing the evolution of the voyage narrative from O'Dwyer to Mask-Connolly, one wonders if O'Dwyer interviewed her while writing his 1964 book.
26 Elizabeth Catherine (Etmanski) Shalla, "Memoirs," 2.
27 See Makowski, *The Polish People in Canada*, 56; Rekowski, *The Saga of the Kashub People*, 15; and "A Personal History of a Barry's Bay Resident," *BBTW*, 4 November 1981.
28 Moltmann, *Germans to America*, 86.
29 *JLAC*, 1859. Appendix 19, Report of the Chief Emigration Agent, 3.
30 Mask-Connolly only listed a few ships from 1872 that had been afflicted by illness and death. These were sourced to a website and not contextualized. Mask-Connolly, *Kashubia to Canada: Crossing on the Agda*, 89, 294.
31 Wagner, *A History of Migration from Germany to Canada*, 64.
32 Radecki and Heydenkorn, *A Member of a Distinguished Family*, 21; Rekowski, *The Saga of the Kashub People*, 14.
33 Rekowski, *The Saga of the Kashub People*, 14.
34 Mask-Connolly, *Polish Pioneer Families*, 12; Mask-Connolly, *Brudenell Revisited*, 3–4.
35 *JLAC*, 1859. Appendix 19, Report of the Chief Emigration Agent, 14.
36 Mask-Connolly refers to the ship as the *Donan*. However, it is recorded as the *Donau*. This error may have been caused by the handwriting in the ships' lists.
37 Campey, *Fast Sailing and Copper Bottomed*, 144–5.
38 Mask-Connolly, *Kashubia to Canada: Crossing on the Agda*, 88. However, the author does not source this claim either.
39 Campey, *Fast Sailing and Copper Bottomed*, 145–55.
40 Eltis, "Free and Coerced Transatlantic Migrations," 271.
41 *JLAC*, 1859. Appendix 19, Report of the Chief Emigration Agent, 4.
42 "An act to amend and consolidate the laws relating to the Carriage of Passengers by Sea," in *The Statutes of the United Kingdom of Great Britain and Ireland*, vols. 15 and 16 (London, 1852), 108–13. See also *An act to*

regulate the Carriage of Passengers in Merchant Vessels. 29th American Congress, 22 February 1847, Session II, Chapter XVI, 9th Statute, 128. Also, "Measurement of Passenger Vessels," *New York Times*, 13 September 1856, 4. On many slave ships, which landed in the Carribbean and Rio, deck space per person was around 3 to 4 feet: Eltis, "Free and Coerced Transatlantic Migrations," 272.

43 Mask-Connolly claimed that 290 persons were on board the *Elbe*. The AAZ said 188. The ship was only 264 tonnes. The figure seems abnormally high and does not fit any patterns.

44 Adams, *Ireland and Irish Migration*, 88, 230.

45 Lee-Whiting, "Why So Many German Immigrants Embarked at Liverpool," 71, 79.

46 According to Catherine Parr Traill, British law in 1852 required ships to provide passengers with the following every week: 2.5 lbs. bread or biscuit, 1 lb. wheaten flour, 5 lbs. oatmeal, 2 lbs. rice, 1.5 lbs. sugar, 2 oz. salt, 2 oz. tea or 4 oz. coffee or cocoa in addition to 3 quarts of water daily. See *The Canadian Settler's Guide*, 32.

47 Bickelmann, "The Emigration Business," 138; and Schöberl, "Emigration Policy," 39. Bickelmann also remarks that Bremen and Hamburg cracked down on the port swindlers known as "*litzer*" by the beginning of the 1850s, well before other European ports. See "The Venture of Travel." All these are in Moltmann, *Germans to America*.

48 Rekowski, *The Saga of the Kashub People*, 62; *Kaszuby Canada, Part One*, dir. Henryk Bartul; Mask-Connolly, as quoted in Finnigan, *Life Along the Opeongo Line*, 194.

49 Mask-Connolly, *Kashubia to Canada: Crossing on the Agda*, 184.

50 Rekowski, *The Saga of the Kashub People*, 62.

51 Mask-Connolly, *Kashubia to Canada: Crossing on the Agda*, 42–3.

52 Graff, "What the 1861 Census Can Tell Us About Literacy," 344.

53 AO, RG1, A-I-7, "Ottawa–Opeongo Road Agent's location returns & reports 1860–1866."

54 AO, RG1, C-IV, Township Papers, Hagarty Twp.

55 These are deduced from multiple land petitions (1860s to the 1890s), AO, RG1, C-IV, Township Papers.

56 Graff gives us an idea of some of the factors that affect "success" in *The Labyrinths of Literacy*, 172.

57 Original copied by Edward Breza, "Mieszkańcywsi Kalisz z początku XIX w," *Pomerania*, no. 7 (1984), 39.

58 Graff, *Literacy Myths, Legacies and Lessons: New Studies in Literacy*, 35, 39. Also see Graff, "What the 1861 Census Can Tell Us about Literacy," 339.

59 Russell, "Forest into Farmland," 132. Similar sentiments are expressed by Wilson, *Tenants in Time*, 18.
60 Radforth, *Bushworkers and Bosses*, 75; and Russell, "Forest into Farmland," 140. Russell notes on page 141 that the rates are lower for the aforementioned district than for others (such as Newcastle at 2.2, Gore at 1.2, or Johnstown at 1.0) perhaps because "a substantial number of farmers went up the Ottawa Valley to work in lumber camps each winter, leaving less time for farm clearing."
61 Such a conclusion is drawn from affidavits in AO RG1, A-I-7, Box 14.
62 Lee, *Lumber Kings and Shantymen*, 72.
63 See "Report of the Minister of Agriculture, 1861" in MG11-CO47, Canada, Miscellanea, Blue Books of Statistics, etc., 1861.
64 Makowski, *The Polish People in Canada*, 57; Rekowski, *The Saga of the Kashub People*, 29; Mask-Connolly, *Polish Pioneer Families*, 8.
65 Crown Lands Agent T.P. French to the Commissioner of Crown Lands P.M. Vankoughnet, 7 October 1859. AO, RG1, A-I-7, Box 14.
66 AO, RG1, A-I-7, Box 14, 08615. "Ottawa–Opeongo Road Agent's Location Returns & Reports 1860–1866."
67 Iacovetta, *Gatekeepers*, 49–62.
68 Basu, *Highland Homecomings*, 199.
69 Rekowski claimed that in Canada "because of their isolation, poverty and lack of schools, the second, third, and fourth generations of Kashubs in Canada reverted to illiteracy and analphabetism and a lower level of culture and education prevailed among them than had existed among the founding fathers." *The Saga of the Kashub People*, 55. This topic could also be an excellent avenue of study.
70 Conrad and Finkel, *History of the Canadian Peoples: Volume II*, 113–16.
71 Miller, *Emigrants and Exiles*, 3–6.
72 Jacobsen, *Special Sorrows*, 2.
73 Unlike Prussian Poland, the Polish Catholic clergy in Galicia were not as active in nationalist politics. Lukowski and Zawadzki, *A Concise History of Poland*, 189, 202. Unlike Prussia, Austria recognized and designated Polish as the official language of Galicia in June 1869: Pekacz, *Music in the Culture of Polish Galicia*, 36. They had a "hands-off" policy of ruling too: Golab, "The Polish Experience in Philadelphia," 45. Bujak's quote appears as cited in Stauter-Halsted, *The Nation in the Village*, 24. Other statistics and claims in this section were gathered from a combination of the aforementioned sources as well as: Magosci and Hann, *Galicia*, 3, 10, 28; Kieniewicz, *The Emancipation*, 204–5; Frank, *Oil Empire*, 28, 42–5; Himka, *Socialism in Galicia*, 4–5; Galush, "Journeys of Spirit and

Space," 8; Gustawicz, "Galicya," 457–8; Dutkiewicz, "Main Aspects," 62–3; and Murdzek, *Emigration in Polish Social-Political Thought*, 142.

74 In this sense, I am trying to invoke Sherry B. Ortner's notion of agency as "expressed largely through an idiom of activity and passivity" and also as the notion of individual intention and desire. See *Anthropology and Social Theory*, 140.

75 Mangalam and Schwartzweller, "Some Theoretical Guidelines," 9–10.

76 Petersen, "A General Typology of Migration," 53.

77 Zubrzycki, *Soldiers and Peasants*, 14.

78 Petersen, "A General Typology of Migration," 58. *The American Heritage Dictionary of the English Language* (710) defines forced as "imposed by force ... against one's will ... involuntary."

79 Mask-Connolly, *Kashubia to Canada: Crossing on the Agda*, 23; and Shalla. "Memoirs," 3.

80 Petersen, "A General Typology of Migration," 58. *The American Heritage Dictionary of the English Language* (905) defines the term "impelled" as "to urge action through moral pressure."

81 Green, "The Politics of Exit," 288.

82 Moogk, "Reluctant Exiles," 9. An example of subsidized passage happened in the Württemburg town of Schwenningen. The residents appropriated 20,000 gulden to assist the emigration of 224 paupers in 1847. Some Hessian and Bavarian villages also shipped poor children to America in the late 1840s: Walker, *Germany and the Emigration*, 75.

83 Fahrmeir, "Nineteenth Century German Citizenships," 730; Torpey, *The Invention of the Passport*, 66.

84 Walker, *Germany and the Emigration*, 93; Bade, *Migration in European History*, 96.

85 Glofcheskie, *The Klopotek-Glowczewski Family Coat of Arms*, 9.

86 Torpey, *The Invention of the Passport*, 76.

87 The papers are deposited in a glass case at the Wilno Heritage Society's museum.

88 Shalla, "Memoirs," 3; Glofcheskie, *The Klopotek-Glowczewski Family Coat of Arms*, 9–10.

89 Sulimierskiego, Chlebowskiego, and Walewskiego, *Słownik Geograficzny Królestwa Polskiego*, Volume 3, 904–5.

90 Dependant, of course, on which community the settler left as Wiele and Leśno were further south than Lipusz by approximately 10 kilometres.

91 Steitz, *Die Entstehung Der Kön-Mindener Eisenbahngesellschaft*; Holborn, *A History of Modern Germany*, 15; Also, *Die Entwicklung der Verkehrsverhaltnisse b) Ost- und Westpreußen 19./20. Jht.* in *Historisch-*

     geographischer Atlas des Preußenlandes, Mortensen, Mortensen, and Wenskus.

92 Canada Legislative Assembly, *Report of the Select Committee to whom was referred the Annual Report of the Chief Emigration Agent and Supplementary Report of the German Assistant at Quebec* (Quebec: Thompson & Co., 1860), 41.

93 *AAZ*, 20 January 1860; Holborn, *A History of Modern Germany*, 377; also *Die Entwicklung der Verkehrsverhaltnisse b) Ost- und Westpreußen 19./20. Jht.* in *Historisch-geographischer Atlas des Preußenlandes*, Mortensen, Mortensen, and Wenskus.

94 Wagner, *A History of Migration from Germany to Canada 1850–1939*, 27–37.

95 Hansen, *German Schemes of Colonization Before 1860*, 53.

96 Bausenhart, *German Immigration and Assimilation in Ontario 1783–1918*, 64. The Quebec route was abandoned in 1871: Paszkowski, *Poles in Australia and Oceania 1790–1940*, 8–9; Starczewska, "The Historical Geography," 12; Radziłowski, "Out on the Wind," 18; Goc, *Native Realm*, 19.

97 The statistics from Berent were taken from various passages in: *Statistische Darstellung des Berenter Kreises ... Berent*, 1863. The daily and yearly wages are from the region of Kartuzy (the district to the north of Berent) c. 1861. See *Topographisch-statistische Beschreibung des Kreises Carthaus ... Danzig*, 1880. I converted the wages from marks to thalers based on the commonly used formula of the time: 1 thaler = 3 marks.

98 For the Hamburg-America see Dutkiewicz, "Main Aspects," 82.

99 See L. Stafford to J. Lowe (30 July 1872), LAC RG17, vol. 68, #6569 and *Renfrew Mercury*, 9 August 1872.

100 Wagner, *Canada*, 15.

101 Kamphoefner, "The Real Guidebooks," 6, 11; and "German Emigration Research," 28. Kamphoefner also suggested that the state used agents as scapegoats to deny "that the mass exodus resulted from genuine social and economic" problems in "German Emigration Research," 28. James M. Bergquist paraphrases the words of Bretting in his review: "Auswanderungsagenturen und Auswanderungsvereinim 19 und 20. Jahrhundert'," 120. See also Keeling, "Costs, Risks and Migration Networks Between Europe and the United States," 121; and Hvidt, "Emigration Agents," 202–3.

102 Gaddis, *The Landscape of History*, 136.

103 Gorecki, "*Viatorto Ascriptitius*," 26.

104 Moodie, *Roughing It in the Bush or Forest Life in Canada*, 3.

105 Gopnik, *Winter*, 82.
106 An examination of Rekowski's claim that the settlers' descendants had a lower level of education after settling in Canada would be an interesting topic and venture. However, it is beyond the scope of this study.
107 As recorded by Lorentz, "An Outline of Cassubian Civilization," in *The Cassubian Civilization*, 18.

CHAPTER FOUR

1 French, *Information for Intending Settlers*.
2 Ickiewicz, *Kaszubi w Kanadzie*, 55, 102. Reprinted in *Pomerania* 7–8, no. 411 (July–August, 2008), 4; Jost, "Polish Kashub Pioneers in Ontario," 20; Zurakowski, *The Proud Inheritance*, 15; Rekowski, *The Saga of the Kashub People*, 26.
3 She copied this statement, without sourcing it, from Peter Hessel, *Destination*, 34. See Mask-Connolly, *Kashubia to Canada: Crossing on the Agda*, 1; Renfrew County was not created until 8 June 1861. See County of Renfrew, "History," http://www.countyofrenfrew.on.ca/menu/about-the-county/history/.
4 Walsh, "Landscapes of Longing," 29–30.
5 *The American Heritage Dictionary of the English Language*, 1897.
6 Hamer, *New Towns in the New World*, 79; See also Quay, *Westward Expansion*, 156.
7 I use the term "resettlement" since the land was settled first by indigenous populations. Ruby and Brown, *Indians of the Pacific Northwest*, 97.
8 See *Information for Emigrants to British North America*, 2nd ed.; Hansen, *German Schemes of Colonization Before 1860*, 54; Walker, *Germany and the Emigration*, 62.
9 Gates, "Official Encouragement to Immigration by the Province of Canada," 25; Parker, "Colonization Roads and Commercial Policy," 31. Parker gives too much credit to the Minister of Agriculture, P.M. Vankoughnet, and too little to William Hutton or French in the production of the guides.
10 Curtis, "Official Documentary Systems and Colonial Government," 411; Walsh, "Landscapes of Longing," 159, 163; See also, Hodgetts, *Pioneer Public Service*, 250–1; Boyce, *Hutton of Hastings*, 218–19.
11 Gates, "Official Encouragement to Immigration by the Province of Canada," 26; Hodgetts, *Pioneer Public Service*, 243. In 1859, A.B. Hawke, the Chief Emigration Agent for Upper Canada (stationed in Toronto), testi-

fied that the agency in Ottawa (headed by Francis Clemow) did not report to him but to A.C. Buchanan, the Chief Emigration Agent at Quebec, and the Bureau of Agriculture. Select Parliamentary Committee on Emigration, *JLAC*, 1859, Appendix 19, 38. Clemow was appointed in 1857 on the recommendation of Buchanan. See also Hodgetts, *Pioneer Public Service*, 121.

12 Walsh, "Landscapes of Longing," 17, 55. There were several Crown Lands Agents responsible for the roads, such as French (Opeongo), Ebeneezer Perry (Addington), M.P. Hayes (Hastings). Spragge, "Colonization Roads in Canada West, 1850–1867," 7.

13 Turner, "William Hutton."

14 NAC RG17, A-I-2, vol. 1490, Reel T-112, 369–70, Hutton and Buchanan to Executive Council, 25 April 1855.

15 Boyce, *Hutton of Hastings*, 186–8; Walsh, "Landscapes of Longing," 164.

16 Hutton, *Canada: Its Present Condition*; Parr Traill, *The Canadian Settler's Guide* (1855); Hutton, *Canada: A Brief Outline*; Vera Foster, *Work and Wages*. Emigrant Office chief A.C. Buchanan also wrote a guidebook. See Macdonald, *Canada*. Hutton's first guidebook was published in the series "Stanford's Emigrant Guides." See Boyce, *Hutton of Hastings*, 189. The guides by Parr Traill and Foster were endorsed by the government as legitimate guides.

17 Walsh, "Landscapes of Longing," 169.

18 Parson, "The Colonization of the Southern Canadian Shield in Ontario," 266; Macdonald, *Canada*, 13.

19 Walsh, "Landscapes of Longing," 159, 194.

20 Boxes of rotting books were found in a basement in 1872. See Macdonald, *Canada*, 32. Quay argued that the informative aspect of guidebooks was dubious since some settlers "found themselves weighted down by the sheer number of things they had to put aboard their wagons." See *Westward Expansion*, 156. Walter Kamphoefner wrote that the effectiveness of guidebooks is often overstated and argued that personal contacts were more influential. See "The Real Guidebooks," 6, 11.

21 Walsh, "Landscapes of Longing," 158–9; Macdonald, *Canada*, 80. Curtis also echoed this, saying that after the Irish famine migrations, immigration policy "focused especially on the attraction of farmers with capital, capable of purchasing the Crown Lands whose capitalization was at the base of colonial financial policy." See "Official Document Systems and Colonial Government," 407.

22 Hodgetts, *Pioneer Public Service*, 255.

23 Report to the Chief Emigration Agent, *JLAC*, 1859, Appendix 19, 8.

24 *Report of the Select Committee to Whom Was Referred the Annual Report of the Chief Emigration Agent, and Supplementary Report of the German Assistant at Quebec*, 41.
25 Francis Clemow cited in Report to the Chief Emigration Agent, *JLAC*, 1859, Appendix 19, 25–6; *Report of the Select Committee*, 41.
26 Lee-Whiting, "Why So Many German Immigrants Embarked at Liverpool," 75. French's publication was indeed translated into German but the paper copy was not given a publication date: T.P. French, *Anweisungfür Ansiedler an die Ottawa und Opeongo Strasse und Umgegend*. (A copy is in the possession of the author.)
27 Walsh, "Landscapes of Longing," 157. The original document is Select Parliamentary Committee on Emigration, *JLAC*, 1859, Appendix 19; Report of William Hutton, Secretary of the Department of Agriculture, 5 May 1857, *JLAC*, Appendix 54. The German version is: William Hutton, *Canada: Ein kurzer Abriss von dessen geographischer Lage, Production, Klima, und Bodenbeschaffenheit, Erziehungs und Municipal-Wesen, &c.*
28 LAC, RG17, A-I-2, vol. 1491, Hutton to French, 15 January 1857; LAC, RG17, A-I-2, vol. 1490, Department of Agriculture – General Letterbooks 1852–1894, Hutton to French, 25 June 1857.
29 Mask-Connolly quoted, but erroneously referred to Sinn as the "Chief Emigration Agent" in *Kashubia to Canada: Crossing on the Agda*, 37–8; also quoted in *Brudenell Revisited*, 3; "2008 Special Year for Canada's Polish Community marking the 150th ANNIVERSARY of the arrival of the first large group of Polish immigrants – the KASHUBS – to Canada in 1858," *NWHS* 7, no. 1 (Spring/Summer 2008), 3–4.
30 This employment was also mentioned by Bassler, "The 'Inudation' of British North America," 108.
31 *Report of the Select Committee*, 37–41.
32 Peter Hessel consulted one edition (1861) of the *DAZ* that outlined free grants along the Opeongo. Unfortunately, he did not write about earlier issues. *Destination*, 45–6.
33 "Briefe eines deutschen Ansiedlers," *DAZ*, 15 August 1853.
34 Wilhelm Sinn, "Einwanderung in Canada im Jahre 1854," *DAZ*, 5 April 1855.
35 As cited by Bassler, "The 'Inudation' of British North America," 99.
36 LAC RG17, A-I-2, vol. 1491. Cameron to Sinn, 11 June 1853.
37 "Briefe aus Canada," *DAZ*, 27 June 1853; "Briefe eines deutschen Ansiedlers in Kanada," *DAZ*, 10 May 1853; "Canada," *AAZ*, 26 June 1857.
38 *The Canadian Agriculturalist* 7, no. 8 (August 1856), n.p.; *DAZ*, 15 September 1856.

39 LAC, RG17, A-I-2, vol. 1491, Hutton to Buchanan, 3 December 1856.
40 *Jubiläums-Büchlein: zurfeier des 50 jährigen Jubiläums der evang.-luther Synode von Canada*, 15. Also, *Report of the Select Committee*, 40. As evidenced in chapter 3, some of the settlers could write their names and some of their signatures were German versions of their given name. Thus, it is not far-fetched to suggest that some of the settlers spoke and understood German.
41 Bassler, "The 'Inudation' of British North America," 108.
42 Hvidt, "Emigration Agents," 183.
43 Lee-Whiting, *On Stony Ground*, 8.
44 *Allgemeine Auswanderung Zeitung*, 8 February 1861. See also Kellenbenz, "Die Auswanderungnach Lateinamericka," 215–42.
45 Wagner, *A History of Migration*, 43. Traditionally, "shipping companies and their agents had announced or advertised sailings." See Charlotte Erickson, *Emigration From Europe*, 228. These agents operated on many different levels. There were emigrant brokers at the port, main agents in the communities inland, and sub-agents throughout the countryside. The business originated around 1836 in Bremen when the shipowner, Robert M. Sloman, started building the emigrant transport business: Bickelman, "The Emigration Business," 136–7. Before 1860, the emigrant traffic business was a case of "every man for himself." The employment of agents was not limited to Prussia. Hvidt analyzed the industry in Denmark and the Companie Générale Transatlantique in Le Havre employed 55 agents and around 200–300 sub-agents. Moltmann, "Steamship Transport of Emigrants from Europe to the United States," 315.
46 LAC, RG17, A-I-2, vol. 1492, Hutton to Wagner, 23 March 1857; LAC, RG17, A-I-2, vol. 1492, 14 May 1858; LAC, RG17, A-I-2, vol. 1492, Hutton to C.P. Roney (in London), 28 July 1858.
47 Gates, "Official Encouragement to Immigration by the Province of Canada," 30; Macdonald, *Canada*, 82. Original source is *JLAC*, 1860, IV, Paper 21, Letters of instruction of A.C. Buchanan of 30 Jan. 1860, and of P.M. Vankoughnet, Commissioner of Crown Lands, 11 February 1860. All that is known of Wagner between 1850 and 1857 is that he was a resident of Ottawa, having escaped Poznań in Prussian-occupied Poland after his participation in the 1848 uprisings. He later became a land surveyor for Lower Canada in 1857 and Upper Canada in 1858. See Gürttler, "William (Wilhelm) Wagner."
48 William Wagner was shocked by the work of other agents for shipping lines or subsidized by American railroad companies, Brazil, and the Cape Colony. He wrote that "these agents ... are the most abominable of

things, and I would be satisfied to have nothing to do with any of them, but I cannot help it." *JLAC*, 1862, IV, Paper 21, Wagner to Vankoughnet, 11 March 1862. The director of the North German Lloyd Line conceded that, in dealing with emigration agents, "we work with the scum of humanity." Rumours were always rife when it came to the reliability of the agents. Around 1850, a rumour circulated in Pomerania that "'a Prussian prince' had obtained estates [in] 'America and Australia' and was offering free passage and support for Prussians." Bade wrote that behind this imaginary "'prince' was probably an overseas or German emigrant agent." See *Migration in European History*, 94, 108. Ingrid Schöberl wrote that there was "many a swindler ... to be found among the agents." Schöberl, "Emigration Policy in Germany and Immigration Policy in the United States," in *Germans to America*, 39.

49 Gates, "Official Encouragement to Immigration by the Province of Canada," 30–1; Macdonald, *Canada*, 81–2; *JLAC*, 1862, Appendix 1, Report of the Select Committee on Immigration and Colonization, 17 May 1862. The same methods of recruiting were used by Dominion agents in Dublin and Glasgow later in the nineteenth century: Marjory Harper, "Enticing the Emigrant," 43–4.

50 LAC, RG17, vol. 2392, William Wagner (in Berlin) to William Hutton, 24 April 1860; See also Gates, "Official Encouragement to Immigration by the Province of Canada," 35. Salaries are available in MG11-CO47, Canada, Miscellanea, Blue Books of Statistics, etc., 1860.

51 Walsh, "Landscapes of Longing," 218; NAC, RG17, A 3.3, vol. 2398, "Report to the Governor General in Council re: investigation of illegal practices by emigration agents," 6 April 1862.

52 See LAC, RG17, A-III-3 vol. 2398, 13–17; LAC, RG17, A-I-2, vol. 1492, Hutton to Buchanan, 12 November 1858 and 29 November 1858; LAC, RG17, A-I-2, vol. 1492, Hutton to Buchanan, 31 October 1857; LAC, RG17, A-I-2, vol. 1490, Department of Agriculture – General Letterbooks 1852–1894, Hutton to Buchanan, 5 July 1858. Also: LAC, RG17, A-I-2, vol. 1490, Department of Agriculture – General Letterbooks 1852–1894.

53 Bassler also wrote that if emigration from Württemberg had not ceased in 1856 he would have been given the position of "consul": "The 'Inudation' of British North America," 107. See also "Report to the Governor General in Council re: investigation of illegal practices by emigration agents," 6 April 1862.

54 Rekowski, *The Saga of the Kashub*, 6, 26–7. Mask-Connolly, *Kashubia to Canada: Crossing on the Agda*, 35; Finnigan, *Life Along the Opeongo Line*, 93; and Prince, *The Kovalskie (Kowalski) Family of Barry's Bay*, 13.

55 Lehr, *Community and Frontier*, 21, 30.

CHAPTER FIVE

1. Tuan, *Space and Place*, 17.
2. *Kaszëbë: Pioneers of the Wilderness*.
3. This reference to stoniness and being able to construct many walls of China is in Radecki and Heydenkorn, *A Member of a Distinguished Family*, 21. Rekowski repeated it without citing it in *The Saga of the Kashub People*, 45. While scanning through microfilm from Buffalo, I found that it was originally written by Fr Dembski to *Polak w Ameryce*, no. 2, Rok. II, 8 May 1888. Dembski also wrote, in Polish, that "the Polish locals have bread but not very much money."
4. Mask-Connolly's comments on a recent television program summed up the notion that settlers were given bad land. "Polish Studio," OMNI-TV Toronto, 2 January 2010.
5. Gjerde, "New Growth on Old Vines," 57.
6. A more recent analysis was made by a former local resident, Derek Murray. He analyzed the farming economy and touched on the shanty market in a graduate research paper but did not recognize the importance of the agro-forestry economy and did not draw upon the literature surrounding this issue. See "Narratives, Transitions and the Spaces Between Old and New," 50–5.
7. Lee-Whiting, "The Opeongo Road," 77–9; Miller, *Straight Lines in Curved Space*, 22; Hessel, *Destination*, 39, 49–51.
8. Ibid., 24; Rekowski, *The Saga of the Kashub People*, 26. Mask-Connolly did not source the quote either: "Where They Settled," in *Kashub/Polish Heritage Stories of Renfrew County*, 5.
9. Finnigan, *The Story of a Canadian Colonization Road*, 93, 191.
10. Prince, *The Kovalskie (Kowalski) Family of Barry's Bay*, 14.
11. Rekowski, *The Saga of the Kashub People*, 27.
12. Basu, *Highland Homecomings*, 188. Similarly, blame is ascribed by French-Canadians toward agents of colonization (French-Canadian elites and Roman Catholic priests) who encouraged peasants to settle on marginal rural land in Eastern Quebec. See Little, *Nationalism, Capitalism, and Colonization in Nineteenth-Century Quebec*, xi–xii.
13. The Polish-Kashubs did not escape from an urban ghetto; they were rural peasants. It appears that his line of thinking was influenced by the wartime experiences of urban Poles.
14. Jost, "New Documentation," 445.
15. Hessel, *Destination*, 10.
16. Rekowski, *The Saga of the Kashub People*, 26–7.
17. Prince, *The Kovalskie (Kowalski) Family*, 14.

18 Gillespie, Wicklund, and Matthews, *Soil Survey of Renfrew County*, 45.
19 A letter to the editor of the *Renfrew Mercury* (20 July 1880) entitled "Why go West? Is the Ottawa Valley Too Poor for Farming, or Is It Too Poorly Farmed?" argues that these areas were more fertile than the higher fields. Printed in Smallfield, *Lands and Resources of Renfrew County*, 12.
20 By the early 1970s, the staff employed to survey Ontario had dwindled almost to zero and Canada Land Inventory staff (60 at its peak) were transferred: McKeague and Stobbe, *History of Soil Survey in Canada*, 23–4.
21 The *Soil Survey of Renfrew County* by Gillespie, Wicklund, and Matthews, does advise readers that "the level of generalization is indicated by the scale on which the information is published" (45). Considering that the accompanying map for Renfrew County has a scale of 1:63360, the generalization of such a study is evident.
22 Scott, *Seeing Like a State*, 46.
23 Ontario Ministry of Agriculture, Food and Rural Affairs, "Classifying Prime and Marginal Agricultural Soils and Landscapes."
24 McLean, "Peopling Glengarry County"; Elliott, *Irish Migrants in the Canadas: A New Approach*, 117–27; Lockwood, "The Pattern of Settlement in Eastern Ontario," 235–57.
25 Department of Lands and Forests, *Map Showing the Exploration Routes through the Huron and Ottawa Territory between the years 1615–1854*. (1946).
26 *JLAC*, 1856, vol. 15, Appendix 54. Originally in several newspapers including the *Canadian Agriculturalist* 8, no. 8 (August 1856) and the *St. Catherines Journal* (28 August 1856); Kennedy, *The Upper Ottawa Valley*, 146; Parker, "Colonization Roads and Commercial Policy," 34; Miller, *Straight Lines in Curved Space*, 18; Hessel, *Destination*, 10; Parson, "The Colonization of the Southern Canadian Shield in Ontario," 263.
27 Tuan, *Space and Place*, 54–6, 86, 166.
28 Gentilcore and Donkin, *Land Surveys of Southern Ontario*, 1.
29 Wilson, *Tenants in Time*, 5.
30 Originally in French, *Information for Intending Settlers*. Repeated in Lee-Whiting, "The Opeongo Road," 79; Kennedy, *The Upper Ottawa Valley*, 152; Hessel, *Destination*, 80; Parson, "The Colonization of the Southern Canadian Shield in Ontario," 263; Shaw, *The Opeongo*, 34. French's previous occupation was gleaned from AO, RG1, A-I-7, Crown land administration subject files, Box 14, #08031–#08035.
31 As cited by Richards, "Lands and Policies," 204.
32 Walsh, "Landscapes of Longing," 53, 58.
33 Graeme Wynn, "Notes on Society and Environment in Old Ontario," 53–6.

34 *Canadian Journal of Science, Industry and Art* (2 September 1852), 46.
35 Thomas C. Keefer, *"Montreal" and "The Ottawa": Two Lectures Delivered Before the Mechanics Institute of Montreal* (Montreal: John Lovell, 1854), 33. NAC, RG 17, A-I-2, vol. 1490, Hutton to French, 7 July 1856.
36 Walsh, "Landscapes of Longing," 69.
37 Parson, "The Colonization of the Southern Canadian Shield in Ontario," 267. Also echoed by Wynn, "Notes on Society and Environment in Old Ontario," 58.
38 *Emigration and Colonization in Canada: A Speech Delivered in the House of Assembly, Quebec, 25 April 1862*, 20.
39 *JLAC*, 1863, no. 5, Appendix, 3. *JLAC*, 1863, Appendix no. 8, Evidence of Ezra Stevens, 7 May 1863.
40 Wynn, "Notes on Society and Environment in Old Ontario," 56; Forkey, *Shaping the Upper Canadian Frontier*, 92. Harris, *The Reluctant Land*, 368.
41 Zeller, *Land of Promise, Promised Land*, 1–3. The nature of these sentiments of expansionism, as Doug Owram pointed out, were primarily English-Canadian. See *Promise of Eden*, 5. The trope of mastering the environment is in French's guidebook when, in closing, he states that settlers should not be afraid of Canadian winters. Without them, "the climate would be less healthful, the soil less fruitful, [and] the valuable products of the forest could never be made subservient to the use of man." *Information for Intending Settlers*, 36.
42 Zeller, *Inventing Canada*, 3–6. One of the beliefs was that if trees were cleared, the sunlight would penetrate the soil to improve the climate. Zeller, *Land of Promise, Promised Land*, 3–9. On a local scale, this belief was echoed earlier by T.P. French and was also present in his claim that the snow purified the air and enriched the earth. *Information*, 35. The struggle to reconcile the disorder of the wilderness against the order of society is hinted at by Owram, *Promise of Eden*, 18–19.
43 He notes, however, that "high modernism must not be confused with scientific practice. It was fundamentally, as the term 'ideology' implies, a faith that borrowed, as it were, the legitimacy of science and technology." Scott, *Seeing Like a State*, 4.
44 Zeller, *Inventing Canada*, 16; Zeller, *Land of Promise, Promised Land*, 9.
45 Lower, "The Assault on the Laurentian Barrier, 1850–1870," 302.
46 Wynn, "Notes on Society and Environment in Old Ontario," 54. The eight million persons calculation was actually made by A.J. Russell a year before Vankoughnet. Using a calculation that factored in the total land, along with lumber allowances, Russell came to this conclusion. *JLAC*, 1854–1855, Appendix MM, 250.

47 Wood, *Making Ontario*, 10.
48 Walsh, "Landscapes of Longing," 89.
49 Ibid., 305.
50 Kirkwood and Murphy, *The Underdeveloped Lands*, 154–8.
51 Finnigan, *Canadian Colonization Road*, 60–76; Wynn, "Notes on Society and Environment in Old Ontario," 55.
52 Walsh, "Landscapes of Longing," 91. See also Thompson, *Men and Meridians*, Volume I, 243.
53 Gentilcore, "Lines on the Land," 60; *JLAC*, 1861, Sessional Paper no. 15, Appendix 36. Annual Report of the Commissioner of Crown Lands. Mask-Connolly included a copy of this map in her book but did not source it, analyze it, or situate its importance within the colonizing project. *Kashubia to Canada: Crossing on the Agda*, 2.
54 *Government Map of Part of the Huron and Ottawa Territory Upper Canada Compiled under the direction of Thomas Devine F.R.G.S.C. &c. Head of Surveyors Branch U.C.* (1861).
55 Gourlay, *Statistical Account of Upper Canada*, 368.
56 Gentilcore and Donkin, *Land Surveys*, 4–6.
57 Kirkwood and Murphy, *The Underdeveloped Lands*, 42.
58 Parr Traill, *The Backwoods of Canada*, 46.
59 One could also argue that the Ottawa to Georgian Bay canal and rail projects to open the tract were also part of the imagined geography for the territory. These were advertised when the tract was opened for settlement. See AO, RG52, Series V-b, Box 1, vol. 1, and French, *Information*, 22.
60 AO, RG1, F-I-8, vol. 28, Russell to Hutton, 7 August 1857. Walsh, "Landscapes of Longing," 108.
61 *JLAC*, 1863, Sessional Paper No. 5, Appendix, no. 41.
62 Walsh, "Landscapes of Longing," 101.
63 *JLAC*, 1861, Appendix 1, 4–5. By this point, the estimated population that the land could hold was reduced to 1,500,000 from the 8,000,000 calculation made several years earlier.
64 AO, RG1, A-I-7, French to Vankoughnet, 15 February 1859. Casting down the statements of some (such as the Wakefieldian approach of selling land to obtain a "better class of settlers," advocated by Russell (AO, RG1, F-I-8, vol. 28, Russell to Hutton, May 1858) that the land was not fertile, French used inventory science and listed the crop yields as proof against the "mere assertions" of some opponents to the free grants scheme. Although the ones he was refuting are unnamed, local authors like Mask-Connolly and Finnigan have taken French's words out of context and do not write about his belief in the hierarchies of knowledge in

the Victorian inventory sciences. The former author, without sourcing the quote, claimed that "T.P. French did everything he could to disprove 'mere assertions of the utter worthlessness of the land along this road for farming purposes.'" Mask-Connolly, "Where They Settled," 5. Finnigan's misuse of this quote is in Finnigan, *Canadian Colonization Road*, 93.

65 This is also evident when French wrote to Vankoughnet hoping to have a settlement of Poles, after a few made their way up the road in 1859, and said that more could be persuaded to arrive. AO, RG1, A-I-7, French to Vankoughnet, 31 August 1859. Presumably, the rest of the potential Poles were the ones sojourning in Renfrew. French also defended his belief that the territory could be transformed into a productive space through effort in a letter to Vankoughnet. RG1, A-I-7, Box 14, French to Vankoughnet, 7 January 1860. What French, the former banker, calculated was the amount of money needed to place a "self-reliant man of family" along the colonization roads. This would lead to progress and development of the individual and the land. *Information*, 14, 15, 21–2.

66 AO, RG52, V-B, Box 2, File 8-6. Bridgeland to Commissioner of Crown Lands, 22 August 1861.

67 Printed in Smallfield, *Lands and Resources*, 12.

68 Cited to an undated *Report to the Ontario Agricultural Commission*. See Jones, *History of Agriculture in Ontario*, 114.

69 Gentilcore, *Land Surveys of Southern Ontario*, 4.

70 *JLAC*, 1854–1855, Appendix MM, 11.

71 Finnigan, *The Story of a Canadian Colonization Road*, 74.

72 *JLAC*, 1854–1855, Appendix MM, 11.

73 Finnigan, *Canadian Colonization Road*, 60–9.

74 Compare Devine's maps to Murray's *Topographic Plan of the River Bonnechere & S.W. Branch of the Madawaska with a sketch of the Headwaters of the Ottonabee* (1853) and this becomes evident.

75 AO, RG1, A-I-7, French to Commissioner of Crown Lands, McDougall, 11 December 1862; AO, RG1, B-IV, vol. 12, William Bell to Thomas Devine, 20 March 1863; AO, RG1, E-6, vol. 9. Also Walsh, "Landscapes of Longing," 107–8, 256.

76 By-Law #80, United Council of the Townships of Hagarty, Sherwood, Jones, Richards, and Burns (24 August 1885) declared their intention "to establish a road around the Prussian Mountains." According to Miller, the road over the hills was closed the following year. *Straight Lines in Curved Space*, 185. The "missing link" was cut and trimmed by volunteers and the Wilno Heritage Society. It opened in 2009 as a walking trail. The idea of using this route as a walking trail was promoted to the Ontario government by Marilyn Miller as early as 1977. See *Straight Lines*, 169.

The calculations were made using the "Barry's Bay 31 F/5" map produced in 1996 by the Centre for Mapping of Natural Resources Canada.

77 AO, RG1, A-I-7, French to Joseph Cauchon, 17 November 1856. AO, RG1, A-I-7, French to Cauchon, 4 December 1855.

78 AO, RG1, A-I-7, French to Commissioner of Crown Lands, L.V. Sicotte, 8 March 1858. AO, RG1, A-I-7, French to Sicotte, 5 June 1858; AO, RG1, A-I-7, #08328.

79 AO, RG1, A-I-7, Box 14, French to Vankoughnet, 7 January 1860.

80 AO, RG1, B-IV, vol. 82, Crown Land Papers, Surveyors Ledger, 1847–1871, 150; AO, RG1, A-I-7, French to Commissioner of Crown Lands, McDougall, 11 December 1862; AO, RG1, B-IV, vol. 82, Crown Land Papers, Surveyors Ledger, 1847–1871, 176.

81 Gentilcore and Donkin, *Land Surveys*, 21.

82 Donna E. Williams mentions that the productivity of the land was still debated in the high levels of government into the late 1860s. See *Hardscrabble*, 27.

83 Walsh, "Landscapes of Longing," 101, 106.

84 Lee, *Lumber Kings*, 18.

85 Lee, *Lumber Kings*, 8. Gaffield makes a similar claim in *Language*, 62. See also Kennedy, *The Upper Ottawa Valley*, 169–70, and MacKay, *The Lumberjacks*, 27.

86 In 1851, John Egan claimed that his timber operations needed "about six thousand barrels of Pork and ten thousand barrels of Flour. We employ about sixteen hundred horses and oxen during the winter, which consume about 60,000 bushels of oats ... and twelve hundred tons of hay. The oats at average cost of two shillings and three pence delivered; hay, four pounds per ton; we thus give employment to hundreds of farmers in the valley of the Ottawa." *JLAC*, 1853, Appendix MMMM, John Egan to A.J. Russell, 14 February 1851. The lumber firm owner, Allan Gilmour, echoed the sentiment that the industry needed settlers to supply certain goods. *JLAC*, 1854–1855, Appendix MM, 236.

87 Lee, *Lumber Kings*, 47.

88 *JLAC*, 1853, Appendix MMMM, John Egan to A.J. Russell, 14 February 1851. A.J. Russell's comments attest to Egan's encouragements. *JLAC*, 1853, Appendix MMMM, 1.

89 Rekowski tried to examine the connections between lumbering and forestry, saying that the government followed the "agrarian myth." He gleaned this from Marilyn Miller's monograph (20) but rambled in his definition of the myth, saying it was "the belief that only agriculture could be the basis of any permanent and stable economy in the area; that lum-

bering must need be only a temporary transitional industry; worse, that the south Ontario shield, all evidence to the contrary could sustain millions of people living off the land and every effort be made to induce would-be farmers, Canadian or European, to settle thereon." *The Saga of the Kashub People*, 39. Miller, an external author, was not clear about the "agrarian myth" herself. Instead she looked at the symbiotic relationship between the lumberer and farmer, analyzing it through the trope of natural resource exploitation rather than using nineteenth-century agricultural paradigms. *Straight Lines*, 8–15.

90 Lower, *Settlement and the Forest Frontier in Eastern Canada*, 30. Also in Little, *Nationalism*, 10; Harris, *The Reluctant Land*, 367.
91 Charles McNamara, *Life in the Lumber Camps of McLaughlin Brothers, Arnprior Ontario* (c. 1940), 92. AO, Charles McNamara Collection, C-120-1-0-1.1.
92 A statement from the Bureau of Agriculture (30 September 1854) attests to this since the Opeongo was opened "benefitting equally the farmer and the lumberer." *JLAC*, 1854–1855, Appendix MM, 11.
93 Lee, *Lumber Kings*, 18.
94 Lower, *Settlement*, 44–5. Jones, *History of Agriculture*, 112.
95 According to A.J. Russell, Egan was one of several outspoken persons who advocated for the creation of the Opeongo. *JLAC*, 1854–1855, Appendix MM, 255.
96 AO, RG1, A-I-7, Box 14, French to Vankoughnet, 7 January 1860. Support for the scheme is also found in: French, *Information*, 27; Jones, *History of Agriculture*, 112; Lower, *Settlement*, 45; Lee, *Lumber Kings*, 18.
97 Harris, *The Reluctant Land*, 367.
98 Lower, *Settlement*, 45. Other agro-forestry schemes were proceeding concurrently in areas such as Lac Megantic, St Maurice, and Lac Saint-Jean: Little, *Nationalism*, 31–3. They were also practised as early as the 1840s in Prescott County. Gaffield, *Language*, 62.
99 Lee, *Lumber Kings*, 228. Also reflected in Little, *Nationalism*, 31.
100 Gaffield, *Language*, 80.
101 Elliott, *The City Beyond*, 48. John Robertson, "Agricultural Report on the County of Carleton," 492–4; Smallfield, *Lands and Resources of Renfrew County*, 5.
102 *The Resources of the Ottawa District* (Ottawa: The Times, 1872), 6–7.
103 Lee, *Lumber Kings*, 226; also reflected in Smallfield, *Lands and Resources*, 6, and Harris, *The Reluctant Land*, 336.
104 Robertson, "Agricultural Report on the County of Carleton," 492–4. Jones, *History of Agriculture*, 112.

105 Elliott, *The City Beyond*, 48.
106 Little, *Nationalism*, 11, 29. The employment statistic is from Lee, *Lumber Kings*, 162.
107 Elliott, *The City Beyond*, 48.
108 Addison, *Early Days in Algonquin Park*, 13.
109 Seguin, *La Conquête du sol au XIXe siècle*, 50–64.
110 To borrow the phrase used by Bruce S. Elliott in a July 2010 conversation.
111 Harris, *The Reluctant Land*, 336.
112 Mask-Connolly, *Brudenell Revisited*, 20–33; Mask-Connolly, *Kashubia to Canada: Crossing on the Agda*, 153, 204–5; Mask-Connolly, *Marriage Matters*, 116.
113 AO, RG1, A-I-7, Box 14, French to Vankoughnet, 7 January 1860.
114 See *Renfrew Mercury*, 4 August 1871. Mask-Connolly, *Kashubia to Canada: The Shulist Story*, 3; and also Shalla, "Memoirs," 3, mentions the women who worked out of their homes. For Portage County, see Koliński, "The Origin and Early Development," 24.
115 Lee-Whiting, "Who Named It Wilno?" *BBTW*, 13 November 1985, 5. Etmanski's example is from Shalla, "Memoirs," 11. Lower defines "jobbers" as "settlers who took a contract from the company to work a piece of the limits not being worked from the main camp." *The North American Assault on the Canadian Forest*, 35.
116 The Oral History Project of the Barry's Bay Public Library, "Faith and Liberty: Oral History with Frank J. Ritza," 16. "Lumbermen Recall the Good Ol' Days," *BBTW*, 15 July 1971.
117 Shalla, "Memoirs," 46.
118 "Land is the Land: John Mintha," 13; "A Local Pastor: Oral History with Rev. Msgr. J.A. Pick," 12; "Lots of Work: An Oral History with Joe Luckasavitch," 2; *BBTW*, 12 January 1977; *BBTW*, 26 January 1977. For general wages see Lee, *Lumber Kings*, 168.
119 Little, *Nationalism*, 33.
120 *Renfrew Mercury*, 25 October 1872.
121 AO, RG1, C-IV, Township Papers; *Renfrew Mercury*, 25 October 1872. The timber rights of the McLaughlin Lumber Company in the nineteenth century covered the majority of the townships of Radcliffe and Brudenell as well as portions of Sherwood and Hagarty Townships: AO, C-277-1-348-0-2, *Plan Shewing the Position of Byers' Creek in the Limits of D. McLaughlin Esq., North of the Madawaska River* (1865?). Also see Lee, *Lumber Kings*, 38, 40.
122 AO, RG1-A, Box 2, "Opeongo Road 1860-1866," Paylist No. 4, Opeongo Road.

123 Smallfield, *Lands and Resources*, 6; Miller, *Straight Lines*, 46–7. Rekowski, *The Saga of the Kashub People*, 53.
124 Gaffield, *Language*, 66–7.
125 Jones, *History of Agriculture*, 113.
126 Miller, *Straight Lines*, 45–6. This localized industry still employed locals, which helps to explain Rekowski's argument that the industry in Wilno and Barry's Bay did not decline until the 1930s and 1940s.
127 Lee, *Forest Products in the Ottawa Valley*, 88, 120.
128 Jones, *History of Agriculture*, 297.
129 MacKay, *Over the Hills to Georgian Bay*, 12.
130 Beauprie, *Destination Algonquin Park*, 27.
131 "U.S. Tariff May Fell Canadian Jobs," *Ottawa Citizen*, 17 October 1986, 4; Kathryn May, "Valley Lumber Mills Seek Tax Break," *Ottawa Citizen*, 10 January 1987, 7; Joshua C. Blank, "Death of a Salesman But Not a Forest: J.R. Booth," *This Week in History: Archives*; Bert Hill, "Big Drop in Lumber Prices Has Effects: Joy and Sorrow; Consumers Get Savings While Profit Margins Tumble for Firms," *Ottawa Citizen*, 24 June 1995, 1. Recently, Murray Brothers Lumber Company Ltd. has formed connections with China in an effort to produce board feet and stay in business.
132 Rekowski, *The Saga of the Kashub People*, 40. He plagiarized these and other statements – word for word – from Miller, *Straight Lines*, 26.
133 Prince, *The Kovalskie (Kowalski) Family*, 15.
134 Walsh, "Landscapes of Longing," 305.
135 This is Little's argument for the St Francis district; however, it can be applied to the Ottawa-Huron Tract too. *Nationalism*, xiv.
136 Lehr, *Community and Frontier*, 6, 11–12.
137 Basu, *Highland Homecomings*, 188.
138 If they even knew how to (or could) return sufficient organic material back to the sandy soil.
139 Rekowski, *The Saga of the Kashub People*, 55.
140 Little, *Nationalism*, xi–xii; Martynowych, *Ukrainians in Canada*, 72; also Lehr, "Governmental Coercion in the Settlement of Ukrainian Immigrants in Western Canada," 180, 184, 192. Thanks are extended to Dr Rhonda Hinther for passing along this information about the Ukrainian community.
141 Joan Finnigan remarked that "even the pig-headed Irish failed along the Opeongo." See Miller, *Straight Lines*, 49. These groups in the Ottawa-Huron Tract were not alone. Gaffield remarked that in Prescott County, "the chronology of immigration, the accessibility of land, and the climatic conditions made the different perceptions of soil particularly important" for settlement. *Language*, 70.

142 Jane Errington used these in reference to British Loyalist settlers. See *The Lion, the Eagle and Upper Canada*, 5; MacGregor, *A Life in the Bush*, 81.

CHAPTER SIX

1 The closest examination was written by Rekowski who gave a rambling account of the history of the Pomeranian region. The chapter immediately following listed the Kashubs as resident without adequately explaining their origins and development as a group. Later on, buried near the end of the book, Rekowski refers, in two sentences, to the possible origins of "Kaszuba" as originating in a label or in a type of clothing worn. *The Saga of the Kashub People*, 1–6, 173.
2 Mask-Connolly, "Translators Thanked & Translators Needed," NWHS 9, no. 1 (Spring/Summer 2010), 20–1.
3 Borzyszkowski, *The Kashubs, Pomerania and Gdańsk*. The newest publication, in English, which looks at the identity of the Kashubs, does not delve into the past: Obracht-Prodzyński, *The Kashubs Today*. Unfortunately, the classic monograph that examines the origins of the Kaszubs has been out of print for decades and is considered a rare book: Lorentz, Fischer, and Lehr-Spławiński, *The Cassubian Civilization*.
4 Hroch, "National Self-Determination," 283. See also Brock, *Folk Cultures and Little Peoples*, 2.
5 McKay, *The Quest of the Folk*, 10; Brock, *Folk Cultures*, 2.
6 McKay, *The Quest of the Folk*, 10, 12.
7 Hroch, "National Self-Determination," 284; Hobsbawm, "Mass-Producing Traditions," 263.
8 Labuda, "The Key Problems," 6.
9 V. Polyakov, "The Valley of the Vistula," 37; Alexander Majkowski, *Historia Kaszubów*, 1; Labuda, "The Key Problems," 12.
10 Polyakov, "The Valley of the Vistula," 37.
11 Macdonald, "The Kashubs on the Baltic," 268. See also Lorentz, Fischer, and Lehr-Spławiński, *The Cassubian Civilization*, 4.
12 Ibid.; and Polyakov, "Vistula," 38. Labuda claimed that Adam was active around the year 1075 AD. "The Key Problems," 12.
13 Polyakov, "Vistula," 50; Macdonald, "The Kashubs on the Baltic," 269.
14 Lorentz, "An Outline of Cassubian Civilization," 4; Labuda, "The Key Problems," 5.
15 *Annales Colbazienses* (1531), MGH SS XIX, 719; Labuda, "The Key Problems," 5.

16 Fischer, "Cassubian and Polish Ethnography: A Comparative Study," in Lorentz, Fischer, and Lehr-Spławiński, *The Cassubian Civilization*, 187–8.
17 Lorentz and Gulgowski, "Der Name Kaschubei," 150–2.
18 Tetzner, *Die Slowinzen und Lebakaschuben*, 1.
19 Borzyszkowski, *The Kashubs*, 12–19.
20 Kashubian Pomeranian Association, *The Unknown Kashubia*, 2. However, Friedrich Lorentz argues that even though the Church hierarchy in Rome used the term "Cassubia," they had only heard of it as a region, not necessarily a people. See Lorentz, "Welches Rechthaben die Kaschuben Westpreussens auf diesen Namen?" in *Mitteilungen des Vereinsfürkaschubiche Volkskunde*, 185–9.
21 Kashubian Pomeranian Association, *The Unknown Kashubia*, 2–3.
22 Labuda, "The Key Problems," 5.
23 Buske, *Pommern*, 99.
24 Ibid., 103.
25 Blaeu, *Theatrum Orbis Terrarum*; Janssonius, *Accurata Prussiae descriptio*; Allard, *Regni Poloniae*; Gustavus, *Auctior et Correctior*; Steutter, *Ductatus Pomeraniae cum magna Maris Balthici*.
26 Lorentz, "An Outline of Cassubian Civilization," 4.
27 Buske, *Pommern*, 20–1.
28 Macdonald, "The Kashubs on the Baltic," 271.
29 Labuda, "The Key Problems," 15; Lorentz, "An Outline of Cassubian Civilization," 10.
30 Topolińska, *A Historical Phonology*, 17; Lorentz, "An Outline of Cassubian Civilization," 7.
31 Lorentz, "An Outline of Cassubian Civilization," 7–8; Labuda, "The Key Problems," 18–19; Polyakoff, *Eagles Black and White*, 79.
32 Labuda, "The Key Problems," 9, 18–19. In the present day, the debate over whether the Kashubian vernacular developed separately from Polish or as a vernacular offshoot is still unsettled. See Perkowski, *A Kashubian Idiolect in the United States*, 101; Stone, "The Language of Cassubian Literature and the Question of a Literary Standard," 521; Topolińska, *A Historical Phonology*, 19; Labuda, "The Key Problems," 15; Obracht-Prondzyński, *Kaszubidzisiaj*, 16–18; Kulas, *Kashub-English-Kashub: Mini Dictionary-Słowôrzk*, vii–x.
33 Brock, *Folk Cultures*, 73.
34 Brock, "Florjan Cenôva and the Kashub Question," 266, 278.
35 Ibid., 267; Also, Brock, *Folk Cultures*, 74. The reference to the "Slav Q" parallels Biblical scholars and their search for the mystical source – Q – in their analysis of the Synoptic Gospels. Brock wrote that he tried to look

for connections between the Kashubian language and "other Slav tongues like Russian ... Lower Lusatian or Czech." See Brock, "Florjan Cenôva," 274.
36 Borzyszkowski, *The Kashubs*, 48.
37 Italics in original. Labuda, "The Key Problems," 22–4.
38 Borzyszkowski, *The Kashubs*, 48–9.
39 Ibid. Also, Fr Gustaw Pobłocki, who knew Cenôva, wrote this of him after his death: "In daily life an ardent Pole, loving his nationality, but in his writings an enemy of the Poles, and especially of the *szlachta*; by baptism and conviction a believing Catholic (though a loose liver and quite indifferent in regard to fulfilling his religious duties), yet – as an author – a supporter of [Russian] Orthodoxy, sneering at Catholic faith, the Pope and the clergy." See Brock, "Florjan Cenôva," 285.
40 Ibid., 266; Brock, *Folk Cultures*, 71.
41 Brock, "Florjan Cenôva," 277–8. Brock, *Folk Cultures*, 79. He even experimented with the spelling of his name but settled on "Cenôva."
42 Lorentz, "An Outline of Cassubian Civilization," 16.
43 Brock, "Florjan Cenôva," 280; Brock, *Folk Cultures*, 81.
44 These movements of people parallel movements in other areas of Poland in the same era. See Praszałowicz, "Jewish, Polish and German Migration," 135–55; Praszałowicz, "Local Community and Nineteenth Century Migrations," 175–88. Finding employment for many Polish people prompted emigration: see Walaszek, "Migracje I Ziemie Polskie," 43–65. The movement of people into the coal producing area in the Ruhr valley was a choice for many Polish people from West Prussia who wished to obtain gainful employment in 1870s: see Kulczycki, "The Herne 'Polish Revolt' of 1899," 149–50. Several groups embarked on transatlantic emigration to areas in the Commonwealth: see Zubrzycki, "Polish Emigration to British Commonwealth Countries," 650–3. Some groups were motivated by religious reasons and were guided by a religious leader: see Starczewska, "The Historical Geography," 11–42.
45 Ramułt, *Słownik języka pomorskiego*; Ramułt, *Statystyka ludności kaszubskiej*.
46 Brock, "Florjan Cenôva," 259. Brock, *Folk Cultures*, 93. Ramułt's figures for America were gleaned from a letter of Derdowski's, who was prone to exaggeration: Perkowski, "The Kashubs – Origins and Emigration to the U.S.," 4.
47 Ramułt, *Słownik języka pomorskiego, czyli kaszubskiego*, XL, XLI.
48 Cenôva echoed this in his article "*Skôrb*." He wrote that Kashubian "is today almost the same as it was a thousand and more years ago, because educated parrots did not distort it. Instead, it is the simple folk who have preserved it." Brock, "Florjan Cenôva," 279.

49 Kashubian Pomeranian Association, *The Unknown Kashubia*, 9.
50 Parallel movements in other areas prove this trend as well. The journal *Folklore* had its start in England in the 1880s.
51 Rekowski, *The Saga of the Kashub People*, 20.
52 Dorson, "The State of Folklorists," 71.
53 Manouelian, "Invented Traditions," 391. Karłowicz's quote is on the same page as well.
54 Hobsbawm argues that, in many cases across Europe, the state was the one that tried to form these formal and informal social inventions of tradition to ensure social cohesion. "Mass Producing Traditions," 263–4.
55 Bhabha, *The Location of Culture*, 145.
56 Błachkowski, *Hafty Polskie Szycie*, 75.
57 Manouelian, "Invented Traditions," 393.
58 Lorentz, "An Outline of Cassubian Civilization," 30, 33–4.
59 Kaszubski Park Etnograficzny, "Teodora and Izydor Gulgowski."
60 Lorentz, "An Outline of Cassubian Civilization," 34. See also Socha-Borzestowski, "A Note on the Folk-Art of Cassubia," 195, 196.
61 Lorentz, "An Outline of Cassubian Civilization," 33; Błachowski, *Hafty Polski Szycie*, 88.
62 Kashubian Pomeranian Association, *The Unknown Kashubia*, 28.
63 Borzszykowski used it but did not cite it: *The Kashubs*, 84.
64 Ibid., 85–6.
65 Benet, *Song, Dance and Customs of Peasant Poland*, 32.
66 Borzyszkowski, *The Kashubs*, 87–8.
67 MacMillan, *Paris 1919*, 496.
68 Brock, *Folk Cultures*, 67.
69 MacMillan, *Paris 1919*, 216.
70 Brock, *Folk Cultures*, 67.
71 Kashubian Pomeranian Association, *The Unknown Kashubia*, 9; Brock, *Folk Cultures*, 66; Martel, *The Eastern Frontiers of Germany*, 111.
72 Martel, *The Eastern Frontiers*, 111.
73 Ibid., 124, 145. See also Brock, *Folk Cultures*, 67.
74 Borzyszkowski, *The Kashubs*, 49.
75 The Prussian census of 1910 created a new category where one could identify oneself as a Kashub. Brock, "Florjan Cenôva," 259.
76 Polyakov, "The Valley of the Vistula," 56; also in MacMillan, *Paris 1919*, 216–17. It is unclear whether there was enough support for a "Kashub" state; however, allying with the Poles was preferable for survival.
77 Labuda, "The Key Problems," 29.
78 Tymieniecki, *History of Polish Pomerania*.

79 For example, Lorentz, *Gramatyka pomorska*; *Tesky pomorskie (kaszubski)*; *Geschichte der Kaschuben*.
80 Gogolewski, "Dialectology in Poland, 1873–1997," 129.
81 Fischer, *Lud Polski: Podręcznik etnografji Polski*; *Zarys etnograifczny wojewodztwa pomorskiego*; *Zwiądek etnograficzny Pomorza z Polska: Przewic propagandize korytarzowej*.
82 Borzyszkowski, *The Kashubs*, 84, 99, 110, 115–17.
83 Ibid., 27–8, 135.
84 Kashubian Pomeranian Association, *The Unknown Kashubia*, 22.
85 Borzyszkowski, *The Kashubs*, 30.
86 Kashubian Pomeranian Association, *The Unknown Kashubia*, 35.
87 Ibid., 22–4.
88 Ibid., 21.
89 Hugh Trevor-Roper used this for the Scottish Highland tradition but it fits with the Kashubian traditions too: "The Invention of Tradition: The Highland Tradition of Scotland," in *The Invention of Tradition*, Hobsbawm and Ranger, eds, 14.
90 See "Introduction: Inventing Traditions," 2–3.
91 Mask-Connolly, "Wilno Heritage Society Recipients of Two Prestigious Awards from Poland in 2009," *NWHS* 8, no. 2 (Fall/Winter 2009), 15.
92 Brock, "Florjan Cenôva," 267.
93 Kashubian Pomeranian Association, *The Unknown Kashubia*, 13–14.
94 Buske, *Pommern*, 19.
95 Borzyszkowski, *The Kashubs*, 19.
96 Kashubian Pomeranian Association, *The Unknown Kashubia*, 14.
97 Koehne, *Zeitschrift für Munz-, Siegel-, und Wappenkunde*, 240.
98 The lifespan of Bogusław X was from 1454–1523 but his reign was from 1474–1523 according to Buske, *Pommern*, 99. Georg I's rule was from 1523–1531. The flag colours are derived from the coat of arms. Again, the record promoted by the KPA is silent on the recency of its adoption.
99 Koehne, *Zeitschrift für Munz-, Siegel- und Wappenkunde*, 240–2.
100 Grote, *Münzenstudien*, 582–3.
101 Koehne, *Zeitschrift für Munz-, Siegel-, und Wappenkunde*, 240–2; Grote, *Münzenstudien*, 582–3.
102 See Buske, *Pommern*, 104. "Hinter Pommern" and "Duchy Wolgast" were the two large territorial entities in 1696.
103 Kashubian Pomeranian Association, *The Unknown Kashubia*, 30.
104 Muzeum Kaszubskiego w Kartuzach, "Kaszëbë" (1999).
105 Błachowski, *Hafty Polski Szycie*, 86–8. Socha-Borzestowski neatly sidesteps this issue in her article by stating that "the expert would probably

notice the occasional Baroque or Rococo theme borrowed by the folk-artist." See "A Note on the Folk-Art of Cassubia," 195.
106 Ibid. See also Pain, *The Heritage of Upper Canadian Furniture*, 199, 307, 314, 483, 514–17; Kostelníček, *Slovenská ornamentika*, Plate III; and Fleming and Rowan, *Folk Furniture*, 112.
107 Błachowski, *Hafty Polski Szycie*, 88.
108 Ibid., 88–9. Originally from "W sprawie przemysłu ludowego na Kaszubach," *Gryf*, no. 4, 26.
109 Muzeum Kaszubskiego w Kartuzach, "Kaszëbë" (1999).
110 Błachowski, *Hafty Polski Szycie*, 89
111 Kashubian Pomeranian Association, *The Unknown Kashubia*, 31.
112 Lorentz, Fischer, and Lehr-Spławiński, *The Cassubian Civilization*, 36.
113 Stelmachowska, *Atlas Polskich Strojów Ludowych*, 6, 7. Similarities are also reflected in Piskowz-Branekova, *Polska Stroke ludowe*, 9.
114 Stelmachowska, *Atlas Polskich Strojów Ludowych*, 67.
115 Kashubian Pomeranian Association, *The Unknown Kashubia*, 1–2.
116 Obracht-Prondzyński, *Kaszubidzisiaj: Kultura-język-tożsamość*, 9.
117 Gunn, *History and Cultural Theory*, 149; see also Perin, "Writing About Ethnicity," 202.
118 Salminen, "UNESCO Red Book," and Toops, "Marlena Porębska," 161.
119 Perin, "Writing About Ethnicity," 202, and others such as Walsh, "Ethnicity, Family and Community," 143; and Gabaccia, "Do We Still Need Immigration History?," 54.
120 Topolińska, "A Historical Phonology of the Kashubian Dialects of Polish," 17.
121 Blank, "From Serfdom to Citizenship," 123.
122 Walser Smith, "Prussia at the Margins," 77. Also see table 2.4 in chapter 2.
123 Sollars, *The Invention of Ethnicity*, xii.

CHAPTER SEVEN

1 Rekowski, *The Saga of the Kashub People*, viii. The reference to "low Polish" is also reiterated by Mask-Connolly in Debbi Christinck, "Wilno's Rich Heritage is Brought Vividly to Life by Researcher," *EL*, 25 February 1999, A12. John Glofcheskie comments on language usage, saying that "standard literary Polish [is the language] which the Kashub recognizes as his Language for writing and reading, for singing hymns, and for all 'official' occasions. His dialect is reserved for the informal daily dealings of life, for his oral literature and for the *frantówka*, that category of short and happy song, so expressive of his good humor." *Folk Music of Canada's Oldest Polish Community*, 3.

2 Jozef Kisielewski, *Ziemia Gromadzi Prochy* (Poznań, 1939). It is now considered a rare book.
3 Rekowski, *The Saga of the Kashub People*, ix–xii.
4 Rekowski, "Are Kashubs Poles?" *BBTW*, 13 August 1986, 6, 20; Rekowski, *The Saga of the Kashub People*, 64–5.
5 Barecki, *Kaszëbë*; Kulas, *Kashub, English, Kashub, Kaszubsczi, Anielsczi, Kaszubsczi Mini Dictionary, Słowôrzk*, viii.
6 Barecki, *Kaszëbë*.
7 Letter from Mask-Connolly to Jozef Borzyszkowski, 5 June 2002. Published in Borzyskowski, *O Kaszubach w Kanadzie*, 535.
8 Schulist, "A Kashubian Treasure on the Top of Our Tongue," 7; and The Kashubian Voice (David Shulist's *nom de plume*) "Jedno Slowo," *BBTW*, 7 July 2009, 13.
9 "Welcome," *Kashub/Polish Heritage Stories of Renfrew County: 1. Wilno and Area* (Wilno Heritage Society, 2000), unnumbered introductory page.
10 Mask-Connolly, "A Summary of Jozef Borzyszowski's Visit to the First Polish Settlement Area of Ontario," *Kashubian Association of North America Newsletter* (*KANA*) (Winter 2001), 6; also "Meetings in Poland – 2009," *NWHS* 8, no. 2 (Fall/Winter 2009), 6–8.
11 Schulist, "A Kashubian Treasure on the Top of Our Tongue," 6–7.
12 See http://www.wilno.org/Events/2005/2005.html, accessed 17 July 2013.
13 WHS, "Culture/Tradition," www.wilno.org/culture/language.html, accessed 18 March 2015. WHS, "Canadian/Kashub Music," www.wilno.org/culture/music.html, accessed 18 March 2015.
14 WHS, "Dance and the Kashub Culture," www.wilno.org/culture/dance.html, accessed 5 August 2011. WHS, "Embroidery," www.wilno.org/culture/embroidery.html, accessed 18 March 2015.
15 Lynne Visutskie, "Wilno Polish Heritage Park" in *Kashub/Polish Heritage Stories of Renfrew County*, 56–7; Mask-Connolly, "Five New Heritage Stones," *KANA* (Summer 2002), 10–11; Mask Connolly, "Four New Family Homestead Stones & New Placement of Stones in 2009," *NWHS* 8, no. 2 (Fall/Winter 2009), 20–1.
16 Higgins, "Polish Day in Wilno," in *Kashub/Polish Heritage*, 42–5.
17 Mask-Connolly, "Wilno's Annual Polish Day Celebration a Huge Success," *KANA* (Summer 2002), 12–13; David Shulist, "Message from the President," *NWHS* 7, no. 1 (Spring/Summer 2008), 2.
18 WHS, "The Polish Kashub Festival," www.wilno.org/culture/festival.html, accessed 5 August 2010.
19 *NWHS* 7, no. 1 (Spring/Summer 2008), 11. The unnumbered back page of the 2009 program for the Opeongo Heritage Cup reflects this as well. Shulist is listed as the founder, commissioner, and promoter.

20 *NWHS* 8, no. 1 (Spring/Summer 2009), 5. In Poland, "Radio Kaszëbë" was started in 2004. It is maintained by the Puck Regional Association: Obracht-Prondsyński, *Kaszubidzisiaj*, 30. See also Debbi Christinck, "Kashubs Celebrate 150 Years in Canada in Annual Celebration in Wilno," *EL*, 7 May 2008, 10.

21 *The Combermere Free Press* (Summer 2008), 4.

22 "Jedno Slowo," *BBTW*, 7 July 2009, 13.

23 "Governor General Announces 75 Caring Canadian Awards"; also Mask-Connolly, "Wilno Heritage Society Recipients of Two Prestigious Awards from Poland in 2009," *NWHS* 8, no. 2 (Fall/Winter 2009), 14–15.

24 "Prime Minister Harper Celebrates Historic Milestone of the Polish Community in Canada," www.wilno.org/events150/Parliament/parliament.html, accessed 5 August 2010. A similar switch happened after the WHS received the "Diploma of the Minister of Foreign Affairs for Outstanding Services for the Promotion of Poland." Commenting on the award, the Polish ambassador to Canada, Piotr Ogrodzinski, was quoted as saying they had received the award for "preserving and promoting the heritage of Polish Kashubs in Canada," but Shulist dumped the Polish label, again, as *BBTW* wrote that Shulist "is quick to point out, in a way the award is intended to honour anyone from the Kashub culture who has helped to keep the traditions alive over generations." See "Wilno Heritage Society Honoured at Ceremony," *BBTW*, 4 November 2009, 3.

25 Blank, "Pitching, Pies and Piety."

26 Shulist, "Why Chicken?" *BBTW*, 8 September 2009, 6.

27 Mask-Connolly, "Wilno Heritage Society Recipients of Two Prestigious Awards from Poland in 2009," 15. Shulist's connections to the EU are not clear in the profile article: Ryan Paulsen, "David Shulist sets sights on Mayoral seat," *BBTW*, 19 May 2010, www.barrysbaythisweek.com/ArticleDisplay.aspx?e=2583860, accessed 5 August 2010.

28 As cited on www.kashub.com – a website without many formal titles. The only contact information is an email address. The user of this email address can be traced to David Shulist, according to the email address provided to Benita Baker of *The Ottawa Citizen* in a 13 November 2010 promotional story (H5).

29 Gillis, "Memory and Identity," 3.

30 Perin, "Writing About Ethnicity," 204; Gunn, *History and Cultural Theory*, 132; Cooley, *Making Music in the Polish Tatras*, 11; McAndrew, "School Spaces and the Construction of Ethnic Relations," 15; Loewen, "The Fragmented Refashioning of American Urban Immigration History," 60–3; Walsh, "Ethnicity, Family, and Community," 143; Conzen, "Immigrants, Immigrant Neighbourhoods, and Ethnic Identity," 604.

31 Walsh, "Ethnicity, Family, and Community," 145; Gabaccia, "Do We Still Need Immigration History?," 53.
32 This problem is not specific to the Kashub group. James Bergquist, in a review of Brenda Lee-Whiting's study of the material culture of German settlers in the Ottawa Valley, questions what specifically categorizes the materials as "German." See "Harvest of Stones: The German Settlement in Renfrew County by Brenda Lee-Whiting," 444.
33 Schulist, "A Kashubian Treasure on the Top of Our Tongue," 6.
34 *NWHS* 8, no. 1 (Spring/Summer 2009), 8.
35 Ickiewicz, "Kaszubi w Kraju Klonowego Liścia," 8.
36 "Jedno Slowo," *BBTW*, 7 July 2009, 13.
37 Hudder, "Kashub vs. Polish," 10.
38 Mask-Connolly, "Salute to One of Our Polish Seniors: Helen Dombroskie nee Lorbetskie," *If you don't know, you Wilno! News from the Wilno Heritage Society celebrating Canada's Polish Kashub Cultural Heritage* (*IYDK*) 5, no. 2 (Fall/Winter 2006), 3; Mask-Connolly, "The Olympics 2010 & Our Pride in Being Canadian," *NWHS* 9, no. 1 (Spring/Summer 2010), 3, 27; Mask-Connolly, "Opeongo Heritage Trail Grand Opening: Saturday, October 10, 2009," *NWHS* 8, no. 2 (Fall/Winter 2009), 11–13; Mask-Connolly, "Foreword," in Kulas, *Kashub, English, Kashub, Kaszubsczi, Anielsczi, Kaszubsczi Mini Dictionary, Słowôrzk*, vi.
39 Geertz, *The Interpretation of Cultures*, 259–60.
40 Anderson and Frideres, *Ethnicity in Canada*, 14; Perin, "Writing About Ethnicity," 204.
41 A postmodernist, at this point, would rightly argue that even though someone might invoke a certain ethnicity, it is impossible for us to accurately pinpoint which of the characteristics they identify with. They would argue that it is impossible to fully ascribe to an ethnicity, since it changes and evolves. My main point here is to highlight the usage of the word *generally*, since very few who define themselves ethnically are true postmodernists.
42 Hansen, *The Problem of the Third Generation Immigrant*, 9–10; Gans, "Symbolic Ethnicity"; Anderson, *Imagined Communities: Reflections on the Origin and Spread of Nationalism*, 6.
43 Cooley, *Making Music*, 11, 61.
44 Iacovetta, "Manly Militants," 218.
45 Vasta, "Immigrants and the Paper Market," 200.
46 These names, of course, cannot be divulged, as part of my ethics approval through Carleton University stipulated that I had to have a signed consent form to include testimony from an oral interview.

47 Interview with Peter T. Glofcheskie (3 July 2010).
48 Interview with Clifford G. Blank (3 July 2010).
49 Kulas, *Kashub, English*, viii.
50 Interview with Tony Bleskie (3 August 2010).
51 Mask-Connolly, *Polish Pioneer Families in the Parish of Brudenell to the Year 1870*, 3.
52 Mask-Connolly, *Marriage Matters*, 5.
53 Anderson, *Imagined Communities*, 145.
54 Barecki, *Kaszëbë*.
55 Mask-Connolly, *Kashubia to Canada: Crossing on the Agda*, 7, 15.
56 Ed Chippior, "Concluding ..." in *English-Polish-Kashub Dictionary*, ed. Stanisław Frymark, back cover.
57 Bòbrowsczi and Kwiatkòwskô, *Kaszëbsczë ABECADŁO*; Kulas, *Kashub, English*, vii–ix, 63. Initially, David Shulist and the WHS encouraged Stan Frymark of Leśno, Poland, to produce a trilingual dictionary. Frymark produced one in 2008 (*English-Polish-Kashub Dictionary*), but once a local resident, Kulas, produced one (*Kashub, English, Kashub, Kaszubsczi, Anielsczi, Kaszubsczi Mini Dictionary, Słowôrzk*), Shulist and the WHS no longer promoted Frymark's.
58 Professor Edward Breza stresses that the Bible, the "Our Father," and Homer's work have been translated into Kashubian. In his mind, it thus resembles a language more than a dialect: Barecki, *Kaszëbë*. Benedict Anderson's research tells us that "print-capitalism gave a new fixity to language, which in the long run helped to build that image of antiquity so central to the subjective idea of the nation." In light of Breza's comments, these comments seem pertinent. Anderson, *Imagined Communities*, 44.
59 Canada, Minister of Supply and Services, *The Cultural Contribution of Other Ethnic Groups*, 13.
60 Walsh, "Ethnicity, Family and Community," 131.
61 "Meetings in Poland," *NWHS* 8, no. 2 (Fall/Winter 2009), 7.
62 Mask-Connolly, "Translators Thanked & Translators Needed," *NWHS* 9, no. 1 (Spring/Summer 2010), 20.
63 Kulas, *Kashub, English*, ix.
64 Disseminated from "Meetings in Poland," *NWHS* 8, no. 2 (Fall/Winter 2009), 7.
65 David Shulist recounted the deep connections with the church in his article "Canadian/Kashub Christmas of Days Gone By," *KANA* (Winter 2000), 6. In closing, he stated: "The language of choice was Kashub. The way of life was God." However, when reflecting on childhood Christmas celebrations, he does not show how the label "Kashub" existed in the vo-

cabulary of local residents. He himself noted the evolution of the way locals viewed their speech: Polish, "low-Polish," and Kashubian (after Rekowski's work was printed): Schulist, "A Kashubian Treasure on the Tip of Our Tongue," 7.

66 Blank, "Pitching, Pies and Piety."
67 Anderson and Frideres, *Ethnicity in Canada*, 41; Allport, *The Nature of Prejudice*, 415.
68 Pakulski, "Polish Migrants in Hobart," 90.
69 Mask-Connolly, "Fr. Archie Afelskie (1937–2009) Had Great Reverence for his Polish-Kashub Forefathers," NWHS 8, no. 2 (Fall/Winter 2009), 16; Barecki, *Kaszëbë*; Mask-Connolly, "Four New Family Stones & New Placement of Stones in 2009," NWHS 8, no. 2 (Fall/Winter 2009), 20. He also said the opening prayer for the 2010 version of "Kashub Day." See also "Meetings in Poland," NWHS 8, no. 2 (Fall/Winter 2009), 8.
70 Mask-Connolly, "Our 3 Polish Parishes – But For How Much Longer?" IYDK 3, no. 1 (Spring/Summer 2004), 13.
71 Schulist, "A Kashubian Treasure," 6. Capitals in original.
72 Interview with Clifford G. Blank (September 2009).
73 See EL, "Chicken Supper at Barry's Bay," 26 September 1924; vol. 34, no. 32, 26 June 1936; "People of Wilno Erecting Splendid New Church," vol. 34, no. 33, 3 July 1936; vol. 36, no. 48, 7 October 1938; vol. 47, no. 36, 24 September 1948; vol. 47, no. 37, 30 September 1948; vol. 48, no. 41, 11 November 1949; vol. 49, no. 30, 28 September 1950; vol. 50, no. 24, 17 August 1951; and vol. 50, no. 28, 28 September 1951.
74 Lorentz, "An Outline of Cassubian Civilization," 67.
75 Shulist, "Canadian/Kashub Christmas of Days Gone By," KANA (Winter 2000), 6. Anna Porter's words come to mind at this point: "History often becomes a political tool to be wielded when needed, distorted when convenient and hidden when harmful to one's cause." See *The Ghosts of Europe*, 53.
76 Frye, *The Bush Garden*, xxiii.
77 Barecki, *Kaszëbë*; Kulas, *Kashub, English*, viii; Schulist, "A Kashubian Treasure," 7.
78 WHS, "Embroidery," www.wilno.org/culture/embroidery.html, accessed 17 July 2013.
79 Instead of using the term "authentic" as something to be discovered, I am, instead, borrowing one of Cooley's implications: that it is a concept that is "constructed in a process of 'authentication.'" See *Making Music*, 137.
80 Ryan Paulsen, "Zen and the Art of Kashubian Embroidery," BBTW, 10 March 2010.

81 Kirshenblatt-Gimblett, "Theorizing Heritage," 369; Hutton, *History as an Art of Memory*, 6; Cooley, *Making Music*, 137; Barford, *The Early Slavs*, 31.
82 Gans, "Symbolic Ethnicity," 3.
83 Gillis, "Memory and Identity," 4; see also Gerber, "Theories and Lives," 53.
84 My definition of "cultural hearth" is influenced by R.J. Johnston, Derek Gregory, and David M. Smith. They write that it is "the centre or place of origin of a cultural group associated with a particular cultural landscape ... Hearths are the 'breeding grounds' of culture groups from which systems associated with them may later diffuse." *The Dictionary of Human Geography*, 2nd ed., 88. Regarding distanciation, see Gerber, "Theories and Lives," 50.
85 Zurakowski, *The Proud Inheritance*, 130; *Kaszuby Canada, Part One*, dir. Henryk Bartul.
86 It can be argued that for the Polish-Kashubs, the emergence from the pioneer phase was controlled also by their physical isolation in the Canadian Shield. Katz and Lehr's comments in this area provide a fascinating point for comparison: "As rural society emerged from the pioneer phase, only distance and physical isolation could ameliorate the onslaught of a homogenous culture." See "Ethnicity, Institutions, and Landscape," 186.
87 Basu, *Highland Homecomings*, 198–9.
88 Gillis, "Memory and Identity," 17; Gans, "Symbolic Ethnicity," 17. This section is also influenced by the thoughts of McKay, *The Quest of the Folk*, 302.
89 Belchem, "Irish and Polish Migration," 12.
90 Walsh, "Performing Public Memory and Re-Placing Home in the Ottawa Valley, 1900–1958," 33; Featherstone, "Localism, Globalism, and Cultural Identity," 345. Also, Janice Kulyk-Keefer described how stories from the old country and her mother's village seemed vivid and alive – even though she had never been there. See *Dark Ghost in the Corner*, 18.
91 *Kaszuby Canada, Part One*, dir. Henryk Bartul.
92 Walsh, "Performing Public Memory," 33.
93 Cooley, *Making Music*, 124.
94 *Kaszuby Canada, Part One*, dir. Henryk Bartul.
95 *NWHS* 9, no. 1 (Spring/Summer 2010), 2.
96 "Polish Studio," OMNI-TV Toronto, 2 January 2010.
97 Błachowski, *Hafty Polski Szycie*, 88; Lorentz, "An Outline of Cassubian Civilization," 33.
98 Swyripa, *Wedded to the Cause*, 25.
99 Joanna Szymanski, "Kashubian Embroidery Rediscovered by 6th Generation Kashub Canadians," *IYDK* 4, no. 1 (Spring/Summer 2005), 3. Also appeared in *BBTW*, 30 March 2005.

100 WHS, "Embroidery," www.wilno.org/culture/embroidery.html, accessed 5 August 2010.
101 Ryan Paulsen, "Can't Rain on This Kashub Parade: Local Kashubs Brave the Elements to Celebrate Their Culture," *BBTW*, 5 May 2010; Paulsen, "Zen and the Art of Kashubian Embroidery."
102 Mask-Connolly, "Karl Rhode – First Kashubian Language Teacher in Canada's First Polish Settlement and Kashubian Community," *NWHS* 10, no. 1 (Spring/Summer 2011), 15.
103 Smolicz and Secombe, "Polish Culture and Education in Australia," 129.
104 Silverman, "Dyngus Days and Kolędy Nights," 34; Gillis, "Memory and Identity," 5.

EPILOGUE

1 Anderson and Frideres, *Ethnicity in Canada*, 37; Kucharska, "Kaszubi w Kanadzie," 163–79.
2 Bourrie, ed., *The Cultural Integration of Immigrants*, 285.
3 Gans, "Symbolic Ethnicity," 1–12.
4 "Parishioners & Friends of St. Hedwig's, Barry's Bay, Send $5000 Donation to Kashubian Parish in Borzyszkowy, Poland," *NWHS* 7, no. 1 (Spring/Summer 2007); "Kanadyjska ofiara," *Kurier Bytowski*, 24 May 2007, 1, 17.
5 Cooley, *Making Music in the Polish Tatras*, 10, 133, 138.
6 McCannell, *The Tourist*, 21, 90–120; Harvey, *Justice, Nature, and the Geography of Difference*, 302; and Cooley, *Making Music*, 150.
7 Shulist bequeathed the title of "Kashub Queen" posthumously to Martha (Palubiski) Linton. Although she sang in Polish and English, wore a "Polish" costume, and never travelled to the Kaszuby area in Poland, Linton's regular performances at the yearly festival branded her as Kashubian, according to Shulist. Thus, those who saw her perform witnessed an authentic cultural experience. Linton left the area, but returned after she found the longing too much to bear: "Martha Linton was 'Queen of Kashub Music,'" *BBTW*, 21 April 2009. Also, the word "imported" here has two meanings. The contemporary "Kashubian costume" was imported from Poland, since, according to the WHS, it was "lost." Also, the adoption of yellow and black as "Kashubian colours" was imported from Poland via the KPA's descriptions of Kashubian culture.
8 At the 2010 celebration, Shulist bestowed the title of "honorary Kashub" on a reporter, Ryan Paulsen, who regularly covers WHS events: Paulsen, "Can't Rain on this Kashub Parade."

9 Stella Yarskavitch recalled how the family would call upon the priest to bless the fields and rid them of bugs as soon as an infestation occurred. *Kaszuby Canada, Part One*, dir. Henryk Bartul.
10 Featherstone, "Localism, Globalism and Cultural Identity," 345.
11 Basu, *Highland Homecomings*, 192; Akenson, *The Irish Diaspora*.
12 Anderson, *Imagined Communities*, 6. In the past, scholars have approached the influence of space, place, and ethnicity relative to urban ethnic neighbourhoods. See Conzen, "Immigrant Neighbourhoods and Ethnic Identity," 603.
13 Perin, "Clio as an Ethnic," 443; see also Clifford, "Museums as Contact Zones," 454.
14 "Park Features," www.wilno.org/Museum/Park_Features/park_features.html, accessed 19 July 2010.
15 Schneider, "Of Pioneers, Victorians and 'Indians,'" 42.
16 Arthur Hazelius opened an outdoor museum in Sweden to display ethnographic pieces in 1891. Since then, the Swedish term "skansen" has been adopted and used to describe outdoor ethnographic museums. Burke, "Popular Culture in Norway and Sweden," 144.
17 Schneider, "Of Pioneers," 42.
18 Lowenthal, "Pioneer Museums," 122; and Schneider, "Of Pioneers," 43.
19 Tivy, "Museums, Visitors and the Reconstruction of the Past in Ontario," 35; Schneider, "Of Pioneers," 43.
20 Lowenthal, "Pioneer Museums," 120; Although Clifford's discourse centred around museums as colonial contact zones, it can also function as a contact zone in many different ways for many different people. Clifford, "Museums as Contact Zones," 438, 445.
21 *NWHS* 8, no. 2 (Fall/Winter 2009), 26.
22 Mask-Connolly, "Summer 2005 – Log Shed opens as New Display Building at Wilno Heritage Park," *IYDK* 4, no. 2 (Fall/Winter 2005), 12.
23 "Kashubian Capital of America," http://polishmuseumwinona.org/about-us/kashubian-capital-of-america, accessed 17 July 2013.
24 See Edstrom, "What Winona Needs," 4 February 2009; "Polish Music at the Museum this Weekend," 7 October 2009; "Celebrate Your Irish at the Polish Museum," 10 March 2010; Porter, "Polish Heritage, Cultural groups to Merge," 7 November 2010; "Polish Egg Decorating Class Creates Beauty," 1 April 2012; "Polish Museum Offers Look to Polish Catholic Past," 9 September 2012, in the *Winona Post*, accessed 17 July 2013, www.winonapost.com.
25 Gerber, "Theories and Lives," 35.
26 Mask-Connolly encouraged locals to visit the museum in Panna Maria, Texas, which claims to commemorate the first Polish settlement in North

America. See "North America's 1st Polish Settlement dates from 1854 at Panna Maria, Texas," *NWHS* 7, no. 1 (Spring/Summer 2008), 16–17. See also *NWHS* 4, no. 1 (Spring/Summer 2005), 18; and Sulpher, "In Search of Kashub Brethren," *NWHS* 7, no. 1 (Spring/Summer 2008), 19.

27 Mask-Connolly, "Canadian Buildings & Exhibit on Kashub Emigration at Museum in Poland," *NWHS* 9, no. 1 (Spring/Summer 2010), 6–9.
28 Darieva, "Rethinking Homecoming," 505.
29 See Blank and Glofcheskie, *Ask My Grandpa*, 10; *NWHS* 12, no. 1 (Spring/Summer 2013); vol. 12, no. 2 (Fall/Winter 2013); vol. 13, no. 1 (Spring/Summer 2014); vol. 13, no. 2 (Fall/Winter 2014).
30 Anderson, *Imagined Communities*, 163–4.
31 Fedorowicz, "The Future of Polish Organizational Life in Canada," 348.
32 Hryniuk and Luciuk, *Canada's Ukrainians*; Luciuk, *Searching for Place*, 277–8; Zembrzycki, *Memory, Identity, and the Challenge of Community Among Ukrainians in the Sudbury Region, 1901–1939*; Hinther and Mochoruk, *Re-imagining Ukrainian Canadians*, 4, 11–13; Gabert, "Locating Identity," 75; Murdzek, *Emigration in Polish Social-Political Thought*, 136; and Koliński, "Polish Rural Settlement in America," 38.
33 See Blank, "Pitching, Pies and Piety," 79; and *EL* 20, no. 11 (20 January 1922).
34 Lehr, *Community and Frontier*, 171.
35 Foucault, *Power*, 330–1.
36 Mask-Connolly, *Marriage Matters*, ii, 1.

BIBLIOGRAPHY

ARCHIVAL SOURCES

Archives of Ontario

Charles McNamara Collection, C-120-1-0-1.1
Department of Crown Lands Administration Subject Files, RG1, A-I-7
Department of Crown Lands Township Papers, RG1, C-IV

Library and Archives Canada

"Annual Report of the Minister of Agriculture." *Journals of the Legislative Assembly of the Province of Canada* (1854–1866)
Canada, Miscellanea, Blue Books of Statistics, etc., MG11-CO47 (1858–1861)
Department of Agriculture, General Letterbooks, RG17, A-I-2
Hansard of the Senate of Canada, 3rd Session, 40th Parliament, Volume 147, Issue 25, 5 May 2010
Harry Hinchley Fonds
Journals of the Legislative Assembly of the Province of Canada (1854–1866)
"Report of the Commissioner of Crown Lands of Canada." *Journals of the Legislative Assembly of the Province of Canada* (1856–1866)
"Report of the Select Committee to whom was referred the annual report of the chief emigration agent, and supplementary report of the German assistant at Quebec (1860)." *Journals of the Legislative Assembly of the Province of Canada*, 1860

Arnprior and District Archives

Peter Hessel Fonds

NEWSPAPERS AND NEWSLETTERS

Allgemeine Auswanderungs Zeitung. Rudolstadt (1856–1862)
The Barry's Bay Review (1960s)

Barry's Bay This Week (1960s–1980s, 2005–2010)
Deutsche Auswanderer Zeitung. Bremen (1852–1864)
The Canadian Agriculturalist 7, no. 8 (August 1856)
The Eganville Leader (1900–1960s, 2005–2010)
The Kamaniskeg Chronicle (Barry's Bay, 1970s)
Kurier Bytowski, 24 May 2007, 1, 17
The Ottawa Citizen
Polak w Ameryce (1888–1890)
Przyjaciel ludu Kaszubskiego, Kashubian Association of North America (1997–2007)
Renfrew Mercury (1871–1880)
News from the Wilno Heritage Society (2002–2015)
Winona Post, Winona, Minnesota

PUBLISHED SOURCES

Adams, William Forbes. *Ireland and Irish Migration to the New World from 1815 to the Famine.* New Haven: Yale University Press, 1932.
Addison, Ottelyn. *Early Days in Algonquin Park.* Whitney: Friends of Algonquin Park, 2006.
Akenson, Donald Harman. *The Irish Diaspora: A Primer.* Toronto: P.D. Meany, 1993.
Allard, Carolo. *Regni Poloniae, Magni Ducatus Lithuaniae, coeterumque Regi Poloniae subditarum regionum tabula,* 1683.
Allport, G.W. *The Nature of Prejudice.* Garden City: Anchor/Doubleday, 1954.
Alvis, Robert E. "Hallowed Ground, Contagious Corpses, and the Moral Economy of the Graveyard in Early Nineteenth-Century Prussia." *Journal of Religion* 84 (April 2004): 234–55.
"An act to amend and consolidate the laws relating to the Carriage of Passengers by Sea." *The Statutes of the United Kingdom of Great Britain and Ireland.* Vols. 15 and 16, 108–13. London, 1852.
"An act to regulate the Carriage of Passengers in Merchant Vessels." *29th American Congress,* 22 February 1847, Session II, Chapter XVI, 9th Statute: 128.
Anderson, Alan B., and James S. Frideres. *Ethnicity in Canada: Theoretical Perspectives.* Toronto: Macmillan, 1981.
Anderson, Benedict. *Imagined Communities.* London: Verso, 1991.
– *Imagined Communities: Reflections on the Origin and Spread of Nationalism.* London: Verso, 2006.
Ansimov, E.V. "Peter I: Birth of the Empire." In *Major Problems in the History of Imperial Russia,* edited by James Cracraft, 82–98. Lexington: D.C. Heath, 1994.

Avery, D.H., and J.K Fedorowicz. *The Poles in Canada*. Ottawa: Canadian Historical Association, 1982.

Bade, Klaus J. *Migration in European History*. Cornwall: Blackwell, 2003.

Barford, P.M. *The Early Slavs: Culture and Society in Early Medieval Eastern Europe*. Ithaca: Cornell University Press, 2001.

Bassler, Gerhard P. "The 'Inundation' of British North America with 'the Refuse of Foreign Pauperism': Assisted Emigration from Southern Germany in the Mid-19th Century." *German Canadian Yearbook* 4 (1978): 93–113.

– "German Overseas Migration to North America in the Nineteenth and Twentieth Centuries." *German Canadian Yearbook* 7, (1983): 8–21.

– *The German Canadian Mosaic Today and Yesterday: Identities, Roots, and Heritage*. Ottawa: German Canadian Congress, 1991.

Basu, Paul. *Highland Homecomings: Genealogy and Heritage Tourism in the Scottish Diaspora*. Abingdon: Routledge, 2007.

Batinski, Michael C. *Pastkeepers in a Small Place: Five Centuries in Deerfield, Massachusetts*. Amherst & Boston: University of Massachusetts Press, 2004.

Bausenhart, Werner. *German Immigration and Assimilation in Ontario, 1783–1918*. Ottawa: Legas, 1989.

Beauprie, Donald J. *Destination Algonquin Park: Tracks to Cache Lake and the Highland Inn*. Renfrew: General Store Publishing House, 2011.

Beckett, John. *Writing Local History*. Manchester: Manchester University Press, 2007.

Behrens, C.B.A. *Society, Government and the Enlightenment: The Experiences of Eighteenth-Century France and Prussia*. London: Thames and Hudson, 1985.

Belchem, John. "Irish and Polish Migration: Some Preliminary Comparative Analysis." In *Irish and Polish Migration in Comparative Perspective*, edited by John Belchem and Klaus Tenfelde, 11–26. Essen: Verlag, 2003.

Belzyt, L. *Sprachliche Minderhciten im polnische Staat 1815–1914: Die preußische Sprachenstatistik in Bearbeitung und Kommentar*. Marburg: Herder-Institut, 1998.

Benet, Sula. *Song, Dance and Customs of Peasant Poland*. New York: Roy, 1951.

Berger, Carl. *The Writing of Canadian History: Aspects of English-Canadian Historical Writing Since 1900*. 2nd ed. Toronto: University of Toronto Press, 1986.

Bergquist, James. "Harvest of Stones: The German Settlement in Renfrew County by Brenda Lee-Whiting." *International Migration Review* 21, no. 2 (Summer 1987): 443–4.

Bhabha, Homi K. *The Location of Culture*. London: Routledge, 1994.

Bickelman, Hartmut. "The Venture of Travel." In *Germans to America: 300 Years of Immigration 1683–1983*, edited by Günter Moltmann, 46–133. Stuttgart: Eugen Heinz, 1982.

Bideleux, Robert, and Ian Jeffries. *A History of Eastern Europe: Crisis and Change.* New York: Routledge, 1998.

Bismarck, Otto. *Reflections and Reminiscences.* New York: Harper & Row, 1968.

Bittermann, Rusty. "On Remembering and Forgetting: Highland Memories Within the Maritime Diaspora." In *Myth, Migration and the Making of Memory: Scotia and Nova Scotia c. 1700–1990*, edited by Marjory Harper and Michael Vance, 253–66. Halifax: Fernwood, 1999.

Błachkowski, Alexander. *Hafty Polskie Szycie. Tom II: Tradycje I wspólczesnosc polskiej sztuki ludowej.* Torun: Stowarzyszenia Twórców Ludowych, 2004.

Blaeu, Guiljel and Ioanne. *Theatrum Orbis Terrarum, sive Atlas Novus in quo Tabulæ et Descriptiones Omnium Regionum*, 1645.

Blank, Clifford G. Interview by Joshua C. Blank, Le Bristol Meridien Hotel, Warsaw, Poland. 2 July 2010.

Blank, Inge. "From Serfdom to Citizenship: Polish Folk Culture from the Era of the Partitions to World War I." In *Roots of the Transplanted: Volume One: Late 19th Century East Central and Southeastern Europe*, edited by Dirk Hoerder and Inge Blank, 111–74. New York: Columbia University Press, 1994.

Blank, Joshua C. "Death of a Salesman but Not a Forest: J.R. Booth." *This Week In History Archives.* Gatineau: Parks Canada, 2005.

– "Pitching, Pies and Piety: Early Twentieth Century St. Hedwig's Parish Picnics." *Historical Studies* 76 (2010): 61–85.

– (Illustrated by Natalie Glofcheskie). *Ask My Grandpa.* Wilno Heritage Society, 2012.

Blank, Joshua C., Angela Lorbetskie, and Theresa Prince. *Sto Lat: One Hundred Years of Faith at St Hedwig's Parish.* Barry's Bay: St Hedwig's Parish, 2014.

Blanke, Richard. *Prussian Poland in the German Empire (1871–1900).* New York: Columbia University Press, 1981.

– "The Polish Role in the Origin of the Kulturkampf in Prussia." *Canadian Slavonic Papers* 25, no. 2 (June 1983): 253–62.

Bleskie, Tony. Interview by Joshua C. Blank, Barry's Bay, 3 August 2010.

Bòbrowsczi, Witold, and Katarzëna Kwiatkòwskô. *Kaszëbsczë ABECADLO.* Gdansk: Dar Gdanska, 2002.

Bodnar, John. *Remaking America: Public Memory, Commemoration and Patriotism in the Twentieth Century.* Princeton: Princeton University Press, 1992.

Böhning, Peter. *Die Nationalpolnische Bewedung in Westpreussen 1815–1871.* Marburg: J.G. Herder-Institut, 1973.

Bolton, Charles. "The New Genealogy." *Utah Genealogical and Historical Magazine* 4 (1913): 126–30.
Borzyszkowski, Józef. *O Kaszubach w Kanadzie: Kaszubsko-kanadyjskie losy I dziedzictwo kultury.* Gdansk: Elblag, 2004.
– *The Kashubs, Pomerania and Gdansk.* Translated by Tomasz Wicherkiewicz. Gdansk: Elblag, 2005.
Boswell, David, and Jessica Evans. *Representing the Nation: Histories, Heritage and Museums.* London: Routledge, 1999.
Bourrie, W.D., ed. *The Cultural Integration of Immigrants.* Paris: UNESCO, 1959.
Boyce, Gerald E. *Hutton of Hastings: The Life and Letters of William Hutton, 1801–1861.* Belleville: The Intelligencer, 1972.
Breton, Raymond. "Institutional Completeness of Ethnic Communities and the Personal Relations of Immigrants." *American Journal of Sociology* 70 (1964): 192–205.
Breza, Edward. "Mieszkańcy wsi Kalisz z początku XIX w." *Pomerania*, no. 7 (1984): 39.
Brock, Peter. "Florjan Cenôva and the Kashub Question." *East European Quarterly* 2, no. 3 (September 1968): 259–94.
– *Folk Cultures and Little Peoples: Aspects of National Awakening in East Central Europe.* New York: Columbia University Press, 1992.
Brody, Hugh. *The Other Side of Eden: Hunters, Farmers and the Shaping of the World.* Vancouver: Douglas & McIntyre, 2000.
Brzeski, Pawel. "Nauczycielka Ontaryjskich Kaszubów." *Pomerania*, no. 267–8 (Lëpinc-Zélnik 1995): 66.
Buchanan, A.C. *Canada: For the Information of Intending Emigrants.* Quebec: John Lovell, 1864.
Bukowczyk, John J. "Polish Americans, Ethnicity and Otherness." *The Polish Review* 43, no. 3 (1998): 299–313.
Burke, Peter. "Popular Culture in Norway and Sweden." *History Workshop*, no. 3 (1977): 143–7.
Buske, Norbert. *Pommern: Territorialstaat und Landesteil von Preussen: ein Überblick über die politische Entwicklung: die Rolle Vorpommerns seit 1945.* Schwerin: Thomas Helms Verlag, 1997.
Butterwick, Richard. "What is Enlightenment (Oświecenie)? Some Polish Answers, 1765–1828." *Central Europe* 3, no. 1 (May 2005): 19–37.
Campey, Lucille H. *Fast Sailing and Copper Bottomed: Aberdeen Sailing Ships and the Emigrant Scots They Carried to Canada 1774–1855.* Toronto: Natural Heritage, 2002.
Canada, Minister of Supply and Services. *The Cultural Contribution of Other Ethnic Groups.* Report Book IV. Ottawa: Queen's Printer, 1970.

Carr, E.H. *What Is History?* 2nd ed. New York: Penguin, 1987.

Chirst, Daniel, ed. *The Origins of Backwardness in Eastern Europe: Economies and Politics from the Middle Ages Until the Early Twentieth Century.* Berkeley: University of California Press, 1989.

Chorzempa, Rosemary A. *Korzenie Polskie: Polish Roots.* Baltimore: Genealogical Publishing Company, 1993.

Christinck, Debbi. "Wilno's Rich Heritage is Brought Vividly to life by Researcher." *Eganville Leader,* 25 February 1999, A12.

Clifford, James. "Museums as Contact Zones." In *Representing the Nation: A Reader: Histories, Heritage and Museums,* edited by David Boswell and Jessica Evans, 435–58. New York: Routledge, 1999.

Climo, Jacob B., and Maria G. Catell. *Social Memory and History: Anthropological Perspectives.* Walnut Creek: AltaMira, 2002

Colombo, John Robert. *Mysteries of Ontario.* Toronto: Hounslow, 1999.

Conrad, Margaret, and Alvin Finkel. *History of the Canadian Peoples: Volume II: 1867 to the Present.* 4th ed. Toronto: Pearson Longman, 2006.

Contenta, Sandro. "Vatican Knew of Abuse in Ontario: Victim: Papal Embassy Officials Told in 1993 Says Man Abused by Former Monsignor." *The Toronto Star,* 28 March 2010.

Conzen, Kathleen Neils. "Immigrants, Immigrant Neighbourhoods, and Ethnic Identity: Historical Issues." *The Journal of American History* 66, no. 3 (December 1979): 603–15.

– "Thomas and Znaniecki and the Historiography of American Immigration." *Journal of American Ethnic History* 16, no. 1 (Fall 1996): 16–25.

Cooley, Timothy J. *Making Music in the Polish Tatras: Tourists, Ethnographers and Mountain Musicians.* Bloomington: Indiana University Press, 2005.

Corrigan, Robert C. *A History of St. Lawrence O'Toole's Parish: To Commemorate its 50th Anniversary, 1934–1984.* St Lawrence Parish: Self-published, 1984.

Cotton, Larry D. *Whiskey and Wickedness: No. 4 Renfrew County, Ontario 1825 to 1900.* Ottawa: Self-published, Doculink, 2008.

"County of Renfrew History." Accessed 5 August 2010. http://www.countyofrenfrew.on.ca/menu/about-the-county/history/.

Cracraft, James, ed. *Major Problems in the History of Imperial Russia.* Lexington: D.C. Heath, 1994.

Craig, Gordan A. *The Politics of the Prussian Army 1640–1945.* New York: Oxford University Press, 1964.

Cross, L.D. *Ottawa Titans: Fortune and Fame in the Early Days of Canada's Capital.* Canmore: Altitude, 2004.

Cruikshank, Juilie. *Do Glaciers Listen?: Local Knowledge, Colonial Encounters, and Social Imagination.* Vancouver: UBC Press, 2005.

Curtis, Bruce. "Official Documentary Systems and Colonial Government: From Imperial Sovereignty to Colonial Autonomy in the Canadas." *Journal of Historical Sociology* 10, no. 4 (1997): 389–417.

Cygan, Mary. "Inventing Polonia: Notions of Polish American Identity, 1870–1990." *Prospects: An Annual of American Cultural Studies* 23 (1998): 209–46.

Czubaty, Jarosław. "'What Is to be Done When the Motherland has Died?' The Moods and Attitudes of Poles After the Third Partition, 1795–1806." *Central Europe*, no. 2 (November 2009): 95–109.

Danborn, David B. *Born in the Country: A History of Rural America.* Baltimore: Johns Hopkins University Press, 1995.

Darieva, Tsypylma. "Rethinking Homecoming: Diasporic Cosmopolitanism in Post-Soviet Armenia." *Ethnic and Racial Studies* 34, no. 3 (March 2011): 490–508.

Davies, Norman. *God's Playground: A History of Poland: Volume 2, 1795 to the Present.* New York: Columbia University Press, 1982.

– *God's Playground: A History of Poland: Volume 1, The Origins to 1795.* New York: Columbia University Press, 2005.

Department of Lands and Forests. *Map Showing the Exploration Routes Through the Huron and Ottawa Territory between the years 1615–1854.* (1946).

Dombroskie, Helen. Interview by Joshua C. Blank, Valley Manor Nursing Home, Barry's Bay, Ontario. 9 February 2009.

Dorson, Robert. "The State of Folklorists from an American Perspective." *Journal of the Folklore Institute* 19, nos. 2–3 (May 1982): 71–105.

Dreschel, Edwin. *Norddeutscher Lloyd Bremen, 1857–1970.* Vancouver: Cordillera, 1994.

Drummond, Andrew J., and Jacek Lubecki. "Reconstructing Galicia: Mapping the Cultural and Civic Traditions of the Former Austrian Galicia in Poland and Ukraine." *Europe-Asia Studies* 62, no. 8 (2010): 1311–38.

Dutkiewicz, Henry. "Main Aspects of the Polish Peasant Immigration to North America from Austrian Poland Between the Years of 1863 and 1910." Thesis, University of Ottawa, 1958.

Dwyer, Philip G., ed. *The Rise of Prussia 1700–1830.* Essex: Pearson Longman, 2000.

Elliott, Bruce S. "Harvest of Stones: The German Settlement in Renfrew County. BRENDA LEE-WHITING." *Archivaria* 22 (Summer 1986): 206–8.

– *The City Beyond: A History of Nepean, Birthplace of Canada's Capital 1792–1990.* Nepean: City of Nepean, 1991.

– *Irish Migrants in the Canadas: A New Approach.* 2nd ed. Montreal & Kingston: McGill-Queen's University Press, 2004.

Elliott, Bruce S., David A. Gerber, and Susan M. Sinke, eds. *Letters Across Borders: The Epistolary Practices of International Migrants*. New York: Palgrave Macmillan and Carleton Centre for the History of Migration, 2006.

Eltis, David. "Free and Coerced Transatlantic Migrations: Some Comparisons." *American Historical Review* 88, no. 2 (April 1983): 251–80.

Errington, Jane. *The Lion, the Eagle, and Upper Canada: A Developing Colonial Ideology*. Montreal & Kingston: McGill-Queen's University Press, 1987.

Evenson, Brad. "Vampires: Scholar Unearths More Than Legends." *Ottawa Citizen*, 27 August 1989, D3.

Fabian, Johannes. *Time and the Other: How Anthropology Makes its Object*. New York: Columbia University Press, 1983.

Fahmeir, Andreas K. "Nineteenth Century German Citizenships: A Reconsideration." *The Historical Journal* 40, no. 3 (1997): 721–52.

Featherstone, Mike. "Localism, Globalism and Cultural Identity." In *Identities: Race, Class, Gender and Nationality*, edited by Linda Martin Alcoff and Eduardo Mendieta, 342–59. Malden: Blackwell, 2003.

Fedorowicz, J.K., ed. *A Republic of Nobles: Studies in Polish History to 1864*. Cambridge: Cambridge University Press, 1982.

Finnigan, Joan. *Some of the Stories I Told You Were True*. Ottawa: Deneau, 1981.

– *Finnigan's Guide to the Ottawa Valley: A Cultural and Historical Companion*. Kingston: Quarry Press, 1988.

– *The Story of a Canadian Colonization Road: Life Along the Opeongo Line*. Renfrew: Penumbra, 2004.

Fischer, Adam. *Lud Polski. Podręcznik etnografji Polski*. Lwów, 1926.

– *Zarys etnograifczny wojewodztwa pomorskiego*. Toruń, 1929.

– *Zwiądek etnograficzny Pomorza z Polska: Przewic propagandize korytarzowej*. Lwów, 1930.

Fleming, John, and Michael Rowan. *Folk Furniture of Canada's Doukhobors, Hutterites, Mennonites and Ukrainians*. Edmonton: University of Alberta Press, 2004.

Forkey, Neil S. *Shaping the Upper Canadian Frontier: Environment, Society, and Culture in the Trent Valley*. Calgary: University of Calgary Press, 2003.

Foster, Vere. *Work and Wages: or, The Penny Emigrant's Guide to the United States and Canada*. 5th ed. London: W&F.G. Gash, 1855.

Foucault, Michel. *Power: Essential Works of Foucault*. Vol. 3. Edited by J. Faubion. London: Penguin, 2002.

Frank, Alison Feig. *Oil Empire: Visions of Prosperity in Austrian Galicia*. Cambridge: Harvard University Press, 2005.

Fraser, Ian Shenstone. "The Renfrew Region in the Middle Ottawa Valley." MA Geography Thesis, Clark University, 1953.

French, T.P. *Information for Intending Settlers on the Ottawa and Opeongo Road and Its Vicinity.* Ottawa, 1857.
Frideres, James S. "Ethnic Organizational Dynamics: The Polish Group in Canada, Henry Radecki." *Canadian Historical Review* 61, no. 4 (1980): 553–4.
Frye, Northrop. *The Bush Garden: Essays on the Canadian Imagination.* Toronto: Anansi, 1995.
– *The Educated Imagination.* Toronto: Anansi, 2002.
Frymark, Stanisław. *English-Polish-Kashub Dictionary.* Self-published: Wilno Heritage Society, 2008.
Gabaccia, Donna R. "Do We Still Need Immigration History?" *Polish American Studies* 55, no. 1 (Spring 1998): 45–68.
Gaddis, John Lewis. *The Landscape of History: How Historians Map the Past.* New York: Oxford University Press, 2002.
Gaffield, Chad. *Language, Schooling, and Cultural Conflict: The Origins of the French-Language Controversy in Ontario.* Montreal & Kingston: McGill-Queen's University Press, 1987.
Galush, William T. "Journeys of Spirit and Space: Religion and Economics in Migration." *Polish American Studies* 59, no. 2 (Autumn 2002): 5–16.
Gans, Herbert. "Symbolic Ethnicity: The Future of Ethnic Groups and Cultures in America." *Ethnic and Racial Studies* 2, no. 1 (January 1979): 1–20.
Gates, Lillian F. *Land Policies of Upper Canada.* Toronto: University of Toronto Press, 1968.
Gates, Paul W. "Official Encouragement to Immigration by the Province of Canada." *The Canadian Historical Review* 15, no. 1 (March 1934): 24–38.
Geertz, Clifford. *The Interpretation of Cultures.* New York: Basic, 1973.
Gentilcore, Louis. "Lines on the Land: Crown Surveys and Settlement in Upper Canada." *Ontario History* 61 (June 1969): 57–73.
Gentilcore, Louis, and Kate Donkin. *Land Surveys of Southern Ontario: An Introduction and Index to the Field Notebooks of the Ontario Land Surveyors 1784–1859.* Toronto: York University, 1973.
Gerber, David A. "Theories and Lives: Transnationalism and the Conceptualization of International Migrations to the United States." In *Transnationalismus und Kulturvergleich*, edited by Michael Bommes, 31–53. Osnabrück: IMS-Beiträge, 2000.
Gillespie, J.E., R.E. Wicklund, and B.C. Matthews. *Soil Survey of Renfrew County.* Toronto: Department of Agriculture, 1964.
Gillis, John R. *The Prussian Bureaucracy in Crisis 1840–1860: Origins of an Administrative Ethos.* Stanford: Stanford University Press, 1971.
– "Memory and Identity: The History of a Relationship." In *Commemorations: The Politics of National Identity*, edited by John R. Gillis, 3–23. Princeton: Princeton University Press, 1994.

Gjerde, Jon. "New Growth on Old Vines – The State of the Field: The Social History of Immigration to and Ethnicity in the United States." *Journal of American Ethnic History* 18, no. 4 (Summer 1999): 40–65.

Gleason, Philip. "Crèvacoeur's Question: Historical Writing on Immigrants, Ethnicity, and National Identity." In *Imagined Histories: American Historians Interpret the Past*, edited by Anthony Molho and Gordon S. Wood, 120–43. Princeton: Princeton University Press, 1998.

Glofcheskie, Bronas Anthony, ed. *Saint Hedwig's Parish Festivities 1980*. Barry's Bay: St Hedwig's Parish, 1980.

Glofcheskie, John Michael. *Folk Music of Canada's Oldest Polish Community*. Ottawa: National Museum of Man, 1980.

– "Polish Hymns from Saint Hedwig's: 1973 Heritage Recording." Audio-CD. Vancouver: Kerry Regier, 2003.

– "Folk Music of Canada's Oldest Polish Community." Audio-CD. Ottawa: Library and Archives Canada, 2006.

Glofcheskie, Peter T. Interview by Joshua C. Blank, Le Bristol Meridien Hotel, Warsaw, Poland. 3 July 2010.

– *The Klopotek-Glowczewski Family Coat of Arms*. Self-published, 2006.

Goc, Michael J. *Native Realm: The Polish-American Community of Portage County 1857–1992*. Friendship, WI: New Past Press, 1992.

Gogolewski, Stanislaw. "Dialectology in Poland, 1873–1997." In *Towards a History of Linguistics in Poland: From the Early Beginnings to the End of the Twentieth Century*, edited by E.F.K. Koener and Aleksander Szwedek, 123–46. Philadelphia: John Benjamins, 2001.

Golab, Caroline, "The Polish Experience in Philadelphia: The Migrant Laborers Who Did Not Come." In *The Ethnic Experience in Pennsylvania*, edited by John E. Bodnar, 39–73. Cranbury: Associated University Press, 1973.

Gołabek, Ks. Marian. "Jubileusz Kaszubskiej parafii w Kanadzie." *Pomerania*, no. 9 (1997): 63–5.

Gopnik, Adam. *Winter: Five Windows on the Season*. Toronto: Anansi, 2011.

Gorecki, Piotr. "*Viator* to *Ascriptitius*: Rural Economy, Lordship, and the Origins of Serfdom in Medieval Poland." *Slavic Review* 42, no. 1 (Spring 1983): 14–35.

Gourlay, R. *Statistical Account of Upper Canada*. Vol. 1. London, 1822.

"Governor General Announces 75 Caring Canadian Awards," [1 April 2009]. Accessed 5 August 2010. http://news.gc.ca/web/article-eng.do?m=/index&nid=440829.

Grabowski, Jan. "Polish Immigrants in Northern Ontario and the Ottawa Valley during the Early Twentieth Century." In *Ottawa: Making a Capital*, edited by Jeffrey Keshen and Nicole St-Onge, 251–62. Ottawa: University of Ottawa Press, 2001.

Graff, Harvey J. "What the 1861 Census Can Tell Us About Literacy: A Reply." *Social History* 8, no. 16 (November 1975): 337–48.
– *The Labyrinths of Literacy: Reflections on Literacy Past and Present.* Pittsburgh: University of Pittsburgh Press, 1995.
– *Literacy Myths, Legacies and Lessons: New Studies in Literacy.* New Brunswick, NJ: Transaction, 2011.
Green, Anna. "Individual Remembering and 'Collective Memory': Theoretical Presuppositions and Contemporary Debates." *Oral History* 32, no. 2 (Autumn 2004): 35–6.
Green, Nancy L. "The Politics of Exit: Reversing The Immigration Paradigm." *The Journal of Modern History* 77 (June 2005): 263–89.
Greene, Victor. *For God and Country: The Rise of Polish and Lithuanian Ethnic Consciousness in America 1860–1910.* Madison: The State Historical Society of Wisconsin, 1975.
Grenville, J.A.S. *Europe Reshaped, 1848–1878.* Oxford: Blackwell Publishers, 2000.
Gross, Michael B. *The War Against Catholicism: Liberalism and the Anti-Catholic Imagination in Nineteenth-Century Germany.* Ann Arbor: University of Michigan Press, 2004.
Grote, Hermann. *Münzenstudien.* Band IV–VI. Leipzig, 1862.
Gürttler, Karen R. "William (Wilhelm) Wagner." *Dictionary of Canadian Biography*, Vol. XII. University of Toronto, 2000. Accessed 5 August 2010. http://www.biographi.ca.
Gustavus, Carolus. *Auctior et Correctior Tabula Chorographica Regni Poloniae Vicinarumque Regionum, ubiitinera.* Nuremburg, 1696.
Gunn, Simon. *History and Cultural Theory.* Harlow: Pearson Longman, 2006.
Ha, Tu Thanh. "Vatican, Canadian Church Officials Tried to Keep Sex Scandal Secret." *The Globe and Mail*, 9 April 2010.
Hagen, William W. "The Partitions of Poland and the Crisis of the Old Regime in Prussia 1772–1806." *Central European History* 9, no. 2 (June 1976): 115–28.
– *Germans, Poles, and Jews: The Nationality Conflict in the Prussian East, 1772–1914.* Chicago: University of Chicago Press, 1980.
Hamer, David Allan. *New Towns in the New World: Images and Perceptions of the Nineteenth-Century Urban Frontier.* New York: Columbia University Press, 1990.
Handlin, Oscar. *The Uprooted: The Epic Story of the Great Migrations that Made the American People.* Boston: Little Brown, 1951.
Hansen, Marcus L. *German Schemes of Colonization Before 1860.* Northampton: Smith College, 1924.
– *The Problem of the Third Generation Immigrant.* Rock Island: Augustana Historical Society, 1938.

- *The Immigrant in American History*. Cambridge: Harvard University Press, 1940.
Harper, Marjory. "Enticing the Emigrant: Canadian Agents in Ireland and Scotland, c. 1870–c. 1920." *The Scottish Historical Review* 83, no. 215 (April 2004): 41–58.
Harris, R. Cole. *The Reluctant Land: Society, Space, and Environment in Canada before Confederation*. Vancouver: UBC Press, 2008.
Harvey, D.C. "The Importance of Local History in the Writing of General History." *Canadian Historical Review* 13, no. 3 (1932): 244–51.
Harvey, David. *Justice, Nature, and the Geography of Difference*. Oxford: Blackwell, 1986.
Haselback, Dieter. "The Social Construction of Identity: Theoretical Perspectives." In *A Chorus of Different Voices: German-Canadian Identities*, edited by Angelika E. Sauer and Matthias Zimmer, 1–19. New York: P. Lang, 1998.
Hessel, Peter D.K. *Destination: Ottawa Valley*. Ottawa: Runge Press, 1984.
- "German Immigration to the Ottawa Valley in the 19th Century." *German Canadian Yearbook* 7 (1984): 67–94.
- *The Algonkin Tribe: A Historical Outline*. Arnprior: Kitchesippi Books, 1987.
Heydenkorn, Benedykt, ed. *A Community in Transition: The Polish Group in Canada*. Toronto: Canadian Polish Research Institute, 1985.
High, Steven. "Sharing Authority: An Introduction." *Journal of Canadian Studies* 43, no. 1 (Winter 2009): 12–39.
Himka, John-Paul. *Socialism in Galicia: The Emergence of Polish Social Democracy and Ukrainian Radicalism (1860–1890)*. Cambridge: Harvard University Press, 1983.
- *Galicia and Bukovina: A Research Handbook About Western Ukraine, Late 19th and 20th Centuries*. Edmonton: Alberta Culture and Multiculturalism, 1990.
Hinther, Rhonda L., and Jim Mochoruk. *Re-imagining Ukrainian Canadians: History, Politics, and Identity*. Toronto: University of Toronto Press, 2011.
Hobsbawm, Eric. "Mass-Producing Traditions: Europe, 1870–1914." In *The Invention of Tradition*, edited by Eric Hobsbawm and Terrance Ranger, 263–307. New York: Cambridge University Press, 2009.
Hobsbawm, Eric, and Terrance Ranger. *The Invention of Tradition*. New York: Cambridge University Press, 2009.
Hodgetts, J.E. *Pioneer Public Service: An Administrative History of the United Canadas, 1841–1867*. Toronto: University of Toronto Press, 1955.
Hoerder, Dirk. "Ethnic Studies in Canada from the 1880s to 1962: A Historiographical Perspective and Critique." *Canadian Ethnic Studies* 26, no. 1 (1994): 1–18.

- "Changing Paradigms in Migration History: From 'To America' to World-Wide Systems." *Canadian Review of American Studies* 24, no. 2 (Spring 1994): 105–26.
- "Immigration History and Migration Studies since 'The Polish Peasant': International Contributions." *Journal of American Ethnic History* 16, no. 1 (Fall 1996): 26–36.
- "The Transplanted: International Dimensions." *Social Science History* 12, no. 3 (Autumn 1998): 255–63.
- *Cultures in Contact: World Migrations in the Second Millennium*. Durham: Duke University Press, 2002.
- "Towards a History of Canadians: Transcultural Human Agency as Seen Through Economic Behaviour, Community Formation, and Societal Institutions." *Social History/Histoire Sociale* 38, no. 76 (2005): 433–59.
- "Individuals and Systems: Agency in Nineteenth and Twentieth Century Labour Migrations." In *European Mobility: Internal, International, and Transatlantic Moves in the 19th and Early 20th Centuries*, edited by Annemarie Steidl, Josef Ehmer, Stan Nadel, and Hermann Zeithofer, 53–68. Goettingen: V&R unipress, 2009.

Holborn, Hajo. *A History of Modern Germany: Volume 3: 1840–1945*. New York: Alfred A. Knopf, 1959.

Hrniuk, Stella, and Lubomyr Y. Luciuk. *Canada's Ukrainians: Changing Perspectives, 1891–1991*. Toronto: University of Toronto Press, 1991.

Hroch, Miroslaw. "National Self-Determination from a Historical Perspective." *Canadian Slavonic Papers* 37, nos. 3–4 (September 1995): 283–98.

Hudder, Christine. "Kashub vs. Polish: What's the Difference?" *Valley Gazette*, 3 May 2012, 10.

Hutton, Patrick H. *History as an Art of Memory*. Hanover: University of Vermont Press, 1993.

Hutton, William. *Canada: Its Present Condition, Prospects and Resources, fully described for the Information of Intending Emigrants*. London: Edward Stanford, 1854.
- *Canada: A Brief Outline of Her Geographical Position, Productions, Climate, Capabilities, Educational and Municipal Institutions, Fisheries, Railroads, &c &c &c.* Quebec: John Lovell, 1858.
- *Canada: ein kulzer Abriss von dessen geographischer Lage, Production, Clima, und Bodenbeschaffenheit, Erziehungs und Municipal-Wesen &c.* Toronto, n.d.

Hvidt, Kristian, "Emigration Agents: The Development of a Business and Its Methods." *Scandinavian Journal of History* 3, no. 1 (1978): 179–203.

Iacovetta, Franca. "Manly Militants, Cohesive Communities, and Defiant Domestics: Writing About Immigrants in Canadian Historical Scholarship." *Labour/Le Travail* 36 (Fall 1995): 217–52.

- *The Writing of English Canadian Immigrant History.* CHA Ethnic Group Series Booklet #22. Ottawa: Canadian Historical Association, 1997.
- "Post-Modern Ethnography, Historical Materialism, and Decentring the (Male) Authorial Voice: A Feminist Conversation." *Social History* 32, no. 64 (November 1999): 275–93.
- *Gatekeepers: Reshaping Immigrant Lives in Cold War Canada.* Toronto: Between the Lines, 2006.

Ibbitson, John. "The Last Stronghold of Kaszuby Culture." *Ottawa Citizen,* 8 September 1992, D1.

Ickiewicz, Kazimierz. *Kaszubi w Kanadzie.* Gdansk: Zrzeszenie Kaszubsko-Pomorskie, 2008.
- "Kaszubi w kraju klonowego liscia." *Pomerania,* nos. 7–8 (July–August 2008): 3–10.

Inoki, Takenori. *Aspects of German Peasant Emigration to the United States, 1815–1914.* New York: Arno Press, 1981.

Isajiw, Wsevolod. "The Process of Maintenance of Ethnic Identity: The Canadian Context." In *Sounds Canadian,* edited by P.M. Migus, 129–38. Toronto: Peter Martin, 1975.
- *Ethnic Identity Retention.* Toronto: Centre for Urban and Community Studies/University of Toronto, 1981.

Jacobsen, Matthew Frye. *Special Sorrows: The Diasporic Imagination of Irish, Polish, and Jewish Immigrants in the United States.* Cambridge: Harvard University Press, 1995.

Janssonius, Joan. *Accurata Prussiae description.* Amsterdam, c. 1645–60.

Jaroszyńska-Kirchmann, Anna D. *The Exile Mission: The Polish Political Diaspora and Polish Americans, 1939–1956.* Athens: Ohio University Press, 2004.

Johnston, R.J., Derek Gregory, and David M. Smith, eds. *The Dictionary of Human Geography.* 2nd ed. London: Blackwell, 1986.

Jones, Robert Leslie. *History of Agriculture in Ontario 1613–1880.* Toronto: University of Toronto Press, 1946.

Jost, Isabelle. "New Documentation on the Settlement of the Western Part of the Ottawa-Opeongo Colonisation Road." *Revue de l'Universite d'Ottawa* 44, no. 4 (1974): 443–52.

Jost, Izabela. *Osadnictwo Kaszubskie W Ontario.* Lublin: Katolicki Uniwersytet Lubelski, 1983.
- "Polish Kashub Pioneers in Ontario." *Polyphony* 6, no. 2 (1984): 20–4.

Jubiläums-Büchlein: zur feier des 50 jährigen Jubiläums der evang luther Synode von Canada. Berlin, 1910.

Kammen, Carol. *On Doing Local History.* 2nd ed. Walnut Creek: AltaMira, 2003.

Kamphoefner, Walter D. "German Emigration Research, North, South and East: Findings, Methods and Open Questions." In *People in Transit: German*

Migrations in Comparative Perspective, 1820–1930, edited by Dirk Hoerder and Jörg Nagler, 19–34. Washington: Cambridge University Press, 1995.
– "The Real Guidebooks: Advice on Immigration Letters back to Germany." Symposium on the Uses of Immigrant Letters, Washington, DC, May 1997, unpublished manuscript.
Karski, Jan. *Story of a Secret State: My Report to the World.* Washington, DC: Georgetown University Press, 2013.
Kaszëbë: Pioneers of the Wilderness. Directed by Darek Barecki. Produced by OMNI-TV/Opeongo Road Production Inc., 2004. Videocassette (VHS).
Kaszubski Park Etnograficzny. "Teodora and Izydor Gulgowski." Waglikowice, n.d.
Kaszuby Canada, Part One. Directed by Henryk Bartul. Produced by Group 44, 1997. Videocassette (VHS).
Kaszuby. National Film Board Production. Directed by André Herman. Produced by William Weintraub, 1975. Videocassette (VHS).
Katz, Yossi, and John C. Lehr. *The Last Best West: Essays on the Historical Geography of the Canadian Prairies.* Jerusalem: Magnes, 1999.
Keefer, Thomas C. *'Montreal' and 'The Ottawa': Two Lectures Delivered Before the Mechanics Institute of Montreal.* Montreal: John Lovell, 1854.
Keeling, Drew, "Costs, Risks and Migration Networks Between Europe and the United States, 1900–1914." In *Maritime Transport and Migration: The Connections Between Maritime and Migration Networks*, edited by Torsten Feys, 113–74. St John's: International Maritime Economic History Association, 2007.
Kellenbenz, Hermann. "Die Auswanderung nach Lateinamericka." In *Maritime Aspects of Migration*, edited by Klaus Friedland, 215–42. Wien: Böhlau, 1989.
Kennedy, Clyde C. *The Upper Ottawa Valley: A Glimpse of History*. Pembroke: Renfrew County Council Press, 1970.
Kennedy, Janice. "Earning Contempt." *Ottawa Citizen*, 19 April 2009, A11.
Kelley, Ninette, and Michael Trebilcock. *The Making of the Mosaic: A History of Canadian Immigration Policy.* Toronto: University of Toronto Press, 2000.
Kieniewicz, Stefan. *The Emancipation of the Polish Peasantry.* Chicago: University of Chicago Press, 1969.
Kirkwood, A., and J.J. Murphy. *The Underdeveloped Lands in Northern and Western Ontario: Information Regarding Resources, Products and Suitability for Settlement – Collected and Compiled from Reports of Surveyors, Crown Land Agents, and Others.* Toronto: Hunter, Rose & Co., 1878.
Kirshenblatt-Gimblett, Barbara. "Theorizing Heritage." *Ethnomusicology* 39, no. 3 (1995): 367–80.

Kisielewski, Jozef. *Ziemia Gromadzi Prochy*. Poznań: Księgarnia św. Wojciecha, 1939.

Klima, Leszek, and Kazmierz Mróz. *Powiat Chojnicki w Świetle Cyfr*. Chojnice: Polskie Towarzystwo Krajoznawcze, 1938.

Kochanowicz, Jacek. "The Polish Economy and the Evolution of Dependency." In *The Origins of Backwardness in Eastern Europe: Economies and Politics from the Middle Ages Until the Early Twentieth Century*, edited by Daniel Chirst, 92–130. Berkeley: University of California Press, 1989.

Koehne, Boris. *Zeitschrift für Munz-, Siegel- und Wappenkunde*. Berlin: Druck & Mittler, 1842.

Koliński, Dennis. "The Origin and Development of Polish Settlements in Central Wisconsin." *Polish American Studies* 51, no. 1 (1994): 21–48.

– "Polish Rural Settlement in America." *Polish American Studies* 52, no. 2 (1995): 21–55.

Köllman, Wolfgang, and Antje Kraus. *Quellen zur Bevölkerungs-, Sozial- und Wirtschaftsstatistik Deutschlands 1815–1875*, Band I. Boppard am Rhein: Harald Boldt Verlag, 1980.

Kos-Rabcewicz-Zubkowski, Ludwig. *Canada Ethnica IV: The Poles in Canada*. Toronto: Polish Alliance Press, 1968.

Kruszewski, Z. Anthony. "Nationalism and Politics: Poland." In *The Politics of Ethnicity in Eastern Europe*, edited by George Klein and Milan J. Reban, 147–84. New York: Columbia University Press, 1981.

Kucharska, Jadwiga. "Kaszubi w Kanadzie: Mechanizmy Identyfikacji Etnicznej." *Etnografia Polska* 30, no. 1 (1986): 163–79.

Kukushkin, Vadim. *From Peasants to Labourers: Ukrainian and Belarusan Immigration from the Russian Empire to Canada*. Montreal & Kingston: McGill-Queen's University Press, 2007.

Kulas, Julian. *Kashub-English-Kashub: Mini Dictionary-Slowôrzk*. Combermere: Self-published, 2009.

Kulczycki, John J. "The Herne 'Polish Revolt' of 1899: Social and National Consciousness among Polish Coal Miners in the Ruhr." *Canadian Slavonic Papers* 31, no. 2 (June 1989): 146–53.

Kulyk-Keefer, Janice. *Dark Ghost in the Corner: Imagining Ukrainian-Canadian Identity*. Saskatoon: Heritage Press, 2005.

Kurelek, William. *The Polish Canadians*. Montreal: Tundra, 1981.

Labuda, Gerard. "The Key Problems of the History of the Kashubs Against the Background of Pomeranian History." *Polish Western Affairs* 30, no. 1 (1989): 3–29.

– *Historia Kaszubów w dziejach Pomorza: Tom I, Czasy sredniowieczne*. Gdansku: Instytut Kaszubski, 2006.

Łajming, Anna. *Czterolistna Koniczyna*. Gdańsk: Instytut Kaszubski, 2011.

Lamberti, Marjorie. "State, Church, and the Politics of School Reform During the *Kulturkampf.*" *Central European History* 19, no. 1 (1986): 63–81.
- *State, Society, and the Elementary School in Imperial Germany.* New York: Oxford University Press, 1989.
Lee, David. *Forest Products in the Ottawa Valley 1850–1925.* Gatineau: Historic Sites and Monuments Board of Canada, 1985.
- *Lumber Kings and Shantymen: Logging, Lumber and Timber in the Ottawa Valley.* Toronto: James Lorimer & Company, 2006.
Lee-Whiting, Brenda. "First Polish Settlement in Canada." *Canadian Geographic Journal* 75, no. 3 (1967): 108–12.
- "The Opeongo Road: An Early Colonization Scheme." *Canadian Geographic Journal* 74, no. 3 (1967): 76–83.
- "The Old Wooden Crosses of Wilno." *The Globe and Mail*, 26 August 1972, 30.
- *Harvest of Stones: The German Settlement in Renfrew County.* Toronto: University of Toronto Press, 1985.
- "Why So Many German Immigrants Embarked at Liverpool." *German Canadian Yearbook* 9 (1986): 71–9.
- *On Stony Ground.* Renfrew: Juniper, 1986.
- "Memories of Canada's First Polish Settlement: Along the Opeongo Road." *The Beaver* 72, no. 1 (1992): 29–33.
Legree, Fr Joseph. *Lift Up Your Hearts: A History of the Roman Catholic Diocese of Pembroke.* Kingston: Brown & Martin, 1988.
Lehr, John C. "Government Coercion in the Settlement of Ukrainian Immigrants in Western Canada." *Prairie Forum* 8, no. 2 (1983): 179–94.
- *Community and Frontier: A Ukrainian Settlement in the Canadian Parkland.* Winnipeg: University of Manitoba Press, 2011.
Little, J.I. *Nationalism, Capitalism, and Colonization in Nineteenth-Century Quebec: The Upper St. Francis District.* Montreal & Kingston: McGill-Queen's University Press, 1989.
Livingstone, David N. *Putting Science in its Place: Geographies of Scientific Knowledge.* Chicago: University of Chicago Press, 2003.
Lockwood, Glenn J. "The Pattern of Settlement in Eastern Ontario 1784–1875." *Families* 30, no. 4 (1991): 235–57.
Loewen, Royden. "The Fragmented Refashioning of American Urban Immigration History." *Urban History Review* 27, no. 2 (March 1999): 60–3.
Lorentz, F. *Tesky pomorskie (kaszubski).* Kraków: Polska Akademia, 1924.
- *Geschichte der Kaschuben.* Berlin: Reimar Hobbing, 1926.
- *Gramatyka pomorska.* Poznań, 1924–1927.
Lorentz, F.R., Adam Fischer, and Tadeusz Lehr-Splawinski. *The Cassubian Civilization.* London: Faber, 1935.

Lorentz, F., and I. Gulgowski. "Der Name Kaschubei." In *Mitteilungen des Vereins für kaschubiche Volkskunde*, 148–52. Leipzig: Otto Harrassowitz, 1910.

Lowenthal, David. "Pioneer Museums." In *History Museums in the United States: A Critical Assessment*, edited by Warren Leon and Roy Rosenzweig, 115–27. Urbana and Chicago: University of Illinois Press, 1989.

Lower, A.R.M. *Settlement and the Forest Frontier in Eastern Canada*. Toronto: Macmillan, 1936.

– "The Assault on the Laurentian Barrier, 1850–1870." *Canadian Historical Review* 10 (1929): 294–307.

Luciuk, Lubomyr. *Searching for Place: Ukrainian Displaced Persons, Canada, and the Migration of Memory*. Toronto: University of Toronto Press, 2000.

Lüdtke, Alf. *Police and State in Prussia 1815–1850*. New York: Cambridge University Press, 1989.

Lukowski, Jerzy. *Liberty's Folly: The Polish-Lithuanian Commonwealth in the Eighteenth Century, 1697–1795*. New York: Routledge, 1991.

– *The Partitions of Poland 1772, 1793, 1795*. New York: Longman, 1999.

Lukowski, Jerzy, and Hubert Zawadski. *A Concise History of Poland*. 2nd ed. Cambridge: Cambridge University Press, 2006.

Macdonald, Gregory. "The Kashubs on the Baltic." *The Slavonic and East European Review* 19, no. 53/54 (1939–40): 265–75.

Macdonald, Norman. *Canada: Immigration and Colonization 1841–1903*. Aberdeen: Aberdeen University Press, 1968.

MacGregor, Alison. "Why the Vampires of Wilno Will Not Die." *Ottawa Citizen*, 31 October 1998, A1.

MacGregor, Roy. *A Life in the Bush: Lessons from My Father*. Toronto: Penguin, 1999.

– *The Weekender: A Cottage Journal*. Toronto: Viking, 2005.

MacKay, Donald. *The Lumberjacks*. Toronto: Natural Heritage, 1998.

MacKay, Niall. *Over the Hills to Georgian Bay: The Ottawa, Arnprior and Parry Sound Railway*. Toronto: Stoddart, 1981.

MacMillan, Margaret. *Paris 1919: Six Months That Changed the World*. New York: Random House, 2003.

Magosci, Robert, and Christopher Hann, eds. *Galicia: A Multicultural Land*. Toronto: University of Toronto Press, 2005.

Majkowski, Alexander. *Historia Kaszubów*. Gdynia, 1938.

Makowski, William B. "Poles in Canada." In *Slavs in Canada: Volume 1*, edited by Yar Slavutych, 19–23. Edmonton: Proceedings of the First National Conference on Canadian Slavs, 9–12 June 1965.

– *History and Integration of Poles in Canada*. Niagara Peninsula: Canadian Polish Congress, 1967.

– *The Polish People in Canada: A Visual History*. Montreal: Tundra, 1987.

Mangalam, J.J., and Harry K. Schwartzweller. "Some Theoretical Guidelines Toward a Sociology of Migration." *International Migration Review* 4, no. 2 (Spring 1970): 5–21.

Manoeulian, Edward. "Invented Traditions: Primitivist Narrative and Design in the Polish Fin de Siècle." *Slavonic Review* 59, no. 2 (Summer 2000): 391–405.

Maracle, Stephen. "Fudging the Truth: A Tradition As Old as Uncle Tom." *The Globe and Mail*, 9 October 2010, F2.

Martel, René. *The Eastern Frontiers of Germany*. London: Williams and Northgate, 1930.

Martynowych, Orest. *Ukrainians in Canada: The Formative Years 1891–1924*. Edmonton: University of Alberta, 1991.

Mask-Connolly, Shirley. *Polish Pioneer Families in the Parish of Brudenell to the Year 1870*. Ottawa: Self-published, Doculink, 1996.

– "Walking the Missing Link of the Opeongo." *Eganville Leader*, 6 October 1999, A5.

– *Kashubia to Canada: The Shulist Story*. Ottawa: Self-published, 2001.

– *Brudenell Revisited: Supplement to Polish Pioneer Families in the Parish of Brudenell to 1870, with additional information, stories & photos*. Ottawa: Self-published, Doculink, 2002.

– *Kashubia to Canada: Crossing on the Agda*. Ottawa: Self-published, Doculink, 2003.

McAndrew, Marie. "School Spaces and the Construction of Ethnic Relations: Conceptual and Policy Debates." *Canadian Ethnic Studies* 35, no. 2 (2003): 14–29.

McCannell, Dean. *The Tourist: A New Theory of the Leisure Class*. Berkeley: University of California Press, 1999.

McGee, Thomas D'Arcy. *Emigration and Colonization in Canada: A Speech Delivered in the House of Assembly, Quebec, 25 April 1862*. Quebec: Hunter, Rose & Lemieux, 1862.

McKay, Ian. "Tartanism Triumphant: The Construction of Scottishness in Nova Scotia, 1933–1954." *Acadiensis* 21, no. 2 (Spring 1992): 5–47.

– *The Quest of the Folk: Antimodernism and Cultural Selection in Twentieth-Century Nova Scotia*. Montreal & Kingston: McGill-Queen's University Press, 1994.

McKeague, J.A., and P.C. Stobbe. *History of Soil Survey in Canada 1914–1975*. Ottawa: Department of Agriculture, 1978.

McLean, Marianne. "Peopling Glengarry County: The Scottish Origins of a Canadian Community." Canadian Historical Association, *Historical Papers* (1982): 156–71.

Medlicott, W.N. *Bismarck and Modern Germany*. London: English Universities Press, 1965.
Miller, Kerby A. *Emigrants and Exiles: Ireland and the Irish Exodus to North America*. New York: Oxford University Press, 1985.
Miller, Marilyn G. *Straight Lines in Curved Space: Colonization Roads in Eastern Ontario*. Toronto: Ministry of Culture and Recreation, 1978.
Moltmann, Günter. *Germans to America: 300 Years of Immigration 1683–1983*. Stuttgart: Eugen Heinz, 1982.
– "Steamship Transport of Emigrants from Europe to the United States, 1850–1915: Social, Commercial and Legislative Aspects." In *Maritime Aspects of Migration*, edited by Klaus Friedland, 309–20. Wien: Böhlau, 1989.
Moodie, Susanna. *Roughing it in the Bush or Forest Life in Canada*. Toronto: Bell & Cockburn, 1913.
Moogk, Peter N. "Reluctant Exiles: Emigrants from France in Canada before 1760." In *Immigration in Canada: Historical Perspectives*, edited by Gerald Tuchinsky, 8–47. Toronto: Copp Clark Longman, 1994.
Morawska, Ewa. "Ethnicity." In *Encyclopedia of Social History*, edited by Peter N. Stearns, 241–4. New York and London: Garland, 1994.
Mordawski, Jan. *Statystyka Ludnosci Kaszubskiej: Kaszubi u Progu XXI Wieku*. Gdansk: Instytut Kaszubski, 2005.
– *Geographia Kaszub*. Gdansk: Zrzeszenie Kaszubsko-Pomorskie, 2008.
Mortensen, Hans, Gertrud Mortensen, and Reinhard Wenskus. *Historisch-geographischer Atlas des Preußenlandes*. Wiesbaden: Franz Steiner Verlag, 1968.
Murdzek, Benjamin P. *Emigration in Polish Socio-Political Thought, 1870–1914*. New York: Columbia University Press, 1977.
Murray, Alexander. *Topographic Plan of the River Bonnechere & S.W. Branch of the Madawaska with a sketch of the Headwaters of the Ottonabee*, 1853.
Murray, Derek. "Narratives, Transitions and the Spaces Between Old and New: A Socio-Economic History of Brudenell, Ontario through the 1871 Census of Canada." Unpublished manuscript, Summer 2009.
Muzeum Kaszubskiego w Kartuzach. "Kaszëbë." 1999.
Nora, Pierre. "Between Memory and History: Les Lieux de Memoire." *Representations* 26 (Spring 1989): 7–25.
O'Brien, Matthew J. "New Wine in Old Skins: New Polish and Irish Immigrants and Polish- and Irish-American Ethnics." In *Irish and Polish Migration in Comparative Perspective*, edited by John Belchem and Klaus Tenfelde, 221–37. Essen: Klartext, 2003.
O'Dwyer, Reverend William C. *Highways of Destiny: A History of the Diocese of Pembroke, Ottawa Valley, Canada*. Ottawa: Le Droit, 1964.

Obracht-Prodzynski, Cezary. *Kaszubi dzisiaj: Kultura-Jezyk-Tozsamosc.* Gdansk: Instytut Kaszubski, 2007.
– *The Kashubs Today: Culture-Language-Identity.* Gdansk: Instytut Kaszubski, 2007.
Ogelman, Nedim. "Ethnicity, Demography, and Migration in the Evolution of the Polish Nation-State." *The Polish Review* 40, no. 2 (1995): 159–79.
Ontario Ministry of Agriculture, Food and Rural Affairs. "Classifying Prime and Marginal Agricultural Soils and Landscapes: Guidelines for Application of the Canada Land Inventory in Ontario." Accessed 16 October 2015. http://www.omafra.gov.on.ca/english/landuse/classify.htm
Ortner, Sherry B. *Anthropology and Social Theory: Culture, Power, and the Acting Subject.* Durham: Duke University Press, 2006.
Our Lady Seat of Wisdom Academy. "Michael O'Brien Named Artist and Writer in Residence." Accessed 5 August 2010. http://www.seatofwisdom.org/news/latest/michael-obrien-namedartist-and-writer-in-residence.html.
Owram, Doug. *Promise of Eden: The Canadian Expansionist Movement and the Idea of the West 1856–1900.* Toronto: University of Toronto Press, 1992.
Pace, Judith L., and Annette Hemmings. "Understanding Authority in Classrooms: A Review of Theory, Ideology, and Research." *Review of Educational Research* 77, no. 1 (March 2007): 4–27.
Pain, Howard. *The Heritage of Upper Canadian Furniture.* Toronto: Van Nostrand-Reinhold, 1978.
Pakulski, Jan. "Polish Migrants in Hobart: A Study in Community Formation." In *Polish People and Culture in Australia*, edited by Roland Sussex and Jerzy Zubrzycki. Canberra: Australian National University, 1985.
Parker, Keith A. "Colonization Roads and Commercial Policy." *Ontario History* 67 (1975): 31–9.
Parr Traill, Catherine. *The Canadian Settler's Guide.* Toronto: McClelland and Stewart, 1969.
– *The Backwoods of Canada.* Toronto: McClelland and Stewart, 1971.
Parson, Helen E. "The Colonization of the Southern Canadian Shield in Ontario: The Hastings Road." *Ontario History* 79, no. 3 (1987): 15–28.
Paszkowski, Lech. *Poles in Australia and Oceania 1790–1940.* Sydney: Pergamon, 1987.
Patterson, Sheila. "This New Canada." *Queen's Quarterly* 62 (1955): 80–8.
Paulsen, Ryan. "Wilno Heritage Society Honoured at Ceremony." *Pembroke Observer*, 25 November 2009, B8.
Pekacz, Jolanta T. *Music in the Culture of Polish Galicia, 1772–1914.* Rochester: University of Rochester Press, 2002.

Peredo, Sandra. "Count Dracula in Canada? They Worry About Vampires in Wilno, Ont." *The Canadian Magazine*, 22 September 1973.

Perin, Roberto. "Clio as an Ethnic: The Third Force in Canadian Historiography." *Canadian Historical Review* 64, no. 4 (1983): 441–67.

– "Writing About Ethnicity." In *Writing About Canada: A Handbook for Modern Canadian History*, edited by John Schultz, 201–30. Toronto: Prentice/Hall, 1990.

Perkowski, Jan L. "The Kashubs: Origins and Emigration to the U.S." *Polish American Studies* 23, no. 1 (January–June 1966): 1–7.

– *A Kashubian Idiolect in the United States*. Bloomington: Indiana University Press, 1969.

– *Vampires, Dwarves, and Witches Among the Ontario Kashubs*. Ottawa: Canadian Centre for Folk Culture Studies, National Museum of Man, 1972.

– *Vampire Lore: From the Writings of Jan Louis Perkowski*. Bloomington: Slavica, 2006.

Petersen, William. "A General Typology of Migration." In *Readings in the Sociology of Migration*, edited by Clifford J. Jansen, 49–63. Toronto: Pergamon, 1970.

Pflanze, Otto. *Bismarck and the Development of Germany: The Period of Unification, 1815–1871*. Princeton: Princeton University Press, 1963.

Piekarski, Adam. *The Church in Poland: Facts, Figures, Information*. Warsaw: Interpress, 1978.

Piskorz-Branekova, Elżbieta. *Polska Stroje ludowe*. Warsaw, 2008.

Poliakoff, Vladimir. *Eagles Black and White: The Fight for the Sea*. London: D. Appleton and Company, 1929.

Polish Cultural Institute. *The Kashubian Polish Community of Southeastern Minnesota*. Chicago: Arcadia, 2001.

Polyakov, V. "The Valley of the Vistula." *The Slavonic and East European Review* 12, no. 34 (July 1933): 36–62.

Pope Pius IX. "Quod Nunquam: On the Church in Prussia," (5 February 1875). Accessed 5 August 2010. http://www.papalencyclicals.net/Pius09/p9quodnu.htm.

Popowska-Taborska, Hanna. *Kaszubszczyzna: Zarys dziejów*. Warszawa: Panstwowe Wydawnictwo Naukowe, 1980.

Porter, Anna. *The Ghosts of Europe: Journeys Through Central Europe's Troubled Past and Uncertain Future*. Vancouver: Douglas & McIntyre, 2010.

Porter, Brian. "Patriotism, Prophecy, and the Catholic Hierarchy in Nineteenth-Century Poland." *Catholic Historical Review* 82, no. 9 (April 2003): 213–39.

Praszalowicz, Dorota. "Jewish, Polish and German Migration from the Prussian Province of Posen/Poznań during the 19th Century." In *Irish and Polish*

Migration in Comparative Perspective, edited by John Belchem and Klaus Tenfelde, 135–55. Essen: Klartext, 2003.

– "Overseas Migration from Partitioned Poland: Poznania and Eastern Galicia as Case Studies." *Polish American Studies* 60, no. 2 (Autumn 2003): 59–81.

– "Local Community and Nineteenth Century Migrations: Poznanian Kloszczewo and Zaniemysl (Prussian Poland)." In *European Mobility: Internal, International, and Transatlantic Moves in the 19th and Early 20th Centuries,* edited by Annemarie Steidl, Josef Ehmer, Stan Nadel, and Hermann Zeithofer, 175–88. Goettingen: V&R unipress, 2009.

Price, Mrs Carl, and Clyde C. Kennedy. *Notes on the History of Renfrew County.* Pembroke: Renfrew County Council, 1961.

Prince, Theresa. *The Kovalskie (Kowalski) Family of Barry's Bay.* Ottawa: Self-published, Doculink, 2006.

Quay, Sara E. *Westward Expansion.* Westport: Greenwood, 2002.

Rabinow, Paul, and Nikolas Rose, eds. *The Essential Foucault: Selections from the Essential Words of Foucault, 1954–1984.* New York: New Press, 2003.

Radecki, Henry, and Benedykt Heydenkorn. *A History of Canada's Peoples: A Member of a Distinguished Family: The Polish Group in Canada.* Toronto: McClelland and Stewart, 1976.

Radecki, Henry. *Ethnic Organizational Dynamics: The Polish Group in Canada.* Waterloo: Wilfrid Laurier University Press, 1979.

Radforth, Ian. *Bushworkers and Bosses: Logging in Northern Ontario, 1900–1980.* Toronto: University of Toronto Press, 1987.

Radziłowski, John. "Out on the Wind: Life in Minnesota's Polish Farming Communities." *Minnesota History* 58, no. 1 (2002): 16–28.

Ramirez, Bruno. *On the Move: French-Canadian and Italian Migrants in the North Atlantic Economy, 1860–1914.* Toronto: McClelland and Stewart, 1991.

Ramułt, Stefan. *Słownik języka pomorskiego, czyli kaszubskiego.* Kraków, 1893.

– *Statystyka ludności kaszubskiej.* Kraków, 1899.

Reczynska, Anna. "Emigration from the Polish Territories to Canada up until World War Two." *Polyphony* 6, no. 2 (1984): 11–19.

Reinerman, Alan J. "Metternich, Pope Gregory XVI, and Revolutionary Poland 1831–1842." *The Catholic Historical Review* 86, no. 4 (October 2000): 603–19.

Rekowski, Fr Aloysius. *The Saga of the Kashub People in Poland, Canada, U.S.A.* Saskatoon: Self-published, 1997.

Renkiewicz, Frank. *The Polish Presence in Canada and America.* Toronto: MHSO, 1982.

Richards, J.H. "Lands and Policies: Attitudes and Controls in the Alienation of Lands in Ontario during the First Century of Settlement." *Ontario History* 50 (1958): 193–209.

Richter, Werner. *Bismarck.* London: Macdonald, 1969.

Ritter, Gerhard. *The Sword and the Scepter: The Problem of Militarism in Germany, Volume 1: The Prussian Tradition 1740–1890*. Coral Gables: University of Miami Press, 1969.
Robertson, John. "Agricultural Report on the County of Carleton." *Journal and Transactions of the Board of Agriculture of Upper Canada* 4, no. 1 (January 1856).
Robinson, J.H., ed. *Readings in European History* 2. Boston: Ginn, 1906.
Ross, Ronald J. "The Kulturkampf: Restrictions and Controls on the Practice of Religion in Bismarck's Germany." In *Freedom and Religion in the Nineteenth Century*, edited by Richard Helmstadter, 172–95. Stanford: Stanford University Press, 1997.
– *The Failure of Bismarck's Kulturkampf: Catholicism and State Power in Imperial Germany, 1871–1887*. Washington: Catholic University of America Press, 1998.
Ruby, Robert H., and John A. Brown. *Indians of the Pacific Northwest: A History*. Norman: University of Oklahoma Press, 1988.
Sadkowski, Tadeusz. *Drewniana Architektura Sakralna Na Pormorzu Gdanskim w XVII–XX*. Gdanskie Towarzystwo Naukowe: Gdansk, 1997.
Salminen, Tapani. "UNESCO Red Book on Endangered Languages: Europe." Accessed 1 June 2015. http://www.helsinki.fi/~tasalmin/europe_report.html.
Salmonowicz, Stanislaw. "The Culture of Eastern Pomerania at the Threshold of the Modern Era." *Acta Poloniae Historica* 81 (2000): 117–44.
Sanford, Albert Hart. "Polish People of Portage County." In *Proceedings of the State Historical Society of Wisconsin*, 259–88. Madison: State Historical Society of Wisconsin, 1902.
Schama, Simon. *Landscape and Memory*. New York: Vintage, 1995.
Schleinitz, W. *Topographisch-statistische Beschreibung des Kreises Carthaus nebst OrtschaftsVerzeichniß. Nach amtlichen Quellen zusammengestellt*. Danzig: Kafemann, 1880.
Schneider, Laura. "Of Pioneers, Victorians, and 'Indians': Rethinking Aboriginal Representation in Ontario's Community History Museums." MA Art History Thesis, Carleton University, 2008.
Schöberl, Ingrid. "Emigration Policy in Germany and Immigration Policy in the United States." In *Germans to America: 300 Years of Immigration 1683–1983*, edited by Gunter Moltmann, 36–43. Stuttgart: Eugen Heinz, 1982.
Schulist, David. "A Kashubian Treasure on the Top of Our Tongue." *Kashubian Association of North America Newsletter* (Summer 2001): 6–8.
Scott, James S. *Seeing Like a State: How Certain Schemes to Improve the Human Condition Have Failed*. New Haven: Yale University Press, 1998.

Séguin, Normand. *La Conquête du sol au XIXe siècle.* Sillery: Boréal, 1977.
Seixas, Peter. "What Is Historical Consciousness?" In *To the Past: History Education, Public Memory & Citizenship in Canada*, edited by Ruth W. Sandwell, 11–22. Toronto: University of Toronto Press, 2006.
Seymour, Andrew. "'Deep Breach of Trust': Sentence Sets Stage for Massive Lawsuits Against Church. Former Pembroke Priest and Vatican Insider Gets Four Years for Sexually Abusing Boys." *Ottawa Citizen*, 15 January 2008, A1, D7.
– "Priest, Church Face Lawsuits: Retired Vatican Official Convicted in January of Sexual Assault." *Ottawa Citizen*, 7 April 2008, C1.
Shalla, Elizabeth. "(1890–1978) Memoirs." Unpublished manuscript.
Shaw, Bernard S. *The Opeongo: Dreams, Despair and Deliverance.* Burnstown: General Store Publishing House, 1994.
Shepherd, William. *Historical Atlas.* New York: Barnes and Noble, 1929.
Showalter, Dennis. "Prussia's Army: Continuity and Change, 1713–1830." In *The Rise of Prussia 1700–1830*, edited by Philip G. Dwyer, 220–36. Essex: Pearson Longman, 2000.
Silverman, Deborah Anders. "Dyngus Days and Koledy Nights: Folk Celebrations in Polish-American Communities." *New York Folklore* 23, nos. 1–4 (1997): 25–37.
Smallfield, Albert, ed. *Lands and Resources of Renfrew County, Province of Ontario: A Hand-book.* Renfrew: Renfrew Mercury, 1881.
Smith, Charles H., and Ian Dyck, eds. *William E. Logan's 1845 survey of the Upper Ottawa Valley.* Gatineau: Canadian Museum of Civilization, 2007.
Smolicz, J.J., and M.J. Secombe. "Polish Culture and Education in Australia: A Review of Some Recent Research and Educational Developments." In *Polish People and Culture in Australia*, edited by Roland Sussex and Jerzy Zubrzycki. Canberra: Australian National University, 1985.
Snyder, Louis L. *The Blood and Iron Chancellor.* Princeton: D. Van Nostrand, 1967.
Socha-Borzestowski, Br. "A Note on the Folk-Art of Cassubia." *Folklore* 81, no. 3 (Autumn 1980): 195–7.
Sollars, Werner, ed. *The Invention of Ethnicity.* New York: Oxford University Press, 1989.
Spragge, George W. "Colonization Roads in Canada West 1850–1867." *Ontario History* 49, no. 1 (1957): 1–17.
Stamplecoskie, Ray. "Vampire Tale Drives Stake Through Wilno." *Ottawa Citizen*, 10 September 1989, A8.
Starczewska, Maria. "The Historical Geography of the Oldest Settlement in the United States." *The Polish Review* 12, no. 2 (Spring 1967): 11–40.

Statistische Darstellung des Berenter Kreises im Regierungsbezirk Danzig mit Berücksichtigung der Geschichte, Physiographie etc. Nebst dem Wissenswerthesten aus sämmtlichen Verwaltungszweigen. Berent, 1863.

Stauter-Halsted, Keely. *The Nation in the Village: The Genesis of Peasant National Identity in Austrian-Poland 1848–1914.* Ithaca: Cornell University Press, 2001.

Steitz, Walter. *Die Entstehung Der Kön-Mindener Eisenbahngesellschaft: Ein Beitrag Zur Frühgeschichte der Deutschen Eisenbahnen und des Preussischen Aktienwesens.* Köln: Rheinisch-Westfälischen Wirtschaftsarchiv, 1974.

Stelmachowska, Bozena. *Szutka Ludowa Na Kaszubach.* Poznań, 1937.

– *Strój Kaszubski.* Wroclaw, 1959.

Steutter, Mattaeus. *Ductatus Pomeraniae cum magna Maris Balthici Et Provinciarum Ad Nexarum Parte Ad delineationem novissimam sculpsit et excudit.* Augsburg, c. 1725.

Stone, Gerald. "The Language of Cassubian Literature and the Question of a Literary Standard." *The Slavonic and East European Review* 50, no. 121 (October 1972): 521–9.

Stolarik, M. Mark. "Multiculturalism in Canada: A Slovak Perspective." *Canadian Ethnic Studies* 35, no. 2 (2003): 123–8.

Sulimierskiego, Filipa, Bronislawa Chlebowskiego, and Wladyslawa Walewskiego. *Slownik Geograficzny Królestwa Polskiego.* Volumes 2–14. Warszawa, 1880–1884.

Sussex, Roland, and Jerzy Zubrzycki, eds. *Polish People and Culture in Australia.* Canberra: Australian National University, 1985.

Svitlana, Krys. "Jan Louis Perkowski: Vampire Lore: From the Writings of Jan Louis Perkowski." *Canadian Slavonic Papers* 51, no. 1 (March 2009): 116–18.

Swyripa, Frances. *Wedded to the Cause: Ukrainian-Canadian Women and Ethnic Identity 1891–1991.* Toronto: University of Toronto Press, 1993.

– "The Mother of God Wears a Maple Leaf: History, Gender, and Ethnic Identity in Sacred Space." In *Sisters or Strangers? Immigrant, Ethnic, and Racialized Women in Canadian History*, edited by Marlene Epp, Franca Iacovetta, and Frances Swyripa, 341–61. Toronto: University of Toronto Press, 2004.

Szulist, W. *Kaszubi Kanadyjscy: Okres Pionierski I Dzien Dzisiejszy.* Gdansk: Arkun, 1992.

Szulist, Wladyslaw. *Towards Heights of Polishness: Kashubian Identity and True Scholarship.* Gdansk: Self-published, 2007.

Tetzner, Franz. *Die Slowinzen und Lebakaschuben.* Berlin, 1899.

The American Heritage Dictionary of the English Language. Boston: Houghton Mifflin Company, 1992.

The Kashubian Pomeranian Association. *The Unknown Kashubia: A Few Things Worth Knowing About Kashubia.* Gdansk, 2008.

The Oral History Project of the Barry's Bay Public Library. "A Local Pastor: Oral History with Rev. Msgr. J.A. Pick. Interviewed by Jenifer McVaugh," 1991.
- "Land is the Land: John Mintha. Interviewed by Jenifer McVaugh," 1991.
- "Needed at Home: Oral History with Mary Smaglinski Burant. Interviewed by Jenifer McVaugh," 1992–93.
- "You Have to Do What Comes to Your Hands: Oral History with Rose (Burchat) Chapeskie. Interviewed by Jenifer McVaugh," 1992–93.

The Resources of the Ottawa District. Ottawa: The Times, 1872.

The Wilno Heritage Society. Accessed 5 August 2010. http://www.wilno.org.

Thistlewaite, Frank. "Migration in Europe Overseas in the 19th and 20th Centuries." XIe Congrès International des Sciences Historiques. *Rapports, V: Histoire Contemporaine*, 32–60. Goteborg/Stockholm/Uppsala: Almquiste Wiksell, 1960.

Thomas, William I., and Florian Znaniecki. *The Polish Peasant in Europe and America. Vol. 1*. New York: Dover, 1958.

Thompson, Don W. *Men and Meridians: The History of Surveying and Mapping in Canada*. Volume 1: Prior to 1867. Ottawa: Queen's Printer, 1966.

Tivy, Mary. "Museums, Visitors and the Reconstruction of the Past in Ontario." *Material History Review* 37 (Spring 1993): 35–51.

Toops, Gary H. "Marlena Porębska: *Das Kashubische: Sprachtod oder Revitalisierung?* Book Review." *Canadian Slavonic Papers* 49, nos. 1–2 (March–June 2007): 160–2.

Topolińska, Zuzanna. *A Historical Phonology of the Kashubian Dialects of Polish*. The Hague: Mouton & Company, 1974.

Torpey, John. *The Invention of the Passport: Surveillance, Citizenship and the State*. Cambridge: Cambridge University Press, 2000.

Tracey, Gerald. "Music of the Kashubs Becomes Part of the Archives Series." *Eganville Leader*, 17 May 2006, 8.

Trencsényi, Balász, and Michal Kopeček. *Discourses of Collective Identity in Central and Southeast Europe (1770–1945): Texts and Commentaries. Volume 1: Late Enlightenment – Emergence of the Modern 'National Idea.'* Budapest: Central European University Press, 2006.

Trzeciakowski, Lech. *The Kulturkampf in Prussian Poland*. Trans. Katarzyna Kretkowska. New York: Columbia University Press, 1990.

Tuan, Yi-Fu. *Space and Place: The Perspective of Experience*. Minneapolis: University of Minnesota Press, 2005.

Turner, Wesley B. "William Hutton." In *Dictionary of Canadian Biography* IX, University of Toronto, 2000. Accessed 5 August 2010. http://www.biographi.ca.

Tymieniecki, K. *History of Polish Pomerania*. Poznań: The Society of Lovers of History, 1929.

Van Horn Melton, James. *Absolutism and the Eighteenth-Century Origins of Compulsory Schooling in Prussia and Austria*. Cambridge: Cambridge University Press, 1988.

Vasta, Ellie. "Immigrants and the Paper Market: Borrowing, Renting and Buying Identities." *Ethnic and Racial Studies* 34, no. 2 (February 2011): 187–206.

Vecoli, Rudolph J. "Contadini in Chicago: A Critique of the Uprooted." *The Journal of American History* 51, no. 3 (December 1964): 404–17.

– "We Study the Present to Understand the Past." *Journal of American Ethnic History* 18, no. 4 (Summer 1999): 115–25.

Village of Barry's Bay 50th Anniversary. Barry's Bay, 1983.

www.kashub.com. Accessed 20 August 2010.

Wagner, Jonathan. *A History of Migration from Germany to Canada 1850–1939*. Vancouver: UBC Press, 2006.

Wagner, William. *Canada: Ein kurzer abriss von dessen Geographischer Lage, sowie Production, Klima und Bodenbeschaffenheit, Erziehungs und Municipal Wesen, Fischereien, Eisenbahnen u.s.w.* Berlin: L. Burckhardt, 1860.

Walaszek, Adam. "Migracje i Ziemie Polskie w Dobie Masowych Wedrówek Zarobkowych." *Przeglad Polonijy* 18, no. 3 (1992): 43–65.

Walker, Mack. *Germany and the Emigration, 1816–1885*. Cambridge: Harvard University Press, 1964.

Walser Smith, Helmut. "Prussia at the Margins: or the World that Nationalism Lost." In *German History from the Margins*, edited by Neil Gregor, Nils Roemer, and Mark Roseman, 69–83. Bloomington: Indiana University Press, 2006.

Walsh, John. "Ethnicity, Family, and Community: German Canadians in Suburban Ottawa, 1890–1914." In *A Chorus of Different Voices: German-Canadian Identities*, edited by Angelika E. Sauer and Matthias Zimmer, 143–65. New York: P. Lang, 1998.

Walsh, John C. "Landscapes of Longing: Colonization and the Problem of State Formation in Canada West." PhD dissertation, University of Guelph, 2001.

– "Performing Public Memory and Re-Placing Home in the Ottawa Valley, 1900–58." In *Placing Memory and Remembering Place in Canada*, edited by James Opp and John C. Walsh, 25–56. Vancouver: UBC Press, 2010.

Walsh, John C., and Steven High. "Rethinking the Concept of Community." *Social History* 32, no. 64 (1999): 255–73.

Wandycz, Piotr S. *The Lands of Partitioned Poland, 1795–1918*. Seattle: University of Washington Press, 1996.

- *The Price of Freedom: A History of East Central Europe from the Middle Ages to the Present*. 2nd ed. New York: Routledge, 2001.
Warmińska, Katarzyna. "To Be or Not to Be a Minority Group? Identity Dilemmas of Kashubian and Polish Tatars." In *Multiple Identities: Migrants, Ethnicity, and Membership*, edited by Paul Spickard, 114–33. Bloomington: Indiana University Press, 2013.
Weber, Max. *The Theory of Social and Economic Organization*. New York: Henderson and Parsons, 1947.
Wells, H.G. *The Outline of History*. New York: Macmillan, 1921.
Wenkstern, Otto. *Prussia and the Poles*. London: Mann Nephews, 1892.
Whitton, Charlotte. *Hundred Years A-Fellen'*. Ottawa: Runge, 1943.
Wieniewski, Ignacy. *Heritage, The Foundations of Polish Culture: An Introductory Outline*. 2nd ed. Toronto: University of Toronto Press, 1981.
Wigzell, Faith. "Perkowski, J.L. 'The Darkling. A Treatise on Slavic Vampirism' (Book Review)." *Slavonic and East European Review* 69, no. 3 (July 1991): 546.
Wilno Heritage Society. *Kashub/Polish Heritage Stories of Renfrew County: 1. Wilno and Area*. Wilno: Self-published, 2000.
Williams, Donna E. *Hardscrabble: The High Cost of Free Land*. Toronto: Dundurn, 2013.
Wilson, Catharine Anne. *Tenants in Time: Family Strategies, Land, and Liberalism in Upper Canada, 1799–1871*. Montreal & Kingston: McGill-Queen's University Press, 2009.
Wood, J. David. *Making Ontario: Agricultural Colonization and Landscape Re-Creation Before the Railway*. Montreal & Kingston: McGill-Queen's University Press, 2000.
Woodsworth, James S. *Strangers Within Our Gates, or, Coming Canadians*. Toronto: F.C. Stephenson, 1909.
- *My Neighbour*. Toronto: Missionary Society of the Methodist Church, 1911.
Wright, Donald. *The Professionalization of History in English Canada*. Toronto: University of Toronto Press, 2005.
Wynn, Graeme. "Notes on Society and Environment in Old Ontario." *Journal of Social History* 13, no. 1 (Autumn 1979): 49–65.
Wytrwal, Joseph A. *America's Polish Heritage: A Social History of the Poles in America*. Detroit: Endurance Press, 1961.
Young, James E. *The Texture of Memory: Holocaust Memorials and Meaning*. New Haven: Yale University Press, 1993.
Zabrovsky, Danna. "Virginia Woman Falls in Love with Ottawa Phantom." *Ottawa Citizen*, 16 August 2010, A1.
Zamoyski, Adam. *The Polish Way: A Thousand-Year History of the Poles and their Culture*. New York: Hippocrene, 1994.

Zeitlin, Richard H. "White Eagles in the North Woods: Polish Immigration to Rural Wisconsin 1857–1900." *The Polish Review* 25, no. 198: 69–92.

Zeller, Susanne. *Land of Promise, Promised Land: The Culture of Victorian Science in Canada*. Ottawa: Canadian Historical Association, 1996.

– *Inventing Canada: Early Victorian Science and the Idea of a Transcontinental Nation*. Montreal & Kingston: McGill-Queen's University Press, 2009.

Zembrzycki, Stacie Raeanna. "Memory, Identity, and the Challenge of Community Among Ukrainians in the Sudbury Region, 1901–1939." PhD dissertation, Carleton University, 2007.

Zubrzycki, Jerzy. "Polish Emigration to British Commonwealth Countries: A Demographic Survey." *International Migration Review* 13, no. 4 (Winter 1979): 650–3.

Zucchi, John E. *Italians in Toronto: Development of a National Identity, 1875–1935*. Montreal & Kingston: McGill-Queen's University Press, 1988.

Zurakowski, Anna. *The Proud Inheritance: Ontario's Kaszuby*. Ottawa: The Polish Heritage Institute-Kaszuby, 1991.

INDEX

1848, revolutions of, 58, 87–9, 98, 185, 287n47

Agda, 49, 104, 106, 129, 277n8
agro-forest economy, 162–9, 172
alcoholism, 89, 123, 249, 250
Allgemeine Auswanderungs-Zeitung, 112, 139, 280n43
American wakes, 121–2
anti-Enlightenment campaign, 86, 89
anti-Semitism, 95, 272n71
authority, types of, 14–15, 20–3, 36

Barry's Bay, Ontario: cultural changes, 177, 216, 230, 235; regional and cultural descriptions, 3–7, 12, 19, 36–52, 161, 170–1, 226, 246, 250. *See also* Wilno
Bell, Robert, surveyor, 154, 159–60
Biernacki, Msgr Peter, 38–9, 218, 264n72
Bismarck, Otto von, 4, 9, 34, 56–9, 67, 73, 77, 80, 83–100
Blank, Clifford, 223, 227, 229, 240
Blank, Frances (Shulist), 30
Booth, John R., 165–7, 171
Borzyszkowski, Jozef, 66–8, 182, 186, 197, 200, 213
Bremen, 107, 109, 114, 127–9, 138–140, 180, 280n47, 287n45,
Bridgland, James W., 158
Brudenell, 6, 38, 49, 116–7, 154–5, 159–60, 166

Buchanan, A.C., 136–41, 285n11
Burritt, Hamlet, 159–60

Campbell, Evelyn, 137
Canadian Museum of Civilization. *See* Museum of Man
canton system, 78, 96
Cassub, origins of title, 179–85
Cenôva, Florjan, 185–8, 198–9, 225, 229–30
Chippior, Ed, 224–6, 234, 242–3, 247
chłopy. *See* peasants
Chojnice, 5, 70–1, 73, 78, 80–1, 126, 128, 185, 195–6
Clemow, Francis, 137, 142, 285n11
clergy in Poland, 60–6, 77–9, 85–95, 281n73
clothing, Kashubian, 184, 198
colonization roads, 3–4, 24, 143, 149, 153, 163–4, 172. *See also* Opeongo Colonization Road
Combermere, 47, 105, 216, 235
Cooley, Timothy, 222, 231, 234, 240

Davies, Norman, 64, 77, 268n13
Dembski, Fr L., 38, 144, 216
Derdowski, Hieronim, 115, 187, 199
Deutsche Auswander-Zeitung, 139, 143
Devine, Thomas, 156–9

Egan, John, 3, 162–3
Eisenstein, Charles, 10, 138–40

Elliott, Bruce S., 53, 165, 169
embroidery: in Ontario, 47, 213–14, 217, 219, 230, 235–6, 240, 243; in Poland, 191, 198, 202–5, 213. *See also* Wilno: embroidery
emigration: agents, 9, 48, 112, 129, 135–45, 156; guidebooks, 134–7; passports, 8, 78, 83, 99, 126
Enlightenment in Prussian Poland, 73, 76, 86
Etmanski, Wojciech, 13, 213, 215, 227, 238

Fedorowicz, Jan, 62–4, 248
Felician Sisters, 40
Fischer, Adam, 29, 181–4, 195–6
folk, concept of, 178–9
Franco-Prussian War, 56, 95
Free Grants and Homesteads Act (1868), 116, 167
free land, 10–11, 57–8, 130, 132–4, 139–140
French, Thomas Patrick, 10–11, 33, 118, 120–1, 132–43, 145–7, 157–61, 166, 229
furniture, 35, 49, 74, 191, 202, 214, 242, 244; folk, 203–4, 230. *See also* Wilno: furniture

Galicia: emigrants from, 4–6; history of, 69, 122–3, 249, 271n3
Gans, Herbert, 222, 232, 239
Gdańsk, 66, 73, 78, 89, 126–8, 182–5, 193, 196–7, 205
genealogy, 25, 50, 59, 85, 177, 212, 233
Geological Survey of Canada, 149, 153
German immigrants, 3, 34–5, 97, 114
Glofcheskie, Beverly, 247
Glofcheskie, John, 29, 31–2, 57, 70, 84
Glofcheskie, Peter, 218, 223, 247

Golden Freedom, 63, 76
Górale, 191, 240
Grand Trunk Railway, 138, 142
griffin, symbol and meaning, 198–201, 213, 216–17, 245
Gross, Michael, 86, 95
Grzondziel, Fr Rafał, 7, 36, 59, 82, 115
Gulgowska, Teodora, 191–3, 202–4, 235
Gulgowski, Izydor, 182, 191–3, 203

Hagarty, Township of, 116, 148, 155–6, 159–161, 165–6
Hagen, William, 66, 74, 76, 79
Hansen, Marcus, 29, 128, 222
Harper, Stephen, 217–18
Hessel, Peter, 34–7, 48, 52, 103, 145, 147
Heydenkorn, Benedykt, 10, 28, 144
Hutton, William, 136–8, 142, 151, 156

Iacovetta, Franca, 10, 14–15, 31, 59, 222
Ickiewicz, Kazmierz, 10, 35, 68, 133
identities: multiple, 13, 221–3, 236; preservation of, 13, 29, 40–2, 188, 198, 206–9, 222–3, 232–3, 238, 246; Ukrainian, 235, 249
infallibility, doctrine of, 60, 91
Instytut Kaszubski, 182, 197
Irish immigrants, 3, 35, 100, 110, 117, 121–2, 137, 149

Jaworska, Mira, 38, 40–1, 223
Jesuits, 77, 89, 90, 93
Jost, Isabella, 10, 28, 33, 57, 82, 105, 133, 147

Kartuzy, 81, 195, 199, 202–5, 243
Kashubian language, creation of, 12, 185–97

Kashubian Pomeranian Association, 12, 177, 182–3, 196–208, 213, 218, 220, 229–30, 236, 246
Kaszub, origins of title. *See* Cassub
Kieniewicz, Stefan, 63, 68, 82
Killaloe, 6, 247–8
kolędy, 41
Kościerzyna, 5, 70–1, 80–1, 126–9, 191, 194–6
Kraków, 46, 62
Kulas, Julian, 211, 221, 223, 225–6
Kulturkampf, 4, 58, 60, 67, 84–95, 100, 188

Landrat, 76, 78
Lee-Whiting, Brenda, 32–35, 49, 52, 57, 97, 114, 134, 137, 140, 145
Leśno, 70–3, 79, 80–2, 89, 96, 125, 225, 253–6
Lewandowski, Maximilian, 202–4
lieux de mémoire, 22, 53, 247
Lipusz, 70–3, 79–82, 89–90, 95–6, 253–6
literacy, 81, 115–21, 131, 188, 225
Lorentz, Friedrich, 29, 180–96, 205, 228

Madawaska River, 162, 164
Makowski, William B., 10, 25–6, 28–9, 32–3, 52, 67, 84, 119–20
Mask-Connolly, Shirley: biographical details, 49–50, 234; curatorial work, 214, 218, 242, 247; on Kashubs and ethnicity, 51–2, 207, 212, 220–5, 227, 229, 250, 256; on literacy, 115, 119, 121; on migration, 10, 101–11, 131, 134, 138, 143; on Poland, 58–9, 67, 70, 78, 84, 95, 207; writing about the land, 11, 143–6

Massachusetts, migrants from, 5, 6, 256, 258n9
McGee, Thomas D'Arcy, 151, 157
memory, fields of, 11, 21–3
Miller, Marilyn, 24, 121, 134, 145, 169–71
Minnesota, 59, 115, 129, 165–6, 245
Murdzek, Benjamin, 86–7, 94, 249
museums: in Ontario, 12, 22, 42, 47, 49, 58, 214, 219, 242–8; in Poland, 191, 199, 217, 236, 245
Museum of Man, 29, 31–2

New York, 106–11, 129
nobility, 46, 62, 64, 68, 76, 78–9, 86–7, 193. *See also szlachta*

O'Dwyer, Fr William, 9–10, 26, 29, 57, 84, 100–5, 124, 131, 258n9
Opeongo Colonization Road: advertisement of, 10, 134, 139; Battle of Brudenell, 49; description and creation of, 154–5, 159–64, 170; settlers on the road, 6, 10, 12, 19, 32–3, 38, 40, 119, 157, 165, 174; timber and timber rights, 168–9
Ottawa-Huron Tract, 143–73

parish picnics, 38, 39
Parr Traill, Catherine, 136, 156
peasants, emancipation of, 9, 60, 62, 69, 76, 92, 122; holdings, 70, 122–3
Perin, Roberto, 29, 43, 59, 208, 242
Perkowski, Jan, 29–31, 36, 51–2
Pick, Msgr Ambrose, 59, 70, 82, 144, 167, 211, 227, 229
Poland, partitioning of, 15, 60–7, 70, 73–4, 87–8, 181–8, 211
Poles in Canada, statistics, 6–7

Polish Canadian Pioneer Centre, 42, 46, 213, 265n86
Polish language instruction, 27, 40–1, 47, 80
Polishness, 37–47, 94, 213, 226–7, 248
Pomerania, 34, 69–70, 74, 100, 140–1, 180–201; dukes of, 181, 193, 196, 200
Pope Gregory XIV, 88, 182
Pope John Paul II, 38, 197
Pope Pius IX, 92–3
Portage County. See Wisconsin
Poznań, 5–6, 50, 80, 94, 196, 287n47
Prince, Adam, 167, 254
Prince, Bernard, 35, 42; sexual abuse convictions, 51–2
Prince, Theresa, 11, 51, 53, 85, 131, 143–7, 171, 234–5
Protestants in Prussian Poland, 66, 81, 94, 208
Prussia: military and militarism, 56, 66, 78, 83, 95–8, 126, 185; railways in, 126–8

Quebec, Port of, 10, 100, 103, 106–12, 129, 136–40

Radecki, Henry, 10, 28, 52, 144
railways in Prussian Poland, 126–8
Ramirez, Bruno, 53, 55, 59
Ramułt, Stefan, 188–9, 206, 225
Rekowski, Fr Aloysius: on Kashubs and ethnicity, 49, 51–3, 102, 173, 189, 207, 210–11, 226, 229; on language, 43, 189–90, 211; on literacy, 115, 119–21; on migration, 9–10, 48, 101–6; on Poland, 48, 58, 67, 70, 84, 134, 143, 229; writing about the land, 11, 144–7, 169, 171, 173

Renfrew County, 3, 6, 26, 34, 42, 116, 134, 140, 147–8, 198
Renfrew Mercury, 158, 164, 166–8
Ritza, Frank, 42, 47, 56, 59, 83, 105, 243
Ross, Ronald, 86, 94
Royal Commission on Bilingualism and Biculturalism, 26–7, 225

schools: in Austrian Poland, 123; in Canada, 6, 27, 37, 40–2, 46–8, 120, 223, 234–6, 247–8; in Prussian Poland, 57–9, 79–85, 92–4, 115, 188, 191, 193, 197, 204; Prussian inspectors, 79, 92, 94, 273n82
Sejm, 63–4
serfs, 60–3, 69, 76, 139
Shalla, Elizabeth (Etmanski), 41, 45, 59, 105
shanties, 119, 162, 164, 167, 170–1
Sherwood, Township of, 46, 117, 119–20, 148, 155, 161, 166
Shulist, David, 43, 210, 212–30, 234
Shulist, Martin, 42, 46–7, 213, 232, 234, 262n39, 265n86
Sims, A.H., 159
Sinn, William, 10, 34–5, 128, 137–45
skansen, 243–5, 248
slaves, 57, 67, 85, 110, 112, 128
soil surveys, Canadian, 11, 33, 144–9
St Hedwig's Parish (Barry's Bay), 26, 38–41, 103, 214, 218, 227, 239
St Mary's Parish (Wilno), 26, 38, 40, 214, 218, 227, 235
St Stanislaus Kostka Parish (Wilno), 5, 38, 242
szlachta, 60–9, 76, 79, 87, 123, 193, 268n13. See also nobility

Thistlewaite, Frank, 27, 55–6

timber industry in the Ottawa Valley, 3, 151, 156, 160–71
Tusk, Donald, 217, 246

Wagner, William, 34, 70, 129, 132, 141, 145
Walsh, John C., 31, 135–7, 143, 151, 161, 172, 219, 225, 233–4
Wandycz, Piotr, 68, 70, 76, 79, 82, 86
Webster. *See* Massachusetts, migrants from
Wends, 34, 201
West Prussia, 58, 66–70, 80–4, 88–94, 98, 186
Wiele, 253–6
Wilno: cultural changes, 177, 210–20, 230–50; embroidery, 45–6, 213–14, 217, 230, 235; furniture, 35, 49, 230–1, 242; in literature, 24–33; regional and cultural descriptions, 3–7, 11–13, 37–52, 144, 147, 170–1, 226, 228
Wilno Heritage Society, 12–13, 50, 53, 58, 102, 177, 210–51; museum, 12, 49, 58, 214, 242–8. *See also* Glofcheskie, Peter; Mask-Connolly, Shirley; and Shulist, David
Wilowski, Fr Edward, 38, 40
Wisconsin, 97, 107, 128–9, 165–6, 249, 256

Zakopane, 191, 194, 240
Zurakowski, Anna, 10, 35–6, 40, 42–3, 51, 67, 133–4, 232